Innovations and Social Media Analytics in a Digital Society

Editors:

Maria José Sousa
Instituto Universitário de Lisboa
Avenida das Forças Armadas
Lisboa, Portugal

Célio Gonçalo Marques
Instituto Politécnico de Tomar
Quinta do Contador, Estrada da Serra
Tomar, Portugal

T0321393

CRC Press
Taylor & Francis Group
Boca Raton   London   New York

CRC Press is an imprint of the
Taylor & Francis Group, an **Informa** business

A SCIENCE PUBLISHERS BOOK

First edition published 2022
by CRC Press
6000 Broken Sound Parkway NW, Suite 300, Boca Raton, FL 33487-2742

and by CRC Press
2 Park Square, Milton Park, Abingdon, Oxon, OX14 4RN

Library of Congress Cataloging-in-Publication Data (applied for)

ISBN: 978-1-032-03943-5 (hbk)
ISBN: 978-1-032-03944-2 (pbk)
ISBN: 978-1-003-18984-8 (ebk)

DOI: 10.1201/9781003189848

Typeset in Times New Roman
by Radiant Productions

Preface

Our society currently faces unimagined challenges on a global scale, in view of the technological acceleration that leads us towards a new Industrial Revolution, referred to as the '4.0 revolution'.

It is already here and the coming years will surprise us with technological and digital innovations that will be around us more and more, every moment of every day. Thus, we are increasingly led to think about institutions, enterprises and people without boundaries of either time or space.

During the last decade, we were astounded at the implementation of innovative digital solutions in every sector of activity, ranging from public administration to defense, health, education, finance, industry, energy, transport and the academia itself.

Decisions were made with greater certainty, with transitional data being processed by tools of analytic treatment in a non-stop temporal continuum. Digital solutions capturing and processing data and making information available for decision making, operational or strategic, through algorithms or people, are already around us, regardless of our awareness of this reality.

In this context, social networks appeared from 2004 onwards (Facebook and Google began in 2004, Twitter in 2006, Instagram in 2010) and promoted a new paradigm—that of each citizen getting an active voice about their environment, through more or less mobile digital devices, as well as that of the new capacity to interact with others in personal, political, business or social issues.

This was a capacity as well as a power not previously granted to society and it brought along new challenges that academia could not ignore.

The present book, comprising 14 chapters developed by international academics, studying innovations and social media analytics in a digital society, clearly shows the pertinence and relevance of research on social media in a digital society.

It sharpens the curiosity and opens up research windows through literature review, presentation of empirical experiment results, paths and research methodologies and through the approach to social media within the most diverse sectors—all this, while leaving a deep impact on education and on the political, economic and health sectors.

To ensure the planet's sustainability, programs of digital, climatic and resilience transformation and transition are being launched worldwide. One of the critical factors for success relates to the acquisition of new knowledge, behaviors and attitudes by all human beings, in a very short period of time.

With this goal in mind, social media constitutes one of the new forces that is able to actively contribute its mite. This work represents an excellent kick starter for an intensive, reliable, safe and ethically correct use of social media in every sector, including those mentioned above.

For these reasons, I wholeheartedly recommend this book, certain that each of us will be enriched by it and awakened to the need to act for the good of the planet.

Maria Helena Monteiro
Professor at (ISCP) Institute of Social and Political Sciences,
University of Lisbon, Portugal;
President of APDSI (Association for the Promotion and
Development of the Information Society), Portugal

Contents

1

Social Media Innovations in Digital Society

Andreia de Bem Machado,[1,]* *João Rodrigues dos Santos*[2] and
António Sacavém[3]

INTRODUCTION

The growth of emerging technologies has reached an exponential rate. Online platforms have stimulated crucial changes in the way people communicate and interact. The introduction of the World Wide Web in 1991 allowed for the emergence of social media (social networks, blogs, etc.) which became a relevant element of research interest in digital society. Social media applications, such as Facebook, Twitter and YouTube, spread content based on people's attitudes and preferences, amplifying information (e.g., rumors, fake news, relevant information, etc.) through the use of advanced algorithms. Moreover, along with the advancement of information technologies, social media started influencing people's mobility and the way individuals relate in the digital world, constituting itself as a game-changing evolution for both people and organizations (Hennig-Thurau et al., 2010). Social media becomes a social regulator since the individuals become more aware of the world around them, attain insights about the essence of different phenomena and settle their own social position in relations and networks (Milenkova et al., 2018). People and organizations are creating their own legacy on social media by using images, messages, movies that they develop, post and debate. Media socialization, as a means to influence social actors with media content, is a key element of social media realm and encapsulates the active participation of human beings and communities while facilitating the integration of social experience. Furthermore, research has found that individuals consume online information that is in tune with

[1] Department of Engineering and Knowledge Management, Federal University of Santa Catarina, Brazil.
[2] Business and Economics Department, IADE/Universidade Europeia, Portugal.
   Email: joao-rodrigues.santos@universidadeeuropeia.pt
[3] Business and Economics Department, Universidade Europeia, Portugal.
   Email: antonio.sacavem@universidadeeuropeia.pt
* Corresponding author: abmachadopapers@gmail.com

their own stereotypes (Cinelli et al., 2020), shaping tribal narratives and polarized world views (Bail et al., 2018).

Individuals and organizations are struggling to follow fast-paced innovations in social media and manage social presence which requires more and more levels of specialization to handle the increased amount of data that are available in the digital world. Learning how to effectively deal with this 'brand new world' exposes people and organizations to new challenges and also to unimaginable opportunities. For example, to facilitate teaching, the higher education sector across the globe is using social media to inspire learning and encourage students. Studying and better understanding of the main innovations that are emerging in the field of social media may contribute to the development of a more informed 'big picture' and uncover how people and organizations are constructing narratives and developing social perceptions.

1. Social Media

Social media reinvented the virtual world, which is characterized as interactive vehicles, as they are a means of unlimited sharing of information and applications, such as texts, images and multimedia files. Social media are sites on the Internet that allow the creation and sharing of information and content, by people and for people, in which the consumer is both producer and consumer of information (Machado, 2020).

The media is a phenomenon of indigital society, asserting itself as a powerful mechanism that can open space for vast opportunities for collaborative communication (Machado, 2020). The media are divided into three platforms: online communities and/or forums, bloggers and social networks. Online communities and forums are created by consumers without commercial interests or ties to companies. Blogs are periodicals or online journals, updated regularly, that have become an important means of disseminating information. Social networks allow greater interaction between a group of people, allowing connectivity and interactivity between different locations in the world (Hennig-Thurau et al., 2010).

Thus, social media is a powerful communication tool in the digital society. The large amount of data generated (Machado, 2020) by the user is a new and useful source of data. Social media is a communication medium that connects people geographically, with no more barriers between time and space, thus allowing for a complete interconnectedness.

2. Digital Society

The indicators regarding the expansion of indigital society are impressive. According to the latest *Measuring the Information Society Report* by the International Telecommunication Union/United Nations (2018), at the end of 2018, more than half of the world population (51.2 per cent) had access to the Internet. The number of cell phone subscriptions is currently higher than that of the world population and the growth rate of subscriptions went up from 4 per cent in 2007 to 69.3 per cent in 2018. Nearly 76.4 per cent of the world population owns a cell phone. Mobile broadband has become one of the defining characteristics of indigital society, as it has allowed access to the Internet through 3G or 4G. In 2018, almost 60 per cent of households had access to broadband Internet via computer, while this percentage did not reach 20 per cent in 2005 (International Telecommunication Union/United Nations, 2018, p. 11). However, these numbers conceal very large geographical differences between countries and, within them, between social groups, translating, among other things, into a great disparity in the use of digital technologies.

The expansion in the use of digital technologies has changed tremendously the way people communicate, connect and relate. There are a few areas of activity that are not involved in this colossal transformation "and it is happening so quickly that most people are not aware of both the scale and the speed of these transformations" (Richards and King, 2014, p. 405).

Digital technologies play a central role in the global daily life, decisively interfering in the performance of companies and professionals and in the forms of access and analysis to the infinity of information and the available data sources. Even the management of public services is no longer an exception. Gil-Garcia, Dawes and Pardo (2018) emphasize that currently "it is hard to imagine any government function or governance process that does not involve extensive use of information and technology" (p. 633).

The digital society is substantially changing access to knowledge and this transition is occurring in a non-linear way—such is its speed. This is a phenomenon liable to "leave some on the way".

Ali (2020), about the exclusion of many citizens from the highly technological labor market today, says that the "knowledge network must be accompanied by the improvement of labor-skill development" (p. 34).

The exponential and non-linear transition paradigm has many associated difficulties, but it also creates opportunities. In this regard, the "technological changes in the short run should work to prepare people for the urgent changing environment and future jobs" (Ali, 2020, p. 34).

The proactivity needed to be prepared for the future is precisely related to the non-linearity of the digital transformation of society, which triggers behavioral and cognitive changes with magnitude to change the pillars of our reality. When processes evolve in a non-linear way, as with the technological transition, as "enter the real world, our ability to predict what will happen decreases dramatically" (Richards and Smart, 2013, p. 11), society must anticipate rather than react.

In fact, "it is not unusual for a discussion about regulation of a new technological innovation to include concern that it is already too late to intervene" (Bard, 2020, p. 42).

One of the great changes resulting from the continuous digital transformation is the difficulty of perceiving time and space, which are confused in thousands of parallel tracks.

An event anywhere on the globe instantly reaches the rest of the world. There is no change in schedule or no need to wait for the newspaper or correspondence by mail. The present occurs to everyone at the same time and allows distant elements to interact with each other, forming between them a time that does not include a beginning or an end, but a continuous change. "As often with emerging and rapidly developing Internet trends, it can be challenging to define what the real-time Web means" (Hermida, 2010, p. 5).

This fact is intrinsically associated with two problems that are difficult to solve: the overabundance of information and the need to provide society with critical thinking.

The overabundance of information consists of the perception that, at present, the reality of any citizen is the reality of the whole world, and not just the reality of their geographical space. A few years ago, the news consisted of a maximum of five or six topics. The news of the present time is made up of millions and millions of news, which, in most circumstances, impact people without any criteria. This environment causes 'mental fatigue'. In this context, Hermida (2010) states that "one of the ways news has become ambient has been through the proliferation of displays in public places carrying 24-hour news channels or showing news headlines" (p. 1). Currently, the so-called 'infoxication' plays a counterproductive role, by hiding, under tons of 'uninteresting' information, what really adds value to the citizen.

In this regard, Yazdi (2020) says that "most recently, the coronavirus pandemic has made the dangers of the proliferation of misinformation abundantly clear" (pp. 6-7).

"The 'abuse' of artificial intelligence must be avoided. To do this, people need to learn how artificial intelligence functions and how to integrate ethical principles into their behavior" (Wulf, 2020, p. 14).

The need to provide society with critical thinking is the second major problem that results from the immense amount of information available today to any individual. This problem is the cause and effect of the first. It is essential to provide society in general with the basic tools to filter the immense tide of information that floods them daily. For example, "many people have seen a massive potential in large digital platforms to turn them into a useful tool to make their false news viral" (Karunakar, 2018, p. 32). It is necessary to separate what is valid from what is not and to absorb value from a context as dangerous as this one, with an overabundance of (un)information. For this purpose, it is crucial to promote the acquisition of skills that enable individuals to mature their criteria. Regarding this matter, Karunakar (2018) mentions the concept of 'media literacy' as fundamental. "Even though it sounds a bit forceful, people should be made aware of ways to verify the legitimacy of the articles [information] circulating" (Karunakar, 2018, p. 2).

Still in this context and in relation to the period that the world society is going through, Romm (2020), from the *Washington Post*, cited by Yazdi (2020), "says they've seen a flood of misinformation on WhatsApp [among other platforms] about the number of people affected by coronavirus, the way the illness is transmitted and the availability of treatments" (p. 7).

In this sense, it is essential to stimulate digital literacy, especially in an environment in which abundant information circulates without barriers and at great speed. This is even more relevant when it comes to guaranteeing all citizens the right conditions for informed and equal access to all job opportunities and social functions.

"Advances in user interfaces also enable computers to respond directly to a wider range of human requests, thus augmenting the work of highly skilled labor, while allowing some types of jobs to become fully automated" (Frey and Osborne, 2017, p. 18).

In this context, designing the 'Europe 2030 Project', the European Union (2010) underlined that "the digital society and other sectors [...] should become the main drivers of growth and job creation in a market of [...] millions of users and consumers" (p. 8).

The European Commission (2011), in its '2020 Strategy', foresaw the 'digital agenda' (p. 8) as one of the great vectors of the strategy. The purpose of this digital agenda is to contribute to fully exploiting the potential of Information and Communication Technologies, in order to promote innovation, economic growth and progress.

From the digital agenda (EC, 2010)—under which the European Commission will continue to act in the name of smart, sustainable and inclusive growth—the following 'pillars' stand out:

Pillar 2: Interoperability and standards;

Pillar 4: Fast and ultra-fast Internet access;

Pillar 5: Research and innovation;

Pillar 6: Improve digital literacy, skills and inclusion;

Pillar 7: ICT benefits to the European society.

This reality, which will continue to intensify continuously, requires the systematic 're-education' of 'citizen-users'.

Today, we are in the decade of 'big data', artificial intelligence (AI) and machine learning (ML). We are at a tipping point, with the remarkable confluence of powerful and inexpensive hardware and storage, the digitization of every aspect of business, social and personal transactions that have created vast treasure troves of digital data, and rapid advances in algorithms and statistical methods (Agarwal, 2020, p. 10).

This represents a massive transformation, almost a disruptive one. It is essential to ensure continuous training for groups at risk of digital and information exclusion. "Digital media enable new tools to be used and promote the development of new skills" (Wulf, 2020, p. 2). Modern business models (next figure) and human resource management today must incorporate 'technological strategies' that guarantee to keep all individuals properly adapted to digital contemporaneity. "Digital transformation changes the way the business functions through the evolution of cyber-physical systems, representing the fourth industrial revolution" (Vidyakala, 2020, p. 198). This premise is fundamental when it comes to human dignity, but also in terms of economics, with particular relevance to human resources, since the exclusion of human resources will correspond to less global productivity and, therefore, less efficiency in taking advantage of the scarce resources that the world society has at its disposal.

For society not to run the risk of 'wasting' human resources (one of the three productive factors), Agarwal (2020) argues that countries, and their decision makers, "must develop curriculum that educate students about the varieties of digital technologies available today and help them understand the capabilities offered by each" (p. 11).

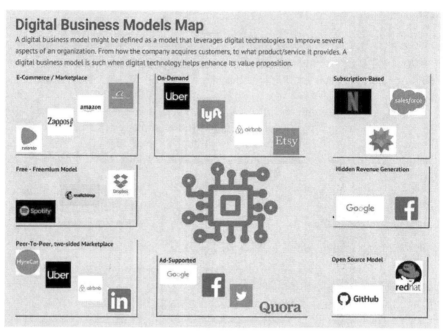

Fig. 1: Digital business model map (Cuofano, S.D.).

This continuous transition of technological paradigm must be based on two assumptions:

Strategic planning of companies and public administration must be based on short-, medium- and long-term logic, assuming, in a calculated way, the risk of an environment in constant digital evolution. Currently, the "successful business models are characterized by digital business innovation which increases their revenues" (Vidyakala, 2020, p. 199). These models require adaptive and open (strategic) planning, scalable in time and space, with the aim of being able to implement continuous changes that allow adapting management needs to the real needs of society. This logic lacks properly adapted human resources. Therefore, to be completely successful, the society must "contribute to the development of digital literacy and multiliteracy and thus to human development" (Wulf, 2020, p. 5).

Traditional hierarchical management models must adapt to a reality of 'masses' provided and enhanced by ICT. "Everyone can participate at any time and feel recognized in the digital public" (Wulf, 2020, p. 5). It is essential to continue to create room for public participation. Failure to do so will lead to compromising situations and, predictably, crises that could have been avoided. The productive process (of whatever type) of the 21st century, highly technological and digital, must know how to manage and incorporate the interesses of 'regular' people, customers and users. Otherwise, ignoring the 'power' of consumers, businesses will not be successful. With relevance to the observation about the empowerment of the 'normal' citizen, Cohen, in 1998, stated that, "arguably, even if publishers currently have power over consumers, digital rights management technologies will eliminate or mitigate this power" (p. 83).

And Cohen was right. In the 21st century, at the height of the digital transition and the so-called Information Society, the average citizen has the last word to say. All areas of the private and public sectors are sensitive to the digital transformation that is developing and to the innovative ways and urgency of their accommodation. It is a world in which the consumer/user is increasingly demanding about the quality of the product or service he/she acquires, and this marks the step of the constant transformation of society's paradigm. In this regard, it is worth mentioning, for example, what is being seen, in general, in public administration at present. "Today, at all levels and in all branches of government, we find tools, applications and emergent technologies being applied to the needs of citizens, service users, public servants and political leaders" (Gil-Garcia et al., 2018, pp. 633-634). The digital transformation is being felt with intensity in all areas of society.

From a strictly economic perspective, Santos (2020) states that "an expansion of the factors of production or a technological improvement allows a country to produce a greater quantity of goods and services, thus shifting the FPP [frontier of production possibilities] to the right" (p. 34), which means more productivity and therefore, better quality of life.

This conjuncture, of technological progress, generates additional efficiency in the management of resources, but its weight in the increase of social welfare, considered globally, is still questionable. It is important to reflect on this digital transformation in the public and private sectors for global and widespread benefit. In 2009, Gheorghiu mentioned that "the concerns about unequal social and economic opportunities have been [...] gathered under the generic name of [...] digital inclusion or e-inclusion" (p. 20).

The intense digital transformation (or digital transition) that has been going on for decades is not merely a business process. According to Mohammad (2020), "revolutionary changes in information and communication systems have shaped cyberspace, which allows [...] to expand the range of information and communication services" (p. 42). The benefits resulting from this reality should be equally distributed.

When it comes to 'digital society', it must necessarily be considered an environment that goes far beyond the business environment. A broad environment (a society, a territory, a country, a continent, or even a 'globalized society') must be considered. In this environment, the protagonist must be human beings. And it is precisely for this reason that digital innovation must move towards a more universal and 'user-friendly' design, taking advantage of the opportunity that increasingly powerful technologies offer.

Furthermore, design and innovation "have the potential to make subtle but meaningful interventions to advance conventional knowledge about digital society" (Alacovska et al., 2020, p. 36).

In fact, regarding design, art and innovation emphasize that "the capacity of both visual and performing arts to synthesize, simplify and convey complex scientific ideas makes the information both more interesting and easier to remember" (Curtis et al., 2012, p. 6).

Perhaps the expression 'digital transformation' should itself be an object of transformation, becoming 'digital social transformation', as it is info-exclusion that we are talking about. This digital (social) transformation must constitute a totally inclusive sphere, where people converge in harmony and take advantage of all creations: buildings, common spaces, companies, industries, services available to the citizen (health, education, culture…). For example, Gilmen (2020) points out that "technology is bringing many benefits to low-income people. […] Internet access gives low-income people the ability to apply for jobs or services and to connect with social justice movements with ease" (p. 10), but in order to really benefit from these advantages, people need to have digital literacy first.

The so-called digital society consists of transforming people's way of life, their habits, the systems of work and production, the way of accessing and using public and private services. It is the transformation of education, health, culture or communication. All of this is based on existing or emerging technologies, which are infiltrating people's lives without real awareness of it: IoT, cloud, virtual reality, mobility technologies, autonomous travel systems (smart cars), robotics. ... Even the privacy of citizens, such as we typically conceive it, is threatened. Solove (2004), for example, in this regard, highlights a reality that remains very current: "a relatively robust amount of law has developed to protect privacy, but it has often failed to be effective when confronted by the problems of the Information Age" (pp. 7-8).

Therefore, these technologies, having no associated accessibility and usability criteria, can, in many circumstances, be more harmful than beneficial. There is a real risk that they may even leave millions of citizens out of the loop, excluding them from the benefits generated by increasing efficiency in resource management. For example, in the particular domain of Internet access, "to convincingly address e-inclusion, the gaps in Internet usage of the older population, people with disabilities, women, and low-education groups, unemployed and less-developed regions [have] to be reduced" (Gheorghiu, 2009, p. 29). The consequences of an 'info-exclusion' reality are disastrous for the dignity of the human being, economies, public spending and society in all its dimensions.

It is true that e-inclusion projects are already being developed all over the world. For example, "one of the main public policies in Argentina is the program 'ConectarIgualdad' [https://www.argentina.gob.ar/educacion/aprender-conectados/ conectar-igualdad]. […]. To guarantee e-inclusion, the program implements various policies in order to develop skills and motorized tools so communities can evolve" (Cortesi et al., 2015, p. 102).

We are on the cusp of a 'big data' revolution. [...] The scale of the 'big data' revolution is such that all kinds of human activities and decisions are beginning to be influenced by 'big data' predictions, including dating, shopping, medicine, education, voting, law enforcement, terrorism prevention and cybersecurity. This transformation is comparable to the Industrial Revolution (Richards and King, 2014, p. 393).

Richards and Smart (2013) wrote that "technologies are now mature enough to leave the research lab and come to the consumer market in large numbers" (p. 3). The figure of the 'digital citizen' ('universal' citizen), who, in 2021, corresponds to a significant part of the world population, will inevitably continue to multiply. This potential must be considered by public and private agents. Their options must include solutions that do not exclude specific sections of the population (cognitive and physical limitations or disabilities, age, specific orientations...) under penalty of contributing to social exclusion and also to negative economic results. In 2009, Gheorghiu said that "throughout the development of the information society, the benefits were not equally distributed inside and among countries" (p. 20).

Still Richards and Smart (2013) point out that digital transformation "has the potential to revolutionize our daily lives and to transform our world in ways even more profound than broad access to the Internet" (p. 3).

In this perspective, it is essential to guarantee the capitalization of this added value for the benefit of citizens' quality of life, without excluding anyone. Digital innovation can play a crucial role here.

3. Methodology

The research method used was the systematic review of literature in an online database, followed by an integrative analysis of the results. The research included in that review is systematically analyzed in relation to its objectives, materials and methods. The approach is mixed, composing a quantitative analysis, which applies statistical and mathematical methods to analyze and build indicators on the dynamics and evolution of the research that has been carried out; and qualitative, which considers an inseparable link between the objective world and the subjectivity of the subject that cannot be translated into numbers, the interpretation of phenomena and the attribution of meanings being the main focus of this research. The quantitative analysis includes the bibliometric analysis of the year of publication, country of occurrence and area of concentration; and the qualitative analysis includes a systematic literature review (RSL). Initially, we tried to work by using the five steps of Torraco (2016), elaborated during the integrative literature review phase described below (Machado et al., 2019), as shown in the following figure:

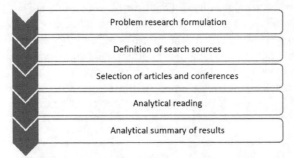

Fig. 2: Organization of the research in five steps.

First phase is the formulation of the research problems that guide this study. This had answered the questions:

(1)   What is social media?

(2)   What does digital society mean?

(3)   What are the innovations of social media in digital society?

To answer these questions, a database search was developed, starting in January 2021 and ending in the same month.

In the second phase, named 'definition of the research sources', some criteria were defined for the selection of the research, such as the delimitation of the research base. We chose to work with the electronic database Scopus (www.scopus.com), considered relevant due to the number of abstracts and references indexed in the space with peer review, as well as its impact in the academic area in the interdisciplinary scope, which is the study area of this research.

Considering the issue of the problem, the third phase is the selection of articles and conferences, with a quantitative analysis taking place through a bibliometric analysis by year of publication, country of occurrence and area of concentration. Considering the research problem, the search terms were delimited, still in the planning phase, namely: 'social media' 'AND' 'digital society'. And, as a basic principle for the search, it was chosen when planning the search to use the terms in the 'title, abstract and keyword' fields, without limiting time, language or any other restriction that could limit the result. From the planning of the research, the data collection recovered a total of 73 indexed works which pointed to the 2009 record, first publication, until 2020.

As a result of this collection, it was identified that these 73 works were written by 164 authors, linked to 128 institutions from 34 different countries. 166 keywords were used to identify and index publications that are distributed in 16 areas of knowledge and eight types of publications. Table 1 shows the result of this data collection in a general bibliometric analysis, when mapping the instructional design theme, in the Scopus database.

The universe of 73 scientific works makes up the sample for a general bibliometric analysis of publications in the area of social media and digital society, without specific limitations, from the consulted database.

The analyzed papers are composed of 73 studies, from the Scopus database. In order to assess the results in more depth for bibliometric analysis, this result was exported to a bibliographic management software, called EndNoteWeb. These data provided the organization of relevant information in a bibliometric analysis, such as temporal distribution; main authors, institutions and countries; type of publication in the area; main keywords; and the most referenced works.

At first, the temporal distribution of the works was analyzed, identifying a very limited level of publications related to the area of analysis in 2009. In 2010,

Table 1: General Bibliometric Data.

Data Base	Scopus
Search terms	'social media' AND 'digital society'
Search fields	*'title, abstract e keywords'*
Total recovered jobs	73
Authors	164
Institutions	128
Countries	34
Key words	166
Knowledge areas	16
Type of publication	8

there was no publication in the area. In 2011, there was only one publication. In 2012, there was an increase in publications with four publications. In 2013, there was no publication. In 2014, there were two publications. In 2015, there was an increase in publications with six published works, followed by 2016 and 2017 with four publications, respectively. In 2018, there was a significant increase with eight publications in the area. And in 2019, there was an increase in publications with 19 published works, followed by another significant increase in 2020 with 24 works. For a better visualization, Fig. 3 was created.

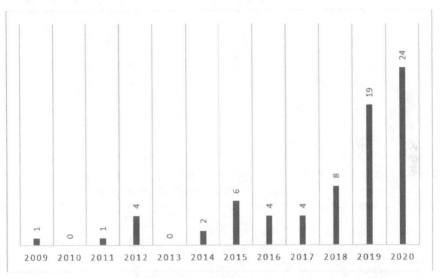

Fig. 3: Time distribution of works.

In 2009, a pioneering work was published and it was entitled, *Using Learning Environments as a Metaphor for Educational Change.* In this article, the author explains that the online learning environment can be seen as the means by which higher education can explore the challenges and opportunities raised through online and digital society (Weller, 2009).

Of the 73 works, there is a varied list of authors, institutions and countries that stand out in the research regarding the theme of social media and digital society.

When analyzing the country with the most publications in the area, it appears that the United Kingdom stands out with 14 per cent of the total publications, with a total of 13 works. In second place stands out the United States with 12 per cent of the publications, that is, 11 works. Figure 4 shows the main countries involved:

Brazil showed itself with only one publication in the area, corresponding to only 2 per cent of the total number of publications, which implies that the discussion is innovative in the country.

Another analysis carried out is related to the identification of prominent authors in the area. In this regard, it was observed that three authors can be referred to as references in the theme: they are Karin Watson, Simon McIntyre, and Anastasia Powell, all with two publications in the area.

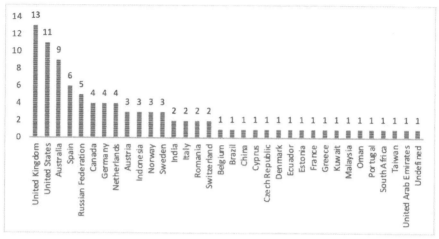

Fig. 4: Distribution by country of work.

From the general survey, it was also possible to analyze the type of documentary research in the area of social media and digital society. It was noticed that the publications are concentrated in articles of scientific journals, with 62 per cent of the total number, and in conference papers, with 25 per cent of the publications. Figure 5 confirms this information in more detail.

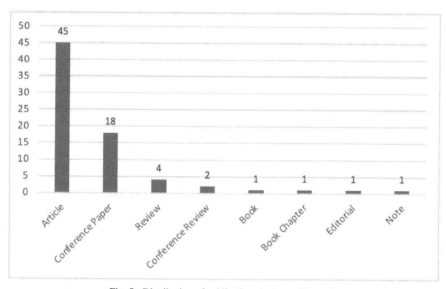

Fig. 5: Distribution of publications by type of journal.

From the bibliometric analysis, based on the recovered work group, in the Scopus database, it was possible to identify the areas of knowledge of the publications. Social sciences stands out with an average of 30 per cent of publications, followed by computer science with 19 per cent, as shown in the following chart (Fig. 6):

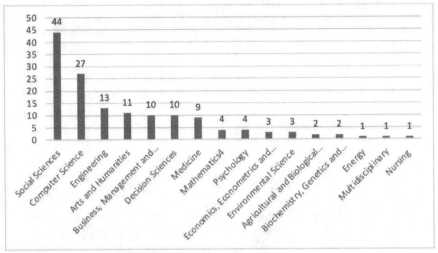

Fig. 6: Journal knowledge area.

Fourth phase is the evaluation of the selection; an evaluation of the quality and the degree of the integrative review—a process dependent on the sample, which includes the sources, the methods and the instruments. In order to select and evaluate the studies, the following inclusion and exclusion criteria were established (Table 2):

Table 2: Criteria for inclusion and exclusion.

	Inclusion Criteria	**Exclusion Criteria**
Scope	Research that addresses innovation in social media in digital society	Research without a focus on innovation in social media in digital society.
Reference Type	Journal articles published or accepted for publication	Conference paper; review; conference review; book; book chapter; editorial and note

Fifth phase is translated into the synthesis process with qualitative and narrative analysis for qualitative and quantitative studies. The synthesis can take the form of a table or model to present the results. The main method that can be used is to reduce data; data display; data comparison; completion and verification design (Whittemore et al., 2005).

So, to answer the research problem: 'What are the innovations of social media in digital society?', 69 articles were excluded, among which those that did not have free access as well as the review documents, book chapter and congress articles that did not contain a relevant relation with the research problem. Thus, to answer the research question, four articles were used, according to the following systematic summary (Table 3).

It is noticed that the relationship of the discussion explained in the previously cited articles is that these address the changes in digital society caused by innovations in social media.

Table 3: Systematic summary.

Year	Author	Title	Innovations of Social Media in Digital Society
2014	Housley et al.	Big and broad social data and the sociological imagination: A collaborative response	The article explains the innovations of social media that demand an interdisciplinary response, but also speak of central sociological concerns that relate to classic issues of social organization.
2017	Romero-Frías and Robinson-García	Social labs in universities: innovation and impact in medialab UGR	The article explains Twitter's innovation and its social impact by analyzing its ability to mobilize and reach in digital society.
2019	Fomicheva et al.	Social media in enabling education	The article explains the trends from digitization to innovation in social media and the subsequent transformation of value awareness in digital society.
2020	Fussey and Roth	Digitizing sociology: continuity and change in the Internet era	The article explains that we are in the era of knowledge production through 'big data'. Social media innovations in digital society are due to ubiquitous computing, machine learning and the 'Internet of Things' and have brought about a social change .

3.1 Social Media Innovations in Digital Society

Digital society was first coined in 2009 and invites a new way to look into innovation and technology. In contemporary society where the customer is the main focus, the commitment towards innovation is very high (Archer-Brown and Kietzmann, 2018) and social media is linked with innovation (Brandtzaeg and Følstad, 2016). Innovations in social media are also a consequence of big social data, generated by users, that is taking place nowadays. Social media communications are emerging at an immense velocity and quantity which facilitate the development of new technologies that are targeted to uncover concealed needs of individuals (Housley et al., 2014). Therefore, knowledge is generated from data and not about data (Kitchin, 2014) which will have an impact on the direction and scope of innovation development.

Almost every sector of society is embedded with digital forms of communication and cooperation. Social media reinvented the traditional narrative and the way individuals interact by redesigning the flow of tacit knowledge (Parinsi and Ratumbuisang, 2020) and stimulating relationships by increasing their visibility. Moreover, social media has been pushing the frontiers between online and offline to a blur space where people and organizations feel the need to be always on. New challenges and opportunities have been emerging from innovation in social media which motivate a renewed interest in the topic. Based on the current review, the interest towards understanding innovation in social media has increased in the last few years. Social media has established a modern dialogue with a vast spectrum of audiences that are transforming the way people and organizations interact. Moreover, knowledge flows underlying the process of innovation have been increasingly managed by social media tools which are drivers and enablers of innovation (Bhimani et al., 2019).

At a fundamental level, some organizations are using social media to provide ideas for improving established goods or services and in order to create new ones. Social media networks have become a source of ideas and guidelines and a way for organizations to become an effective part of the online community. Some companies have even developed an internal social media network, of their own, for internal and external interactions (Bhimani et al., 2019).

Innovations in social media have been used to co-create new products and services (Cheng and Krumwiede, 2018) to achieve competitive advantage (Pérez-González et al., 2017) and to launch innovative solutions to the marketplace (Roberts et al., 2016). Beyond social networking websites, multi-directional interactive apps (e.g., feedly), as well as blogs, are incrementing participation among individuals that move in distinctive social bubbles and stimulating the interaction between users since they have accessible interfaces and reveal low obstacles to entry (Bhimani et al., 2019). Since social media have been drawing attention for their ability to activate emotional responses in individuals (Fussey and Roth, 2020), they have also opened a new opportunity for organizations to better understand customers' affective needs throughout automated sentiment analysis (e.g., media toolkits) and doing so, developing specific communication strategies to increase engagement with particular brands, products and services. Sentiment analysis software examines content and describes the emotional tone of a narrative which is produced in a social media platform.

When organizations use the social media tools in the correct manner, they can achieve multiple advantages, including reaching new targets, developing innovative ideas, integrating relevant insight into individuals' behaviors and needs, establishing an adjusted narrative that is in tune with automatic sentimental analysis and increasing customer participation. In sum, social media is a key element of indigital society, adding multiple layers of complexity in the way individuals and organizations make sense and interact with the world around and innovation social media promoting new channels for human beings to understand each other and make informed choices faster than ever. Nevertheless, social media innovation is posing new challenges that research is starting to address, like increased polarization, since social media can restrain individuals from being confronted to data that may differ from their current beliefs (Bail et al., 2018).

4. Final Considerations

The digital society is substantially changing access to knowledge and the way it is produced. Society is increasingly disciplinary and specialized and is becoming an environment in which the areas of knowledge are not precisely defined and activities and learning depend more and more on the individual.

Considering this scenario, and in order to answer the problem posed in this chapter, it is indisputable that social media innovations in digital society are related to technological transformations that have caused important implications for practically all activities. Among these innovations, it is possible to highlight the applications that allow more and more connectivity and interactivity, such as SmarHub solutions, among others that allow greater interaction between electronic equipment, people and the social environment.

However, people need training to help them live and work in this borderless society and to avoid excessive social fragmentation, segregation and excessive emotional and cognitive burdens. To achieve this, it is very important to provide individuals with self-regulatory learning skills.

The innovations of social media in digital society are linked to a world in transition where skills and competences are not static; learning has been innovated for a hybrid proposal. This incremental social change stems from the nonlinearity of digital transformation, which occurs exponentially and is rapidly changing all dimensions of the world.

In this sense, the emergence of this new intellectual digital dimension may negatively affect some less prepared individuals and even contribute to the social exclusion of some. If the individual is unable to process or understand the current technology and, therefore, how information is produced and circulates in the present, he gradually isolates himself from a reality that he considers complex and very intricate, which does not differentiate users.

Without the ability to access information rationally and to extract value from it, without the capacity to face the eruption of Information and Communication Technologies and without the capacity to understand the intense digital transformation, the citizen ends up being excluded.

And this is a serious problem in a scenario where the notion of time changes systematically, in which everything changes very quickly, and is literally reinvented every moment. Jobs that have been with us for centuries cease to exist in favor of others adjusted to the contemporary context, which mainly involves sharing, opening, and digital intermediation on a global scale.

There is no doubt that the digital transformation of society is based on new technologies and the ability to communicate globally. These vectors require the individual and society to be re-educated every moment. To achieve this goal that digital innovation should assume an increasing preponderance, it is necessary to ensure tools that facilitate collective inclusion.

In order to accompany this intense transformation, society in general and business activities and employers in particular, should consider, at every moment, the best strategy to effectively address the intense digital transformation and encourage the inclusion of all people in the process.

Due to the multisectoral scope of digital transformation, practically transversal to all the domains of society, the immense public and private services generated (health, education, transport, management, culture, communication, varied infrastructures, among others), under the umbrella of this transformation, must be implemented by necessarily using existing technology, but with the guarantee that it is well adjusted to the plurality of capacities of the citizens that make up society.

For this reason, companies and public administration entities cannot fail to adapt their ways of acting and to consider in this process the well-being of users/ consumers. As long as it is properly 'calibrated', the increasingly digital society will undoubtedly constitute an asset that guarantees the improvement of the quality of life of citizens. At this level, digital innovation, conceptually considered, has an important role to play.

In this perspective, the digital transformation represents a great opportunity to conceive a more egalitarian society and to generate consumption and wealth without excluding people, through technological solutions appropriate to the functional, economic and social diversity of the population, taking into account their different capacities and realities. Technology must evolve to serve individuals. The human being, as a user/consumer of public and private goods and services, must be the epicenter of the technological resources managed by companies and public administration. To achieve this result, the technological solutions must be user-friendly and fully accessible to the global universe of users.

Research at this level still has a long way to go. There are not so many studies on the subject, especially of a specialized nature. Therefore, for future work, it is suggested, for example, that the investigation may focus on tools that allow companies, entities, public administration and society in general to adapt their ways of acting and to consider effectively the well-being of users/consumers in a scenario of constant technological transition.

References

Agarwal, R. 2020. Digital transformation: A path to economic and societal value. *Revista CEA,* 6(12).

Alacovska, A., Booth, P. and Fieseler, C. 2020. State-of-the-Art: The role of the arts in the digital transformation. *Arts Formation Report Series,* 2020.

Ali, M.M. 2020. Digitization of the emerging economy: An exploratory and explanatory case study. *Journal of Governance & Regulation,* 9(4): 25–36.

Archer-Brown, C. and Kietzmann, J. 2018. Strategic knowledge management and enterprise social media. *Journal of Knowledge Management,* 27(6): 1288–1309.

Bard, J.S. 2020. Developing a legal framework for regulating emotion AI. *27 B.U.J. Sci. and Tech. L., University of Florida Levin College of Law Research Paper,* 21(1).

Bhimani, H., Mention, A.L. and Barlatier, P.J. 2019. Social media and innovation: A systematic literature review and future research directions. *Technological Forecasting and Social Change,* 144: 251–269.

Brandtzaeg, P. B. and Følstad, A. 2016. Social media use and innovations: Introduction to the special issue. *The Journal of Media Innovations,* 3(1): 1–3.

Cheng, C.C. and Krumwiede, D. 2018. Enhancing the performance of supplier involvement in new product development: The enabling roles of social media and firm capabilities. *Supply Chain Management: An International Journal,* 23(3): 171–187.

Cinelli, M., Brugnoli, E., Schmidt, A.L., Zollo, F., Quattrociocchi, W. and Scala, A. 2020. Selective exposure shapes the Facebook news diet. *PloS ONE,* 15(3).

Cohen, J.E. 1998. Lochner in cyberspace: The new economic orthodoxy of 'Rights Management'. *Michigan Law Review,* 97(2): 462–563.

Cortesi, S., Gasser, U., Adzaho, G., Baikie, B., Baljeu, J., Battles, M., . . . Burton, P. 2015. *Digitally Connected: Global Perspectives on Youth and Digital Media.* London: Berkman.

Cuofano, G. (N.D.). *Digital Business Models Map: The Most Popular Digital Business Model Types* (PNG).

Curtis, D.J., Reid, N. and Ballard, G. 2012. Communicating ecology through art: What scientists think. *Ecology and Society,* 17(2): 3.

European Commission. 2010. A Digital Agenda for Europe: Communication from the Commission to the European Parliament, the Council, the European Economic and Social Committee and the Committee of the Regions, *European Commission*; retrieved from: https://eur-lex.europa.eu/legal-content/en/ALL/?uri=CELEX%3A52010DC0245.

Fomicheva, T.V., Kataeva, V.I., Sulyagina, J.O., Evstratova, T.A. and Chardymsky, M.G. 2019. Digitization of the population in Russia: Technologies and levels of interaction. *International Journal of Recent Technology and Engineering*, 8(2): 4728–4731.

Frey, C.B. and Osborne, M.A. 2017. The future of employment: How susceptible are jobs to computerisation? *Technological Forecasting and Social Change*, 114: 254–280.

Fussey, P. and Roth, S. 2020. Digitizing sociology: Continuity and change in the Internet era. *Sociology*, 54(4): 659–674.

Gheorghiu, R. and Unguru, M. 2009. Beyond connectivity: Future challenges for E-inclusion policies. *Romanian Journal of European Affairs*, 9(2): 20–32.

Gil-Garcia, J.R., Dawes, S.S. and Pardo, T.A. 2018. Digital government and public management research: Finding the crossroads. *Public Management Review*, 20(5): 633–646.

Hennig-Thurau, T., Malthouse, E.C., Friege, C., Gensler, S., Lobschat, L., Rangaswamy, A. and Skiera, B. 2010. The impact of new media on customer relationships. *Journal of Service Research*, 13(3): 311–330.

Hermida, A. 2010. From TV to twitter: How ambient news became ambient journalism. *Media/Culture Journal*, 13(2): 1–6.

Housley, W., Procter, R., Edwards, A., Burnap, P., Williams, M., Sloan, L., Rana, O., Morgan, J., Voss, A. and Greenhill, A. 2014. Big and broad social data and the sociological imagination: A collaborative response. *Big Data & Society*, 1(2): 513–530.

International Telecommunication Union/United Nations. 2018. *Measuring the Information Society Report*, vol. 1; retrieved from: https://www.itu.int/en/ITU-D/Statistics/Documents/publications/ misr2018/MISR-2018-Vol-1-E.pdf.

Karunakar, J. 2018. The practice of journalism in the digital age. *e-journal - First Pan IIT International Management Conference, 2018*; retrieved from: http://dx.doi.org/10.2139/ssrn.3752989.

Machado, A.D.B. 2020. Social media concepts-development of theoretical. *International Journal of Cultural Heritage*, 5: 1–10.

Machado, A.D.B., Sousa, M.J., Nawaz, F. and Martins, J.M. 2020. Impacts of the integration of Chinese managers in the Western economies the case of Brazil. *Transnational Corporations Review*, 12(3): 319–328.

Milenkova, V., Peicheva, D. and Marinov, M. 2018. Towards defining media socialization as a basis for digital society. *International Journal of Cognitive Research in Science, Engineering and Education*, 6(2): 21.

Mohammad, A. 2020. Development of the concept of electronic government construction in the conditions of synergetic threats. *Technology Audit and Production Reserves*, 3.2(53): 42–46.

Parinsi, M.T. and Ratumbuisang, K.F. 2017. Indonesian mobile learning information system using social media platforms. *International Journal of Mobile Computing and Multimedia Communications (IJMCMC)*, 8(2): 44-67.

Perassi, R. and Meneghel, T. 2011. *Conhecimento, mídia e semiótica na área de Mídia do Conhecimento, Mídias do conhecimento, Florianópolis: Padion*, 1: 47–72.

Pérez-González, D., Trigueros-Preciado, S. and Popa, S. 2017. Social media technologies' use for the competitive information and knowledge sharing, and its effects on industrial SMEs' innovation. *Information Systems Management*, 34(3): 291–301.

Richards, N.M. and King, J.H. 2014. Big data ethics. *Wake Forest Law Review*, 49: 393–432.

Richards, N. and Smart, W. 2016. How should the law think about robots? *In:* Calo, R., Froomkin, A.M. and Kerr, I. (Eds.). *Robot Law*, 3–22, Northampton, MA: Edward Elgar Publishing.

Roberts, D.L., Piller, F.T. and Lüttgens, D. 2016. Mapping the impact of social media for innovation: The role of social media in explaining innovation performance in the PDMA comparative performance assessment study. *Journal of Product Innovation Management*, 33: 117–135.

Romero-Frías, E. and Robinson-García, N. 2017. Social labs in universities: Innovation and impact in medialab UGR. *Comunicar. Media Education Research Journal*, 25(1).

Santos, J.R. 2020. *Economia Indispensável*, Lisboa: Lisbon International Press.

Solove, D.J. 2004. The Digital Person: Technology and Privacy in the Information Age. *GWU Law School Public Law Research Paper*, 121.

Torraco, R.J. 2016. Writing integrative literature reviews: Using the past and present to explore the future. *Human Resource Development Review*, 15(4): 404–428.

Vidyakala, K. 2020. Digital transformation and business models. *AutAut Research Journal,* 11(8): 198–201.

Weller, M. 2009. Using learning environments as a metaphor for educational change. *On the Horizon,* 17(3): 181–189.

Whittemore, R. and Knafl, K. 2005. The integrative review: Updated methodology. *Journal of Advanced Nursing,* 52(5): 546–553.

Wulf, C. 2020. *Artificial Intelligence as a Challenge to Society and Education: Global Youth at Digital Trajectories in the Anthropocene,* Free University of Berlin.

Yazdi, M.V. 2020. The digital revolution and the demise of democracy. *Tulne Journal of Technology and Intellectual Property,* 23.

2

Social Media Analytics and Innovation in a Digital Society
A Literature Review

Albérico Rosário,[1] *Ricardo Raimundo*[2] and *Rui Cruz*[3,]*

INTRODUCTION

Social media (SM in further text) are omnipresent in our lives and more and more in firms. Companies are determined to become or stay innovative in ever more complex environments (Barlatier and Mention, 2019), creating new ways to join into diverse innovative ecosystems (Accoto et al., 2016). Thus, new ways of doing business compel firms to create and absorb knowledge throughout innovative processes, by linking both internal and external contexts and knowledge (Dahlander and Piezunka, 2014).

Knowledge is considered a competitive advantage nowadays (Iglesias-Sánchez et al., 2019) as it is innovatively integrated (Nijssen and Ordanini, 2020), along with the emergence of new applications of information and communication technologies (ICTs in further text), as, for instance, SM (Pohjola and Puusa, 2016) and within such environments of collaboration and interaction, the test for firms is to understand the advantages of SM (Mount and Martinez, 2014; Scuotto et al., 2017) and its interplay with the innovation processes (Jussila et al., 2012; Mention et al., 2019). Hence, research efforts focus on understanding the role of SM in processing knowledge within organizations (Corral de Zubielqui et al., 2019; Scuotto et al., 2017) and beyond (Bugshan, 2015; Jussila et al., 2012; Mention et al., 2019). With respect to

---

[1] GOVCOPP – Uniton Governance, Competitiveness and Public Policies - Universidade de Aveiro; IADE - Faculty of Design and Communication of UE – Universidade Europeia, Portugal.
Email: alberico@ua.pt

[2] ISEC Lisboa, Instituto Superior de Educação e Ciências, Portugal.
Email: ricardo.raimundo@iseclisboa.pt

[3] UNIDCOM - Unidade de Investigação em Design e Comunicação; IADE - Faculty of Design and Communication of UE – Universidade Europeia, Portugal.

* Corresponding author: rui.cruz@universidadeeuropeia.pt

accomplishing a competitive advantage (Jiao et al., 2020; Pacauskas et al., 2014), SM has been employed by companies either for marketing (Nijssen and Ordanini, 2020), involving the customer in new product assessment (Filieri, 2013), or new product development in co-creation (Antikainen and Niemelä, 2016; Ross, 2017), whilst the growing involvement of stakeholders in these innovation processes, along with augmenting efficiency of ICTs, has compelled companies to acquire SM-related tools (Barlatier and Mention, 2019; Díaz-Díaz and Pérez-González, 2016; Ooms et al., 2015).

Social media has therefore become a means to assess customer preferences and knowledge, co-creating concepts in partnership with users/costumers and supporting new product development by close interaction (Ernst et al., 2013). It has also been employed by interesting case study companies for social networking and to create a strategy that emphasizes co-evolution of innovation/resources in SMEs (Dobusch and Kapeller, 2018; Hitchen et al., 2017). For instance, the case of Citilab Living Lab shows that SM provides an area for developing innovative solutions, using a citizen-centered design approach and for fostering the co-creation of user-generated content, while opening the culture of innovation to the general public (Leminen et al., 2014). Likewise, the case of Santander City Brain contributes to widen the knowledge on ambitious SM projects implemented by local public administrations for e-government, as it proves that virtual SM are effective innovative tools for civil society (Díaz-Díaz and Pérez-González, 2016).

SM and innovation are therefore strongly related (Filieri, 2013). Managers have claimed that companies should adopt SM tools and deliver an environment where consumers and firms could interact with one another (Ooms et al., 2015). The issue has then extended throughout social networks with regard to its implications in innovation and competitive strategy (Scuotto et al., 2017). As a result, SM is shaping businesses (Mount and Martinez, 2014) and innovation (Drexler et al., 2014), while the need to innovate is paramount in a competitive and customer-centric market (Nijssen and Ordanini, 2020) of strategic knowledge (Ferguson, 2011).

In this way, most publication trends tend to point towards the mediating role of SM in driving open innovation by new collaborative ways (Barlatier and Mention, 2019; Pacauskas et al., 2014), new forms of socialization (Ooms et al., 2015) and capability building (Kastelle and Ohr, 2013). The ensuing cases of SM and (open) innovation in literature relate this with themes of crowdsourcing (Afuah, 2014), social networking (Dobusch and Kapeller, 2018), co-creation (Ross, 2017), new product development (Pacauskas et al. 2014), particularly through case studies (Pohjola and Puusa, 2016) and some emphasized regions (Corral de Zubielqui et al., 2019), as in the case of creation and development of a B2B social community support platform transformed into a relevant business asset (Accoto et al., 2016). Furthermore, the public sector is also improving SM for innovation while only a few studies emphasize how open innovation environment facilitates and fosters scientific and innovation-oriented cooperation among different public stakeholders (Gryczka, 2015).

Nevertheless, this relationship between SM and innovation on the basis of distinct (open) innovation terms (e.g., crowdsourcing) has not been sufficiently theorized in literature (Yang et al., 2020). Hence, the aim of this Systematic

Bibliometric Literature Review (LRSB) is three fold. Firstly, we identify trends in the increasing research on SM and innovation. Secondly, we categorize the SM and (open) innovation subthemes in distinct categories, enhancing thus the current SM paradigm. Finally, we identify ensuing research gaps and future research directions. The originality of the paper relies on its LRSB method, together with extant review of articles that have not been categorized so far.

1. Methodological Approach

A Systematic Bibliometric Literature Review (LRSB) of 'Social Media' and 'Open Innovation' follows the suggestions of Rosário (2021), Rosario et al. (2021) and Rosario and Cruz (2019). An LRSB improves: (i) the validity of a review by providing a clear set of steps that can be followed if the study is replicated; (ii) the accuracy of a review by providing evidence to support arguments closely related to research questions; and (iii) the results, which allow for synthesis and analysis of accumulated knowledge.

We view LRSB as a 'guiding tool', enabling us to shape the review according to our research goals, rather than a methodology with a concrete set of rigid rules. In this sense, LRSB allows for comprehensive knowledge about the subject, as well as its evolution over time, identifying researchers, publications and the nature of the most relevant articles (Rosário, 2021; Rosário et al., 2021; Rosário and Cruz, 2019; Sacavém, et al., 2019). The SCOPUS scientific article database, which is most important for peer-reviewed journals in the academic world, was used. However, we consider that the study has the limitation of considering only the SCOPUS database, excluding other academic databases. Thus, we proceeded as follows: (i) defining the research question; (ii) locating the studies; (iii) selecting and evaluating the studies; (iv) analysis and synthesis; (v) presenting the results; and (vi) concluding the results. This methodology ensures that the LRSB is comprehensive, replicable and answers the research questions (Rosario, 2021; Rosario et al., 2021; Rosario and Cruz, 2019; Sacavém et al., 2019). The literature search includes peer-reviewed scientific articles published until February 2021. The literature search was delimited to the subject areas of business, management and accounting; and the keywords used for the search were 'Social Media' and 'Open Innovation' to ensure the selection of relevant sources for the research.

The process generated 72 scientific documents that are subsequently analyzed in narrative form to delve deeper into the content and possible derivation of shared themes that directly answer the article's research question (Rosario, 2021; Rosario et al., 2021; Rosario and Cruz, 2019; Sacavém et al., 2019). Of the 72 scientific documents selected, 39 are articles, 19 are book chapters, nine are conference papers, three are reviews, one is a book and one is a conference review.

1.1 Publication Distribution

Peer-reviewed articles on the topic can be traced as far back as 2011. The years with the largest number of peer-reviewed articles on the subject, are 2016 and 2017, reaching 11. Peer-reviewed publications distribution on topics were sorted out as followed (Table 1):

Table 1: Journals with peer-reviewed publications on topic between 2010 and 2020.

Journals	Number of Peer-reviewed Publications
27th Bled eConference: eEcosystems Proceedings	1
Journal of Knowledge Management	1
Advanced Fashion Technology and Operations Management	1
Advanced Series in Management	1
Asian Journal of Technology Innovation	1
Atas da Conferencia da Associacao Portuguesa de Sistemas de Informaçâo	1
Australasian Journal of Information Systems	1
British Journal of Management	1
Business and Economic Horizons	1
Business Model Innovation Concepts Analysis and Cases	1
California Management Review	1
Creating and Capturing Value through Crowdsourcing	1
Creativity and Innovation Management	1
European Business Review	1
European Journal of Futures Research	1
IMETI 2013-6th International Multi-Conference on Engineering and Technological Innovation Proceedings	1
Industrial Management and Data Systems	1
Information and Management	1
Information Technology and Management	1
International Journal of Entrepreneurship and Innovation;	1
International Journal of Information Systems in the Service Sector	1
International Journal of Innovation and Technology Management	1
International Perspectives on Business Innovation and Disruption in the Creative Industries Film Video and Photography	1
Journal of Business Research	1
Journal of Enterprise Information Management	1
Journal of Innovation and Knowledge	1
Journal of Organizational and End User Computing	1
Journal of Retailing and Consumer Services	1
Journal of Strategic Information Systems	1
Long Range Planning	1
Marketing Intelligence and Planning	1
Open Innovation New Product Development Essentials from the PDMA	1
Open Innovation through Strategic Alliances Approaches f or Product Technology and Business Model Creation	1
Phantom Ex Machina Digital Disruption's Role in Business Model Transformation	1
Picmet 2016 Portland International Conference on Management of Engineering and Technology Management for Social Innovation Proceedings	1
Proceedings 2019 IEEE International Conference on Engineering Technology and Innovation ICE ITMC 2019	1
Public Administration and Information Technology	1

Table 1 cont. ...

...Table 1 cont.

Journals	Number of Peer-reviewed Publications
Publishing Research Quarterly	1
Research Policy	1
Revolution of Innovation Management the Digital Breakthrough (vol. 1)	1
Strategies and Communications for Innovations an Integrative Management View for Companies and Networks	1
Strategy and Communication for Innovation	1
Tourism Planning and Development	1
UCLA Anderson Business and Information Technologies Bit Project (A Global Study of Technology and Business Practice 2016)	1
Technological Forecasting and Social Change	5
Journal of Business Strategy	4
Journal of Product Innovation Management	4
Lecture Notes in Business Information Processing	3
International Journal of Technology Marketing	2
Managing Open Innovation Technologies	2
Open Innovation a Multifaceted Perspective	2
Strategic Direction	2
Strategy and Communication for Innovation	2
Integrative Perspectives on Innovation in the Digital Economy	2

Figure 1 summarizes the published peer-reviewed literature for the 2010–2020 period.

It is possible to observe that between 2016 and 2017, there was great interest in marketing information publications.

In Table 2 we analyze for the *Scimago Journal & Country Rank (SJR)*, the best quartile and the H index by publication. *The Journal of Marketing* is the most quoted publication with 8,630 (SJR), Q1 and H index 233. There is a total of 16 publications on Q1, eight journals on Q2 and five journals, Q3 and three journals on Q4. Journals from best quartile Q1 represent 30 per cent of the 53 journals titles; best quartile Q2 represents 15 per cent, best quartile Q3 represents 9 per cent, and finally, best Q4

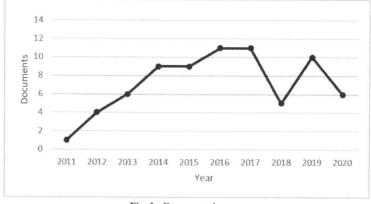

Fig. 1: Documents by year.

Table 2: Scimago journal and country rank impact factor.

Title	SJR	Best Quartile	H Index
Research Policy	3,250	Q1	224
Journal of Product Innovation Management	3,130	Q1	135
California Management Review	2,770	Q1	124
Journal of Strategic Information Systems	2,700	Q1	82
Information and Management	2,400	Q1	153
Long Range Planning	2,010	Q1	96
Journal of Business Research	1,870	Q1	179
Technological Forecasting and Social Change	1,820	Q1	103
British Journal of Management	1,520	Q1	103
Industrial Management and Data Systems	1,390	Q1	96
Journal of Retailing and Consumer Services	1,340	Q1	75
Journal of Innovation and Knowledge	1,060	Q1	15
Creativity and Innovation Management	0,970	Q1	55
Journal of Enterprise Information Management	0,800	Q1	56
European Business Review	0,600	Q1	39
Publishing Research Quarterly	0,490	Q1	14
Tourism Planning and Development	0,520	Q2	27
Journal of Business Strategy	0,490	Q2	36
International Journal of Entrepreneurship and Innovation	O,450	Q2	14
Information Technology and Management	0,420	Q2	35
Journal of Organizational and End User Computing	0,370	Q2	30
Marketing Intelligence and Planning	0,620	Q2	64
Australasian Journal of Information Systems	0,300	Q2	15
European Journal of Futures Research	0,300	Q2	4
Asian Journal of Technology Innovation	0,340	Q3	12
International Journal of Technology Marketing	0,330	Q3	4
Lecture Notes in Business Information Processing	0,260	Q3	44
International Journal of Innovation and Technology Management	0,260	Q3	17
International Journal of Information Systems in the Service Sector	0,220	Q3	11
Strategic Direction	0,120	Q4	10
Advanced Series in Management	0,110	Q4	9
Business and Economic Horizons	0,140	Q4	4
Picmet 2016 Portland International Conference on Management of Engineering and Technology Management for Social Innovation Proceedings	0,130	-*	0
27th Bled eConference eEcosystems Proceedings	-*	-*	4
IMETI 2013 6th International Multi Conference on Engineering and Technological Innovation Proceedings	-*	-*	3
Economics Concepts Methodologies Tools and Applications	-*	-*	-*
Managing Open Innovation Technologies	-*	-*	-*
Open Innovation a Multifaceted Perspective	-*	-*	-*
Strategy and Communication for Innovation Integrative Perspectives on Innovation in the Digital Economy	-*	-*	-*

Table 2 cont. ...

...Table 2 cont.

Title	SJR	Best Quartile	H Index
Advanced Fashion Technology and Operations Management	_*	_*	_*
Atas Da Conferencia Da Associacao Portuguesa De Sistemas De Informacao	_*	_*	_*
Business Model Innovation Concepts Analysis and Cases	_*	_*	_*
Creating and Capturing Value through Crowdsourcing	_*	_*	_*
International Perspectives on Business Innovation and Disruption in the Creative Industries Film Video and Photography	_*	_*	_*
Open Innovation New Product Development Essentials from the PDMA	_*	_*	_*
Open Innovation through Strategic Alliances Approaches for Product Technology and Business Model Creation	_*	_*	_*
Phantom Ex Machina Digital Disruption S Role in Business Model Transformation	_*	_*	_*
Proceedings 2019 IEEE International Conference on Engineering Technology and Innovation ICE ITMC 2019	_*	_*	_*
Public Administration and Information Technology	_*	_*	_*
Revolution of Innovation Management the Digital Breakthrough (vol. 1)	_*	_*	_*
Strategies and Communications for Innovations an Integrative Management View for Companies and Networks	_*	_*	_*
Strategy and Communication for Innovation	_*	_*	_*
UCLA Anderson Business and Information Technologies Bit Project: A Global Study of Technology and Business Practice 2016	_*	_*	_*

Note: *data not available.

represents 6 per cent each of the titles of 41 journals. Finally 21 publications without data representing 40 per cent of all publications.

As evident from Table 2, the significant majority of articles on sport sponsorship is an area of marketing rank on the Q1 best quartile index.

The subject areas covered by the 19 scientific articles were: Business, Management and Accounting (72); Economics, Econometrics and Finance (24); Computer Science (18); Decision Sciences (13); Engineering (9); Social Sciences (9); Psychology (5); Mathematics (3); Medicine (2).

The most quoted article was 'Product development and management association's KIJK comparative performance assessment study' from Markham and Lee (2013), with 121 quotes published in the *Journal of Product Innovation Management* 3, 130 (SJR), the best quartile (Q1) and with H index (135). The published article focuses on the study of practices that leads to better commercial performance of 453 companies from the Product Development and Management Association (PDMA).

In Fig. 2 we can analyze the evolution of citations of articles published between 2010 and 2021. The number of quotes shows a positive net growth with an R2 of 47 per cent for the period 2010–2021, with citations reaching 324 in 2020 .

The h-index was used to ascertain the productivity and impact of the published work, based on the largest number of articles included that had at least the same

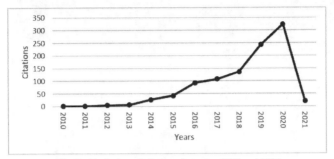

Fig. 2: Evolution of citations between 2010 and 2021.

number of citations. Of the documents considered for the h-index, 15 have been cited at least 15 times.

In Fig. 3, a bibliometric study was carried out to investigate and identify indicators on the dynamics and evolution of scientific information using the main keywords. The study of bibliometric results, using the scientific software VOSviewe, aims at identifying the main research keywords in studies of Social Media and Open Innovation. The linked keywords can be examined in Fig. 4 making it possible to make clear the network of keywords that appear together/linked in each scientific article, allowing us to know the topics studied by the researchers and to identify future research trends. In Fig. 5 is presented a profusion of bibliographic coupling with a unit of analysis of cited references.

2. Theoretical Perspectives

In this section, the main trends in literature are presented. An analysis was performed to analyze the reviewed studies and define thematic areas of research that embrace central issues dealt by the above-mentioned reviewed studies (Figs. 3 and 4). These main thematic areas embrace innovation and open innovation, which encapsulated noteworthy subthemes. The review suggests that research efforts are aimed at building new knowledge to improve new product development (NPD in further text), co-creation, social networking, crowdsourcing, particularly with regard to some regions, particularly Australia, and through distinct case studies based on the effectiveness and efficiency of SM. Additionally, literature also shows that inherent knowledge data processing and resource planning were carried out along these innovation processes. In this way, the main themes that come out in this LRSB and where some authors are key (Fig. 5) are the following:

2.1 The SM in Open Innovation Literature

The results of the review indicate that research in the area of innovation and SM has been largely aimed at the development of concepts related with the application of SM in open innovation.

Firstly, the open innovation paradigm is deemed as strategically aligned by leveraging ways to market their in-house technologies, sharing ideas and intellectual property (IP) and by integrating external knowledge through strategic alliances, collaborative partnerships and conceptual frameworks for supporting government

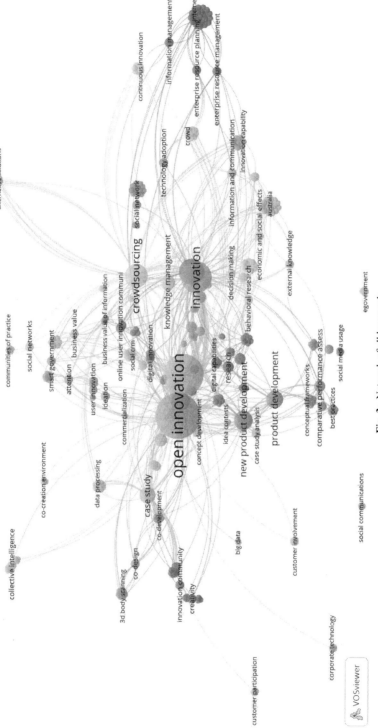

Fig. 3: Network of all keywords.

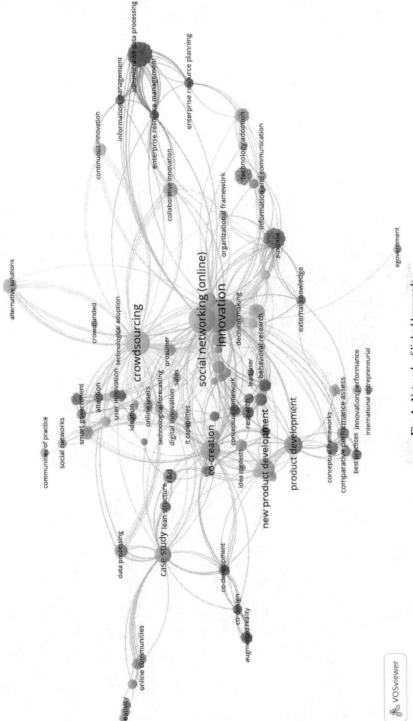

Fig. 4: Network of linked keywords.

Fig. 5: Network of bibliographic coupling.

innovation (Malsbender et al., 2014). In this way, bringing internal and external actors together to create new products and services is key for survival, while SM platforms are able to assist companies in bringing together diverse actors (Culpan, 2014). Open innovation provides, on the one hand, a conceptual lens to examine the SM context of stakeholder networks (De Moor and Aakhus, 2012), while, on the other hand, it breeds scientific and innovation-oriented cooperation among stakeholders, like users, companies, universities and public institutions (Gryczka, 2015).

Secondly, open innovation relies on SM as a strategy for fostering innovation (Barlatier and Mention, 2019) by using crowds to innovate continuously (Cherinka et al., 2013) and, given the role of lead-users in the innovation process, these can be integrated through different SM applications and corporate innovation management. The issue is how to balance strategy and innovation, since strategy is about where to focus resources, which markets to enter and how data can be interpreted to drive business growth, whereas innovation is about integrating research and user feedback to accomplish new products (Ernst et al., 2013).

Thirdly, SM impacts inbound open innovation on capabilities for companies' absorptive capacity of knowledge through boundary-spanning tools that can be used to build and increase absorptive capacity (Ooms et al., 2015) and integrate SM (open) innovation with more classic R&D activities (Barlatier and Josserand, 2019). Indeed, SM in NPD should be accompanied by carefully aligned R&D—marketing cooperation and ensuing results in knowledge integration in terms of innovation (Nijssen and Ordanini, 2020).

Fourthly, paramount to absorptive capacity is the related concept of dynamic capability in SM, in the way it combines diverse capabilities to facilitate customer interaction by networking in the innovation process (Jussila et al., 2012), combining open source technologies, social capital and communication altogether (Ferguson, 2011) and merging innovation with strategy to strengthen innovative capabilities (Kastelle and Ohr, 2013). Also, it supports decision-making and knowledge management (Markham and Lee, 2013) as well as augmenting SM creativity based on innovation and entrepreneurship (Ratten, 2016), as is the case of dynamic capabilities in terms of Online User Innovation Communities OUIC (Dong and Wu, 2015). Dynamic capabilities impact, therefore, the innovation process by an open and collaborative culture (Mention et al., 2019), foster novel forms of digital innovation and web-entrepreneurship (Agostinho et al., 2015), and embed knowledge-processing capabilities in new product development (Jiao et al., 2020). Moreover, digital capabilities positively relate to radical and incremental innovation (Torres de Oliveira et al., 2020) and convert SM into organizational innovation (Bhimani et al., 2019; Patroni et al., 2020).

Fifthly, SM impacts open innovation through distinct ICT tools, such as 'big data' in terms of strategic foresight, focusing, for example, on the utilization of various data channels and SM for generation of interactive knowledge (Drexler et al., 2014) and technology (Mount and Martinez, 2014), as, for instance, in terms of SM Networks for innovation search (Scuotto et al., 2017).

Finally, SM platforms might particularly benefit SMEs and entrepreneurs by connecting customers by their 'social strategy' (Candi et al., 2019) because innovation tends to be mediated by open innovation and SM usage (Freixanet et al., 2020), an important strategic tool for some sectors (e.g., tourism) that positively impacts NPD and competitiveness (Iglesias-Sánchez et al., 2019). Overall, (open) innovation is presented in SM literature to deliver solutions to commercialization and attract attention over new user innovations and smart forms of government, comprehending both public and private stakeholders (Afuah, 2014; Qutaishat and Alex, 2018).

2.2 Social Media and Social Networking

Little was known about how SM differs when either crowds or communities networking are concerned and how tensions could be resolved with increasing openness (Dobusch and Kapeller, 2018). While some streams of literature explore the use of SM networks in small- and medium-sized enterprises (SMEs), innovation oriented, with scarce resources for open innovation (Hitchen et al., 2017), others highlight SM networking to the general public. Particularly in terms of typology of participation processes within social networks, the factors that can influence the way citizens participate through the Internet (Guilló, 2015) and the added value in the network, since SM-based E-learning can be seen as a network of actors interacting with each other (Andersson et al., 2012).

Furthermore, to strategically link firms and users it is essential to build social software in terms of social networks that support partnerships/collaborations for socially-oriented growth (Reid et al., 2016), in how organizations and customers may strategically use online communities to adapt change and attain new capabilities (Wagner et al., 2017) and key lead users (Ernst and Brem, 2017).

2.3 Social Media and Crowdsourcing

The concept of crowdsourcing has gained popularity and has received good acceptance in the organizations while exploring how a crowd acts as a problem solver and generates ideas that lead to open innovation, principally in terms of crowd funding and technology adoption (Singh, 2015).

Firstly, literature explores how crowd-funding platforms enhance the effectiveness of crowdsourcing innovations, whilst applying assurance mechanisms to handle different innovation tasks and motivate more seekers to use the crowdsourcing innovations (Yang et al., 2020).

Secondly, it examines the antecedent conditions that inform management decisions to adopt crowdsourcing techniques as a means of value creation, such as community engagement (Rowe et al., 2015), while it studies crowdsourcing theoretical concepts (López Maciel et al., 2017), its IT capabilities and increasing innovating importance to organizations (Singh, 2015).

Thirdly, literature explores the use of crowdsourcing, particularly from the continuous innovation perspective of business-to-business (B2B) companies (Kärkkäinen et al., 2016), in particular with regard to the use of crowds for open innovation (Zhu et al., 2017) and test of conceptual commercial feasibility (Šundic and Leitner, 2017).

Finally literature addresses the issue of strategic SM platforms and crowdsourcing interplay as a marketing communication tool for innovating and for accessing social capital, innovating through a sharing paradigm of social capital and communication (Ferguson, 2017; Mustafa and Mohammad, 2017).

2.4 Social Media and Co-creation

Co-creation has gained growing attention as a key business model for some companies, while relying on digital technologies. Some use innovative concepts and processes to create premium products for a demanding consumer segment, around digital technology and practices enabling co-creation strategies (Ross, 2017), whilst most literature explores the co-creation approach through case studies focusing on how to engage consumers, both through the consumers' and producers' perspectives (Antikainen and Niemelä, 2017). Moreover, some literature provides a review of users' motivations and how they can be motivated and rewarded for their contribution to co-creation (Antikainen and Niemelä, 2016), whereas attempting to understand the user roles and innovative solutions in co-creation media (Leminen et al., 2014).

2.5 Social Media and New Product Development

In the vein of co-creation, NPD is an issue closely related with innovation and comparative performance assessment (Fig. 4). Literature focuses on the transition from traditional consumer-relationship management (CRM), to social CRM and PORM (prosumer-oriented relationship management) to respond to consumer creative engagement desires, allowing to generate a creative community enabled for open innovation, in terms of knowledge management and communication channels (Potra et al., 2016). Thus literature deals with the issue of enabling an easier dissemination of knowledge through open innovation, SM and more efficient integration of knowledge into NPD and ensuing R&D (Pacauskas et al., 2014).

To accomplish this, it needs to expand the scope of innovation beyond the firms' boundaries into the national culture, particularly regarding reverse innovation and innovation at the bottom-of-the-pyramid (BOP), underscoring, therefore, the link between national culture and NPD (Barczak, 2012). Moreover, most studies emphasize the interplay between SM and online communities in co-creation for open innovation and in the light of NPD for the business sector (Bugshan, 2015).

Finally, literature explores the interplay between sustainability and SM-driven open innovation (SMOI) for a firm's NPD process and performance, while summoning market insights and enhancing customer focus (Du et al., 2016). In doing so, it approaches NPD and SM by allowing users to easily create, edit, or share content, as, for instance, through LinkedIn, Facebook, or Twitter that, overall, embody a rich source of external knowledge to be used for NPD and also provide knowledge on customer needs and technological solutions (Roberts et al., 2016).

2.6 Social Media Illustrated in Some Case Studies and Regions

The afore-mentioned subthemes related with SM and innovation have been approached principally through case study analyses in an attempt to unveil distinct nuances from diverse contexts. Thus, on the one hand, group dynamics of a community of practice have been examined through case study by considering its entire life cycle to decide whether the community will remain worthwhile (Pohjola and Puusa, 2016). On the other hand, some literature emphasize the individual mind through open innovation processes, upon a targeted communications strategy (Karczewski and Zistl, 2017).

Notwithstanding that emphasis is put on the various organizational factors that contribute to SM use for supporting either a more open or closed innovation process (He and Wang, 2016) as, for instance, in the case of the platform Santander City Brain that underlines the contribution s to broaden the knowledge on ambitious SM projects that are implemented by local public administrations (Díaz-Díaz and Pérez-González, 2016). Also, studies on the development of a B2B social community as a social-support platform for the business ecosystems are enhanced, in analyzing B2B clients through an efficient peer support dynamic and development of market connections (Accoto et al., 2016).

These pieces of literature were complemented with other approaches, called Analytical Open Innovation (AOI), in which open innovation is used for the elicitation of service needs, its quality levels and identification of cost/value synergies (Nayebi and Ruhe, 2014). Moreover, comparative studies developed using the Web platform www.Fkjk.org ascertained the desired future among young people from different European countries, in which social networks will empower them to deal with future challenges (Guillo, 2013). Other noteworthy case studies are regarding the enhancement of innovation outputs that companies can attain by involving customers at the 'fuzzy front end' of the NPD process, providing them valuable, original, new and feasible ideas to foster product and service innovation and trigger innovation (Filieri, 2013).

Finally, an important factor found in the review is that some geographical regions were favored in literature. In doing so, Australia was revealed to be an enhanced context, where external knowledge flowing from market-based actors was examined, sourced by SM influence on innovation and business performance, together with the extent to which human resource management practices moderate such a relationship (Corral de Zubielqui et al., 2019).

3. Discussion

3.1 Innovation

The development of an innovation process relies on both the firm's resources and the design of knowledge sharing, providing a conceptual lens to examine the socio-technical conversational context of stakeholder networks (De Moor and Aakhus, 2012). Innovation processes foster global coordination between stakeholders and SM—a driver to assist firms in managing innovation and highlighting external contributions (Dahlander and Piezunka, 2014). Barlatier and Mention (2019) consider SM as a framework to guide managerial action for strategies for innovation, making an integrative set of building blocks for developing further studies in an open and collaborative environment available. Likewise, Cherinka et al. (2013) provide an assessment of applicability and challenges for implementation in large organizations, while Ernst et al. (2013) deliver a conceptual framework for integrating lead-users through different SM applications and integration of SM in corporate innovation management, like boundary-spanning tools to be used in building and increasing absorptive capacity (Ooms et al., 2015).

According to Drexler et al. (2014), SM provides insights into the massive amount of data and offers a model that can be used to predict spreading of content for open innovation; therefore, research on interplay between SM technology and organizational change remains essential.

Mount and Martinez (2014) identify SM as tools that allow a range of organizational and technological adaptations that managers can implement to ensure that they innovate. Accordingly, Scuotto et al. (2017) emphasize the increasing significance taken on by the adoption of SM networks to improve innovation search, in terms of innovation and knowledge management literature. These views are consistent with Barlatier and Josserand (2019), highlighting the key success factors of SM in controlling cost and disruption of open innovation, leveraging the integration of SM along with open innovation strategies and R&D activities.

Alternatively, Candi et al. (2019) suggest that SMEs that put effort into connecting with customers on SM are likely to reap both customers' involvement in innovative SM and new knowledge of value for innovation, allowing the organization to seize strategic opportunities. It all depends on the innovation management model and the positive impact of open innovation in new product development (Iglesias-Sánchez et al., 2019).

The SM has significant representation in current innovation literature and several scholars have identified the triggering role of SM in managing knowledge flows across stakeholders (Scuotto et al., 2017), bringing together internal and external actors to create and innovate through SM platforms (Nijssen and Ordanini, 2020).

SM presents, therefore, distinct features in terms of innovation (Ernst and Brem, 2017). Freixanet et al. (2020), for instance, concludes on the relationship between international entrepreneurial orientation (IEO) and innovation performance, both led by SM usage, evidencing the benefits of IEO and its underlying SM mechanisms. In contrast, Afuah (2014) investigates how organizations can use innovation/ SM in business models to take advantage of entrepreneurial opportunities. Others emphasized the role of SM in facilitating customer interaction in the innovation process (Jussila et al., 2012), in guiding organizations toward SM practices of high potential for realizing the social capital in audiences (Ferguson, 2011).

These theoretical approaches describe SM for innovation as a process in which social approaches are integrated into the day-to-day activities of an organization (e.g., strategy), whilst SM can be leveraged to strengthen important innovation capabilities (Kastelle and Ohr, 2013) towards higher product performance (Markham and Lee, 2013) and service innovation in terms of 'government' (Malsbender et al., 2014).

Social media is therefore deemed as breeding existing innovation environments, expanding the dynamicity of the Web-entrepreneur through open-source platforms for management that result in added value to the firm (Agostinho et al., 2015), either by interactive working on SM creativity (Ratten, 2016), or by online user innovation communities OUIC-enabled capabilities to increase value (Dong and Wu, 2015).

The detailed reading of articles found that the SM paradigm is present in most pieces of writing. On one hand, it is addressed as the key role of SM capabilities in customer participation in NPD (Jiao et al., 2020), while, on the other, it is offered as a typology of SM dynamic capabilities (Torres de Oliveira et al., 2020) that, together with the level of stakeholder engagement, enable the conversion of consumer capabilities on SM into organizational innovation (Patroni et al., 2020; Mention et al., 2019). In sum, SM is therefore seen as both a facilitator and medium of innovation (Bhimani et al., 2019), while gathering user feedback to stimulate innovation (Ogink and Dong, 2019).

3.2 Social Networking

Due to the digital developments in this era, SM is considered as a tool that allows exchange of knowledge creation between people, in particular when knowledge is scattered amidst diverse stakeholders (Scuotto et al., 2017). Moreover, stress within communities may be resolved with increasing openness in strategy-making, as crowds are better compatible with more exclusive strategy-making practices (Dobusch and Kapeller, 2018). The use of SM to connect outside the firm has been the key issue of innovation performance, allowing firms to collaborate easily with diverse groups, thus creating a strategy that emphasizes co-evolution and a framework for open innovation in SMEs (Hitchen et al., 2017). Likewise, SM has enabled value creation from organizational competences for innovation through a typology of processes within social networks on different types of participation processes (Guilló, 2015), in which the more value a network can accrue, the richer the network's ability is to generate knowledge (Andersson et al., 2012).

In this way, as firms absorb new knowledge and face new tests related to innovation, they augment the need for virtual and socially-oriented growth projects (Reid et al., 2016). Consequently, online communities perform a key role as they assist organizations in adapting to a change, allowing them to sense/seize opportunities and re-configure organizational assets (Wagner et al., 2017), even if dependent on the group of lead users (Ernst and Brem, 2017).

To summarize, SM allows firms to absorb knowledge by involving groups of stakeholders (e.g., employees, clients) at various stages of the innovation project (Scuotto et al., 2017), allowing them to share capabilities, which in the end represent a competitive advantage for the innovation process.

3.3 Crowdsourcing

It has been argued that the motivation for use of crowdsourcing from stakeholders drives the innovation process, relying on both user's behavior and task characteristics that might provide guidance to design the innovation task (Yang et al., 2020). The process of designing a knowledge-sharing and engagement platform demands the task to be crowd sourced, a community of interest to be engaged and a structural capability to facilitate the effective engagement of the crowd (Rowe et al., 2015).

Therefore, crowdsourcing can be deemed as the enablement of innovation, either by identifying knowledge gaps, creating concepts on SM crowdsourcing (Singh, 2015), or by identifying crowdsourcing platforms in the development of B2B innovations along the innovation process of product development (Kärkkäinen et al., 2016). In that case, Zhu et al. (2017) present a framework on how to use internal and external crowds best to source new ideas and solution pathways, based on three key components (task, crowd and outcome) and their interrelationships. In this vein, others attempt to apply crowdsourcing effectively, comparing the outcomes of open co-creation approaches and enhancing the importance of lead users (Šundic and Leitner, 2017) and reviewing the theoretical concepts related to crowdsourcing (López Maciel et al., 2017).

Also, other streams of literature put the emphasis on the audiences of these online social networks that enable innovation. It is noteworthy to explore the characteristics of audiences in planning for innovation (Ferguson, 2017), together with the kind of platforms that have been used to get crowd engagement and to communicate with users. Finally, it is central to identify both the social networks related to the business and their key audiences (Mustafa and Mohammad, 2017) to better manage change (Ooms et al., 2015).

In sum, SM and crowdsourcing trigger organizational absorptive capacities, co-innovation activities and ensure competitive advantage (He and Wang, 2016), allowing, therefore, to seize business opportunities and reorganize users' content (Dong and Wu, 2015). As a consequence, innovation literature is currently reliant on SM/crowdsourcing when it comes to organizing knowledge sharing among stakeholders (Scuotto et al., 2017; Filieri, 2013).

3.4 Co-creation

As already mentioned, social media are expected to create profit and ameliorate margins, while improving the innovation process. Some studies show that if SM tools are used appropriately, organizations would augment their interactivity with other stakeholders, gain new clients and develop new products to fill a new need, which is the case of digital fashion that evidence co-creation strategies in brand-stretch and creation of added value, including professional advice (Ross, 2017). Consumers seem to be, therefore, interested in having long-term relationships with producers through co-creation processes, to produce better products, gain new insights (Antikainen and Niemelä, 2017) and attain a rewarding strategy (Antikainen and Niemelä, 2016).

To achieve these goals, SM can support innovative value co-creation by promoting dialogue among stakeholders, openness through a common platform of ideas/resources and encourage collaboration among teams (Ross, 2017). To summarize, SM provides fertile ground in developing innovative solutions for fostering co-creation of content, while being possible to open the innovation to the general public, focusing on user-generated content and communities for innovation ideation (Leminen et al., 2014).

3.5 New Product Development

NPD allows users to easily create, edit, or share content through SM and innovation practices, towards the achievement of competitive advantage. In doing so, we identify diverse streams of literature that emphasize NPD in distinct perspectives. Firstly, it refers to the use of SM as a tool to design and manage technologies, such as the PoRM (Prosumer-oriented Relationship Management) theory with implications in the design of future relationship management technologies (Potra et al., 2016). Secondly, literature refers to the practices involved in the NPD-related processes linked with the firm's innovation context and SM functionalities. Key types of changes were found that affect NPD-related processes, together with important factors in integrating SM into NPD process (Pacauskas et al., 2014). Thirdly, some authors focused on the relationship between national culture and new product development (NPD) in particular with respect to reverse innovation and innovation at the bottom-of-the-pyramid (BOP) (Barczak, 2012). In this vein, we believe that, in the light of culture, some people feel empowered by SM to come online, get involved in social interaction and share their experiences about a new product with other peers (Bugshan, 2015). Finally, another stream of literature focuses mostly on the organizational strategic capability and performance dependent upon the organizational and NPD process, either suggesting a strategic approach to a sustainability embedded in the NPD process of SM based open innovation (Du et al., 2016), or identifying factors influencing the relationship between SM and NPD performance in the form of information from SM channels (Roberts et al., 2016).

3.6 Case Study and Regions

Due to the diverse theoretical perspectives currently in use, the case study has been often applied in distinct contexts and we can conclude that ICT played a major role by increasing awareness of the community in its group dynamics, either more corporate or general public oriented (Pohjola and Puusa, 2016), as, for instance, through the building of a diversified service portfolio (Nayebi and Ruhe, 2014).

In what comes to the corporate perspective, some studies have tested, for instance in Siemens, the communications concept and its interdepartmental implementation following the open innovation paradigm (Karczewski and Zistl, 2017), whilst others focused on the role of the community in terms of strategic/innovative business development, namely in B2B in the company and its business ecosystems (Accoto et al., 2016). In addition, some pieces of literature have shown that customers provide valuable ideas for fostering innovation by illustrating how, for instance, a company has used the strategic information gathered from customers to develop new products (Filieri, 2013).

In contrast, with respect to the general public, other studies have revealed that some situational factors could affect the use of SM both for closed innovation and open innovation (He and Wang, 2016). It is noteworthy to mention the political context, as SM can be useful for civil society to set the political agenda and influence political discourse, provided the government is involved and a community manager follows a secured community platform (Díaz-Díaz and Pérez-González, 2016). Also, the exchange of knowledge on these situational factors through social networks will empower the community to cope with their opportunities and threats (Guillo, 2013). Case studies, both on firms and general public, could therefore be of interest to ascertain influencing key factors for SM innovation in varying contexts.

Finally, it is noteworthy to mention that some contexts have been favored when it comes to studies related with SM and innovation in n particular, Australia, in terms of how external knowledge flows from market-based actors sourced by SM influence, concluding that while knowledge flows are positively related to innovativeness, the relationship between external knowledge flows via SM depend on the importance a firm places on modern HRM practices (Corral de Zubielqui et al., 2019).

4. Conclusion

To summarize, we can conclude that SM has modified the way organizations interact with their contexts as SM relates with innovation in terms of marketing, process, organizational, technical and open innovation. Nevertheless, SM tools, are based on creativity and high levels of interaction between users enabling fast interactions, whereas source ideas to develop existing and new products can be seen as enhancing competitive advantage.

This LRSB provides an overview of the current trends of SM paradigms in innovation in our digital society. This paper has identified the most current SM and innovation theories. Additionally, it unveils the principal SM theories currently being used, as well as their categorization of SM in the sub themes of innovation, crowdsourcing, social networking , co-creation and new product development. This article is thus a step towards integrating the current research trends on SM and innovation, revealing the wider understanding of theory and context nuances, as SM is considered strategic in a firm's value, able to create a culture of innovation.

In a more detailed review, it is shown that the adoption of crowdsourcing, arising from stakeholders, could drive innovation activity, while online social networks enable managers to identify the networks related to their business and to interact with key audiences.

In the same vein, some innovative companies and public entities use SM to source ideas for improving existing products or for new product development.

Overall, the predominant theoretical perspectives used in current literature fail to encapsulate some issues of SM in its innovation process. In particular the emphasis on public SM seems to be highly identified with customer behavior. Consequently, a significant gap exists in the study of public innovation through SM. Also, most studies focus on specific contexts and regions, studying organizations and individuals as a unit of analysis, being therefore required to explore the SM innovation interaction from an integrative and holistic perspective instead of the sole role either of companies or users. Nevertheless, the pluralism of viewpoints in current literature confirms that there is no singular approach when it comes to SM use and innovation processes.

This study has several limitations. Firstly, the LRSB identifies current trends in the area. However the review used only the databases Scopus and EBSCOHost, which means that it might have omitted some relevant articles, even if the representation was high. However, due to our methodological strictness, we would have reduced the chances of an omitted article of significant implication for the analysis. Secondly, future studies building on this piece of literature could more accurately address the SM impact on innovation and behavior at diverse levels of connections, mainly on the public domain. Future studies could draw on the analysis provided in this LRSB to advance the knowledge of SM and innovation.

Acknowledgements

We would like to express our gratitude to the editor and the referees. They offered extremely valuable suggestions or improvements. The authors were supported by the GOVCOPP Research Center of Universidade de Aveiro and UNIDCOM research center of Universidade Europeia.

References

Accoto, C., Valtolina, E. and Mandelli, A. 2016. Social media in B2B: Myopen community at Bticino. pp. 145–166. *In:* Vandana Mangal, Andreina Mandelli, Uday Karmarkar, and Antonella La Rocca (Eds.). *The UCLA Anderson Business and Information Technologies (BIT) Project: A Global Study of Technology and Business Practice (2016).*

Afuah, A. 2014. Business model innovation: Concepts, analysis and cases. *Business Model Innovation: Concepts, Analysis and Cases*, 1–358.

Agostinho, C., Lampathaki, F., Jardim-Goncalves, R. and Lazaro, O. 2015, June. Accelerating web-entrepreneurship in local incubation environments. pp. 183–194. *In:* Persson, A. and Stirna, J. (Eds.). *International Conference on Advanced Information Systems Engineering*, Springer, Cham.

Andersson, P., Jarméus, P., Masog, S., Rosenqvist, C. and Sundberg, C. 2013. Creating value through open innovation in social E-learning. pp. 151–162. *In:* Eriksson Lundström, J., Wiberg, M., Hrastinski S., Edenius, M. and Ågerfalk, P. (Eds.). *Managing Open Innovation Technologies.* Springer, Berlin, Heidelberg.

Antikainen, M. and Niemelä, M. 2016. How to motivate and reward customers in an online co-creation process? pp. 347–372. *In:* Maria Antikainen and Marketta Niemelä (Eds.). *Open Innovation: A Multifaceted Perspective: Part II.*

Antikainen, M. and Niemelä, M. 2017. How to co-create local food products with consumers? *International Journal of Technology Marketing*, 12(1): 71–89.

Barczak, G. 2012. The future of NPD/innovation research. *Journal of Product Innovation Management*, 29(3): 355–357.

Barlatier, P.J. and Josserand, E. 2018. Delivering open innovation promises through social media. *Journal of Business Strategy.*

Barlatier, P.J. and Mention, A.L. 2019. How social media can fuel innovation in businesses: A strategic roadmap. *Journal of Business Strategy.*

Bhatti, S.H., Santoro, G., Sarwar, A. and Pellicelli, A.C. 2021. Internal and external antecedents of open innovation adoption in IT organisations: Insights from an emerging market. *Journal of Knowledge Management.*

Bhimani, H., Mention, A.L. and Barlatier, P.J. 2019. Social media and innovation: A systematic literature review and future research directions. *Technological Forecasting and Social Change*, 144: 251–269.

Bugshan, H. 2015. Open innovation using Web 2.0 technologies. *Journal of Enterprise Information Management*, 28(4): 595–607.

Candi, M., Roberts, D.L., Marion, T. and Barczak, G. 2018. Social strategy to gain knowledge for innovation. *British Journal of Management*, 29(4): 731–749.

Cherinka, R., Miller, R. and Prezzama, J. 2013. Emerging trends, technologies and approaches impacting innovation. pp. 92–97. *In:* IMETI 2013, *Proceedings of the 6th International Multi-Conference on Engineering and Technological Innovation-IMETI.*

Culpan, R. 2014. Open innovation business models and the role of interfirm partnerships. pp. 17–39. *In:* Culpan, R. (Eds.). *Open Innovation through Strategic Alliances.* Palgrave Macmillan, New York.

Dahlander, L. and Piezunka, H. 2014. Open to suggestions: How organizations elicit suggestions through proactive and reactive attention. *Research Policy*, 43(5): 812–827.

De Moor, A. and Aakhus, M. 2013. It's the conversation, stupid!. pp. 17–33. *In:* Eriksson Lundström J., Wiberg, M., Hrastinski, S., Edenius, M. and Ågerfalk, P. (Eds.). *Managing Open Innovation Technologies.* Springer, Berlin, Heidelberg.

de Zubielqui, G.C., Fryges, H. and Jones, J. 2019. Social media, open innovation and HRM: Implications for performance. *Technological Forecasting and Social Change*, 144: 334–347.

Díaz-Díaz, R. and Pérez-González, D. 2016. Implementation of social media concepts for e-government: Case study of a social media tool for value co-creation and citizen participation. *Journal of Organizational and End User Computing (JOEUC)*, 28(3): 104–121.

Dobusch, L. and Kapeller, J. 2018. Open strategy-making with crowds and communities: Comparing Wikimedia and Creative Commons. *Long Range Planning*, 51(4): 561–579.

Dong, J.Q. and Wu, W. 2015. Business value of social media technologies: Evidence from online user innovation communities. *The Journal of Strategic Information Systems*, 24(2): 113–127.

Drexler, G., Duh, A., Kornherr, A. and Korošak, D. 2014. Boosting open innovation by leveraging big data. *Open Innovation*. John Wiley Sons, Inc., S, 299–318.

Du, S., Yalcinkaya, G. and Bstieler, L. 2016. Sustainability, social media driven open innovation, and new product development performance. *Journal of Product Innovation Management*, 33: 55–71.

Ernst, M., Brem, A. and Voigt, K.I. 2014. Innovation management, lead-users, and social media— Introduction of a conceptual framework for integrating social media tools in lead-user management. *In:* Olivas-Luján, M.R. and Bondarouk, T. (Eds.). *Social Media in Strategic Management.* Emerald Group Publishing Limited.

Ernst, M. and Brem, A. 2017. Social media for identifying lead users? Insights into lead users' social media habits. *International Journal of Innovation and Technology Management*, 14(04): 1750022.

Ferguson, S.D. 2011. Strategic planning for communication of innovation: Crowdsourcing as social capital. pp. 229–242. *In:* Michael Hülsmann and Nicole Pfeffermann (Eds.). *Strategies and Communications for Innovations*. Springer, Berlin, Heidelberg.

Ferguson, S.D. 2013. Audience-centered approaches to strategic planning: accessing social capital through sharing platforms on social media. pp. 315–328. *In:* não encontrei (Eds.). *Strategy and Communication for Innovation*. Springer, Berlin, Heidelberg.

Filieri, R. 2013. Consumer co-creation and new product development: A case study in the food industry. *Marketing Intelligence and Planning.*

Freixanet, J., Braojos, J., Rialp-Criado, A. and Rialp-Criado, J. 2021. Does international entrepreneurial orientation foster innovation performance? The mediating role of social media and open innovation. *The International Journal of Entrepreneurship and Innovation*, 22(1): 33–44.

Gryczka, M. 2014. ICT usage as a key prerequisite for open knowledge environment creation. *Business and Economic Horizons*, 10(4): 348–361.

Guillo, M. 2013. Futures, communication and social innovation: U sing participatory foresight and social media platforms as tools for evaluating images of the future among young people. *European Journal of Futures Research*, 1(1): 17.

Guilló, M. 2015. Futures of participation and civic engagement within virtual environments. pp. 41–57. *In:* Jenifer Winter and Ryota Ono (Eds.). *The Future Internet*. Springer, Cham.

He, W. and Wang, F.K. 2016. A process-based framework of using social media to support innovation process. *Information Technology and Management*, 17(3): 263–277.

Hitchen, E.L., Nylund, P.A., Ferràs, X. and Mussons, S. 2017. Social media: Open innovation in SMEs finds new support. *Journal of Business Strategy.*

Iglesias-Sánchez, P.P., Correia, M.B. and Jambrino-Maldonado, C. 2019. Challenges of open innovation in the tourism sector. *Tourism Planning & Development*, 16(1): 22–42.

Jiao, Y., Wu, Y. and Lu, Q.S. 2020. Improving the performance of customer participation in new product development: the moderating effect of social media and firm capabilities. *Asian Journal of Technology Innovation*, 28(2): 284–304.

Jussila, J.J., Kärkkäinen, H. and Leino, M. 2012. Social media's opportunities in business-to-business customer interaction in innovation process. *International Journal of Technology Marketing*, 22, 7(2): 191–208.

Kärkkäinen, H., Jussila, J., Multasuo, J. and Helander, N. 2016. Can crowdsourcing platforms be used in B2B innovation? pp. 393–421. *In:* Anne-Laure Mention and Marko Torkkeli (Eds.). *Open Innovation: A Multifaceted Perspective: Part II.*

Kastelle, T. and Ohr, R. 2013. The role of social media for innovation. pp. 427–436. *In:* Nicole Pfeffermann, Tim Minshall and Letizia Mortara (Eds.). *Strategy and Communication for Innovation*. Springer, Berlin, Heidelberg.

Leminen, S., Westerlund, M., Sánchez, L. and Serra, A. 2014. Users as content creators, aggregators and distributors at Citilab Living Lab. *In:* Robert De Fillippi and Patrik Wikström (Eds.). *International*

Perspectives on Business Innovation and Disruption in the Creative Industries, Edward Elgar Publishing.

Maciel, G.T.L., Palacios, A.P. and Rosas, E.L.G. 2017. *Una revisión de la literatura sobre* crowdsourcing, *Journal of Innovation & Knowledge*, 2(1): 24–30.

Malsbender, A., Hoffmann, S. and Becker, J. 2014. Aligning capabilities and social media affordances for open innovation in governments. *Australasian Journal of Information Systems*, 18(3).

Markham, S.K. and Lee, H. 2013. Product development and management association's comparative performance assessment study (2012). *Journal of Product Innovation Management*, 30(3): 408–429.

Mention, A.L., Barlatier, P.J. and Josserand, E. 2019. Using social media to leverage and develop dynamic capabilities for innovation. *Technological Forecasting and Social Change*, 144: 242–250.

Mount, M. and Martinez, M.G. 2014. Social media: A tool for open innovation. *California Management Review*, 56(4): 124–143.

Mustafa, S.E. and Adnan, H.M. 2017. Crowdsourcing: A platform for crowd engagement in the publishing industry. *Publishing Research Quarterly*, 33(3): 283–296.

Nayebi, M. and Ruhe, G. 2014, June. Analytical open innovation for value-optimized service portfolio planning. pp. 273–288. *In:* Lassenius, C. and Smolander, K. (Eds.). *International Conference of Software Business*. Springer, Cham.

Nijssen, E.J. and Ordanini, A. 2020. How important is alignment of social media use and R&D – Marketing cooperation for innovation success? *Journal of Business Research*, 116: 1–12.

Ogink, T. and Dong, J.Q. 2019. Stimulating innovation by user feedback on social media: The case of an online user innovation community. *Technological Forecasting and Social Change*, 144: 295–302.

Oliveira, R.T., Indulska, M., Steen, J. and Verreynne, M.L. 2020. Towards a framework for innovation in retailing through social media. *Journal of Retailing and Consumer Services*, 54.

Ooms, W., Bell, J. and Kok, R.A. 2015. Use of social media in inbound open innovation: Building capabilities for absorptive capacity. *Creativity and Innovation Management*, 24(1): 136–150.

Pacauskas, D., Durgam, P. and Fomin, V.V. 2014. How companies can modify R&D for integrating social media activities into the new products development. *Bled eConference*, 39.

Patroni, J., von Briel, F. and Recker, J. 2020. Unpacking the social media-driven innovation capability: How consumer conversations turn into organizational innovations. *Information and Management*, 103267.

Pohjola, I. and Puusa, A. 2016. Group dynamics and the role of ICT in the life cycle analysis of community of practice-based product development: A case study. *Journal of Knowledge Management*.

Potra, S., Izvercian, M. and Miclea, S. 2016. Changes in CRM approach: Refined functional blocks for customer creative engagement in services. *International Journal of Information Systems in the Service Sector (IJISSS)*, 8(1): 45–57.

Qutaishat, A.M.A. and Alex, K. 2018. *Open Innovation for Smart Government: A Literature Review*, Paper presented at the *Atas da Conferencia da Associacao Portuguesa de Sistemas de Informacao*, October.

Rashid, Y., Waseem, A., Akbar, A.A. and Azam, F. 2019. Value co-creation and social media: A systematic literature review using citation and thematic analysis. *European Business Review*, 315: 761–784.

Ratten, V. 2016. Social media innovations and creativity. *In:* Alexander Brem and Eric Viardot (Eds.). *Revolution of Innovation Management: The Digital Breakthrough*, 1: 199–220.

Reid, I., Papalexi, M. and Slater, N. 2017. The influence of socially-oriented growth of virtual teams: A conceptual model. pp. 237–249 *In:* Anshuman Khare, Brian Stewart and Rod Schatz (Eds.). *Phantom Ex Machina*. Springer, Cham.

Roberts, D.L., Piller, F.T. and Lüttgens, D. 2016. Mapping the impact of social media for innovation: The role of social media in explaining innovation performance in the PDMA comparative performance assessment study. *Journal of Product Innovation Management*, 33: 117–135.

Rosário, A.M.F.T. and Cruz, R.N. 2019. Determinants of innovation in digital marketing. *Journal of Reviews on Global Economics*, 8: 1722–1731.

Rosário, A. 2021. Research-based guidelines for marketing information systems. *International Journal of Business Strategy and Automation*, 21: 1–16.

Rosário, A.T., Fernandes, F., Raimundo, R.G. and Cruz, R.N. 2021. Determinants of nascent entrepreneurship development. *Handbook of Research on Nascent Entrepreneurship and Creating New Ventures*, 172–193.

Ross, F. 2020. Co-creation via digital fashion technology in new business models for premium product innovation: Case-studies in menswear and womens wear adaptation. pp. 1147–1172. *In:* Information Resources Management Association (USA). *Sustainable Business: Concepts, Methodologies, Tools, and Applications*. IGI Global.

Rowe, M., Poblet, M. and Thomson, J.D. 2015, June. Creating value through crowdsourcing: the antecedent conditions. pp. 345–355. *In:* Bogumił Kamiński, Gregory Kersten and Tomasz Szapiro (Eds.). *International Conference on Group Decision and Negotiation*. Springer, Cham.

Sacavém, A., Cruz, R.V., Sousa, M., Rosário, A. and Gomes, J.S. 2019. An integrative literature review on leadership models for innovative organizations. *An integrative Literature Review on Leadership Models for Innovative Organizations*, 1741–1751.

Scuotto, V., DelGiudice, M., Della Peruta, M.R. and Tarba, S. 2017. The performance implications of leveraging internal innovation through social media networks: An empirical verification of the smart fashion industry. *Technological Forecasting and Social Change*, 120: 184–194.

Singh, P. 2014. Social media crowdsourcing: Supporting user-driven innovation by generating ideas, *International Journal of Online Marketing (IJOM)*, 4(2): 1–14.

Strategic Direction. 2019a. Framing the social media puzzle: A primer for strategists. *Strategic Direction*, 35(7): 2527. https://doi.org/10.1108/SD-04-2019-0072-.

Strategic Direction. 2019b. Innovating through social media: Using the power of social media to enhance open innovation. *Strategic Direction*, 35(4): 26–27. https://doi.org/10.1108/SD-01-2019-0015.

Šundic, M. and Leitner, K. 2018. Co-creation from a telecommunication provider's perspective: A comparative study on innovation with customers and employees. pp. 236–267. *In:* Christopher, L. Tucci, Allan Afuah and Gianluigi Viscusi (Eds.). *Creating and Capturing Value through Crowdsourcing*.

von Karczewski, J. and Zistl, S. 2017. Disrupting communication: innovation communications in the digital age. *In:* Pfeffermann N. and Gould, J. (Eds.). *Strategy and Communication for Innovation*, Springer, Cham.

Wagner, D., Wenzel, M., Wagner, H.T. and Koch, J. 2017. Sense, seize, reconfigure: Online communities as strategic assets. *Journal of Business Strategy*.

Yang, Y., Dong, C., Yao, X., Lee, P.K. and Cheng, T.C.E. 2020. Improving the effectiveness of social media-based crowdsourcing innovations: Roles of assurance mechanism and innovator's behavior. *Industrial Management and Data Systems*.

Zhu, H., Sick, N. and Leker, J. 2016, September. How to use crowdsourcing for innovation?: A comparative case study of internal and external idea sourcing in the chemical industry. pp. 887–901. *In:* PICMET '16. *2016 Portland International Conference on Management of Engineering and Technology (PICMET)*, IEEE.

3

Social Learning Analytics in Education
A Literature Review

Célio Gonçalo Marques,[1,*] *Ana Marta Rodrigues*[1] and
Ana Paula Ferreira[2]

INTRODUCTION

The rise of digital technology and its impact on the daily lives of citizens in all aspects of their professional and personal lives has been the focus of various international bodies. Aware of this reality and of the need to prepare institutions and citizens for an effective and safe use of digital technology, the European Commission (2020) presented the Digital Education Action Plan (2021–2027), which defines its vision for high quality, inclusive and accessible digital education in Europe. The plan is a call for action to strengthen cooperation at European level, to learn from the Covid-19 crisis during which technology is being used in education and training on an unprecedented scale and to adapt education and training systems to the digital age.

True integration of digital technology in the educational context brings countless benefits, not only for the systems themselves, but also for students and faculty, allowing more innovative pedagogical practices and consequently more motivation and improved educational success.

The virtual environments in which these educational activities take place are diverse, from Learning Management Systems (LMS) to social networks. These platforms generate huge amounts of data that can effectively support decision making at various levels: the academic institutions themselves, in strategic decision making,

---

[1] Laboratory of Pedagogical Innovation and Distance Learning (LIED.IPT), Center for Technology, Restoration and Art Enhancement (Techn & Art), Instituto Politécnico de Tomar, Portugal.
Email: ana.rodrigues@ipt.pt
[2] Center for Technology, Restoration and Art Enhancement (Techn & Art), Instituto Politécnico de Tomar, Portugal.
Email: anapaula.ferreira@ipt.pt
* Corresponding author: celiomarques@ipt.pt

such as the implementation of models capable of understanding and supporting student learning; the academic staff, who can tailor teaching strategies; and even the students themselves, who can monitor activities and learning.

This 'measurement, collection, analysis and reporting of data about learners and their contexts for purposes of understanding and optimizing learning and the environments in which it occurs' (Long and Siemens, 2011; Siemens, 2011)—Learning Analytics—becomes more and more important as it allows modeling, predicting and optimizing learning processes.

However, in a paradigm where collaborative learning environments are increasingly privileged, namely social media (e.g., Facebook, Twitter, blogs or forums), the interactions between stakeholders and the contributions they make in the improvement of the education/training system gain greater focus. The data generated in these environments has an enormous potential and makes the study of social learning analytics (SLA) a crucial area. SLA focuses on how learners construct knowledge in their cultural and social settings (Ferguson and Shum, 2012).

The systematic analysis of the amount of data generated by learning platforms and the interactions created in learning communities, formal or informal, bring important contributions that can support institutions by providing data on how the students learn. In this way, they contribute to the improvement of teaching and learning processes, enabling the personalization of pedagogical approaches which, in this way, are adapted to the specific needs of students, as well as to the development of tools which facilitate and improve the work of students and faculty.

In this context, the present paper aims to present a longitudinal overview of the research carried out between January 2012 and 2020 in the area of SLA, characterizing how SLA is used in different educational contexts.

The specific objectives of this study are: (a) to characterize the research trends on SLA; (b) to describe the research methods used in the presented studies; (c) to identify the stakeholders; (d) to identify the areas of interest in SLA based on the future research proposed in the studies.

The methodology used in this study was systematic literature review and followed the seven steps proposed by the Cochrane standard for systematic reviews (Higgins and Thomas, 2021): (1) formulate the research questions; (2) locate and select the studies; (3) assess the quality of the studies; (4) collect the data; (5) analyze and present the results; (6) interpret the results; (7) improve and update the reviews.

The chapter is organized into four sections. The background outlines the theoretical framework of the research conducted and the conceptual basis of the study. The research design and methodology justify the methodological options underlying the research and describe the instruments and procedures used in the data collection and processing phases. Then, in the third section, the results are presented and discussed, duly integrated in the respective theoretical-methodological support. The fourth section contains the conclusions and looks at some current challenges in this area of research. This section also mentions the limitations of this study and presents directions that may be further explored in future research.

1. Background

Technology has given rise to more fluid, democratic and accessible learning spaces (Laat and Prinsen, 2014), transforming educational practices (Ehlers, 2011) and giving prominence to more collaborative, interactive and participatory learning (Tucker et al., 2013). Chen et al. (2018), p. 1 note that "learning in all settings is arguably a social process that cannot be fully accounted for by cognition and behavior of the individual". The importance of the social process is also highlighted by Siemens (2015) who states that learning is more effective when it is collaborative and social in nature.

It should be noted that "learning in a social context is a meaning-making process, where this meaning can be based upon prior experiences as well as the more immediate social context in which something is learned; meaning is made through negotiation among the various actors participating in a learning context" (Laat and Prinsen, 2014, p. 53). The spaces provided by Learning Management Systems, social media tools and MOOCS stand out (Kaliisa et al. 2019).

The importance of these new environments and the wealth of data they provide elevate the importance of the concept of Learning Analytics which, as we saw earlier, focuses on the massive use of data to improve learning (Clow, 2013). Not only do these tools provide vast amounts of data, but they easily enable its tracking, extraction and aggregation (Dawson, 2010).

Studying data to assess learners' patterns in these learning environments leads us to the concept of social learning analytics (SLA), a subset of learning analytics (Adraoui et al., 2017; Ferguson and Shum, 2012; Shum and Ferguson, 2012). "Social learning analytics make use of data generated by learners' online activity in order to identify behaviors and patterns within the learning environment that signify an effective process" (Ferguson and Shum, 2012, p. 8).

According to Shum and Ferguson (2012, p. 5) "the focus of social learning analytics is on processes in which learners are not solitary, and are not necessarily doing work to be marked, but are engaged in social activity, either interacting directly with others (for example, messaging, friending or following) or using platforms in which their activity traces will be experienced by others (for example, publishing, searching, tagging or rating)".

This research area is quite recent and the first reference we found on the term is from 2010: "Towards a social learning space for open educational resources", by Shum and Ferguson (2010), p. 10. The main focus of this concept is the learners, i.e., data is collected, analyzed and used to understand learners' behavior in order to provide improvements in the teaching-learning process (Gašević et al., 2015).

This data can be obtained directly from the platforms (e.g., LMS or from MOOCs) or through an Application Programming Interface (API) in the case of social media tools, such as Twitter, Facebook, Instagram, Wikipedia, YouTube, among others (Aguilar et al., 2019). The huge amount of data generated is sometimes seen as 'big data', which must be properly classified, mixed, filtered and processed (Monca et al., 2016), in order to contribute to the improvement of the teaching and learning process (Merceron et al., 2015).

Ferguson and Shum (2012) propose a taxonomy that divides SLA into five categories. Category (1) Social Network Analytics (SNA) addresses interpersonal relationships, connection between individuals, contacts, resources or ideas (usually with representations by sociograms, graphs or maps showing the overall picture of these relationships). Category (2) Discourse Analytics focuses on language as a primary tool for knowledge construction. The approach to Social Learning Discourse Analytics employs a structured deliberation of mapping the platform under study, to study what learners pay attention to, what viewpoints they assume, how topics are distributed among participants and how semantic relations are between individuals. The remaining three, meanwhile, are 'socialised categories', and labeled as being specialized, applied in social settings. Category (3) Content Analytics refers to user-generated content on Web 2.0, Learning Management Systems or other platforms from which it is possible to extract dialogues, tags, ratings, reputation, textual content, multimedia, video or metadata, which the instructor can use to improve courses. Category (4) Disposition Analytics focuses on intrinsic motivations for learning and innovation. It is used to provide the learners with a perception of a set of dimensions which allow description of mood, engagement, type of activities and personal approach to learning. The last category (5) Context Analytics, is about data generated in context, referring to technological support as well as formal and informal content in learning.

Laat and Prinsen (2014), in their study on social learning analytics in higher education, group the examples of SLA tools and practices into three categories: (1) increase awareness and participation; (2) increase awareness and cultivate networks; and (3) cultivate networks and value creation.

The study of SLA is particularly relevant within the field of Learning Analytics,[1] which in turn stands out within the field of a cademics analytics, a concept that besides the educational aspects also focuses on the administrative and business side (Campbell et al., 2007; Goldstein and Katz, 2005).

The challenges of SLA are diverse and are related to several domains, particularly the pedagogical component, technical aspects (use of 'big data' and artificial intelligence), methods and ethical issues; therefore, we considered the preparation of a systematic literature review on the subject to be of utmost importance.

2. Research Design and Methodology

This research, which falls within the SLA thematic area, aims to present a longitudinal overview of the research carried out in this area between January 2012 and 2020, characterizing how SLA is used in different educational contexts.

Given the research characteristics, the chosen methodology was the systematic literature review, which involves the clear formulation of research questions, the correct definition of the selection criteria and the presentation of conclusions that provide new information on the topic under study (Thomas et al., 2012) because as

---

[1] According to Shum and Ferguson (2012) the concept of Learning Analytics originated from the concepts of business intelligence and Data Mining and the latter, in turn, gave rise to the concept of Educational Data Mining.

Torraco (2005, p. 362) argues: "The result of a comprehensive synthesis of literature is that new knowledge or perspective is created despite the fact that the review summarizes previous research". In this sense and taking into account the desired objectives, four research questions were formulated:

RQ1: What are the research trends of the SLA field in education?

RQ2: What research methods are used?

RQ3: Who are the stakeholders?

RQ4: What are the suggestions for future research?

The Cochrane standard for systematic reviews (Higgins and Thomas, 2021) was selected for this systematic review and the seven steps specified therein were followed: after formulating the research questions (1), the studies to be included in the corpus for analysis were located and selected, (2) and their critical appraisal was performed (3). Subsequently, data were collected (4), analyzed and organized with a view to their presentation (5), which allowed for their interpretation (6). Finally, based on the results obtained, improvement proposals were put forward and the reviews were updated (7).

The procedures followed in each of these steps as well as the data collection instruments are described below.

2.1 Data Collection Procedures and Tools

After formulating the research questions, the data sources were defined to select the studies to be included. We selected the databases with the greatest current impact: Scopus and Web of Science. Both are of a multidisciplinary nature and can converge in a wide range of fields. It was also determined to identify relevant conferences in SLA-related areas. As there was no conference with this specific title, the Learning Analytics and Knowledge Conference organized by the Society for Learning Analytics Research (SoLAR) has been considered. The ACM Digital Library was used to access the conference papers.

2.2 Research Parameters and Inclusion and Exclusion Criteria

A wide range of academic literature has emerged with the topic 'Learning Analytics', whereas the term 'Social Learning Analytics' appears in the sources accessed only from 2012; therefore, it was agreed to limit the documents to the 2012–2020 period.

In all three databases selected, the search parameter was: *Social Learning Analytics*, written only in English and including all types of publications. This literature search was conducted in February 2021.

- *Search in ACM Digital Library*: In the 2012–2020 period, the title 'Social Learning Analytics' searched only in the 'International Conference on Learning Analytics and knowledge', returned 17 results. The system of creating lists in the binder available in the platform itself has been used.
- *Search in Scopus*: The same previous criteria were used and the exclusion of scientific papers in other languages was added (in this case, only Spanish was

identified) returning 73 results. Scopus allows creating listings in CVS format which were then accessed through Microsoft Excel.

- *Search in Web of Science*: The same criteria of the Scopus database were used and 47 results were returned.

A total of 137 publications were identified: 17 results in ACM Digital Library; 73 results in Scopus; and 47 in Web of Science. The Excel listings extracted from the data sources themselves allowed access to a set of relevant information, such as full abstracts, titles, keywords, author identification, document type, year, country, among others.

Identifying Repetitions and Selecting Documents for the Study Context: Before reading the abstracts, the lists of all results in the three databases were merged to identify possible duplications. The Scopus list was used as a reference, since it was the list with the largest number of results. Of the Web of Science results, only four publications were not in the Scopus list; in the ACM Digital Library list, no new publications were identified. Therefore, 77 publications were considered.

Once repetitions have been eliminated, the titles and abstracts of the publications were read. 'Learning Analytics' themes were identified which, having many similarities with the topic under study, were erroneously inserted in the database lists. We also identified documents whose research was inserted in another context outside education. In total, 36 documents were excluded for not matching the scope of SLA and education.

This phase was completed and 41 documents were considered which, based on the abstract, referred to the concept of SLA in education. These were read in full and, for this purpose, a code consisting of a letter and a number was assigned to identify and categorize them: the A-list from the Scopus data source; and the B-list from the Web of Science data source. In this full-text reading process, we identified some publications that met the abstract criteria, but did not contain some of the conditions defined at the beginning of the analysis, including:

- One publication in Italian and one in Spanish (they contained an abstract in English) that were only identified when selected for full reading (Margottini and Rossi, 2020; Motz et al., 2018);
- One publication whose content we could not access (Ouyang, 2015);
- Three publications (Ahn, 2013; Nistor et al., 2017; Nistor et al., 2018) were eliminated because during the analysis it was found that they did not report specifically to the field of education, i.e., two articles were specific to blogs not related to education and another intended to measure literacy in social media (also not related to education);
- Three papers (Abu Khousa and Atif, 2016; Adraoui et al., 2018a; Hernández-García and Conde-González, 2016) were eliminated because we detected that they were different perspectives of studies already considered in this research, which would be redundant for the analysis in question.

After this process, 30 documents were considered which constitute the corpus of analysis of this study.

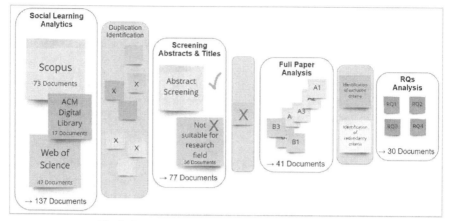

Fig. 1: Research and selection parameters used in the study.

Given the amount of existing information, it was necessary to develop a framework, identifying data or patterns that can answer research questions (Lessard-Hébert et al., 2013) in order to present and interpret the findings; steps recommended by Miles et al. (2019).

After data reduction, which allowed for the identification of significant patterns (Patton, 2014), the data were organized and presented, i.e., the collected information was structured in order to draw conclusions and make decisions, as mentioned by Miles et al. (2019). This data analysis is essential because it allows researchers to compare information and identify patterns and relationships relevant to the study. All collected material was therefore organized and systematized using a mixed content analysis through several analysis frameworks.

3. Results and Discussions

According to the established inclusion and exclusion criteria, 30 documents produced between 2012 and 2020 were analyzed. As shown in Fig. 2, the year 2017 contributed the most number of publications (eight).

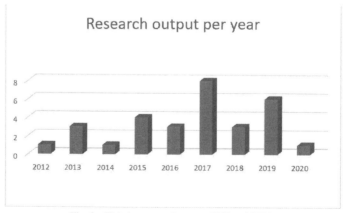

Fig. 2: SLA documents between 2012 and 2020.

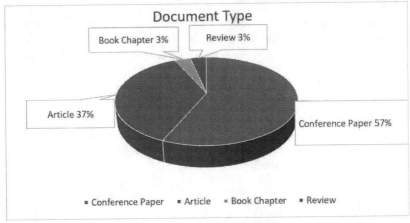

Fig. 3: Document type between 2012 and 2020.

In terms of typology, the majority are conference papers (57 per cent) followed by scientific papers (37 per cent). As for the remaining ones (book chapter and review), they are represented in this analysis with only one document each (Fig. 3).

Regarding the conferences (17 publications), the ACM International Conference contributed with the most number of publications (five) followed by Computers in Human Behavior (two) and Business Information Processing (two).

Below are the results related to the research questions of the study:

RQ1: What are the research trends of the SLA field in education (between January 2012 and 2020)?

The publications were grouped into five categories, following the taxonomy in SLA proposed by Ferguson and Shum (2012). We can see that the categories of Social Network Analytics and Content Analytics gathered more research papers (Table 1).

It should be noted that nine publications were classified into two categories (Aguilar et al., 2019; Babu et al., 2017; Chen et al., 2018; Clauss et al., 2019; Díaz-Lázaro et al., 2017; Hernández-García and Suárez-Navas, 2017; Kaliisa et al., 2019;

Table 1: Categorization of publications according to the taxonomy proposed by Ferguson and Shum (2012).

Category	Document
Social Network Analytics (SNA)	(Adraoui, Retbi et al., 2018b; Adraoui et al., 2017; Chaparro-Peláez et al., 2015; Chen et al., 2018; Hernández-García et al., 2015; Hernández-García and Suárez-Navas, 2017; Kaliisa et al., 2019; Ouyang, 2019; Rienties and Toetenel, 2016; Schreurs et al., 2013; Zampieri and Oliveira, 2017; Zhuhadar et al., 2013; Zorrilla and de Lima Silva, 2019).
Discourse Analytics	(Díaz-Lázaro et al., 2017; Kaliisa et al., 2019).
Content Analytics	(Aguilar et al., 2019; Chen et al., 2018; Clauss et al., 2019; Díaz-Lázaro et al., 2017; Haya et al., 2015; Hernández-García and Suárez-Navas, 2017; Lenk and Clauss, 2020; Ouyang, 2019; Zhuhadar et al., 2013).
Disposition Analytics	(Babu et al., 2017; Nistor et al., 2019; Pesare et al., 2017).
Context Analytics	(Aguilar et al., 2019; Babu et al., 2017; Clauss et al., 2019).

Ouyang, 2019; Zhuhadar et al., 2013) and another nine publications were not put in any of the categories because their contents did not specifically address any of them (Dahlberg, 2017; Dascalu et al., 2016; Dascalu et al., 2018; Ferguson and Shum, 2012; Hickey et al., 2014; Khousa et al., 2015; Manca et al., 2016; Viberg and Dahlberg, 2013; Williams, 2017).

The analysis of the keywords of the publications allowed the identification of 144 expressions or words from which the keyword cloud in Fig. 4 was generated. The most frequent expression is 'Social Learning Analytics' (17) followed by 'Learning Analytics' (10), 'Social Learning' (7) and 'Social Network Analysis' (7).

We also counted the words used in the titles (Table 2). The most frequent word is 'Learning' (36) followed by the words 'Social' (24), 'Analytics' (19) and 'Online' (10).

Fig. 4: Keyword cloud.

Table 2: Most common title words.

Position	Word	Frequency
1°	Learning	36
2°	Social	24
3°	Analytics	19
4°	Online	10
5°	Education	6
6°	Collaboration	4
7°	Interactive	4
8°	Community	3
9°	Higher	3
10°	Design	3
11°	Tool	3
12°	Engagement	3

Note: From a total of 130 different title words

Table 3 shows the research questions that were found. It should be noted that the research questions were not always clearly referred to in the documents under analysis.

Table 3: Identified research questions.

Document	Research Questions
(Lenk and Clauss, 2020)	RQ1. Which support does the e-tutor need to monitor and analyze online collaboration? RQ2. How can this support be provided?
(Nistor et al., 2019)	RQ 1: What are students' attitudes and perceptions of B-LABS? RQ2: How far can students follow the recommended learning scenario? RQ3: What are the cognitive effects of the seminar?
(Aguilar et al., 2019)	Our hypothesis that the activities/tools of the best students are the base to improve the performance of the rest of students, selecting those learning activities/tools included in the learning style of each student, to personalize his/her learning process, is an initial information that can exploit SaCI.
(Kaliisa et al., 2019)	We address the following RQ: What are the opportunities of SLA in terms of generating relevant insights about students' online learning processes which teachers can use to make timely and informed pedagogical decisions?
(Chen et al., 2018)	RQ1. Did students use the SLA toolkit? To what extent did students find the toolkit useful? To what extent did students find the toolkit usable? RQ2. To what extent did the toolkit foster social engagement in online discussions? RQ3. To what extent did the toolkit facilitate conceptual engagement reflected in the content of student posts?
(Hernández- et al., 2015)	RQ1. Are social network parameters of the different actors related to student outcomes in online learning? RQ2. Are global social network parameters related to overall class performance? RQ3. Can visualizations from social network analysis provide additional information about visible and invisible interactions in online classrooms that help in improving the learning process?
(Zhuhadar et al., 2013)	RQ1. What was the impact of using of the Social Multimedia System in general on faculty members' overall satisfaction with their courses compared to other courses in which the Social Multimedia System was not used? RQ2. What was the impact of using of the Social Multimedia System in general on students' learning experience and success compared to other courses in which the Social Multimedia System was not used?
(Clauss et al., 2019)	RQ1. How often is a participant present on the platform compared to other learners? RQ2. How has the activity of the users changed over the course of the project and the different assignments? RQ3. Which communication tool is used the most/least and thus has the highest/lowest acceptance among the participants? RQ4. Which participants communicate most/least? RQ5. Do participants actively participate in the discussion with group members? RQ6. Is there a continuous communication over a longer period of time?
(Ouyang, 2019)	Whether, to what extent, and how does the IntVisRep tool and relevant supporting pedagogies foster individual knowledge construction, social interaction and group knowledge advancement?

Note: Documents not containing clearly expressed research questions were not included in this table.

The research objectives of the studies were divided into five types: Strength of Relationships and Interactions (A); Learning Process (B); Learner Engagement (C); Performance or Assessment (D); SLA Theoretical Framework (E). This division took into account the verbs and intentions specified in the research objectives (Table 4).

Table 4: Objectives identified in the documents under analysis (n = 30).

Type	Research Objectives	
A. Strength of relationships & interactions	To analyze and measure social network relationships.	(Adraoui et al., 2017; Adraoui, Retbi et al., 2018b; Chaparro-Peláez et al, 2015; Schreurs et al., 2013; Zampieri and Oliveira, 2017; Zorrilla and de Lima Silva, 2019).
	To observe the emerging visible and invisible social network structures from student/ instructor interactions.	(Hernández-García et al., 2015).
B. Learning Process	To contribute to learning design (integrate learner with SLA tools).	(Haya et al., 2015; Nistor et al., 2019).
	To foster interactive, collaborative learning in online discussions, engaging learning more effectively.	(Ouyang, 2019; Zhuhadar et al., 2013).
	To have insights into how students learn (habits and collaboration in online environments).	(Kaliisa et al., 2019; Díaz-Lázaro et al., 2017).
	To observe and analyz e learning styles.	(Aguilar et al., 2019).
	To monitor student progress	(Hernández-García and Suárez-Navas, 2017; Lenk and Clauss, 2020).
C. Learner Engagement	To have insights into student's preferences, to measure the engagement in online discussion.	(Babu et al., 2017; Chen et al., 2018; Pesare et al., 2017).
D. Performance or Assessment	To produce measurable indicators for supporting assessment	(Clauss et al., 2019; Williams, 2017).
	To predict and understand performance of students in blended and online environments.	(Rienties and Toetenel, 2016).
E. Theoretical SLA	To highlight the importance and relevance of SLA educational challenges.	(Dascalu et al., 2018; Manca et al., 2016).
	How learning analytics is perceived and perspectives.	(Hickey et al., 2014; Viberg and Dahlberg, 2013).
	To reflect about knowledge management, suggesting SLA in MOOCs.	(Viberg and Messina, 2013).
	To provide some insights mapping the socio-cultural continuum in order to explore where and how learning opportunities emerge.	(Dahlberg, 2017).
	To provide model and concepts about Communities of Practice (CoP).	(Khousa et al., 2015).
	To describe early work towards SLA and encourage learners to help shaping analytics and their associated recommendations.	(Ferguson and Shum, 2012).

The 'Learning Process' and the analysis of 'Strength of Relationships and Interactions' are the categories with more publications, 10 and six respectively.

RQ2: What research methods are used?

Analysis of the methodological plan used by researchers in the publications presented here points to some diversity in the studies conducted, although there is a prevalence of case studies:

- Case study (Clauss et al., 2019; Haya et al., 2015; Hernández-García and Suárez-Navas, 2017; Hernández-García et al., 2015; Hickey et al., 2014).
- Design-based research methodology (Hickey et al., 2014; Nistor et al., 2019; Ouyang, 2019).
- Ethnographic study (Dahlberg, 2017).

It should be noted that in some of the publications the methodological plans of the studies are not clearly identified.

With regards to data collection techniques, most studies use documentary analysis of the data collected from the platforms. The questionnaire is also found in several studies (Table 5).

As for data processing tools, these were chosen by taking into account the following aspects: data capture; data extraction; algorithms for community detection; content analysis; statistical analysis; descriptive statistics; graphic data processing. Table 6 shows that the most used tools were SPSS with statistical analysis (4); Gephi for descriptive statistics (5) and GraphFES for data extraction (2).

RQ3: Who are the stakeholders?

Of the 30 publications analyzed, 90 per cent refer to SLA in higher education with 10 per cent of the articles not identifying the level of education. When analyzing the learning environments, 37 per cent of the articles focus on LMS, 30 per cent on social media tools, 10 per cent on Massive Open Online Courses (MOOCs), one on a proprietary platform and one on MOOCs and social media tools. It should also be noted that 17 per cent of the publications do not portray any specific learning environment (Fig. 5).

Table 5: Data collection techniques.

Data Collection Techniques	ID Document
Documentary Analysis	(Adraoui et al., 2017; Aguilar et al., 2019; Babu et al., 2017; Chaparro-Peláez et al., 2015; Chen et al., 2018; Clauss et al., 2019; Dahlberg, 2017; Dascalu et al., 2018; Díaz-Lázaro et al., 2017; Ferguson and Shum, 2012; Haya et al., 2015; Hernández-García and Suárez-Navas, 2017; Hernández-García et al., 2015; Hickey et al., 2014; Kaliisa et al., 2019; Khousa et al., 2015; Lenk and Clauss, 2020; Manca et al., 2016; Nistor et al., 2019; Ouyang, 2019; Pesare et al., 2017; Rienties and Toetenel, 2016; Schreurs et al., 2013; Viberg and Dahlberg, 2013; Williams, 2017; Zampieri and Oliveira, 2017; Zorrilla and de Lima Silva, 2019).
Questionnaire Survey	(Dascalu et al., 2018; Dascalu et al., 2016; Lenk and Clauss, 2020; Nistor et al., 2019; Zhuhadar et al., 2013; Zorrilla and de Lima Silva, 2019).

Note: Some documents use more than one data collection technique.

Table 6: Tools identified.

Objective	Tools	Documents
Data collection	SQL query	(Aguilar et al., 2019).
Statistical Analysis	SPSS	(Díaz-Lázaro et al., 2017; Hernández-García et al., 2015; Nistor et al., 2019; Rienties and Toetenel, 2016).
	Anova	(Nistor et al., 2019).
Descriptive Statistics	ORA Software	(Zorrilla and de Lima Silva, 2019).
	Gephi	(Chaparro-Peláez et al., 2015; Díaz-Lázaro et al., 2017; Hernández-García and Suárez-Navas, 2017; Hernández-García et al., 2015; Schreurs et al., 2013).
	Facebook Graph API	(Zorrilla and de Lima Silva, 2019).
	Twitter AP	(Zorrilla and de Lima Silva, 2019).
Data extraction	Netvizz	(Díaz-Lázaro et al., 2017).
	GraphFES	(Chaparro-Peláez et al., 2015; Hernández-García and Suárez-Navas, 2017).
	SNAPP	(Chaparro-Peláez et al., 2015).
Algorithms for community detection	ForceAtlas2	(Adraoui et al., 2018b; Chen et al., 2018).
	Louvian Blondel	(Adraoui et al., 2018b; Chen et al., 2018).
	Mind Maps	(Clauss et al., 2019).
	Pajek	(Adraoui et al., 2017; Schreurs et al., 2013).
Graphic data processing	NetDraw	(Schreurs et al., 2013).
	NodeXL	(Schreurs et al., 2013).
	JUNG	(Schreurs et al., 2013).
	ELLI	(Ferguson and Shum, 2012).
	Coh-Metrix	(Kaliisa et al., 2019).
Content Analysis	Nvivo	(Díaz-Lázaro et al., 2017).
	Network Text Analysis	(Haya et al., 2015).
	AutoMap	(Haya et al., 2015).

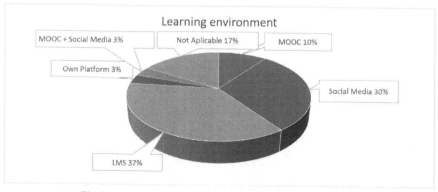

Fig. 5: Learning environments from the SLA analysis documents.

Concerning LMS, Moodle is identified in six articles and there are also two references to Canvas. In terms of social media, social networks are highlighted, namely Facebook (3), Elgg (2) and Twitter (1). There is also the analysis of wikis (1), blogs (1) and other social media platforms such as SocialLearn (2), Adobe Conect (1) and JustLearn (1). There is also an own platform (wikisate).

The target of analyzed articles are students' interactions (100 per cent), with 16.7 per cent of the publications being also analyzed as to teachers' interactions.

Spain is the country with the most papers (five) followed by the United States of America (five) and the United Kingdom (four). The list includes 18 countries from Europe (64 per cent), America (21 per cent), Asia (9 per cent) and Africa (6 per cent) (Fig. 6).

RQ4: What are the suggestions for future research?

The data concerning the proposals for future research presented in the papers are organized into three major categories (Table 7):

A. Improvement of the platform and/or its features;
B. Validation, further development or continuation of the study;
C. Analysis of the implications in the improvement of the teaching/learning process, i.e., both in terms of faculty and students.

In respect of the category 'A. Platform/tool(s) improvement', the proposals focus on the following aspects: improvement of the graphical representation (Ferguson and Shum, 2012; Zorrilla and de Lima Silva, 2019); introduction of new features (Lenk and Clauss, 2020), particularly with regard to discourse analysis (Zorrilla and de Lima Silva, 2019); provision of information to improve collaboration (Ouyang, 2019); incorporation of new learning models (Aguilar et al., 2019); integration of new data on learners, i.e., demographic, personal and socio-cultural data (Rienties and Toetenel, 2016); integration of rules that ensure data privacy and protection (Manca et al., 2016).

Fig. 6: Distribution per country from the SLA analysis.

Table 7: Future research categories.

Category	Sub-category	Documents
A. Platform/tool(s) improvement	Graphic Representation	(Ferguson and Shum, 2012; Zorrilla and de Lima Silva, 2019).
	Features	(Lenk and Clauss, 2020; Zorrilla and de Lima Silva, 2019).
	Information made available	(Ouyang, 2019).
	Learning models	(Aguilar et al., 2019).
	Student data	(Rienties and Toetenel, 2016).
	Data privacy and protection	(Manca et al., 2016).
B. Validation, further development or continuation of the study	Continuity of work	(Adraoui et al., 2018b; Adraoui et al., 2017; Ferguson and Shum, 2012; Pesare et al., 2017; Viberg and Dahlberg, 2013).
	Study validation	(Dahlberg, 2017; Kaliisa et al., 2019; Khousa et al., 2015).
	Model generation	(Dascalu et al., 2018).
	Increase in the number of participants	(Adraoui et al., 2017; Hickey et al., 2014).
	Making more data available on the platform	(Rienties and Toetenel, 2016).
C. Analysis of implications for improving teaching and learning	Implications for students	(Chen et al., 2018; Clauss et al., 2019; Hernández-García et al., 2015; Nistor et al., 2019; Schreurs et al., 2013).
	Implications for faculty	(Díaz-Lázaro et al., 2017; Zorrilla and de Lima Silva, 2019).

When it comes to the category 'B. Validation, further development or continuation of the study', there are several publications that point to the need to further develop the study, in order to: continue the work conducted (Adraoui et al., 2017; Adraoui et al., 2018b; Ferguson and Shum, 2012; Pesare et al., 2017; Viberg and Dahlberg, 2013); validate the study conducted (Dahlberg, 2017; Kaliisa et al., 2019; Khousa et al., 2015), namely by creating models (Dascalu et al., 2018), increase the number of participants (Adraoui et al., 2017; Hickey et al., 2014) or make more data available on the platform (Rienties and Toetenel, 2016).

Finally, the category 'C. Analysis of implications for improving teaching and learning', the proposals left by the researchers concern the main actors of the education process:

- Students, notably to understand their activity within formal and informal education (Nistor et al., 2019); to support learning by providing visual data to students (Aguilar et al., 2019) or tools to support goal achievement (Chen et al., 2018), academic performance (Hernández-García et al., 2015) or to motivate them to learn (Clauss et al., 2019; Schreurs et al., 2013).
- Faculty members/instructors, to support the teaching process, namely in identifying the relationship between the methodologies used and student engagement (Zorrilla and de Lima Silva, 2019) or in supporting the design of new teaching experiences (Díaz-Lázaro et al., 2017).

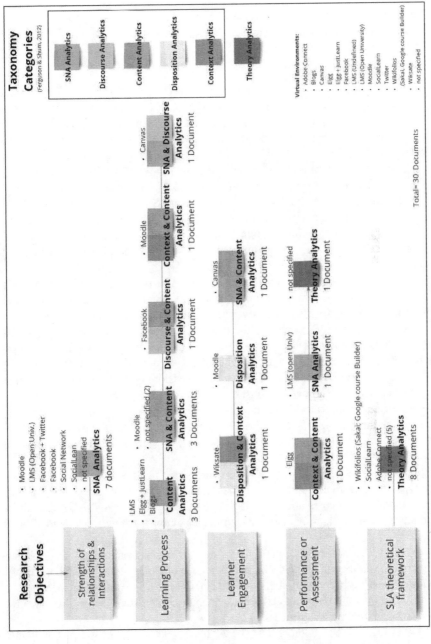

Fig. 7: Conceptual Map: Relationship between research objectives, taxonomy categories and virtual environments.

Figure 7 summarizes three dimensions previously analyzed in the research questions presented in this study.

It shows the distribution of publications by research objectives and, simultaneously, their classification according to Fergu son and Shum's taxonomy (2012), with the virtual environments addressed in the study.

4. Conclusion

This study presents a systematic literature review in the area of SLA and a longitudinal overview of the research conducted between January 2012 and 2020 in educational settings. We started this study with 137 publications identified by the data sources; however, after applying the selection criteria defined for the study, the research focused on 30 publications.

Regarding SLA trends in education (RQ1) and following the categories proposed in the SLA taxonomy by Ferguson and Shum (2012), it can be seen that the most addressed themes are: Social Network Analytics and Content Analytics.

Concerning the objectives of the study, it is possible to group them into five typologies: (a) Strength of Relationships & Interactions; (b) Learning Process; (c) Learner Engagement; (d) Performance or Assessment; and (e) SLA Theoretical Framework.

The works whose research objective is to measure the Strength of Relationships and Interactions (A) generally use more visual representations, such as Sociograms or MindMaps, which provide a visual overview of the distribution of these interactions. Most of the publications related to the learning process research objective (B) fall into the Content Analytics category and focus on the content generated in the groups, using both quantitative and qualitative methods. In the objective Learner Engagement (C), the publications focus on learners' preferences, aiming at measuring motivation and engagement. Performance or Assessment (D) presents studies whose focus is on the production of indicators to support assessment or the prediction of performance. Finally, the theoretical SLA objective (E) comprises a variety of papers that include evidence on the importance of SLA in education, knowledge management; models and concepts and surveys on the subject.

In an attempt to identify possible patterns, correlations were calculated between the types of objectives and the categories of the taxonomy; however, the analysis did not identify any correlation. Nor is an evolutionary trend revealed between older and more recent work, only distinctive strategies of approaching learning in a social context.

As for the methods used (RQ2), there is no prevalence of a particular methodology, although there is a higher incidence of case studies. In these studies, a range of tools has been used, such as Gephi and GraphFES to obtain and extract data, algorithms for community detection, content analysis, statistical analysis, descriptive statistics and graphic data processing.

With regard to stakeholders (RQ3), we found that most studies focus on higher education (90 per cent), which may be related to the affiliation of their authors. About two-thirds of the papers focus on LMS (37 per cent) and on social media tools (30 per cent). In what concerns LMS, Moodle is the most referred to, whereas in terms of social media, the highlight goes to Facebook. The target of the papers analyzed are the students' interactions, but 16.7 per cent of the publications also analyze the teachers' interactions. It does not seem to us that there is a predominance of publications by region. The papers are distributed across 18 countries in Europe, America, Asia and Africa.

The suggestions for future research (RQ4) include one of the areas of greatest interest for this research, as they point to paths to follow, taking into account the results obtained in the studies. The content analysis of the proposals presented by the researchers point to three major categories:

(1) Improvement of the platform and/or its features, namely at the level of: improvement of the graphic representation; introduction of new features, such as discourse analysis; provision of information to improve collaboration; incorporation of new learning models; integration of new student data, including demographic, personal and socio-cultural data; integration of rules ensuring data privacy and protection.

(2) Validation, further development or continuation of the study, namely by creating models, increasing the number of participants, making more data available on the platform.

(3) Analysis of the implications in improvement of the teaching process, with proposals that help faculty members/instructors to identify the relationship between the methodologies used and the involvement of students or in supporting the design of new teaching experiences; and students, by providing features that allow them to understand their activity, providing visual data or tools that support the achievement of learning objectives and that contribute to the improvement of their academic performance or to motivate them to learn.

The results show that Ferguson and Shum's (2012) categories of analysis, when studying SLA, point to a prevalence of studies focusing on Social Network Analytics and Content Analytics. The results also point to a positive impact on the analysis of the relationships and interactions that are established between the various actors of the educational process as well as on the improvement of the learning process as they:

- show the relationship between the methodologies used by faculty members/ instructors and the involvement of students/trainees, in order to identify the most appropriate and to support the design of new teaching experiences;
- provide tools that support and motivate students, both in supporting and monitoring learning objectives and in improving their academic performance.

5. Limitations and Future Research

This study presents the limitations that arise from the methodological options taken during the research, namely, the criteria chosen for the selection of the texts under analysis, which resulted in a reduced amount of expert studies found in the data sources. This analysis certainly does not allow us to analyze the full potential of

SLA, especially considering the times we live in, as a result of the pandemic situation and the European investment in the area of digital technology.

In fact, the time lag between the implementation of innovative pedagogical practices in this area, their study and the publication of results is usually long; therefore, it is likely that there are many innovative researches in the area of SLA which have not yet been published. In addition, technological tools and solutions that contribute to the improvement of teaching/learning practices using SLA are beginning to emerge at a greater pace, and it is not possible for research to monitor and study these innovations at the same pace as they emerge.

The number of publications in the area of SLA will increase significantly in the future; therefore, it will be pertinent to continue this research through a systematic literature review in order to enhance the development of future work. Regarding the recommendations for future research arising from this study, they are related to two main aspects:

- the improvement of the platforms being used, so that they can collect data considered essential for SLA, namely, demographic and socio-cultural data, which will allow a more holistic view of the student, ensuring the issues related to data protection (ethical issues);
- the creation of support tools that allow the design of new teaching experiences, capable of identifying appropriate models for each individual faculty member/ instructor and the profile of their students.

Given the relationship that seems to exist between SLA and the personalization of educational pathways, this is an extremely relevant and pertinent area of research. In this sense, it will also be important to study how virtual environments have adapted to the demands arising from the pandemic and to check their suitability to the contexts, in order to identify good practices that can be disseminated.

Acknowledgements

Laboratory of Pedagogical Innovation and Distance Learning, *Instituto Politécnico de Tomar* (IPT), Portugal.

References

Abu Khousa, E. and Atif, Y. 2016. Virtual social spaces for practice and experience sharing. pp. 409–414. *In:* Li, Y., Chang, M., Kravcik, M., Popescu, E., Huang, R., Kinshuk and N.S. Chen (Eds.). *State-of-the-Art and Future Directions of Smart Learning*. Springer, Singapore.

Adraoui, M., Retbi, A., Idrissi, M.K. and Bennani, S. 2017. Social learning analytics to describe the learners' interaction in online discussion forum in Moodle. *2017 16th International Conference on Information Technology Based Higher Education and Training* (ITHET 2017), IEEE – Institute of Electrical and Electronics Engineers.

Adraoui, M., Idrissi, M.K. and Bennani, S. 2018a. Network visualization algorithms to evaluate students in online discussion forums : A simulation study. *2018 International Conference on Intelligent Systems and Computer Vision* (ISCV 2018), 1–6, IEEE – Institute of Electrical and Electronics Engineers.

Adraoui, M., Retbi, A., Idrissi, M.K. and Bennani, S. 2018b. Evaluate learning communities in the online social media: Facebook groups. *Proceedings of the 12th International Conference on Intelligent Systems: Theories and Application*, 1–6, ACM International Conference Proceeding Series.

Aguilar, J., Buendia, O., Pinto, A. and Gutiérrez, J. 2019. Social learning analytics for determining learning styles in a smart classroom. *Interactive Learning Environments*, 5: 1–17.

Ahn, J. 2013. What can we learn from Facebook activity? Using social learning analytics to observe new media literacy skills. *Proceedings of the Third International Conference on Learning Analytics and Knowledge*, 135–144, ACM International Conference Proceeding Series.

Babu, M.K., Gopalakrishnan, G., Girish, S. and Suryanarayan, S. 2017. Implementation and measurement of technology enabled social learning in engineering education. *Proceedings 5th IEEE International Conference on MOOCs, Innovation and Technology in Education* (MITE 2017), 31–36.

Campbell, J., DeBlois, P. and Oblinger, D. 2007. Academic analytics: A new tool for a new era. *EDUCAUSE Review*, 42(4): 40–57.

Chaparro-Peláez, J., Acquila-Natale, E., Iglesias-Pradas, S. and Suárez-Navas, I. 2015. A web services-based application for LMS data extraction and processing for social network analysis. pp. 110–121. *In:* Palacios-Marqués, D., Ribeiro Soriano, D. and Huarng, K.H. (Eds.). *New Information and Communication Technologies for Knowledge Management in Organizations.* Springer International Publishing.

Chen, B., Chang, Y.H., Ouyang, F. and Zhou, W. 2018. Fostering student engagement in online discussion through social learning analytics. *The Internet and Higher Education*, 37(October 2019): 21–30.

Clauss, A., Lenk, F. and Schoop, E. 2019. Enhancing international virtual collaborative learning with social learning analytics. *Proceedings 2019 2nd International Conference on New Trends in Computing Sciences* (ICTCS 2019), 1–6.

Clow, D. 2013. An overview of learning analytics. *Teaching in Higher Education*, 18(6): 683–695.

Dahlberg, G.M. 2017. A multi-vocal approach in the analysis of online dialogue in the language-focused classroom in higher education. *Educational Technology and Society*, 20(2): 238–250.

Dascalu, M.-I., Bodea, C.-N., Stancu, S. and Purnus, A. 2016. Social learning analytics: A mandatory step for e-education success in the danube region. pp. 409–414. *In:* Boja, C., Doinea, M., Ciurea, C.C., Pocatilu, P., Batagan, L., Velicanu, A., Popescu, M.E., Manafi, I., Zamfiroiu, A. and Zurini, M. (Eds.). *Proceedings of the 15th International Conference on Informatics in Economy* (IE 2016), Education, Research and Business Technologies.

Dascalu, M.-I., Bodea, C.-N., Mogos, R.I., Purnus, A. and Tesila, B. 2018. A survey on social learning analytics: Applications, challenges and importance. pp. 70–83. *In:* Silaghi, G.C., Buchmann, R.A. and Boja, C. (Eds.). *Informatics in Economy.* Springer International Publishing.

Dawson, S. 2010. 'Seeing' the learning community: An exploration of the development of a resource for monitoring online student networking. *British Journal of Educational Technology*, 41(5): 736–752.

De Laat, M. and Prinsen, F.R. 2014. Social learning analytics: Navigating the changing settings of higher education. *Research & Practices in Assessment*, 9(Winter 2014): 51–60.

Díaz-Lázaro, J., Solano Fernández, I. and Sánchez-Vera, M. 2017. Social learning analytics in higher education. An experience at the primary education stage. *Journal of New Approaches in Educational Research*, 6(2): 119–126.

Ehlers, U.D. 2011. Extending the territory: From open educational resources to open educational practices. *Journal of Open, Flexible and Distance Learning*, 15(2): 1–10.

European Commission. 2020. *Digital Education Action Plan (2021–2027)*; retrieved on April 27, 2021, from: https://ec.europa.eu/education/education-in-the-eu/digital-education-action-plan_en.

Ferguson, R. and Shum, S.B. 2012. Social learning analytics: Five approaches. *Proceedings of the 2nd International Conference on Learning Analytics and Knowledge*, 23–33, ACM International Conference Proceeding Series.

Gašević, D., Dawson, S. and Siemens, G. 2015. Let's not forget: Learning analytics are about learning. *TechTrends*, 59(1): 64–71.

Goldstein, P.J. and Katz, R.N. 2005. *Academic Analytics: The Uses of Management Information and Technology in Higher Education*, vol. 8. Bolder, Colorado: EDUCAUSE Center for Applied Research.

Haya, P.A., Daems, O., Malzahn, N., Castellanos, J. and Hoppe, H.U. 2015. Analyzing content and patterns of interaction for improving the learning design of networked learning environments. *British Journal of Educational Technology*, 46(2): 300–316.

Hernández-García, Á., González-González, I., Jiménez-Zarco, A.I. and Chaparro-Peláez, J. 2015. Applying social learning analytics to message boards in online distance learning: A case study. *Computers in Human Behavior*, 47: 68–80.

Hernández-García, Á. and Conde-González, M.Á. 2016. Bridging the gap between LMS and social network learning analytics in online learning. *Journal of Information Technology Research*, 9(4): 1–15.

Hernández-García, Á. and Suárez-Navas, I. 2017. GraphFES: A web service and application for moodle message board social graph extraction. pp. 167–194. *In:* Kei Daniel, B. (Ed.). *Big Data and Learning Analytics in Higher Education: Current Theory and Practice*. Springer International Publishing.

Hickey, D.T., Kelley, T.A. and Shen, X. 2014. Small to big before massive: Scaling up participatory learning analytics. *Proceedings of the Fourth International Conference on Learning Analytics and Knowledge*, 93–97, ACM International Conference Proceeding Series.

Higgins, J. and Thomas, J. 2021. *Cochrane Handbook for Systematic Reviews of Interventions* (version 6.2), London: Cochrane.

Kaliisa, R., Mørch, A.I. and Kluge, A. 2019. Exploring social learning analytics to support teaching and learning decisions in online learning environments. pp. 187–198. *In:* Scheffel, M., Broisin, J., Pammer-Schindler, V., Ioannou, A. and Schneider, J. (Eds.). *Transforming Learning with Meaningful Technologies*. Springer International Publishing.

Khousa, E.A., Atif, Y. and Masud, M.M. 2015. A social learning analytics approach to cognitive apprenticeship. *Smart Learning Environments*, 2(1): 14.

Lenk, F. and Clauss, A. 2020. Monitoring online collaboration with social learning analytics. *In:* Anderson, B.B., Thatcher, J., Meservy, R.D., Chudoba, K., Fadel, K.J. and Brown, S. (Eds.). *26th America's Conference on Information Systems* (AMCIS 2020), Association for Information Systems.

Lessard-Hébert, M., Goyette, G. and Boutin, G. 2013. *Investigação qualitativa: fundamentos e práticas* (5ª Edição), Lisboa: Instituto Piaget.

Long, P. and Siemens, G. 2011. Penetrating the fog: Analytics in learning and education. *EDUCAUSE Review*, 46(5): 31–40.

Manca, S., Caviglione, L. and Raffaghelli, J.E. 2016. Big data for social media learning analytics: Potentials and challenges. *Journal of E-Learning and Knowledge Society*, 12(2): 27–39.

Margottini, M. and Rossi, F. 2020. Self-regulation processes and feedback in online learning. *Journal of Educational, Cultural and Psychological Studies*, 43(June): 193–209.

Merceron, A., Blikstein, P. and Siemens, G. 2015. Learning analytics: From big data to meaningful data. *Journal of Learning Analytics*, 2(3): 4–8.

Miles, M.B., Huberman, A.M. and Saldana, J. 2019. *Qualitative data analysis: A Methods Sourcebook*, 4th ed., SAGE Publications.

Motz, R., Cervantes, O. and Echenique, P. 2018. Sentiments in social context of student modeling. *Proceedings 13th Latin American Conference on Learning Technologies* (LACLO 2018), 484–491.

Nistor, N., Panaite, M., Dascalu, M. and Trausan-Matu, S. 2017. Identifying socio-cognitive structures in online knowledge building communities using cohesion network analysis. *Proceedings 2017 19th International Symposium on Symbolic and Numeric Algorithms for Scientific Computing* (SYNASC 2017), 271–274.

Nistor, N., Dascalu, M., Serafin, Y. and Trausan-Matu, S. 2018. Automated dialog analysis to predict blogger community response to newcomer inquiries. *Computers in Human Behavior*, 89(August): 349–354.

Nistor, N., Dascalu, M. and Trausan-Matu, S. 2019. Joining informal learning in online knowledge communities and formal learning in higher education: instructional design and evaluation of a blended- learning seminar with learning analytics support. *Interaction Design and Architecture(s)*, 43: 110–127.

Ouyang, F. 2015. Explore the potentials of applying social learning analytics to understand students' learning experiences in a ning-based online learning community. *Proceedings 7th International Conference on Education and New Learning Technologies* (EDULEARN15), 6832–6838.

Ouyang, F. 2019. Devising an interactive social learning analytics tool to foster online collaborative learning. pp. 1064–1165. *In:* Lund, K., Niccolai, G.P., Lavoué, E., Hmelo-Silver, C., Gweon, G. and Bake, M. (Eds.). *A Wide Lens: Combining Embodied, Enactive, Extended, and Embedded Learning in Collaborative Settings*, 13th International Conference on Computer Supported Collaborative Learning, Conference Proceedings, vol. 2. International Society of the Learning Sciences.

Patton, M.Q. 2014. *Qualitative Research and Evaluation Methods. Integrating Theory and Practice*, fourth edition, Sage Publications.

Pesare E., Roselli, T. and Rossano, V. 2017. Engagement in social learning: detecting engagement in online communities of practice. pp. 151–158. *In:* Kantola, J.I., Barath, T., Nazir, S. and Andre, T. (Eds.). *Advances in Human Factors, Business Management, Training and Education*. Springer International Publishing.

Rienties, B. and Toetenel, L. 2016. The impact of 151 learning designs on student satisfaction and performance: Social learning (analytics) matters. *Proceedings of the Sixth International Conference on Learning Analytics & Knowledge*, 339–343. ACM International Conference Proceeding Series.

Schreurs, B., Teplovs, C., Ferguson, R., De Laat, M. and Buckingham Shum, S. 2013. Visualizing social learning ties by type and topic: Rationale and concept demonstrator. *Proceedings of the Third International Conference on Learning Analytics and Knowledge*, 33–37, ACM International Conference Proceeding Series.

Shum, S.B. and Ferguson, R. 2010. Towards a social learning space for open educational resources. *In: Seventh Annual Open Education Conference* (OpenED2010), p. 10.

Shum, S.B. and Ferguson, R. 2012. Social learning analytics. *Educational Technology & Society*, 15(3): 3–26.

Siemens, G. 2005. Connectivism: A learning theory for the digital age. *International Journal of Instructional Technology and Distance Learning*, 2(1): 3–10.

Siemens, G. 2011. *1st International Conference on Learning Analytics and Knowledge*; retrieved on February 17, 2021, from: https://tekri.athabascau.ca/analytics/.

Thomas, J.R., Nelson, J.K. and Silverman, S.J. 2012. *Métodos de pesquisa em atividade física* (6ª Edição), Porto Alegre: Artmed.

Torraco, R.J. 2005. Writing integrative literature reviews: guidelines and examples. *Human Resource Development Review*, 4(3): 356–367.

Tucker, B.G., Kazmer, D.O., Bielefeldt, A.R., Paterson, K., Pierrakos, O., Soisson, A. and Swan, C. 2013. Principles of sustaining partnerships between higher education and their larger communities: Perspectives from engineering faculty engaged in learning through service. *International Journal for Service Learning in Engineering, Humanitarian Engineering and Social Entrepreneurship*, 48–63.

Viberg, O. and Dahlberg, G.M. 2013. MOOCs' structure and knowledge management. *Proceedings of the 2st International Conference on Computers in Education* (ICCE 2013), pp. 385–390.

Williams, P. 2017. Assessing collaborative learning: Big data, analytics and university futures. *Assessment and Evaluation in Higher Education*, 42(6): 978–989.

Zampieri, G. and Oliveira, I. 2017. A proposal of a visualization tool in Moodle's Wiki to measure participants' interaction applying graph theory and social learning analytics techniques. *Proceedings 9th International Conference on Education and New Learning Technologies* (EDULEARN17), 4436–4441.

Zhuhadar, L., Yang, R. and Lytras, M.D. 2013. The impact of social multimedia systems on cyberlearners. *Computers in Human Behavior*, 29(2): 378–385.

Zorrilla, M. and de Lima Silva, M. 2019. Sociograms: An effective tool for decision making in social learning. *Technology, Knowledge and Learning*, 24(4): 659–681.

4

State-of-the-Art on Social Presence and Its Implications for Distance Education
A Bibliometric Analysis in the *Web of Science* Database in the 2000–2020 Period

Maria Carolina Rodrigues,[1,*] *Luciana Aparecida Barbieri da Rosa,*[2]
Maria José Sousa,[3] *Waleska Yone Yamakawa Zavatti Campos,*[4]
Francies Diego Motke[2] and *Larissa Cristna Barbieri*[5]

INTRODUCTION

Today's society is marked by constant changes within the types of interaction and communication between people, as humans are social beings. After birth, we are drawn to individuals of our family and from the social environment (Wallon, 1995). For this reason, we grow first in family groups, expanding to the work environment, recreation and the academic environment. In this context, Vygotsky (1991, 2000) argues that the concept of knowledge is substantially a social practice. In this regard, Cubero and Luque (2004) say that "learning processes are based on the idea that human activities are positioned in cultural contexts and are mediated by language and other symbolic systems."

Given this, Short et al. (1976) developed the *Theory of Social Presence*, where they define social presence as "the degree of another person's salience in interaction and the consequent salience of interpersonal relationship." Thus, throughout the

---

[1] Cinturs - University of Algarve, Portugal.
[2] Federal University of Santa Maria, Brazil.
  Email: lucianaaparecidabarbieri@yahoo.com.br; fdmotke@gmail.com
[3] Instituto Universitário de Lisboa.
  Email: maria.jose.sousa@iscte-iul.pt
[4] Pontifical Catholic University of Rio de Janeiro - PUC/Rio, Brazil.
  Email: waleskazavatti@alumni.usp.br
[5] Faculdade de Educação São Luis - FESL, Brazil.
  Email: barbierila@hotmail.com
* Corresponding author: mcmrodrigues@ualg.pt

years and with the development of research, the concept of social presence has become more widespread with the study of Gunawardena and Zittle (1997), who analyzed social presence in the virtual environment, identifying the changes that were influenced by each element of the virtual environment having more impact than the environment.

Social presence is defined by Garrison (1990, 1991) as the individual's ability to project himself or herself socially (and affectively) in virtual environments. Garrison et al. (2000) present three essential elements for social presence: Open communication, group connection and affective expression. In this context, the concept was pertinent as Lowenthal (2010) emphasizes that it is amongst the most important concepts to elucidate the condition of interaction in virtual environments and one of the essential obstacles to collaborative learning within the virtual environment.

At this juncture, social presence is a fundamental piece for the conception of qualification in distance education from the student's point of view (Cobb, 2009). In addition, Lisboa and Coutinho (2011) explain that "social presence is about creating a supportive environment in such a way that participants feel comfortable and secure in expressing their ideas. It is fundamental for a community because it prepares its members to develop the flexibility to detail their opinions, views and, above all, to respect the variety of opinions within the group. Along this way, it becomes an extremely important assistance for the cognitive presence to become effective, once individuals are prepared to be in a very collaborative way, to debate ideas with solid arguments and within ethical principles, thus favoring critical reflection, and at last learning."

To have such a relationship between the topic and the virtual learning environment, a high degree of social presence is crucial; that is, the conception of teaching strategies equals those of face-to-face courses and thus, making the virtual learning environment (AVA) appropriate for scholars (Mackey and Freyberg, 2010). In keeping with Tu (2000), the better the relation between students, the greater the motivation for collaborative learning.

However, if social presence does not exist, that is, if there is low socialization, AVA could also be affected. Tu and Mcisaac (2002) state that it is not exclusively the amount or periodicity of the fundamental interactions but the essence itself. In this perspective, the perception of social presence was analyzed by Shih and Swan (2009), in asynchronous conversations in the virtual learning environment. They explained that the influence within the teaching-learning process emerges from the tutor from previous discussions to achieve success in the distance learning modality.

The studies of Boling et al. (2012), Hill et al. (2009) and Onrubia et al. (2010) emphasize that in the communication of the Moodle environment, there is a significant absence of visual communication, that is, interaction, expression, gestures among others. Thus, strategies should focus on teaching-learning that allow students to interact, with the virtual sphere being a facilitator, for the transmission of knowledge. Therefore, the so-called technological resources can act within the virtual environment as a moderator with different mechanisms that can be used individually or in association with other methods within AVA, as identified in the studies by Borup et al. (2012), Deschryver et al. (2009), Dunlap and Lowenthal (2009) and Jin (2009), in using tools to measure the level of social presence.

Park and Kim (2020) introduced social presence driven by interactive communication technologies and empirically investigated their roles in online learning. The authors found that the interactivity of communication technologies improved students' perception of social presence in online education, relieving those educators who hesitate to include a brand-new interactive technology in their curriculum because of the uncertainty of its effectiveness. They also found that social presence contributes to student satisfaction in online learning, confirming that social presence is driven by interactive communication technologies that significantly affect the online learning experience (Park and Kim, 2020).

According to the above, it is evident that interactivity emerges from the performance and dynamics of individuals' interactions. Hence, social presence in distance learning is crucial. However, distance learning is not a replacement type of teaching. For Moore and Kearsley (2007), the primary institutional experiences go back to 1878 and 1881, being, the fastest-growing educational modality today.

For this reason, some investigations analyze these themes and their state- of- the- art in depth. Due to the importance of expanding and exploring what has been researched in the Portuguese and international scenarios, the following question of the study is: What is the panorama of the scientific development on social presence and distance education available within the WoS database? The present study aims to analyze the characteristics of scientific production on social presence and distance education from the analysis of scientific articles published in journals indexed in the *Web of Science* (WoS) database, from 2000 to 2020.

The data was collected using the category 'Social Presence' and 'Distance Education' or 'Distance Learning' or distance-learning or distance teaching or Education at a Distance or EaD. The selection criteria were within the period ranging from 2000 to 2020. Furthermore, as the interpretation of the data allowed confirmation of the growth of scientific production, the main authors who wrote on the subject were identified, among other characteristics, and investigated articles within that period to show the context in which the terms were cited.

The survey results showed that the year with the highest number of publications was 2020 in the WoS. The most prominent institution in terms of publications was the University of California system, located in California, with 143 publications. In addition, Kesim (2020) wrote the article, 'A Study of the Graduate Theses on Distance Learning Administration', in Turkey, from 1999 to 2019. The study was structured as follows: Introduction, a systematic review of literature, performing a panorama on the main concepts of social presence in distance education and state- of- the- art of Portuguese and international studies on the theme; methodology, which describes the procedures adopted in the research; main results, with the analysis of the topic developed in the study and the discussion of the results found, followed by conclusion, limitations and future lines of research and ending with the bibliographic references used in this article.

1. Theoretical Reference

1.1 Social Presence in Distance Education

The massive growth of the demand and offer of learning through distance education mediated by new technologies could be a reality that may bring simple access and spatial and temporal flexibility to the participants. However, there are important, often unknown, constraints that must be considered about social presence in distance education (Vivas et al., 2017).

Distance education has been increasingly mediated by computers, reinforcing the requirement to watch the standard of communication between students and teachers, since verbal language is not found concatenated to visual communication within the virtual scenario. Therefore, the actual interaction depends on the standard of communication established between the actors of distance education—a situation called 'social presence'. For Coelho and Tedesco (2017), consistent with Tu (2000), social presence is one of the most important factors to be considered within the scope of distance education because of the impact of computer-mediated communication on learning.

Social presence can be often understood as the result of discursive interaction established during a constructive path, promoting a sense of community and creating positive relationships with learning activities (Remesal and Colomina, 2013). According to Sung and Mayer (2012), the social presence in virtual learning environments is related to the personal connection between students and instructors in online courses. The authors analyzed the five factors that frame social presence: social respect, sharing, the openness of ideas, social identity and intimacy.

Biocca et al. (2003) propose new theoretical designs and measurements of social presence, intending to make the theory on the topic more robust and effective. Therefore, they need to be considered as criteria of analysis on social presence and cognitive psychological issues resulting from technological intervention and the role of technology in social interaction—the latter being potentiated by social presence. In summary, specific virtual learning environments provide a greater quantity and quality of social interactions, promoting an adequate, social space which is conducive to a way of community, trust and interpersonal relationships. Although some people argue that distance education may be isolating, students in online learning environments also seek social relationships (Akcaoglu and Lee, 2016; Kreijns et al., 2007, 2013).

In a recent study, Dilling et al. (2020) indicated that there is no statistically significant difference in the perceptions of students at community colleges about the presence of teaching and the social presence between the traditional in-person and online learning environment. The authors entail that they can often achieve an equally strong teaching presence and social presence within the online learning environment (Dilling et al., 2020).

1.2 State- of- the- art on Social Presence in Distance Education: A Longitudinal Study

Numerous studies of social presence have focused on the elaboration of constructs or application of instruments to measure social presence in several contexts (Caspi and Blau, 2008; Tu, 2002). Another vital aspect addressed by the work on this topic is the importance of social presence for the success of collaborative learning, communication and interaction. The importance of social presence in distance courses lies especially within the impact associated with learning. This happens because the standard of online interaction can improve social presence and, therefore, support collaborative learning through tools, such as videos, forums, constant teacher intervention, among others (Borup et al., 2012; Collins et al., 2019; Kim and Timmerman, 2016; Remesal and Colomina, 2013; Thomas et al., 2017).

Numerous criteria are associated with the perception of social presence and the satisfaction of online courses. Among these factors, we highlight the educational design with flexible characteristics to the various kinds of learning, constant online presence, the quality of instructors and the realisation of integrated discussions through forums that provide constructive interaction of knowledge (Ke, 2010). In this same line, a quantitative study by Kim et al. (2011) shows that integration of media, quality of the education instructor and environmental interactivity are significant predictors of social presence, having a clear impact on learning satisfaction.

Other recent studies also show that an exceptional level of social presence positively relates to collaborative learning and student satisfaction (Oyarzun and Conklin, 2018; Oyarzun et al., 2018; Richardson et al., 2017; So and Brush, 2008; Zhan and Mei, 2013). However, to Weidlich and Bastiaens (2017), the social nature of the learning environment fosters the establishment of social interactions, thus engendering social presence, which in turn leads to the quality of learning experience, but not satisfaction.

The Community model of Inquiry Framework (CoI), developed by Garrison et al. (2000), consists of social presence, teaching presence and cognitive presence. In the mentioned model, social presence is the mediating variable between teaching presence and cognitive presence. Numerous studies were conducted on applying this model to exploring the three constituent elements of the tutorial experience (Borup et al., 2012; Boston et al., 2014; Feng et al., 2017). We can see that emotional involvement is an important part of promoting social presence. The active learning of students is influenced by the social presence, emotional involvement and teacher-student interaction. This way, the dynamic posture of the student is also affected by the issues related to social presence and emotion within the search for knowledge (Molinillo et al., 2018).

2. Methodology

This research is divided into three stages: the definition of the research strategy, the eligibility criteria for data collection and the analysis of the results. The database used was the Main Collection of the *Web of Science* (WoS), with the application of terms 'social presence' and 'distance education' or 'distance learning' or 'distance teaching' or 'Education at a Distance or EaD' in the search field of WoS, using the Boolean operators – AND, OR.

In the second stage, the survey of the eligibility criteria, the period between 2000 and 2020, was defined. The chosen approach combined the terms hoping to contemplate, in a single survey, a study that encapsulated the topic, which initially resulted in 5,533 articles/books/proceedings. Finally, in the third stage, the most cited publications were compared with the authors, who published the most in the same period. Figure 1 shows the research steps.

To capture the most recent evolution of studies within the area, the period chosen was the decade from 2000 to 2020, and, after refining the research, the number of articles resulted in a total of 2,199.

In the present article, the technique of quantitative and statistical bibliometry was used. For Pimenta et al. (2017), this has a fundamental role within the analysis of the behavior and performance of the production of scientific knowledge and exposure of relevant literature in various research areas. In line with the authors Tague-Sutckiffe (1992) and Garousi (2015), bibliometry is defined as a collection of mathematical and statistical techniques and procedures that allow, among others, to live the diffusion of the assembly and dissemination of scientific knowledge in a given subject, to judge the expansion of this product in books, articles, documents, newspapers. To research scientific papers with similar properties, it is fundamental to standardize the physical description and content of these documents, mentioning the relevant items and the researched literature's dispersion concepts (Café and Bräscher, 2008). The data collected from the WoS database was processed, organized and visualized in step with Fig. 2.

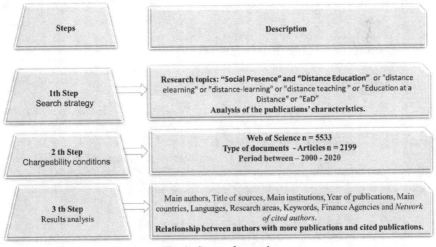

Fig. 1: Stages of research.

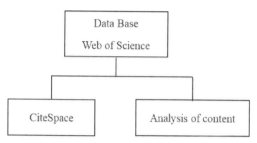

Fig. 2: Tools and methods for data processing.

Therefore, according to the steps described in Fig. 1, the bibliometric analysis of the study was performed and presented below. The networks were created using CiteSpace v.5.7.R1 which, as Chen and Leydesdorff (2014) described it, is a Java application for detecting, visualizing and analyzing emerging trends and critical changes in scientific literature, favoring the understanding of the complex relations established in the different domains of knowledge.

In CiteSpace, parameters, such as time (between 2000 and 2020) and node type (country and institutions, category, keyword, references), were defined. The networks are formed by nodes (authors, journals, institutions, countries, research areas, keywords) whose size is proportional to their collaboration in the literature. The links are connections that show the intensity and frequency of relationships. According to the authors Chen and Song (2019), the purple-coloured rings point to high intermediation centrality, which is important in connection with other nodes.

3. Results

The research results, which supported the acceptable Boolean operators for refinement, are presented to broaden the scope of research to incorporate the largest possible number of works in the years 2000 to 2020. We found 2,199 scientific articles when it comes to social presence and distance education or distance-learning or distance teaching or Education at a Distance or EaD.

3.1 General Characteristics of the Publications

The general characteristics of publications associated with *Social Presence* and *Distance Education* or *distance learning* or *distance-learning* or *distance teaching* or *education at a Distance* or *EaD* are as follows: 1. Authors, 2. Title of sources, 3. Institutions, 4. Year of publications, 5. Countries, 6. Languages, 7. Research areas, 8. Keywords and 9. Finance Agencies. Afterwards, the number of publications per author and the number of citations is presented.

3.1.1 Main Authors

The first analysis regarded the author's relevance. Figure 3 presents the authors and the number of published articles on the subject within the analyzed period.

It is observed that the authors who published the most were Bozkurt, A., Dotterl, S. and Francke, W. with 11 publications.

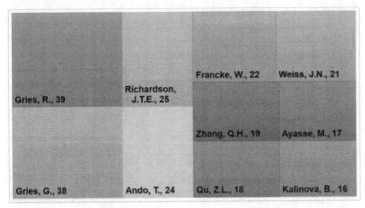

Fig. 3: Distribution of articles by authors.

3.1.2 Title of Sources

Table 1 shows the most influential papers with the most scientific articles published on the topic, highlighting the *Journal of Chemical Education* with 194 articles published.

Most of the publications were found in journals of their respective field, which shows that they will be a reference for the articles on these subjects. There are also publications of articles in multidisciplinary journals.

Table 1: Distribution of articles by title of sources.

Publication Titles	Count
Journal of Chemical Education	194
Journal of Chemical Ecology	168
International Review of Research in Open and Distributed Learning	129
Information Technologies and Learning Tools	81
Computers Education	76
Lecture Notes in Computer Science	68
Turkish Online Journal of Distance Education	68
Distance Education	59
Telemedicine and E-Health	49
Computer Applications in Engineering Education	44

3.1.3 Main Institutions

The institutions of the authors with most published works are related to the topics that are presented in Table 2.

Technological and pedagogical evolution in distance and network teaching nowadays allows healthy competition between higher education institutions. The authors at the University of California System published the largest amount of scientific articles on the subject.

Table 2: Distribution of articles by main institutions.

Affiliations	Count
University of California System	143
Open University, UK	138
University of South Africa	134
Ministry of Education Science of Ukraine	85
State University System of Florida	80
United States Department of Agriculture	78
Universidad Nacional de EaD	65
University of California, Los Angeles	60
University of North Carolina	55
Pennsylvania Commonwealth System of Higher Education	49

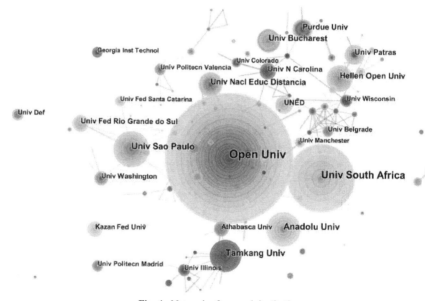

Fig. 4: Network of research institutions.

From the analysis of the network of institutions with most research on social presence and distance education, it is evident that the institutions of authors who publish on the subject form networks among themselves, acting as partners in the construction of knowledge: Brazilian universities that are part of the network, such as the University of São Paulo, the Federal University of Rio Grande do Sul and the Federal University of Santa Catarina; North American institutions like the University of Wisconsin, University of North Carolina, University of Colorado, University of Washington and Illinois; European university authors also research and publish on the topic, such as the Polytechnic University of Madrid and Valencia, the University of Bucharest and the University of Manchester; the University of South Africa is the most important African representative in the network. Special emphasis should be

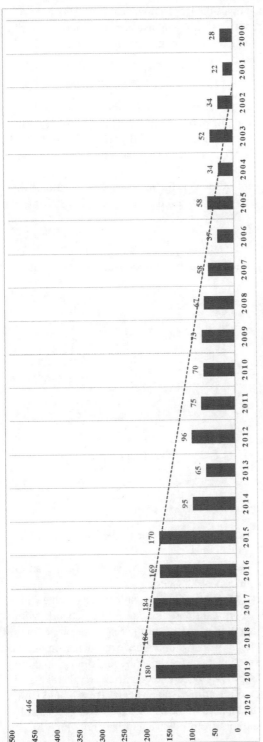

Fig. 5: Total publications distributed per year.

given to The Open University, which owns the largest node in the network and which can be justified by the fact that it is one of the largest distance education universities in the world. It is concluded that the network among research institutions is vast, favoring the exchange of knowledge.

3.1.4 Annually Published Articles

At this point, research followed the growth of the publications in the database in the period under study. The distribution of publications over time shows a trend of growth or decline in the study area, as Huang et al. (2020) refer. This reflects the interest of researchers on the topic. The total scientific production in the period under analysis was 2,199 publications.

In *Web of Science*, from the point of view of the number of publications, there is a boom in their number in the year 2020, followed by the years 2018, 2017, and 2019.

3.1.5 Main Countries

At this point, the bibliometric analysis identified the number of articles distributed by the countries of origin (Fig. 6).

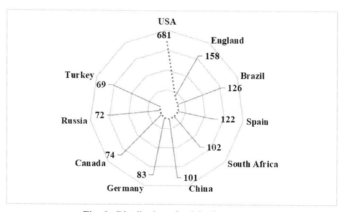

Fig. 6: Distribution of articles by country.

It is highlighted that it will be an area of interest for further research in USA, England, Brazil, Spain, South Africa and China.

Figure 7 shows the networks established between the authors of the articles focusing on the countries where the authors are located.

From the analysis of the network of countries, it is possible to see that the United States is the country with the most significant participation in the network, with a high centrality of intermediation as announced by the purple ring in its circle. In this way, the USA is configured as a country whose authors have an increased number of publications in the area, added to the fact that they have the role of intermediating relations and establishing networks among different countries. England has the second-largest node in the network, followed by Brazil, Spain, Russia, and China. In general, it is possible to see that the authors of the articles on the subject establish numerous research networks with authors from other countries and which has the

Fig. 7: Country network.

potential to be helpful for the area of studies and research on social presence and distance education.

3.1.6 Main Languages

Regarding the languages of the works published in the study area, 7,449 are published in English, as shown in Fig. 8.

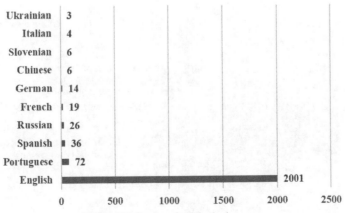

Fig. 8: Distribution of articles by language.

3.1.7 Research Areas

Regarding the primary research areas in *social presence and distance education or distance learning or distance teaching or education at a distance or EaD,* we have Education Educational Research, Computer Science, Chemistry and Engineering (Table 3).

Table 3: Research areas.

Research Areas	Count
Education Educational Research	1,137
Computer Science	265
Chemistry	220
Engineering	209
Environmental Sciences Ecology	107
Biochemistry Molecular Biology	100
Health Care Sciences Services	92
Information Science Library Science	80
Entomology	67
Business Economics	58

Figure 9 shows the network of research categories of studies on social presence and distance education.

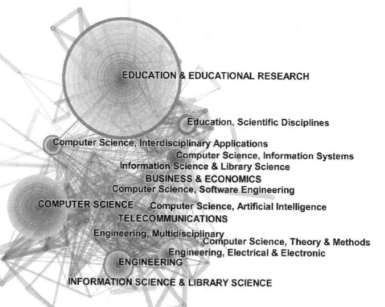

Fig. 9: Research areas network.

It is possible to conclude that studies on the subject are multidisciplinary and interdisciplinary, because multiple relationships exist between research areas. Moreover, the network nodes interact with each other through numerous edges. Finally, from the network, it is seen that the field of study is multidisciplinary due to containing several nodes and including several actors related to each other.

The following section will analyze the keywords in the articles.

3.1.8 Most Used Keywords

The keywords represent a source of access to scientific articles, briefly show the content, research methods, and/or tools used in the studies, a position corroborated by researchers Wang et al. (2018), who state that the keywords of the articles can obtain essential information for research in a given area (Fig. 10).

The most commonly used keywords were: Distance Learning, E-learning, Social Presence, Distance Education, Education, Distance E-learning, Learning Systems, Online Learning, Community of Inquiry, Teaching Presence, which strengthen the selection of the bibliographical portfolio, as it is cohesive with the objective of the research in higher education, learning management system, technology, motivation (Fig. 10).

Fig. 10: Keywords of the research articles (Wordle).

In a complementary way, for the analysis of the co-occurrence of the most present keywords in the articles (titles, author, keywords and abstract), the CiteSpace software was used, which culminated in the network in Fig. 11, to scientifically measure the most relevant themes in the studies on 'social presence' and 'distance education'.

The size of the nodes in the keyword network demonstrates that the most significant and recurring word in works on the subject is distance learning, followed by e-learning. The next most significant keywords are higher education, learning management system, technology, motivation, ICT, Moodle, collaboration, blended learning, distance education, internet, web, design and satisfaction. The analysis of the keywords reveals that the field is marked by the connection of areas, such as education, technology, and management, unveiling that the subject is composed of transversal knowledge in practical terms.

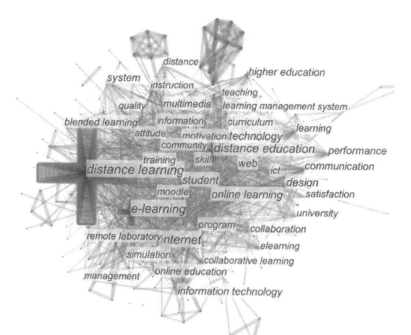

Fig. 11: Keywords research.

3.1.9 Funding Agencies

We present the funding agencies at this point (Fig. 12).

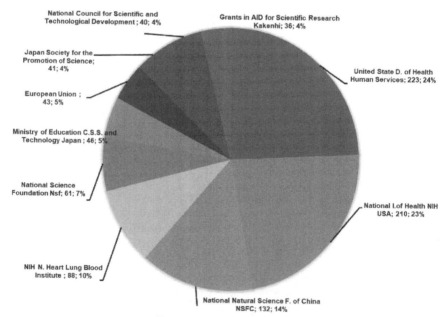

Fig. 12: Study finance agencies.

Concerning the funding agencies of the work, including the theme in research, it was found that all of them have the same number of publications: United States Department of Health Human Services, National Natural Science Foundation of China, National Institutes of Health, USA (NIH), European Union (E.U.), National Science Foundation, among others.

3.2 Most Cited Articles from 2000 and 2020

Among the data from the *Web of Science* on social presence and distance education, from 2000 to 2020, it is essential to highlight the prominent publications in the number of citations.

It is important to note that of the 20 most cited articles, the most relevant articles are: (i) *A study of the graduate theses on distance learning administration in turkey from 1999 to 2019*, by Kesim, E., published in the Turkish online journal of distance education, in 2020; (ii) *Precariousness and privatisation of public policies in distance education*, by Mattos, M., and Silva, M., published in the *Journal Education*, in 2020; and, (iii) *Distance education (EAD) training for the formation of archival documentary heritage preservation agents in the Federal University of Rio Grande (FURG)* by Schwarzbold, KCM and Cordenonsi, A.Z., published in the *Journal Open Access*, in 2015.

We carried out the network analysis of the most referenced authors in the selected works in a complementary way. Thus, the network in Fig. 13 contains the authors cited by articles on the theme of social presence and distance education.

From the analysis of the network present in Fig. 13, it is evident that the network of the authors most cited in the references of the studies raised is a dense network, whose principal authors are Anderson, T.; Bandura, A., Garrison, D.R.; Keegan, D.; Moore, M.G., among others.

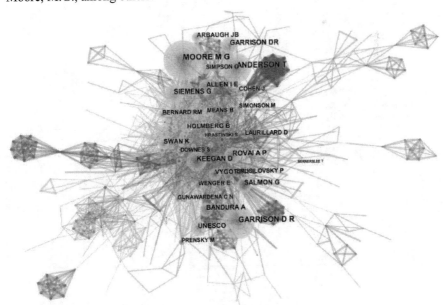

Fig. 13: Network of cited authors.

Table 4: Most cited articles.

Cit.	Title	Authors	Journal	Year
315	E-Learning, online learning, and distance learning environments: Are they the same?	Moore, J.L.; Dickson-Deane, C. and Galyen, K.	*Internet and Higher Education,* 14(2): 129–135	2011
235	Three-dimensional virtual worlds and distance learning: two case studies of Active Worlds as a medium for distance education	Dickey, M.D.	*British Journal of Educational Technology,* 36(3): 439–451	2005
155	3-D Object Retrieval With Hausdorff Distance Learning	Gao, Y.; Wang, M.; Ji, R.; Wu, X. and Dai, Q.	*IEEE Transactions on I. Electronics,* 61(4): 2088–2098	2014
121	Interaction in distance-learning courses	Bouhnik, D. and Marcus, T.	*Journal of The American Society for Inf. Science and Technology,* 57(3): 299–305	2006
102	Exploring multiplexity: Social network structures in a computer-supported distance learning class	Haythornthwaite, C.	*Information Society,* 17(3): 211–226	2001
98	The automatic control telelab - A Web-based technology for distance learning	Casini, M.; Prattichizzo, D. and Vicino, A.	*IEEE Control Systems Magazine,* 24(3): 36–44	2004
94	The automatic control telelab: A user-friendly interface for distance learning	Casini, M.; Prattichizzo, D. and Vicino, A.	*IEEE Transactions on Education,* 46(2): 252–257	2003
92	Predicting students' performance in distance learning using machine learning techniques	Kotsiantis, S.; Pierrakeas, C. and Pintelas, P.	*Applied Artificial Intelligence,* 18(5): 411–426	2004
91	Evaluating the effectiveness of distance learning: A comparison using meta-analysis	Allen, M.; Mabry, E.; Mattrey, M.; Bourhis, J.; Titsworth, S. and Burrell, N.	*Journal of Communication,* 54(3): 402–420	2004
87	EAD and PEBD: Two Energy-Aware Duplication Scheduling Algorithms for Parallel Tasks on Homogeneous Clusters	Zong, Z.; Manzanares, A.; Ruan, X. and Qin, X.	*IEEE Transactions on Computers,* 60(3): 360–374	2011
84	Distance learning techniques for ontology similarity measuring and ontology mapping	Gao, W.; Farahani, M. R.; Aslam, A. and Hosamani, S.	*Cluster Computing – The Journal of Networks, Software Tools and Applications,* 20(2): 959–968	2017

Table 4 contd. ...

...Table 4 contd.

Cit.	Title	Authors	Journal	Year
81	Constructivist pedagogy in conventional on-campus and distance learning practice: an exploratory investigation	Tenenbaum, G; Naidu, S; Jegede, O. and Austin, J.	*Learning and Instruction,* 11(2): 87–111	2001
80	A developmental model for distance learning using the Internet	Passerini, K; Granger, M.J.	*Computers and Education,* 34(1): 1–15	2000
79	College students' perceived threat and preference for seeking help in traditional, distributed, and distance learning environments	Kitsantas, A. and Chow, A.	*Computers and Education,* 48(3): 383–395	2007
77	Late-phase 3 EAD. A unique mechanism contributing to the initiation of atrial fibrillation	Burashnikov, A. and Antzelevitch, C	*Pace-Pacing and Clinical Electrophysiology,* 29(3): 290–295	2006
73	Evaluation of classroom-based, Web-enhanced, and Web-based distance learning nutrition courses for undergraduate nursing	Buckley, K.M.	*Journal of Nursing Education,* 42(8): 367–370	2003
70	Five facets of social presence in online distance education	Sung, E. and Mayer, R.E.	*Computers in Human Behavior,* 28(5): 1738–1747	2012
70	Technology acceptance and social networking in distance learning	Lee, J.S.; Cho, HC; Gay, G; Davidson, B. and Ingraffea, A.	*Educational Technology and Society,* 6(2): 50–61	2003
65	Student perspectives on videoconferencing in teacher education at a distance	Gillies, D.	*Distance Education,* 29(1): 107–118	2008
64	Examining Motivation in Online Distance Learning Environments: Complex, Multifaceted, and Situation-Dependent	Hartnett, M.; George, S.A. and Dron, J.	*International Review of Research in Open and Distributed Learning,* 12(6): 20–38	2011

4. Final Considerations

The present study aimed to understand the characteristics of the scientific production related to the topic of social presence and distance education in the *Web of Science* database. It carried out bibliometric research to reach the goal, obtaining 2,199 publications related to these themes, mainly in the following areas: Education, Educational Research, Computer Science, Chemistry and Engineering.

When evaluating the international scientific literature on social presence and distance education, the publication data indicates that scientific production grew with slight fluctuations between 2000 and 2014. In 2015 and 2019, growth remained constant, but in 2020 there was a boom in production, much due to the mandatory confinement caused by the pandemic in the global village. Most published studies are in the *Journal of Chemical Education, Journal of Chemical Ecology*, and *International Review of Research in Open and Distributed Learning*, which stand out with the most significant number of publications.

It has been found that the USA leads the ranking of countries that published the most on the subject, and the English language dominates with 2001 publications, with, again, 2020 being the year with the most significant number of publications. The most prominent institution was the University of California System, located in California, with 143 publications. It was observed that the authors who most published were Bozkurt, A., Dotterl, S. and Francke, W., with 11 publications.

Regarding the most used keywords in the article, we have Distance Learning, E-learning, Social Presence, Distance Education, Education, Distance E-learning, Learning Systems, Online Learning, Community of Inquiry, Teaching Presence. Consequently, it strengthens the selection of the bibliographical portfolio, as it is cohesive with the objective of the research in higher education, learning management system, technology, motivation.

In the conjunction analysis of keywords carried out using the CiteSpace software, we found that the nodes' size in the keyword shows the most critical and recurring word in the works on the topic is distance learning, followed by e-learning, higher education, learning management system, technology, motivation, ICT, Moodle, collaboration, blended learning, distance education, Internet, web, design and satisfaction.

The analysis of the keywords reveals that the field is marked by the connection of areas, such as Education, Technology and Management, unveiling that the subject is composed of transversal knowledge in practical terms.

The authors of the 20 most cited articles in *Web of Science* on the most relevant articles are:

(i) 'A study of the graduate theses on distance learning administration in Turkey from 1999 to 2019', by Kesim, E., published in the Turkish online journal of distance education, in 2020.

(ii) 'Precariousness and privatisation of public policies in distance education' by Mattos, M. and Silva, M., published in the *Journal Education*, in the year 2020.

The main limitation of this study is that it uses only the *Web of Science* database. Nevertheless, it suggests future studies to expand the search form on topics in other fields. Furthermore, the need persists for more scientific events on the topic, as well as for the development of methodological analyses to identify further gaps in the field.

References

Akcaoglu, M. and Lee, E. 2016. Increasing social presence in online learning through small group discussions. *International Review of Research in Open and Distance Learning*, 17(3): 1–17.

Allen, M., Mabry, E., Mattrey, M., Bourhis, J., Titsworth, S. and Burrell, N. 2004. Evaluating the effectiveness of distance learning: A comparison using meta-analysis. *Journal of Communication*, 54: 402–420.

Biocca, F., Harms, C. and Burgoon, J.K. 2003. Toward a more robust theory and measure of social presence: Review and suggested criteria. *Presence* (Camb.), 12(5): 456–480.

Boling, E.C., Hough, M., Krinsky, H., Saleem, H. and Stevens, M. 2012. Cutting the distance in distance education: perspectives on what promotes positive, online learning experience. *Internet and Higher Education*, 15(2): 118–126.

Borup, J., West, R.E. and Graham, C.R. 2012. Improving online social presence through asynchronous video. *Internet and Higher Education*, 15(3): 195–203.

Boston, W., Gibson, A.M., Ice, P., Richardson, J. and Swan, K. 2014. An exploration of the relationship between indicators of the community of inquiry framework and retention in online programs. *Journal of Asynchronous Learning Networks*, 13(3): 67–83.

Bouhnik, D. and Marcus, T. 2006. Interaction in distance-learning courses. *JASIST*, 57: 299–305.

Buckley, K. 2003. Evaluation of classroom-based, web-enhanced, and web-based distance learning nutrition courses for undergraduate nursing. *The Journal of Nursing Education*, 42: 367–370.

Burashnikov, A. and Antzelevitch, C. 2006. Late-Phase 3 EAD. A unique mechanism contributing to initiation of atrial fibrillation. *Pacing and Clinical Electrophysiology: PACE*, 29: 290–295.

Café, L. and Bräscher, M. 2008. *Organização da informação e bibliometria, Encontros Bibli: Revista Eletrônica de Biblioteconomia e Ciência da Informação, Especial*, 54–75.

Casini, M., Prattichizzo, D. and Vicino, A. 2003. The automatic control telelab: A user-friendly interface for distance learning. *IEEE Transactions on Education*, 46(2): 252–257.

Casini, M., Prattichizzo, D. and Vicino, A. 2004. The automatic control Telelab. *Control Systems, IEEE*, 24: 36–44.

Caspi, A. and Blau, I. 2008. Social presence in online discussion groups: Testing three conceptions and their relations to perceived learning. *Social Psychology of Education*, 11(3): 323–346.

Chen, C. 2006. CiteSpace II: Detecting and visualizing emerging trends and transient patterns in scientific literature. *Journal of the American Society for Information Science and Technology*, 57(3): 359–377.

Chen, C. and Leydesdorff, L. 2014. Patterns of connections and movements in dual-map overlays: A new method of publication portfolio analysis. *Journal of the American Society for Information Science and Technology*, 65(2): 334–351.

Cobb, S.C. 2009. Social presence and online learning: A current view from a research perspective. *Journal of Interactive Online Learning*, 8(3): 241–254.

Coelho, W.G. and Tedesco, P.C.D.A.R. 2017. *A percepção do outro no ambiente virtual de aprendizagem: Presença social e suas implicações para Educação a Distância. Revista Brasileira de Educação*, 22(70): 609–624.

Collins, K., Groff, S., Mathena, C. and Kupczynski, L. 2019. Asynchronous video and the development of instructor social presence and student engagement. *Turkish Online Journal of Distance Education*, January, 53–70 .

Cubero, R. and Luque, A. 2004. *Desenvolvimento, educação e educação escolar: A teoria sociocultural do desenvolvimento e da aprendizagem. In:* Coll, C., Marchesi, Á. and Palacios, J. (Orgs.). *Desenvolvimento psicológico e educação*, second edition, Porto Alegre: Artmed, 2: 94–106.

DeSchryver, M., Mishra, P., Koehleer, M. and Francis, A. 2009. Moodle vs. Facebook: Does using Facebook for discussions in an online course enhance perceived social presence and student interaction? pp. 329–336. *In*: Gibson, I., Weber, R., McFerrin, K., Carlsen, R. and Willis, D. (Eds.). *Proceedings of Society for Information Technology & Teacher Education International Conference 2009.* Chesapeake, VA: Association for the Advancement of Computing in Education (AACE).

Dickey, M. 2005. Three-dimensional virtual worlds and distance learning: Two case studies of Active Worlds as a medium for distance education. *British Journal of Educational Technology*, 36: 439–451.

Dilling, J., Varga, M.A. and Mandernach, B.J. 2020. Comparing teaching and social presence in traditional and online community college learning environments. *Community College Journal of Research and Practice*, 44(10-12); 854–869.

Dunlap, J. and Lowenthal, P. 2009. Tweeting the night away: using twitter to enhance social presence. *Journal of Information Systems Education*, 20: 129–136.

Feng, X., Xie, J. and Liu, Y. 2017. Using the community of inquiry framework to scaffold online tutoring. *International Review of Research in Open and Distance Learning*, 18(2): 162–188.

Gao, W., Farahani, M., Aslam, A. and Hosamani, M. 2017. Distance learning techniques for ontology similarity measuring and ontology mapping [353]. *Cluster Computing*, 20.

Gao, Y., Wang, M., Ji, R., Wu, X. and Dai, Q. 2014. 3-D object retrieval with hausdorff distance learning. *Industrial Electronics, IEEE Transactions on*, 61: 2088–2098.

Garousi, V. 2015. A bibliometric analysis of the Turkish software engineering research community. *Scientometrics*, 105(1): 23–49.

Garrison, D.R. 1990. An analysis and evaluation of audio teleconferencing to facilitate education at a distance. *American Journal of Distance Education*, 4(3): 13–24.

Garrison, D.R. 1991. Critical thinking and adult education: A conceptual model for developing critical thinking in adult learners. *International Journal of Lifelong Education*, 10(4): 287–303.

Garrison, D.R., Anderson, T. and Archer, W. 2000. Critical inquiry in a text-based environment: Computer conferencing in higher education. *The Internet and Higher Education*, 2(2-3): 1–19.

Garrison, D.R., Anderson, T. and Archer, W. 2000. Critical inquiry in a text-based environment: Computer conferencing in higher education. *The Internet and Higher Education*, 2(2-3): 87–105.

Garrison, D.R. and Arbaugh, J.B. 2007. Researching the community of Inquiry Framework: Review, Issues, and Future Directions. *The Internet and Higher Education*, 10(3): 157–172.

Garrison, D.R., Cleveland-Innes, M. and Fung, T.S. 2010. Exploring causal relationships among teaching, cognitive and social presence: Student perceptions of the community of inquiry framework. *Internet and Higher Education*, 13(1-2): 31–36.

Gillies, D. 2008. Student perspectives on videoconferencing in teacher education at a distance. *Distance Education*, 29(1): 107–118.

Gunawardena, C.N. 1995. Social presence theory and implications for interactive and collaborative learning in computer conferences. *International Journal of Educational Telecommunications*, Charlottesville, 1(2-3): 147–166.

Gunawardena, C.N. and Zittle, F.J. 1997. Social presence as a predictor of satisfaction within a computer-m ediated conferencing environment. *The American Journal of Distance Education*, 11(3): 8–26.

Hartnett, M., George, A. and Dron, J. 2011. Examining motivation in online distance learning environments: complex, multifaceted, and situation-dependent. *International Review of Research in Open and Distance Learning*, 12: 20–38.

Haythornthwaite, C. 2001. Exploring Multiplexity: Social Network Structures in a Computer-Supported Distance Learning Class. *Inf. Soc.*, 17: 211–226.

Hill, J., Song, L. and West, R. 2009. Social learning theory and web-based learning environments: A review of research and discussion of implications. *American Journal of Distance Education*, 23: 88–103.

Huang, L., Zhou, M., Lv, J. and Chen, K. 2020. Trends in global research in forest carbon sequestration: A bibliometric analysis. *Journal of Cleaner Production*, 252: 1–17.

Jae-Shin, L., Cho, H., Gay, G., Davidson, B. and Ingraffea, A. 2003. Technology Acceptance and Social Networking in Distance Learning. *Educational Technology & Society*, 6.

Jin, S.A. 2009. Modality effects in Second Life: The mediating role of social presence and the moderating role of product involvement. *Cyberpsychol. Behav. Dec.*, 12(6): 717–721.

Ke, F. 2010. Examining online teaching, cognitive and social presence for adult students. *Computers and Education*, 55(2): 808–820.

Kim, J. 2011. Developing an instrument to measure social presence in distance higher education. *British Journal of Educational Technology*, 42(5): 763–777.

Kim, J., Kwon, Y. and Cho, D. 2011. Investigating factors that influence the social presence and learning outcomes in distance higher education. *Computers and Education*, 57(2): 1512–1520.

Kim, J. and Timmerman, C.E. 2016. Effects of Supportive Feedback Messages on Exergame Experiences. *Journal of Media Psychology*, 30(1): 29–40.

Kitsantas, A. and Chow, A. 2007. College students' perceived threat and preference for seeking help in traditional, distributed, and distance learning environments. *Computers & Education*, 48(3): 383–395.

Kotsiantis, S., Pierrakeas, C. and Pintelas, P. 2003. *Preventing Student Dropout in Distance Learning Using Machine Learning Techniques* (Vol. 2774).

Kotsiantis, S., Pierrakeas, C. and Pintelas, P. 2010. Predicting students' performance in distance learning using machine learning techniques. *Applied Artificial Intelligence*, May–June 2004, 411–426.

Kreijns, K., Kirschner, P.A., Jochems, W. and van Buuren, H. 2007. Measuring perceived sociability of computer-supported collaborative learning environments. *Computers and Education*, 49(2): 176–192.

Kreijns, K., Kirschner, P.A. and Vermeulen, M. 2013. Social aspects of CSCL environments: A research framework. *Educational Psychologist*, 48(4): 229–242.

Lisboa, E.S. and Coutinho, C.P. 2011. *Comunidades virtuais: Sistematizando conceitos, Revista Científica de Educação a Distância Paidei@*, 2(4): 1–22.

Lowenthal, P. 2009. *The Evolution and Influence of Social Presence Theory on Online Learning*, 124–139.

Mackey, K. and Freyberg, D. 2010. The effect of social presence on affective and cognitive learning in an international engineering course taught via distance learning. *Journal of Engineering Education*, 99(1): 23–34.

Mattos, M. and Silva, M. 2020. *Precarização e privatização das políticas públicas na educação a distância, Educação* (UFSM), 45(e34): 1–22.

Molinillo, S., Aguilar-Illescas, R., Anaya-Sánchez, R. and Vallespín-Arán, M. 2018. Exploring the impacts of interactions, social presence and emotional engagement on active collaborative learning in a social web-based environment. *Computers and Education*, 123: 41–52.

Moore, M.G. and Kearsley, G. 2007. *Educação a distância: U ma visão integrada , Traduzido por Roberto Galman*, São Paulo: Thomson Learning.

Moore, J.L., Dickson-Deane, C. and Galyen, K. 2011. e-Learning, online learning, and distance learning environments: Are they the same? *The Internet and Higher Education*, 14(2): 129–135.

Onrubia, J., Colomina, R. and Engel, A. 2010. *As comunidades virtuais de aprendizagem baseadas no trabalho em grupo e na aprendizagem colaborativa. In:* Coll, C. and Monereo, C. (Orgs.). *Psicologia da educação virtual: A prender e ensinar com as tecnologias da informação e da comunicação*, Porto Alegre: Artmed.

Oyarzun, B. and Conklin, S. 2018. *Instructor Social Presence Effects on Learner Social Presence, Achievement, and Satisfaction*, 625–634.

Oyarzun, B., Stefaniak, J., Bol, L. and Morrison, G.R. 2018. Effects of learner-to-learner interactions on social presence, achievement and satisfaction. *Journal of Computing in Higher Education*, 30(1): 154–175.

Palloff, R.M. and Pratt, K. 2004. *O aluno virtual: U m guia para trabalhar com estudantes online, Porto Alegre: Artmed*, 216 p.

Park, C. and Kim, D.-G. 2020. Exploring the roles of social presence and gender difference in online learning. *Decision Sciences Journal of Innovative Education*, 18: 291–312.

Passerini, K. and Granger, M. 2000. A developmental model for distance learning using the Internet. *Computers & Education*, 34: 1–15.

Pimenta, A.A., Portela, A.R.M.R., Oliveira, C.B. and Ribeiro, R.M. 2017. *A bibliometria nas pesquisas acadêmicas, SCIENTIA: Revista de Ensino, Pesquisa e Extensão*, 4(7): 1–13.

Remesal, A. and Colomina, R. 2013. Social presence and online collaborative small group work: A socio-constructivist account. *Computers and Education*, 60(1): 357–367.

Richardson, J.C., Maeda, Y., Lv, J. and Caskurlu, S. 2017. Social presence in relation to students' satisfaction and learning in the online environment: A meta-analysis. *Computers in Human Behavior*, 71: 402–417.

Russo, T. and Benson, S. 2005. Learning with invisible others: Perceptions of online presence and their relationship to cognitive and affective learning. *Educational Technology and Society*, 8(1): 54–62.

Shih, L. and Swan, K. 2005. Fostering social presence in asynchronous online class discussions. pp. 602–606. *In: Conference on Computer Support for Collaborative L earning*, 6: 2005, Taipei, International Society of the Learning Sciences.

Short, J., Williams, E. and Christie, B. 1976. *The Social Psychology of Telecommunication*, New York: John Wiley.

So, H.J. and Brush, T.A. 2008. Student perceptions of collaborative learning, social presence and satisfaction in a blended learning environment: Relationships and critical factors. *Computers and Education*, 51(1): 318–336.

Sung, E. and Mayer, R. 2012. Five facets of social presence in online distance education. *Computers in Human Behavior*, 28: 1738–1747.

Swan, K., Richardson, J.C., Ice, P., Garrison, D.R., Cleveland-Innes, M. and Arbaugh, J.B. 2008. Validating a measurement tool of presence in online communities of inquiry. *E-Mentor*, 2(2): 1–12.

Tague-Sutcliffe, J. 1992. An introduction to informetrics. *Inf. Process Manag.*, 28(1): 1–3.

Tenenbaum, G., Naidu, S., Jegede, O. and Austin, J. 2001. Constructivist pedagogy in conventional on-campus and distance learning practice: An exploratory investigation. *Learning and Instruction*, 11: 87–111.

Thomas, R.A., West, R.E. and Borup, J. 2017. An analysis of instructor social presence in online text and asynchronous video feedback comments. *Internet and Higher Education*, 33: 61–73.

Tu, C.H. 2000. Online learning migration: From social learning theory to social presence theory in a CMC environment. *Journal of Network and Computer Applications*, 23(1): 27–37.

Tu, C.H. 2002. The measurement of social presence in an online learning. *International Journal on E-Learning*, 1(2): 34–45.

Tu, C.H. 2002. The impacts of text-based CMC on online social presence. *The Journal of Interactive Online Learning*, 1(2): 1–24.

Tu, C.H. and Mcisaac, M. 2002. The relationship of social presence and interactions in online classes. *The American Journal of Distance Education*, 16(3): 13–150.

Vivas, J.R., Terroni, N.N. and Ricci, L. 2017. *Retricciones del canal de comunicación efectos psicosociales en entornos educativos*, *Psicologia Escolar e Educacional*, 6(1): 21–29.

Vygotsky, L.S. 1991. *A formação social da mente*, 4th. ed., São Paulo: Martins Fontes.

Vygotsky, L.S. 2000. *A formação social da mente: O desenvolvimento dos processos psicológicos superiores, Tradução de José Cipolla Neto*, São Paulo: Martins Fontes.

Wallon, H. 1995. *A evolução psicológica da criança*, Lisboa, Portugal: Edições 70.

Wang, Z., Zhao, Y. and Wang, B. 2018. A bibliometric analysis of climate change adaptation based on massive research literature data. *Journal of Cleaner Production*, 199: 1072–1082.

Weidlich, J. and Bastiaens, T.J. 2017. Explaining social presence and the quality of online learning with the SIPS model. *Computers in Human Behavior*, 72: 479–487.

Zhan, Z. and Mei, H. 2013. Academic self-concept and social presence in face-to-face and online learning: Perceptions and effects on students' learning achievement and satisfaction across environments. *Computers and Education*, 69: 131–138.

Zong, Z., Manzanares, A., Ruan, X. and Qin, X. 2011. EAD and PEBD: Two Energy-Aware Duplication Scheduling Algorithms for Parallel Tasks on Homogeneous Clusters. *Computers, IEEE Transactions on*, 60: 360–374.

5

Using Google Trends and Twitter to Analyze the Phenomenon of Telework during the Covid-19 Pandemic
A Social Media Analytics Review and Study

António Pimenta de Brito

INTRODUCTION

The field of Social Media Analytics (SMA) is fast developing informatic tools and frameworks to collect, monitor, analyze, summarize, and visualize social media data, usually driven by specific requirements for a target application or problem statement (Rathore et al., 2017). This spontaneous, big and complex data can be very useful for business or scientific intentions.

SMA is a recent area of study in the social sciences, but it already has applications in various sectors of activity. Although, there is a serious problem that could jeopardize access to this information, namely for the social sciences, the massive amount of data that has evolved from SMA can be a very profitable business (Batrinca and Trealeven, 2015). Moreover, data analytics, a fashionable discipline, and data analyst as a trendy profession, was followed by the increased cost that started to exist to access it. Consequently, there is a risk of creating inequality in the access to this data and fosters a culture of knowledge consumerism and closed access to data. Today large amounts of data are owned by big social media companies and their partners. In addition, the most used programming languages to get advantage of SMA data, take, for example, programming languages as R or Python, are difficult to dominate for those who do not have programming skills; not to mention other languages, that have a somewhat opaque methodology (Yun and Kim, n.d.). Therefore, this study

BRU-ISCTE/ ISEC Lisboa, ISCTE-Instituto Universitário de Lisboa, Portugal; ISEC Lisboa - Instituto Superior de Educação e Ciências, Portugal.
Email: acpbo@iscte-iul.pt

aims to experiment on SMA tools that are both reliable and can be used by social scientists who are acquainted with social phenomena and research methodologies, but who are not necessarily skilled programmers. Thus it is hoped that knowledge may not be restricted to a few people but grants free, ethical and transparent access to information and technology.

Telework is a field of study that interconnects technology with the human element. It has been studied in research for some time, but the Covid-19 pandemic has brought in a new component. It is not something planned, as usual, and is not only meant to improve business efficiency but a reaction to a natural catastrophe (Belzunegui-Eraso and Erro-Garcés, 2020; Pew Research Center, 2020b).

SMA tools, like Twitter, Facebook and Google Trends have a long history of effectiveness in analyzing catastrophes (Fan and Gordon, 2014; Kim et al., 2018; Lai and To, 2015; Muralidharan et al., 2011; Rathore et al., 2017; Zhao et al., 2017). The main goal of this study is to understand how people perceived telework during the Covid-19 pandemic: positive, negative, or neutral. To answer this question, first of all, an overview about SMA is necessary: the most important literature, business and research uses of these tools. Then, the ability of these tools to analyze the phenomenon of telework in the context of the Covid-19 pandemic is assessed, using Google Trends and Social Media Macroscope's SMILE (Social Media Intelligence & Learning Environment) Twitter repository (Yun et al., 2019), created in the academic field. Secondly, the research methodology and explanation of what these tools are and why they can be reliable to analyze such phenomena is presented. The next phase announces the results obtained when using the chosen SMA tools. With Google Trends the approach is to analyze how the word 'telework' was searched in its search engine, during the period of the outbreak of Covid-19 and social distancing, in the U.S. In the tool SMILE, two datasets of 10,500 tweets automatically generated are analyzed and answered to the main research question: the perception of Americans regarding telework, in this period. Finally, conclusions about the analysis will be drawn, highlighting the limitations existent and suggest future research directions.

1. Theoretical Framework

1.1 From Social Media to Big Data

Social networks have changed the face of the world, namely communication and the way information is accessed (Kaplan and Haenlein, 2010). Previously, the mediator between facts and the public was traditional media; today, more than ever, personal expression has never been more democratic, and content creation can be done by everyone, all the time, and this privilege is not that of a journalist, painter, or poet. Another aspect is the unprecedented way in which it is possible to meet and interact with people we know and do not know (Drews and Schemer, 2010). It has raised many questions, such as the regulation of this information and interaction, but it is undeniable that, in addition to a form of expression with endless potential, it is also a data repository of great use for companies and scholars.

Kaplan and Haenlein (2010, p. 61) defined social media as "a group of Internet-based applications that build on the ideological and technological foundations of Web 2.0 and that allow the creation and exchange of user-generated content."

Social media appears in the so-called Web 2.0. In the first phase of the Internet, the Web 1.0 was read-only and with a passive participation of the user, without being able to develop and publish content. In this second phase came the revolution of social networks with high interactivity and user participation in the production of contents (Almeida, 2017). This content, from comments to posts, blogs, chats, Wikis, customer reviews and relevant relationships, brought huge interactivity until then not seen and generated what is called 'Big Data'. Twitter and Facebook are examples of this. Twitter, a micro-blogging platform, alone generates about 500 million tweets daily or several terabytes (one terabyte = 1,000,000,000,000 bytes) of data (Park et al., 2015).

Each social network has its segment, use and functionality. Social media platforms are classified into various online forums, such as social networking (Facebook and LinkedIn), media sharing (YouTube, Flickr, and Instagram), blogging (Tumblr and WordPress), messaging (WhatsApp, snapchat, Facebook messenger), collaborative websites (Wikipedia), virtual worlds (Second Life), commerce communities (Snapdeal and Pepper Fry) and social bookmarking (StumbleUpon) (Mangold and Faulds, 2009).

According to the Pew Research Center (2019), in 2005, only 5 per cent of adult Americans used at least one social network; in 2011, it grew to half of all Americans; in 2019, 72 per cent of Americans already used some type of social network. At what other time in history did we manage to have so much data automatically generated about the population without resorting to a census, survey, questionnaire or focus group? According to Statista, nowadays 3.78 billion people use social networks in the world (Tankovska, 2021).

Along with this interactivity, connectivity and community, came Web 3.0, which is called the Semantic Web, because not only do there exist addresses on the Internet, content that can be edited and shared among users, but now the Internet helps the user to find what one wants: the Smart web. So, with Web 2.0 came the revolution of content, but the majority of all that data tends to be unstructured. With Web 3.0 and especially Web 4.0, tools and methodologies began to be developed that would make this data, from unstructured to structured, from raw data into valuable knowledge to generate useful insights, be it in the natural sciences or in the social sciences.

Web 4.0 has several definitions and encompasses several dimensions and each of them offers a different, but complementary view of the 4.0 paradigm. Social networks, technologies such as the Internet of Things, 'Big Data', artificial intelligence and M2M (machine to machine communication) offer a comprehensive image of the Web 4.0 application (Almeida, 2017).

1.2 Social Media Analytics—What it is and its Utility

Social Media Analytics (SMA) develops precisely in the context of 'Big Data' and Web 4.0. If the large amount of information started to circulate on the networks, it could no longer be stored and processed efficiently. 'Big Data' is also a vague and multifaceted term but in general, it seeks to define a new paradigm in which the way of storing and processing data has been revolutionized. Cloud computing appears as a storage and processing tool and the opportunity generated by massive data collection at the organizational level brought social media the same opportunity. Kitchin (2014, p. 68) describes 'Big Data' with the following characteristics: "huge in volume, high in velocity, diverse in variety, exhaustive in scope, fine-grained in resolution, relational in nature, and flexible in trait."

It remains to be asked if it is possible to find data for research in as much quantity and speed as that of social networks? If compared with traditional academic research, it will be necessary, depending on the methodology, to collect data for the study. Whatever the method, quantitative, qualitative or other, will it find samples as gigantic and rich, automatically generated, as those of social media? It is true that specific tools are needed to extract, treat and generate insights, but it is undeniable to say that there has never been so much data to work with; raw material with which to extract useful and real-time insights for companies and organizations.

Academic studies on Social Media Analytics have not yet been around for a long time. Since 2005, it has become popular to study social networks in academic research. Studies in Social Media Analytics have existed since 2010, but those that matter, from a perspective of applying this knowledge to business and organizational problems in general, only appear from 2015 onward (Rathore et al., 2017). Previously, they were focused more on methodologies and definitions of social media, but studies on the application of Social Media Analytics to the problems of economic and governmental activities were not common (Rathore et al., 2017).

Compared with traditional research methodologies, such as empirical studies based on surveys, there are advantages of SMA as it can analyze stakeholder knowledge from user-generated content in a consistent manner, without introducing biases from the responses (Rathore et al., 2017). Even when analyzing employee data through Twitter, there is evidence that supports that these methods can bridge the shortcomings of traditional questionnaires by limiting time and space and the bias generated (Gelbard et al., 2018).

Social media is especially important when one can mix the knowledge of social sciences and that of computerized expertise, the computational social science (Cioffi-Revilla, 2010; Lazer et al., 2009). As it has been said since the beginning of the SMA revolution, "what does existing sociological network theory, built mostly on a foundation of one-time snapshot data, typically with only dozens of people, tell us about massively longitudinal data sets of millions of people, including location, financial transactions, and communications? These vast, emerging data sets on how people interact surely offer qualitatively new perspectives on collective human behaviour" (Lazer et al., 2009, p. 722). Using quantitative techniques (computational statistics, machine learning and complexity) and 'Big Data' for data mining and simulation modeling (Cioffi-Revilla, 2010), it is proven that to get better results from SMA, automation along with human interpretation can foster better results than both of them apart (Pääkkönen et al., 2020).

Twitter is a large contributor in the 'Big Data' phenomenon (Bruns and Stieglitz, 2013). Its data repository and the corresponding tools for processing that data are among the most used from the existing social networks (Batrinca and Treleaven, 2015). This micro-blogging platform is very popular in the SMA realm due to various reasons. One of them is the access to data: unlike other social networks, Twitter does not have their users' data prohibited, facilitated by the Public API (application programming interface) with its relatively easier access, compared with other APIs such as Facebook's (Park et al., 2015); secondly—and this is a stronger reason—its high traceability, if we want to make associations, design and establish relationships between networks: "Research may focus on finding networks of friends. Twitter, on the other hand, allows different types of relationships through such Twitter features as 'follow', 'reply', 'retweet', 'favourite' and 'hashtag'. These intrinsic features of Twitter create more complex and larger networks in the conversational environment and thus enable the speedy dissemination of social issues" (Thelwall et al., 2011; cited by Park et al., 2015, p. 4) and facilitates word of mouth through the number of opinions and the speed of retweeting (Jansen et al., 2009).

Finally, it has a wide range of applications. It can be used for professional (networking, learning and promotion) or organizational goals (hiring, stakeholder engagement, market sensing and new product/service development) (Rathore et al., 2017).

1.3 Social Media Analytics' Use in Various Sectors

SMA is used in different sectors of activity. In the public administration sector, for example, for the analysis of public responses, extracted from social media before, during and after disasters, have the potential to improve situational knowledge in an emergency and disaster management practices (Muralidharan et al., 2011). Another example of the application of these tools is in political science. Social media platforms enable direct and transparent channels of engagement between citizens, politicians and governments and is a powerful tool for decision making (Bertot et al., 2012; Stieglitz and Dang-Xuan, 2013).

The Cambridge Analytic a scandal was a bad and a good example of the use of SMA for political intents. A good example in a sense that Social Media Analytics were effective. They tracked down preferences, profiles, segments and that data were used to target and communicate to specific audiences. But it illustrated the darker side of SMA, when there is a suspicion that ethical principles were not followed. Privacy and its access are the 'thorniest challenges' in SMA (Lazer et al., 2009, p. 722). In the two cited applications of SMA to the political realm, the authors propose ethical solutions—either to manually access to the Twitter public timeline or the Facebook partially accessible timeline, or through the source of data from social media brands through their public API's (Bertot et al., 2012; Stieglitz and Dang-Xuan, 2013).

In urban planning, it is important to understand how people circulate and populate the city. Through the intersection of methodologies, there are studies based on geotagged tweets that follow that goal (Shelton et al., 2015).

Another area of business in which the application of Social Media Analytics tools has already been studied is the field of finance. For example, through market sentiment analysis, is modelled from Google Trends on the Covid-19 pandemic. This is then analyzed against the time series of daily closing stock prices, using augmented vector autoregression (VAR). In this way, the effect of market sentiment on stock prices was analyzed (Ding et al., 2020).

In the area of tourism, these tools also have applications. Park et al. (2016) chose Tweets that used the hashtag from cruise travel-related topics, which could enable better tourist engagement.

1.4 Social Media Analytics—Methodologies and Tools

A popular methodology of SMA is text analytics, network analysis and visualization. In a study that was carried out, a sample of several studies, based on various sectors, demonstrated that the most used methodological approaches tried in different industries when analyzing data from social media is word frequency and sentiment analysis, followed by frequency distribution, regression, topic modelling, content analysis, graph centrality and density and tags analysis (Rathore et al., 2017).

They also include data mining, that is knowledge discovery that extracts hidden patterns from huge quantities of data, using sophisticated differential equations, heuristics, statistical discriminators (e.g., hidden Markov models) and artificial intelligence machine learning techniques (e.g., neural networks, genetic algorithms and support vector machines) (Batrinca and Treleaven, 2015). This methodology includes classification, clustering, association rule discovery and regression (Rathore et al., 2017).

There is a vast range of Social Media Analytics tools. Easy availability of API's provided by Twitter, Facebook and news services has led to an 'explosion' of data services and software tools for scraping and sentiment analysis, and Social Media Analytics platforms (Batrinca and Treleaven, 2015). But there is a problem, as pointed out: the difficult access for academic purposes. It is recommended that there be more public funding to access this data that could be made available via the cloud. Otherwise, large amounts of data and knowledge would only be the property of some private, public companies or privileged academics presiding over these data from which they would produce papers that could not be criticized, reviewed and replicated (Batrinca and Treleaven, 2015).

1.5 Teleworking

Remote work is not a new topic in the discipline of OB. This has been studied since the 1970's (Blount, 2015). It is defined as work performed at home or a satellite office to reduce commuting (Shin et al., 2009). Recently, with the outbreak of the Covid-19 pandemic, this catastrophe emerged as a drive for the mandatory use of this means of work (Pew Research Center, 2020b). For this reason, teleworking did not appear as a pressing need for the usual reasons for which it was requested: "enhanced organizational flexibility, curtailed business overhead costs, improved worker productivity, effective worker recruitment and retention, and reduced commuting time for workers" (Shin et al., 2009, p. 86), but because an external circumstance required it (Belzunegui-Eraso and Erro-Garcés, 2020).

The forces that cause organizational change are commonly mentioned in the literature. One of the drives for change is environmental forces that require managers to implement comprehensive change programs. They are planned and unplanned (Burke, 2018). Covid-19 presents itself as an unplanned change for many organizations that have been forced to adopt telecommuting as the major form of work in their company. Teleworking is generally studied as a planned change, as the organization proactively aims to increase the indicators presented above and usually related to productivity and cost reduction.

Telework has been studied substantially but despite this, it is a topic with some methodological deficiencies as its definition is not unanimous (Shin et al., 2009). Also, most of the studies focus on trying to understand if telework is good or bad, and the findings are often inconclusive (Boell et al., 2016). Equally rarely has it been studied as a phenomenon of unplanned and reactive change, but as a proactive innovation strategy. Nevertheless, to the best of the knowledge of this study, very few studies have attempted to analyze the relationship between telework and the safety problems of employees and/or citizens emanating from natural disasters, terrorist attacks, or health alert alarms (Belzunegui-Eraso and Erro-Garcés, 2020). Finally, social media can be a precious tool to understand and support telework: "Social media can support job design in different ways. First, it can support practices such as remote working" (Dossena, 2019, p. 209).

According to the Pew Research Center (2020b), in a study conducted on 10,332 adults in the US in October 2020 during the Covid-19 pandemic, the main point in favor of teleworking is the advantage of increased flexibility and a common drive for teleworking is the fear of being infected. Those who are most benefited/adapted to telework are older adults, with an academic degree and who adapt well to technologies; but on the negative side, comes the question of felt isolation. People who are harmed the most are those who cannot do their job online. Young people seem to adapt poorly, as well as parents with children under the age of 18. According to the study, "majorities of workers say they have seen little change in various aspects of their work lives compared with before the outbreak." Other conclusions that the study had was that people who now claim that their work can mostly be done by telecommuting, 70 per cent did not do it before the pandemic and more than half want to continue doing it in the future. But most workers in general say that their work cannot be done mostly from home.

There is indeed a great divide between those who can and cannot do teleworking. The division seems to be between those who can't help but "wait at tables or give haircuts" (Pew Research Center, 2020a) and those who can continue to do their work online, especially among those who have a university degree.

Finally, this study aims to understand if the analyzed sample demonstrates this division and inconclusiveness (Boell et al., 2016) that exists in society in relation to the perception of telework.

2. Empirical Research Approach

2.1 Google Trends and SMILE

The methodological approach adopted is to use two SMA tools and try to understand what the perceptions of people are towards telework: positive, negative or neutral. On the one hand, Google Trends and its search engine analysis tool was used, on the other, a sample of Tweets from SMILE tool was considered.

The decision for these two tools was done in order to overcome the problem of the difficult access of social media data for social science researchers, as previously stated. Namely the Social Media Macroscope (Yun et al., 2019), which sought to overcome the difficulty mentioned by Batrinca and Treleaven (2015). Through public funding, this open access platform created within the academy, provides free social media tools and data with little need for access or computer technical knowledge.

The Google Trends index represents the search volume of keywords by Google users, and it serves to indicate market sentiment and the public's attention to an event or incident (Liu et al., 2019). It has some limitations and biases, but, nevertheless, Google Trends has served and still serves as an excellent tool for infoveillance and infodemiology (Rovetta, 2020).

Using Google Trends, up to five topics can be compared at a time and also see how often these topics have been mentioned and in which geographic regions the topics have been searched for the most (Batrinca and Treleaven, 2015). Google Trends is a useful tool, not to predict the future, but to predict the present. It is utilized to measure, for example, the impact of unemployment, economic forecasts from the central banks or epidemiology (Choi and Varian, 2012). Google Trends has already proven to be a reliable tool for scientific inferences. It provides a way to quantify Web interest in a specific topic more efficiently than any other historically used methods (e.g., population surveys) (Amber et al., 2016; Dreher et al., 2018; Havelka et al., 2020; Mohamad and Kok, 2019).

The most used method is to collect users' research data and correlate it with hard data. For example, assessing market sentiment and its relationship to stock price fluctuations (Ding et al., 2020); collecting research data from users regarding tourist destinations and demand data from tourist destinations, they are used to make demand forecasts and consumer preferences in the field of tourism (Höpken et al., 2019). Google Trends can also be significant to analyze a consequence of a natural disaster or catastrophe; in this case, it is an epidemic.

SMM allows access to Twitter data and further analysis, with various perspectives. From there, after the automated output of tweets, one can analyze the data the desired way. A possible approach to the output of macroscope data is to use content analysis to treat and draw conclusions from the data of social media, namely tweets from Twitter—an approach which has been demonstrated to have reliable results in other studies and particularly in the event of catastrophes (Fan and Gordon, 2014; Kim et al., 2018; Lai and To, 2015; Muralidharan et al., 2011; Rathore et al., 2017; Zhao et al., 2017). Content analysis is a research technique for making replicable and valid inferences from texts (or other meaningful matter) to the contexts of their use (Krippendorff, 2018), but we will use the computerized tools that SMM makes available, so that it authentically is a Social Media Analytics approach. Otherwise, by manually analyzing the tweets, it would be a traditional approach, even if the collection phase was automated.

SMM's goal is "to provide the next generation of solutions to allow for researchers to conduct ethical, legal and reproducible social media research" (Yun et al., 2019, p. 3). The first tool in the SMM is SMILE which provides open-source functions that collect social media data and analyze it. The tool currently provides access to real time data from Twitter and Reddit (in 2018 it provided historical data, but from the current information, no more) and a suite of open-source tools to perform text-pre-processing, sentiment analysis, network analysis, machine learning text classification (Pedregosa et al., 2011), name entity recognition and phrase detection.

SMILE offers two methods of searching Twitter for data via Twitter's API. Both methods are facilitated by using the GraphQL query language to interact with Twitter's REST API. Searching of tweets connects to Twitter's Search API endpoint to collect and return up to 180,000 posts from the last seven days that match the keywords one provides.

Searching 'Twitter Users' connects to Twitter's User Search endpoint to collect and return up to 1,000 accounts that match the keywords you provide. SMILE also offers the option to search the historical backlog of Twitter data. The initial objective was to provide a database that included tweets collected from Twitter's one per cent streaming API since May 2018.

The project envisioned that "the SMM would bring people closer to a place where social researchers can focus primarily on the research question at hand, rather than all the technology details that surround the answering of that question" (Yun et al., 2019, p.8).

According to SMM, since the website was publicly launched in September 2018, it has had researchers from more than 70 institutions using the environment, and there have been over 1,200 new sessions of their tools (SMILE and BAE) started by these researchers.

In the SMM platform, the user can immediately utilize two open-source applications from its catalogue, SMILE and BAE, which can receive contributions from other apps from other developers. The SMILE application offers several computerized data analytics tools to process data from social networks. In the past, it was possible to have access to the historical Twitter repository, but this feature has recently been discontinued and now it is only possible to search for tweets from the last week in which the user is searching.

There is evidence that tweets can be useful to understand employee perceptions (Van Zoonen et al., 2016) inserted in the field of the so-called HR analytics (Marler and Boudreau, 2016), but there is no work, at least to the knowledge of this study, that uses SMA tools to treat Twitter data with organizational research purposes (Marler and Boudreau, 2016). As said, the majority of the studies use traditional research methodology, for example, analysis of Twitter data with content analysis or sentiment analysis methodology manually generated.

It is easy to find studies that demonstrate the usefulness of social media in HR practices (Sinha et al., 2012); however, the same author highlights that you need 'tools' to analyze social media data. The same author mentions various studies that prove the utility of social media for HR purposes, but they all use traditional research methodologies based on social media data.

2.2 Data Collection and Treatment Methodology

In the case of Google Trends, the way the term 'telework' evolved in user searches carried out in the United States was investigated, beginning shortly before the declaration of Covid-19 as a pandemic (March 2021) until February 2021.

From SMM-SMILE, 500 tweets and 10,000 tweets from different time frames, where the term 'telework' was mentioned, were extracted, be it in post, hashtag, mentions or retweets (forwarding the post). These two datasets of Twitter posts happen, the first, between March 5th and March 12th and the second, between March 28th and April 3rd, 2021. The geographic location of the tweets is restricted to the United States and randomly chosen. The entirety of tweets where the word 'telework' is mentioned are displayed and the respective metadata, that is, the 'descriptive analysis'—the user's personal description—are made available at the tool's output. From here four computerized tools of SMILE were chosen and an answer to this question was searched : "What is the perception of the sample about telework, positive, negative or neutral?"

As Yun and Kim (n.d.) advise, as a start, natural language pre-processing analysis was performed in order to assess what the main words and subjects concerned with 'telework' in the corpus are. Then an auto phrase mining analysis was applied. The next step was to draw a network analysis and finally a sentiment analysis. The first dataset was used in all analyses, the second only in the network analysis, in terms of comparison. In the natural language pre-processing tool, the process of 'tokenization' was experimented—the task of isolating smaller portions of the text, by dividing the written text into meaningful units, such as words, sentences, or topics. The next step was 'lemmatization' and 'stemming', which reduce word forms of common base words. 'Part-of-speech tagging' is the process of making up a word in a text (corpus) as corresponding to a particular part of speech, based on its definition and its context (Bird, 2006; Yun et al., 2019). Two outputs of SMILE in natural language pre-processing are the frequency chart and the tree where interaction with each phrase taken out of the tweets is possible.

The next step is auto phrase mining. Citing Shang et al. (2018), the authors of the framework used in this tool: "Phrase mining refers to the process of automatic extraction of high-quality phrases (e.g., scientific terms and general entity names) in a given corpus (e.g., research papers and news). Representing the text with quality phrases instead of n-grams can improve computational models for applications, such as information extraction/retrieval, taxonomy construction and topic modeling' (Shang et al., 2018; Yun et al., 2019). It is a text summarization approach used when the goal is to resume large amounts of text or find patterns automatically in it. Here, this technique will be used in order to discern what is discussed and stated in the tweets in which the word 'telework' is mentioned. What topics are related? What associations? What patterns? In the auto phrase mining display, the download of the dataset is done and then it is necessary to choose the minimum support value, that is the level of repetition that has to have a sentence to show in the results as significant. After choosing the threshold, the algorithm is run. The result/output of SMILE is the visualization of the phrases—a preview of the phrases with the highest score of significance that are part of this dataset.

The next methodological approach was sentiment analysis (Hutto and Gilbert, 2014; Yun et al., 2019), sometimes known as 'opinion mining' or 'emotion AI'— referring to the use of natural language processing, text analysis, computational linguistics and biometrics to systematically identify, extract, quantify and study affective states and subjective information. Here the output of the dataset concerning the percentage of tweets that have a positive, negative or neutral perception of the subject of telework was received.

Finally, the network analysis tool was deployed. 'Network analysis' is the process of investigating structures through the use of networks and graph theory. It characterizes networked structures in terms of 'nodes' (individual actors, people, or things within the network) and the ties, edges, or links (relationships or interactions) that connect them (Hagberg et al., 2008; Yun et al., 2019). In this case, the network is a social media network—Twitter—and it functions the same way. Here, a user is connected to others, either through a follower/follower relationship, or, for example, by retweeting a post from this user. In these relationships, users are linked, in turn, to other users, forming a network based on the same type of relationship. Through this type of follower/follower relationship, almost all users are related in some way to any other user on Twitter. Through the affinities and connections between users, we can find hidden patterns, centralities, hub users on the social network (the ones that concentrate most of the connections), and, from here, draw conclusions about the way information circulates and why it circulates and what information and influence each actor represents (Park et al., 2015). The network nodes and connections for the two different dated datasets will be displayed and compared.

3. Results and Discussion

The example of teleworking in the context of the Covid-19 pandemic was chosen, to exemplify the usefulness of Google Trends and SMM analytics tools in the area of OB and HR research and how they can facilitate the work of social science researchers who do not have computing and programming skills. An experiment was conducted to analyze what the dataset perception is about telework: either positive, negative or neutral. Below, in the Google Trends dashboard, the word 'telework' was typed and revealed often—it was mentioned between January 1st of 2020 and February 22nd of 2021. As seen in Fig. 1, the maximum factor 100 mention of the word 'telework' on the search engine was reached exactly when the effect of the Covid-19 pandemic announcement was felt in the world (March–April 2020) and specifically in the U.S.

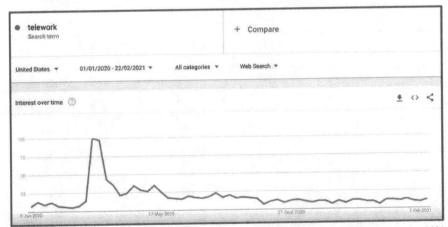

Fig. 1: Google Trends output of the word "telework" in the USA, in the period between January 1st, 2021 and February 22nd, 2021.

Google Trends precisely demonstrates the disproportionate attention that the subject had before and after the Covid-19 outbreak. It is difficult not to draw a causal relationship between Covid-19 and the significant occurrence of searches in the subject 'telework'. The tool also allows an analysis by sub-region (Fig. 2).

Google Trends (Fig. 3) presents the number of mentions of related topics. The most related topics with 'telework' present in American Google searches were 'telecommuting–topic', followed by 'Employment topic' and 'Job topic' (Fig. 3). Regarding 'related queries', on top was 'federal telework', followed by 'telework jobs' and 'telework policy':

A causal effect between the Covid-19 outbreak and the emergence of telework can definitely be drawn, mainly around March–April 2020, the date of the announcement of the World Health Organization (WHO) of this epidemic as 'pandemic', March 11th (Adhanom, 2020). From the Google Trends data output, it can be concluded that the federal program of telework (www.telework.gov) was a top concern for Americans during the Covid period (Fig. 3).

"Exactly one year ago today (March 15th, 2021), the Office of Management and Budget posted (on a Sunday night), guidance instructing agencies to offer 'maximum telework' to employees in the Washington, D.C. metro area" (Ogrysko, 2021).

Washington, D.C. is exactly the place of the U.S. with the majority of Google searches for the word 'telework' (Fig. 2). These Google results can be very useful to understand people's main concerns on the topic—which are to draw conclusions and to act upon them, from a business, organizational, political, scientific, social or any other level. From this output it is also evident that the topic 'employment' is

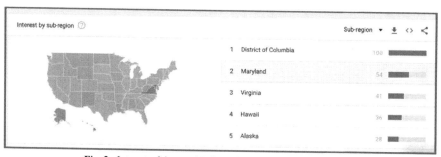

Fig. 2: Interest of the word 'telework' by sub-region of the USA.

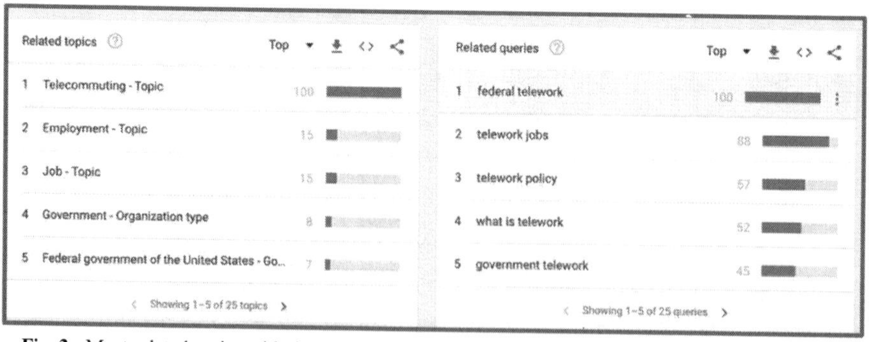

Fig. 3: Most related topics with the word 'telework' and top related queries done on Google Trends.

very important, considering that, from a quick analysis of the occurrences, 'telework jobs' and 'Employment topic' are present in the second most searched term of 'related queries' and 'related topics', respectively (Fig. 3). Also, present are three occurrences of job-related issues ('Employment topic', 'job topic', 'telework jobs') connected with telework and the Covid-19 circumstances, as both the numbers of unemployment skyrocketed following the outburst of the pandemic, face-to-face work drastically decreased and those unemployed were trying to find remote jobs (Pew Research Center, 2020a), both in the U.S. and in the whole world. This is supported by more statistics, precisely in the district of Columbia (Congressional Research Service, 2021, p. 6). Regarding unemployment rates in the US in the Covid-19 year, the official data follows on Google Trends: *"increased from 3.5 per cent in February 2020 to 4.4 per cent in March 2020, peaked at 14.8 per cent in April, and then fell to 6.7 per cent in December"* (Congressional Research Service, 2021, p. 5).

Therefore, statistical data and observed facts back Google Trends' outputs entirely, if there was still any doubt regarding the tool's reliability. Finally, the frequency of the search term 'what is telework' can sound curious in a first impression but can be backed by the case that we are pointing out in this study: telework was more present following the Covid-19 outbreak, not because it was a planned change but in reaction to this 'environmental' episode.

In the tool SMILE, the aim was to analyze Twitter data and try to understand what knowledge could be envisioned about the phenomenon of telework and what was the perception of the tweeter about the subject. How the word 'telework' behaved in tweets was tracked down in a given time frame. Visual and quantitative output is given by the system in a user-friendly way. Between the time frame of two weeks (first dataset), from March 5th to 12th, 500 randomly chosen tweets mentioning the word 'telework' were analyzed.

From the initial search and the first dataset output, various analyses of the tweets can be performed, starting from the manual content analysis of the *.csv file. The file automatically gives various fields: the tweet, the user description, date of post, etc., upon which we can perform filtering, searches, categorization and classification. It would not be needed to carry on proving the advantages of SMM because this functionality is already useful, since researchers that do not use SMA tools know what is involved when they manually extract tweets for analysis—both, the time-consuming task of manually collecting different tweets by user and the privacy and regulatory issues that are involved. It is known that the data of SMM are public and can be used without the mentioned constraints, but as SMA is further discussed, there is a need to use computerized tools. Below, how often tweets are published daily can be seen (Fig. 4), based on the second dataset of 10,000 tweets. It is concluded that the theme 'telework' is present during the week, especially in the hours of leaving work, between six p.m. and seven p.m.

Following the automatic generation of a set of tweets, SMILE makes available various SMA tools based on machine learning where it can be made into various machine learning analyses.

For this study, natural language pre-processing was used, followed by automated phrase mining, sentiment analysis and, lastly, network analysis. From the output of the

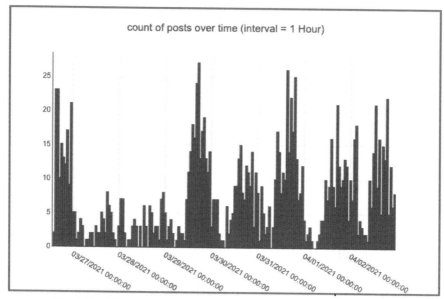

Fig. 4: SMILE output, count of tweets in a time frame, second dataset analyzed.

500 and 10,000 tweets, several types of results were received. From private tweets, corporate tweets, to announcements or the dissemination of studies on teleworking, the information received is very rich and can be the target of the analysis and classification that it is needed. Given below are some examples of tweets extracted:

"@PhysWiz @LukeDyks Exactly. I like to telework, and it works for me and my family. However, I'd like to go in one to two days a week. But really, it should just be left flexible, to best meet the needs of the workers".

"@thegarance but if in-person work isn't necessary, why require it? Teaching is best in-person, but office work isn't necessarily. Even without Covid, telework just makes sense for a lot of people—the virus just helped make it clear".

"@kdrum I hope you're right. I was a big fan of telecommuting a few years ago, until I realized how lonely and isolating telework can be".

The first dataset that is in the time frame of March 5th to 12th was used for all analytics tools: natural language pre-processing, automated phrase mining, sentiment analysis and network analysis. Finally, in the network analysis, the second dataset was also used, the one that ranges from March 28th to April 3rd of 2021, for a question of comparison.

The following outputs were obtained by computing natural language pre-processing, the words that appear most related to telework (Fig. 5):

The most frequent words that appear are 'telework', 'plan', 'march', 'covid-19', 'women'—all terms similar to what was found in Google searches, although with a bit more of noise, but even so a good starting point to dig deeper into the data.

Further on, an interactive tree complements this graphic (Fig. 6), showing a grade level of significance of the words with phrases. The tree presents in a larger font "to my organization planning to scale", more related to teleworking. That is,

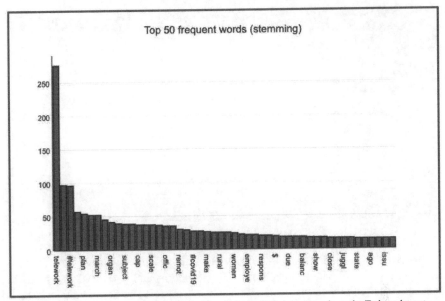

Fig. 5: Natural language pre-processing output (I) – top 50 frequent words on the Twitter dataset.

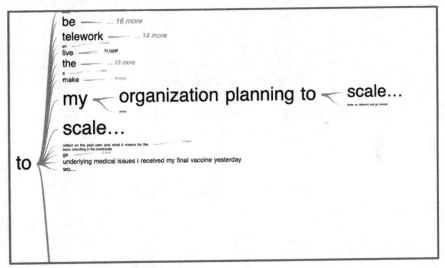

Fig. 6: Natural language pre-processing (II) – Tree.

words mentioned on Twitter have a component of professional content in private accounts, in which users comment on social network how their company is reacting to teleworking.

By clicking in 'telework', from left to right in the tree (Fig. 7), the phrases present in the dataset that are more related to this term can be accessed. These are phrases that express less weight in the dataset, yet we can know that, for telework, it is more associated with 'following my maternity leave', 'effectively sometimes',

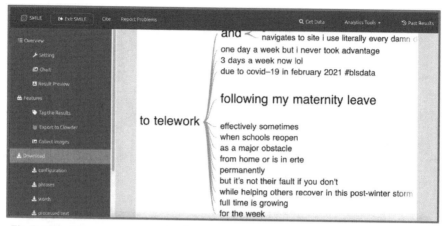

Fig. 7: Natural language pre-processing (III): Most common sentences regarding the word 'telework'

'When schools reopen', 'one day a week but I never took advantage', 'full time is growing', 'due to Covid-19 in February 2021', 'permanently', etc. All terms that we can associate with this issue: work life balance, Covid-19, home-based telework, an increase of this type of work, setbacks of telework, etc., but nothing of a completely undeniable and consistent pattern to put the opinion of the sample definitely on one side or another, yet valuable information about the phenomenon.

The second step of natural language pre-processing is auto phrase mining, as there's a tentative figuring out of how this dataset behaved in terms of 'high quality phrases' (Yun and Kim, n.d.) most connected with the search term. Below is shown a cloud of phrases related to the main topic 'telework' (Fig. 8). The one that showed

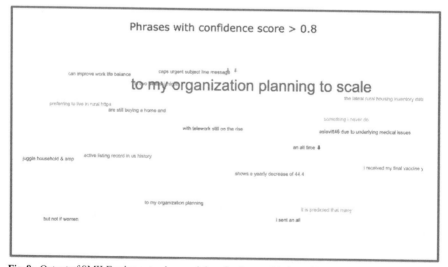

Fig. 8: Output of SMILE using auto phrase mining, for the word 'telework' mentioned in random sample of tweets between March 5th and 12th, 2021.

the most significance was 'to my organization planning to scale', in addition to other significant phrases on the telework theme most present in the analyzed tweets: 'with telework still on the rise', 'can improve life work balance', 'prefer to live in rural'. It can be concluded that there are more significant insights into the phenomenon. The algorithm shows us that people see telework as a good thing for the work-life balance as it has a connection with the search for more places furthest from the cities and, especially, organizations are generally reorganizing for this type of remote work.

Next, the results of the network analysis are treated (Fig. 9). From the graph, it can be concluded that there is a hub, a user that concentrates most of the connections on the network and from which most retweets about 'telework' leave. In fact, when there's an opportunity to understand who is the user that concentrates the majority of the connections on him, this is verified: The user is @DrTomFrieden, with maximum 36 retweets in 500 nodes (tweets) produced. He is precisely an American infectious disease and public health physician. He serves as president and CEO of 'Resolve to Save Lives'—a $225 million, five-year initiative to prevent epidemics and cardiovascular disease. He was the director of the U.S. Center s for Disease Control and Prevention (CDC) (Wikipedia, 2021). He is someone influential in the field of infectious diseases, an area which has now become very attached to teleworking.

This analysis is also done for a larger dataset—10 000 tweets (Fig. 10), in a more recent time frame and verified for the same effect. There is a small number of users around whom most connections are concentrated. This verification follows the investigation on the area: "Investigating central users in networks like Twitter helps identify influential actors in communication and information diffusion" (Park et al., 2015, p. 5). The user @HeMandoKay concentrates more retweets around her (N.48). There are still only six more users with no more than 16 retweets, but who

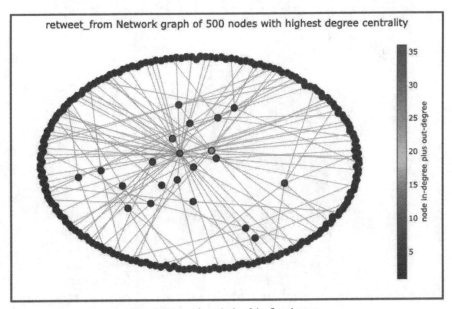

Fig. 9: Network analysis of the first dataset.

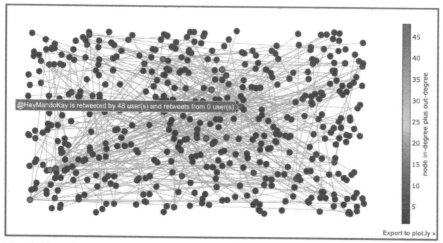

Fig. 10: Network analysis of the second dataset where the user @HeyMandoKay concentrates the highest number of retweets.

still concentrate on the most connections around them, after the central user, in red. The others remain, hundreds of posts, that have no retweets, and therefore have little connectivity and centrality in the network.

Finally, a sentiment analysis is performed on the dataset and the output was as given in Fig. 11. The main conclusion is that the content created, the sample of tweets, do not tend towards one strong tendency, either to perceive teleworking as only positive or only negative. Rather, it sees 10.8 per cent as positive and

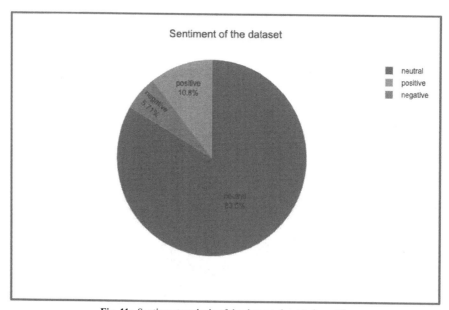

Fig. 11: Sentiment analysis of the dataset about 'telework'.

approximately 83.5 per cent as neutral. This output is in line with the evidence of the national survey and the literature (Boell et al., 2016; Pew Research Center, 2020b). There is no clear perception of people, but rather divided or neutral, regarding this phenomenon, which shows both positive and negative points and, above all, there are numerous circumstances that influence the negative or positive view of telework. For the positive view, namely, having a job capable of being able to work remotely, being a middle-aged adult without children under the age of 18 and used to new technologies, having a college degree and not living alone (Pew Research Center, 2020b).

4. Conclusion, Limitations and Future Directions

Social Media Analytics tools, like Google Trends and Twitter's SMILE repository were used to understand how people perceived 'telework' in the U.S. during the Covid-19 pandemic. The result is that the retrieved data follows the literature regarding telework and brings new insights. The contributions of this study are: (1) Contribution to the OB research about Social Media Analytics and its applicability, explaining a phenomenon like 'telework'. This phenomenon in the Covid-19 pandemic is rather a reaction to a catastrophe than a planned strategy of work efficiency and is not well studied by research (Belzunegui-Eraso and Erro-Garcés, 2020). In this study, Google Trends and SMILE confirm this; (2) it is proven what the literature affirmed, 'telework' is a topic that is not unanimous and inconclusive (Boell et al., 2016; Pew Research Center, 2020) and somewhat neutral in public opinion as there's a lot of different circumstances and types of work people perform. First, the majority of American jobs aren't suitable for 'telework'. Secondly, the ones that are, have a divided opinion; (3) both Google Trends and SMILE SMA tools were very useful and proved that the literature was right about them being trustworthy; (4) the use of these tools contributes for the promotion of a culture of free, ethical and broad access to science; (5) finally, it is a useful and actualized overview over the topic of SMA.

This study has some limitations. Regarding the SMILE tool, despite being widely used, it needs more dissemination and studies. In addition, it needs more public and private support and contributions, as its data source has been reduced over time. But the advantages are more than the liabilities. Any SMA tool is imperfect and may have limitations in the analysis (Yun and Kim, n.d.). Finally, the conclusions drawn from the U.S. are not necessary to extrapolate to another country.

For future research directions, a more detailed and semi-automated content analysis of the sample of tweets could be performed; also, the demographics could be segmented by age, gender, user profile; lastly, the user profile data could be crossed with the tweets to understand better telework.

References

Adhanom, T. 2020, March 11. *WHO Director-General's Opening Remarks at the Media Briefing on Covid-19-11 March 2020*. https://www.who.int/director-general/speeches/detail/who-director-general-s-opening-remarks-at-the-media-briefing-on-covid-19---11-march-2020.

Almeida, F. 2017. Concept and dimensions of Web 4.0. *International Journal of Computers and Technology*, 16(7).

Amber, K.T., Bloom, R. and Hu, S. 2016. Association of google search volume index peaks for skin cancer w ith skin cancer awareness month – Reply. *JAMA Dermatology*, 152(1): 113–114.

Baccianella, S., Esuli, A. and Sebastiani, F. 2010, May. Sentiwordnet 3.0: An enhanced lexical resource for sentiment analysis and opinion mining. *In:* Calzolari, N., Choukri, K., Maegaard, B., Mariani, J., Odijk, J., Piperidis, S., Rosner, M. and Tapias, D. (Eds.). *Proceedings of the Seventh International Conference on Language Resources and Evaluation (LREC'10).*

Batrinca, B. and Treleaven, P.C. 2015. Social Media Analytics: A survey of techniques, tools and platforms. *Ai & Society*, 30(1): 89–116.

Belzunegui-Eraso, A. and Erro-Garcés, A. 2020. Teleworking in the context of the Covid-19 crisis. *Sustainability*, 12(9): 3662.

Bertot, J.C., Jaeger, P.T. and Grimes, J.M. 2012. Promoting transparency and accountability through ICTs, social media, and collaborative e-government. *Transforming Government: People, Process and Policy.*

Bird, S. 2006. NLTK: The natural language toolkit. pp. 69–72. *In:* Curran, J. (Ed.). *Proceedings of the COLING/ACL on Interactive Presentation Sessions.* Association for Computational Linguistics.

Blount, Y. 2015. Pondering the Faultlines of anywhere working (Telework, Telecommuting): A literature review. *Foundations and Trends in Information Systems*, 1(3): 163–276.

Boell, S.K., Cecez-Kecmanovic, D. and Campbell, J. 2016. Telework paradoxes and practices: The importance of the nature of work. *New Technology, Work and Employment*, 31(2): 114–131.

Bruns, A. and Stieglitz, S. 2013. Towards more syste- matic Twitter analysis: Metrics for tweeting activities. *International Journal of Social Research Methodology*, 16(2), 91–108. doi: 10.1080/13645579. 2012.756095.

Burke, W.W. 2018. *Organization Change: Theory and Practice*, 5th ed., Sage, USA.

Cioffi-Revilla, C. 2010. *Computational Social Science*, Wiley Interdiscip. Rev. Comput. Statistics, 2(3): 259–271.

Choi, H. and Varian, H. 2012. Predicting the present with Google Trends. *Economic Record*, 88: 2–9.

Congressional Research Service (2021, Jan.). Unemployment Rates during the COVID-19 Pandemic. *In:* Falk, G., Romero, P.D., Nicchitta, I.A. and Nyhof, E.C. (Eds.). Brief. https://fas.org/sgp/crs/misc/ R46554.pdf.

Ding, D., Guan, C., Chan, C.M. and Liu, W. 2020. Building stock market resilience through digital transformation: Using Google Trends to analyze the impact of Covid-19 pandemic. *Frontiers of Business Research in China*, 14(1): 1–21.

Dossena, C., Mizzau, L. and Mochi, F. 2019. Social Media in HRM: A humanistic management perspective. *In: HRM 4.0 for Human-c entered Organizations.* Emerald Publishing Limited 23: 201–219.

Dreher, P.C., Tong, C., Ghiraldi, E. and Friedlander, J.I. 2018. Use of google trends to track online behavior and interest in kidney stone surgery. *Urology*, 121: 74–78.

Drews, W. and Schemer, C. 2010. eTourism for all? Online travel planning of disabled people. pp. 507– 518. *In: Information and Communication Technologies in Tourism 2010*, Springer, Vienna.

Fan, W. and Gordon, M.D. 2014. The power of Social Media Analytics. *Communications of the ACM*, 57(6): 74–81.

Gelbard, R., Ramon-Gonen, R., Carmeli, A., Bittmann, R.M. and Talyansky, R. 2018. Sentiment analysis in organizational work: Towards an ontology of people analytics. *Expert Systems*, 35(5): e12289.

Hagberg, A., Swart, P.S. and Chult, D. 2008. *Exploring Network Structure, Dynamics, and Function using Network X* (No. LA-UR-08-05495; LA-UR-08-5495), Los Alamos National Lab.(LANL), Los Alamos, NM (United States).

Havelka, E.M., Mallen, C.D. and Shepherd, T.A. 2020. Using Google Trends to assess the impact of global public health days on online health information seeking behavior in Central and South America. *Journal of Global Health*, 10(1).

Höpken, W., Eberle, T., Fuchs, M. and Lexhagen, M. 2019. Google Trends data for analyzing tourists' online search behavior and improving demand forecasting: The case of Åre, Sweden. *Information Technology and Tourism*, 21(1): 45–62.

Hutto, C. and Gilbert, E. 2014, May. Vader: A parsimonious rule-based model for sentiment analysis of social media text. *In: Proceedings of the International AAAI Conference on Web and Social Media*, 8(1).

Jansen, B.J., Zhang, M., Sobel, K. and Chowdury, A. 2009. Twitter power: Tweets as electronic word of mouth. *Journal of the American Society for Information Science and Technology*, 60(11): 2169–2188.

Kaplan, A.M. and Haenlein, M. 2010. Users of the world, unite! The challenges and opportunities of Social Media. *Business horizons*, 53(1): 59–68.

Kim, H., Jang, S.M., Kim, S.H. and Wan, A. 2018. Evaluating sampling methods for content analysis of Twitter data. *Social Media and Society*, 4(2): 2056305118772836.

Kitchin, R. 2014. *The Data Revolution: Big Data, Open Data, Data Infrastructures and Their Consequences*. Thousand Oaks, CA: Sage.

Krippendorff, K. 2018. *Content Analysis: An Introduction to Its Methodology*, Sage Publications.

Lai, L.S. and To, W.M. 2015. Content analysis of social media: A grounded theory approach. *Journal of Electronic Commerce Research*, 16(2): 138.

Lazer, D., Pentland, A., Adamic, L., Aral, S., Barabasi, A.L., Brewer, D. and Van Alstyne, M. 2009. Social science. Computational social science. *Science*, New York, NY, 323(5915): 721–723.

Liu, Y., Peng, G., Hu, L., Dong, J. and Zhang, Q. 2019. Using Google Trends and Baidu index to analyze the impacts of disaster events on company stock prices. *Industrial Management & Data Systems*, 120(2): 350–365.

Mangold, W.G. and Faulds, D.J. 2009. Social media: The new hybrid element of the promotion mix. *Business Horizons*, 52(4): 357–365.

Marler, J.H. and Boudreau, J.W. 2017. An evidence-based review of HR Analytics. *The International Journal of Human Resource Management*, 28(1): 3–26.

Mohamad, M. and Kok, H.S. 2019. Using Google Trends data to study public interest in breast cancer screening in Malaysia. *Asian Pacific Journal of Cancer Prevention, APJCP*, 20(5): 1427.

Muralidharan, S., Rasmussen, L., Patterson, D. and Shin, J.H. 2011. Hope for Haiti: An analysis of Facebook and Twitter usage during the earthquake relief efforts. *Public Relations Review*, 37(2): 175–177.

Ogrysko, N. 2021, March. From maximum telework, to what's next? *Federal News Network*. https://federalnewsnetwork.com/mike-causey-federal-report/2021/03/from-maximum-telework-to-whats-next/.

Pääkkönen, J., Laaksonen, S.M. and Jauho, M. 2020. Credibility by automation: Expectations of future knowledge production in social media analytics. *Convergence*, 26(4): 790–807.

Park, S.B., Ok, C.M. and Chae, B.K. 2016. Using Twitter data for cruise tourism marketing and research. *Journal of Travel and Tourism Marketing*, 33(6): 885–898.

Pedregosa, F., Varoquaux, G., Gramfort, A., Michel, V., Thirion, B., Grisel, O. and Vanderplas, J. 2011. 'Scikit-learn: Machine learning in Python'. *Journal of Machine Learning Research*, 12(Oct.): 2825–2830. *URL: http://jmlr. org/papers/v12/pedregosa11a. html*.

Pew Research Center (2019, June). *Social Media Fact Sheet*. https://www.pewresearch.org/internet/fact-sheet/social-media/.

Pew Research Center. 2020a. *Telework may Save U.S. Jobs in Covid-downturn, especially among college graduates*. https://www.pewresearch.org/fact-tank/2020/05/06/telework-may-save-u-s-jobs-in-covid-19-downturn-especially-among-college-graduates/.

Pew Research Center. 2020b. *How the Coronavirus Outbreak has – and hasn't – Changed the Way Americans Work*. https://www.pewresearch.org/social-trends/2020/12/09/how-the-coronavirus-outbreak-has-and-hasnt-changed-the-way-americans-work/.

Rathore, A.K., Kar, A.K. and Ilavarasan, P.V. 2017. Social Media Analytics: Literature review and directions for future research, *Decision Analysis*, 14(4): 229–249.

Rovetta, A. 2021. Reliability of google trends: analysis of the limits and potential of web infoveillance during covid-19 pandemic and for future research. *medRxiv*, 2020–12.

Shang, J., Liu, J., Jiang, M., Ren, X., Voss, C.R. and Han, J. 2018. Automated phrase mining from massive text corpora. *IEEE Transactions on Knowledge and Data Engineering*, 30(10): 1825–1837.

Shelton, T., Poorthuis, A. and Zook, M. 2015. Social media and the city: Rethinking urban socio-spatial inequality using user-generated geographic information. *Landscape and Urban Planning*, 142: 198–211.

Shin, B., El Sawy, O.A., Sheng, O.R.L. and Higa, K. 2000. Telework: existing research and future directions. *Journal of Organizational Computing and Electronic Commerce*, 10(2): 85–101. doi:10.1207/S15327744JOCE1002_2.

Sinha, V., Subramanian, K.S., Bhattacharya, S. and Chaudhary, K. 2012. The contemporary framework on social media analytics as an emerging tool for behavior informatics, HR analytics and business process, *Management: Journal of Contemporary Management Issues*, 17(2): 65–84.

Stieglitz, S. and Dang-Xuan, L. 2013. Social media and political communication: A social media analytics framework. *Social Network Analysis and Mining*, 3(4): 1277–1291.

Tankovska, H. 2021, January 28. *Number of Social Network Users Worldwide from 2017 to 2025*. Statista; retrieved on February 15, 2021, from: https://www.statista.com/statistics/278414/number-of-worldwide-social-network-users/.

Thelwall, M., Buckley, K. and Paltoglou, G. 2011. Sentiment in Twitter events. *Journal of the American Society for Information Science and Technology*, 62(2): 406–418.

van Zoonen, W., Verhoeven, J.W. and Vliegenthart, R. 2016. How employees use Twitter to talk about work: A typology of work-related tweets. *Computers in Human Behavior*, 55: 329–339.

Wikipedia (2021, May 3). Tom Frieden. https://en.wikipedia.org/wiki/Tom_Frieden.

Yun, J.T., Vance, N., Wang, C. et al. 2019. The social media macroscope: A science gateway for research using social media data. *Future Generation Computer Systems*. https://doi.org/10.1016/j.future.2019.10.029.

Yun, J.T. and Kim, S.W. (n.d.). *Lesson 4–1.3 N-gram Frequency Count and Phrase Mining*, Coursera; retrieved on 13 March, 2021, from: https://www.coursera.org/lecture/applying-data-analytics-business-in-marketing/lesson-4-1-3-n-gram-frequency-count-and-phrase-mining-AvJ3M.

Zhao, X., Zhan, M. and Wong, C.W. 2017. Segmenting and understanding publics in a social media information sharing network: An interactional and dynamic approach. *International Journal of Strategic Communication*, 12(1): 25–45. https://doi.org/10.1080/1553118x.2017.1379013.

6

Social Analytics and Information Technology

*Samsun M. Basarici** and *Yılmaz Kilicaslan*

INTRODUCTION

Nature has shown many different ways of creating life. The essential thing about life is that it requires great cooperation. We see cooperation starting at an atomic level through cells forming complex organisms. As these structures get complicated, cooperation also gets complicated. It does not require so much to build stable structures at an atomic level but at higher levels, things are much more complicated. Living beings have created tribes, cliques, states, etc., to survive. Maybe it is not wrong to say that the 'survival of the fittest' is strongly tied to the ability of creating strong communities. These forms of living together ensure the viability of the species.

Different species created different forms of living together; bees have their hierarchically structured beehives, ants have their hierarchically structured ant colonies, so do wolves, lions, etc., have their prides and so on. As one of the most sophisticated species, the human species also has built different structures, like tribes, societies, etc. What makes human beings different from other living beings is that they possess the ability to examine the structures built and think about them. Besides, the knowledge and intellect of studying them can shape them and as well as they get shaped by them.

This chapter concerns the social structures, namely social networks, created by humans and their studies using information technologies as a tool of investigation. We will first give a brief overview of the history of social networks analysis, starting with sociological and psychological research and extend it up to the usage of information technologies. After the historical overview we will define the terms related to social analytics from the point of view of information technologies. Introducing the main mathematical tool, namely graph theory, and information technological approaches, we will extend the terminology to social media network analysis. Sentiment analysis

Department of Computer Engineering, Engineering Faculty, Aydın Adnan Menderes University, Turkey.
  Emails: yilmaz.kilicaslan@adu.edu.tr
* Corresponding author: sbasarici@adu.edu.tr

with IT tools will be examined as an example of IT usage for social analytics in more detail. The chapter will conclude with some future perspectives and suggestions. Finally, it is noteworthy that this chapter is not meant to be an exhaustive and comprehensive study on social analytics and information technology. It should be regarded as an introductory motivation and occasion for the reader to have access to the topic.

1. A Brief Historical Overview on Social Network Analysis

Sociology as a scientific and positivist discipline started with the works of the French mathematician and philosopher Isidore Marie Auguste François Xavier Comte, in the 19th century. He was also the eponym of this discipline. According to his definition, "Sociology is the study of human behavior" (Comte, 1830). In his doctrine of positivism, he formulated two universal laws applicable to all sciences including astronomy, geology, chemistry, biology, and sociology which he called *physique sociale* (social physics) in his early works. He saw social sciences as the last and highest science. In his opinion social sciences were the 'Queen Science' of human societies and by far the most complex and challenging in the scientific field. Comte's Theory of Sciences can be summarized as given in Fig. 1.

As it is beyond the scope of this chapter here, it would only be mentioned that creating a framework on such a solid base enabled many great minds, like Maximilian 'Max' Carl Emil Weber, David Émile Durkheim, Karl Marx, Friedrich Engels, Maurice Duverger and others to establish sociology as a foundational and independent scientific area.[1]

The sociology of the 19th century, until the beginning of the 20th century, concentrated more on behavioral approaches. Sociology was trying to get established as an independent and strong discipline. The mastermind of network analysis in

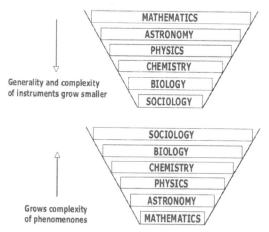

Fig. 1: Comte's theory of sciences (Wikipedia, 2021a).

---

[1] Although some of Marx's and Engels's works are considered as "sociological classics", they are more considered as the cofounders of modern sociology.

sociology was Georg Simmel. At the beginning of the 20th century, Simmel claimed that interdependencies should be the main objective of sociology to establish it as a strong and independent discipline. He postulated that sociology should deal more with the forms of socialization through these interdependencies rather than the contents. Therewith, he put the analysis of relational characteristics and the ties and relationships of individuals into the centre of sociology as postulated in the structural analysis (Simmel, 1890). He was one of the first scientists to put the group into the foreground of his studies. He assumed that groups have a significant influence on individuals and that group membership is an expression of the choice of an individual (Simmel, 1908). He also introduced two different types of groups—organic and rational groups where the first one includes the family and the neighborhood and the latter refers to groups like the military, organizations, etc., which are formed by the individual. According to Simmel, the first type of these groups are groups where the individuals are born into and individuals do not have an influence on them. The second type of groups are formed by individuals, or individuals voluntarily join them, and have the chance to shape or change them. With the works of Simmel, the theoretical foundations of network analysis were created.

Although Simmel's work on network analysis was very much theoretical, it is commonly accepted that the founder of network analysis is Jacob Levy Moreno. He was the first researcher to show the relationship among individuals in small groups, which he called *sociogram*. Consequently, he called his method of measuring social relationships *sociometry* (Jansen, 2003). The drawback of his method was that sociograms were suitable for small groups and were meant to visualize the structures rather than their analysis. Nevertheless, it was the first application of such an approach which is still used in many modern applications, albeit in more sophisticated and complex forms.

Looking at the development of network analysis, one can see two different lines which cross each other at various points. There is a clear socio-psychological trend starting with Gestalt theory going through Field theory, sociometry, balance theories, group dynamics, etc., up to graph theory. The other clear line starts with structural-functional anthropology. These two development lines evolved separately but starting at the beginning of the 1970s, all previous works converged and formed the social network analysis approaches that we can nowadays see. Thanks to researchers like Ronald Breiger, Ronald Burt and others, social media analysis gained a profound basis. These trends can be seen in Fig. 2, as a significant body of good work can be found on the historical development of social network analysis and as a more detailed examination would be out of the scope of this chapter, no further explanation will be given in this chapter.[2]

It is obvious that different researchers and schools have their own points of views as to how social network analysis should be done. The focus differs according to the vantage point. Nevertheless, if a scientific area wants to be established and recognized as a serious and independent field, some features should be incorporated

---

[2] A very good examination of the history of social network analysis can be found in (Scott, 2000); more brief overviews in (Hansen et al., 2020) or (Jansen, 2003).

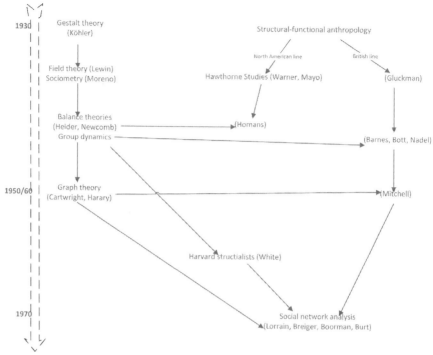

Fig. 2: Development of social network analysis (based on Scott, 2000).

into these researches. As for social network analysis, Linton C. Freeman proposed four features:

1. "Social network analysis is motivated by a structural intuition based on ties linking social actors.
2. It is grounded in systematic empirical data.
3. It draws heavily on graphic imagery, and
4. It relies on the use of mathematical and/or computational models" (Freeman, 2004).

Bringing Fig. 2 in line with Freeman's postulates, one can see that the research from the 1930s corresponds to point one of Freeman's feature list, both on the left and right part of the graphics. After having a solid theoretical basis for Simmel's thoughts, Moreno created the tools that fulfill not only one, but mainly point three of Freeman's postulates. Other research, especially the Hawthorne Studies, satisfy point two as the first research approaches. Many different mathematical and statistical tools and methods used in social network analysis accomplish Freeman's feature four. Some of them will be explained in much more detail later but maybe the strongest tools used come from the field of graph theory that found its way into sociology in the decade between 1950 and 1960 mainly with the works of Harary and Cartwright (Cartwright and Harary, 1956; Harary et al., 1966; Harary, 1969; inter alia).

2. Definitions, Methods and Tools in Social Network Analysis

Social networks have always been pervasive in our daily lives but with the prevalent use of information technologies in modern societies, social networks evolved to become social media networks. Social media is shaping societies in many profound ways. It is imperative to create better tools and methods to understand them. We need newer approaches and utensils to create satisfactory documentation and visualization of these networks to understand 'human behavior' just like Comte proposed centuries ago and as Hansen et al. stated, "to create better social media environments, we will need to better understand the dynamics and patterns of existing platforms" (Hansen et al., 2020). For this purpose, first it is needed to define the terms used with respect to and in context of information technologies in connection with sociology.

Although it is a simple and somewhat clear truth, it should be stated again that social media networks are networks. The science dealing with the study of patterns of connections is *network science*. Network science deals with all kinds of patterns of connections in physical and also in social occurrences. Tools, methods and methodologies of network science can be applied to local area networks in computer engineering, to swarm behavior of *Sturnus vulgaris*, electricity networks, city or country maps, neural networks, etc. A network consists of entities or things which are called *nodes*, *vertices*, *agents*, *items* or *entities* and, in case of social networks, also people. They can represent people, workgroups, teams, institutions, countries, cities, etc. They can also represent things like Web pages, videos, documents and so on. Considering all kinds of connections among a group of people and things, one can define *social networks* as being created from such a kind of collection of connections. From that point of view, it is evident that social networks are a subset of networks. These kinds of networks are created whenever people interact with other people, institutions or artifacts. This interaction may be direct, e.g., one person sending an email or a letter to another person or it may be indirect, e.g., broadcasting a video on YouTube. The connections between the vertices are called *edges*, *ties*, *links*, *relationships* or *connections*. They can represent a friendship, a relationship, a transaction, some shared attributes like students of a class, members of a club, etc. Edges can be *directed* or *asymmetric*. Such kinds of edges have a clear starting vertex, an origin and a clear end vertex, a destination. Their visual appearance in a graph is mostly an arrow from one vertex to another vertex. A line without an arrow in a graph is called an *undirected*, *symmetric* or *mutual* edge. Directed edges can be reciprocated or not, e.g., if one person sends a letter to another person, the receiver can answer this letter with another letter or not. Another property of an edge is its *weight*; an edge can be *weighted* or *unweighted*. Unweighted edges are also called *binary edges* because they only show the existence or non-existence of an edge. In contrast to them, weighted edges include some values that are related to that edge. These values show the strength of a connection. Commonly, for the analysis, edges are stored and represented in matrices or edge lists.

Consequently, the application of the tools, methods, etc., of network science to social networks is called *social network analysis*. It is a systematic methodology, created to evaluate social media networks. The main tool in use is graph theory. Graph theory is a subfield of discrete mathematics and theoretical informatics and is a powerful mathematical tool both to visualize and analyze networked structures, more precisely sets of edges and vertices, their properties and their relationships. The founder of graph theory was the Prussian mathematician, physicist, astronomer, geographer, logician and engineer Leonhard Euler. He shaped many different areas of mathematics but also areas, like music theory, mechanics, optics, etc. It is thanks to him that we have terms like 'mathematical function' in analysis.

Graph theory was founded in 1736 and it was based on the solution of the so-called *Königsberger Brückenproblem*—in English, known as 'Seven Bridges of Königsberg'. Königsberg was a Prussian city which is now in the territory of Russia and called Kaliningrad. It was built on both sides of the River Pregel. In the middle of the river channels, there were two large islands called Kneiphof and Lomse. The islands were connected to the mainland and to each other with a total of seven bridges. The question was whether someone could walk the city while passing each river once and only once. To cut a long story short, Euler could prove that it was impossible to pass all these bridges once and only once. For his proof, he reformulated the problem into a form which is now known as a graph theoretical approach. The problem and its graph theoretical visualization is shown in Fig. 3.

The field of graph theory is one of the best researched areas both in mathematics and computer science. So, it would be unnecessary and a battology to go further into the depth of graph theory here. Good overview can be found in (Gross and Yellen, 1999), a more comprehensive study in (Gross and Yellen, 2004) or in (Alsina, 2007) with some interesting applications.

In the previous section it was stated that the father of network analysis was Jacob Levi Moreno with his sociometry. He introduced the sociograms in his ground-breaking work in 1934 (Moreno, 1934). In this work he claimed that the "growth of the individual organism as a unity from simpler to more highly differentiated levels is well recognized." To analyze this claim, he conducted research on school pupils and showed the relationships in a graphical form. Based on Moreno's work, Martin Grandjean combined Moreno's results with graph theoretical approaches and computational resources to visualize Moreno's research again (Grandjean, 2015). Figure 4 shows Moreno's sociograms compared to the newer computational approach.

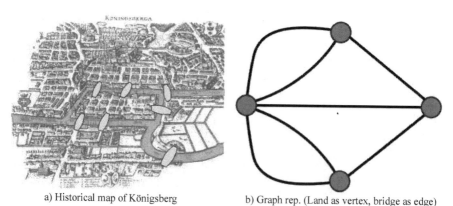

a) Historical map of Königsberg   b) Graph rep. (Land as vertex, bridge as edge)

Fig. 3: Seven bridges of Königsberg (Wikipedia, 2021b).

Class Structure, 8th Grade

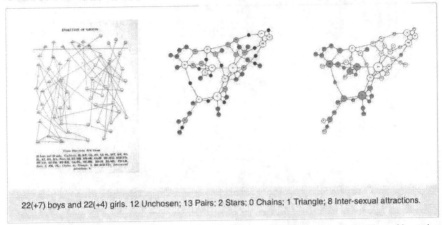

22(+7) boys and 22(+4) girls. 12 Unchosen; 13 Pairs; 2 Stars; 0 Chains; 1 Triangle; 8 Inter-sexual attractions.

Fig. 4: *Left*: Moreno's original network from 1934; *center*: network showing the number of incoming connections with dark gray = 0, white = 3 or more; *right*: network indicating girls in gray and boys in white (Grandjean, 2015).

Tools and methods of graph theory can be used both for visualization and for analysis of social networks. A good example of both visualization and analysis is demonstrated by Stanley Milgram with a series of experiments and research, starting in 1967. All these experiments are known as 'small-world experiment' and have triggered a series of work in various areas. The question was: "Starting with any two people in the world, what is the probability that they will know each other?" (Milgram, 1967). The reformulation of the question in 1969 was: "What is the probability that any two people, selected arbitrarily from a large population, such as that of the United States, will know each other?" (Travers and Milgram, 1969). At first glance this question and the problem per se might look like an intellectual curiosity but "the importance of the problem 'lies' … in the fact that it brings under discussion a certain mathematical structure in society, a structure that often plays a part…" (Milgram, 1967). The researchers conducted several experiments asking arbitrary selected citizens of the USA to send a letter to a given target person. If the participant knows the target person, it should deliver the letter directly to that person; otherwise, the letter should be forwarded to somebody from whom the participant thinks that he/she might know the target person. Each person should sign their name on the letter so that the researchers could see how many steps it took to deliver the letter at the end of the experiment, that is, when the letter reached the target person. In terms of graph theory, each step from one person to the other one is called a *hop*. After a series of experiments Milgram and his colleagues found that on an average it needs only six hops to deliver a letter from one arbitrary selected person to a target as seen in Fig. 5.[3] The results of these experiments are sometimes also referred to as 'six degrees of separation', although Milgram and his colleagues never used this term.

---

[3] In fact, the average path length was about 5.5 or 5.6.

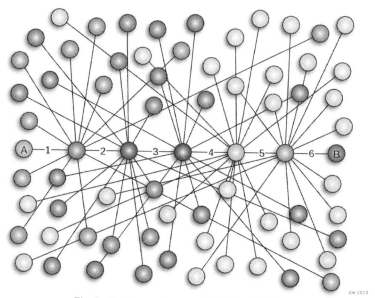

Fig. 5: Six degrees of separation (Wikipedia, 2021c).

In many cases social networks are considered from an individual's point of view. In these cases, the individual is called *ego* and the connected people are called *alters*. When networks include only people connected to a specific ego, they are called *egocentric networks*. Considering egocentric networks, *degrees* can be defined; A basic *1-degree* ego network consists only of the ego and it alters. A *1.5-degree* ego network is an extended 1-degree network. It not only includes the ego and the alters, but also connections between all the alters. Another extension is given with *2-degree* networks which include the 1.5-degree networks plus all the alters' alters. It can be that some of the alters of the alters are not connected to ego. A good example of such a kind of network can be seen in Fig. 5. Networks of degrees like 2.5 or 3 could also be created but in practice, they are not used very much because of their large sizes and unmanageability. With tools of artificial intelligence and 'big data' analysis, it could be feasible to examine such kinds of higher degree networks too.

Networks are also examined by their completeness. "A 'full' or 'complete' network contains the subset of people or entities who match some interest or attribute and includes information about the set of connections among them all" (Hansen et al., 2020).

Networks connecting the same type of entities are called *unimodal*. The examples of all previously shown networks are all unimodal. In the case of the class structure shown in Fig. 4, the vertices are all school pupils, and the edges are all relationships between them. In Fig. 5, all vertices are again people with edges as their relationships. In applications like Facebook, Twitter or web sites, like Imdb.com or Amazon.com, there are connections not only between people but also between people and documents, like pictures, videos, Web pages, etc. In such cases where the vertices can be of different types, the network is called *multimodal*. The analysis of multimodal networks is cumbersome and their handling is more difficult than unimodal networks. For the sake of better and meaningful analysis, such kinds of multimodal networks are often transformed into simpler unimodal networks. The same definitions and thoughts also apply to the edges; in many practical applications, edges are considered to be only of one type, like two people who send each other e-mails or messages. In such cases, the networks show a *uniplex relation* symbolized as a single connection between the entities. In fact, the interaction and relationship between people can be of much broader complexity, e.g., a woman can be the wife of a man but also his manager at work. For such kinds of relationships networks with different type of edges could be constructed, although they are not very common. Such kinds of networks with multiple connection types are called *multiplex networks*.

Initially the measurement of social networks was based on simply counting the connections. With the increase of computational power and strong computational tools, more sophisticated and complex measures have been developed in network analysis. According to Hansen et al., some basic concept of the measurement methods can be summarized as follows:

- *Density*: Density can be defined as the division of existing relationships by the total number of possible relationships which could be presented in a network.

- *Centralization*: Centralization as an aggregate metric designates the "amount to which the network is centred on one or just a few important nodes".

- *Degree centrality*: Degree centrality is a "simple count of the total number of connections linked to a vertex". It is regarded as a sort of 'popularity measure'. Although it measures popularity, it should be noted that it does not differentiate between quality and quantity.

- *Degree*: "Degree is the measure of the total number of edges connected to a particular vertex."

- *Distance*: The distance is given as the minimum number of neighbour-to-neighbour hops from one vertex to another. In the context of social media analytics, the vertices are considered as people and the distance is measured between people who are not neighbors.

- *Geodesic distance*: The shortest path between two people.

- *Structural hole:* A 'structural hole' is a term for recognizing a missing bridge.

- *Closeness centrality*: Closeness centrality measures each individual's position in the network. It captures the average distance "between each vertex and every other vertex in the network". If we assume that nodes can only pass messages to their existing connections or can only influence them, a low closeness centrality indicates that this node which is considered to be people is directly connected or 'just a hop away'. In contrast, nodes in distant or peripheral spots can have high closeness centrality scores. This case designates that these nodes/vertices/people need a high number of hops to connect to these peripheral locations, which is also an indication of more connections (Hansen et al., 2020).

All the aforementioned metrics are mathematically well defined. As graphs are defined as $G = \{V, E\}$, a degree of a vertex can be defined as $C_D = deg\ (v)$; hence, the degree centrality for the whole graph can be given as $C_D = \dfrac{\sum_{i=1}^{|v|}[C_D(v^*) - C_D(v_i)]}{H}$ with v^* being the node with the highest degree in graph G.[4]

Another mathematical tool for social analytics is the matrix. As it is well-known, matrices are constructed of columns and rows and their intersections are called *cells*. The rows and columns represent different entities, actors, etc., and the cells represent the judgement of one entity about the other entity. Matrices are used to easily visualize social network data and allow identification of ties more easily than verbal descriptions.

Other mathematical and statistical tools are also used for both representing and visualizing social media networks, like maps, distributions, etc. Although many different tools and methods could be used in social analytics, the main tools are matrices and graphs. Therefore, further examination of other tools and methods will be omitted here.

With the advent of information technologies and computers, social analytics also changed. The immense computational capacities and power of computers is both a curse and a blessing for social analytics. Now it is possible to visualize and analyze amounts of data very fast. On the other hand, the pervasiveness of information technology devices means the increase in data and also raises the complexity of networks. Today we are speaking about 'big data' but technologies, like the Internet of Things, and approaches like Industry 4.0 will push the 'big' into the direction of 'huge'. The good news, for example about IoT, is that data is and will be generated in machine-readable form so that automated analysis becomes easier after being freed of the burdens of data collection and preparation. Artificial intelligence, data mining, machine learning and all related computer science tools promise a better handling of social media networks and a better understanding of human interactions.

The next subsection will give an example of the usage of information technology tools for the analysis of a very human trait—the sentiment.

3. Usage of IT Tools for Social Network Analysis: Sentiment Analysis

As Pathak et al. (2020) point out: "The drastic shifts from read-only to read-write access to the Web lead the people to interact with each other through social media networks, like Wikis, online forums, communities, etc. Due to this, user-generated content through social media platforms is increasing tremendously. Specifically, Web-based data of the form—opinionated text, reviews of products and services has been one of the most contributing factors in social big data" (p. 2).

It is the field of study called 'sentiment analysis' that is concerned with the question of how to 'understand' such opinionated and largely unstructured big data.

In this chapter we endeavour to answer the following questions:

1. What is sentiment analysis?
2. How is sentiment analysis carried out?

---

[4] A summary of the mathematical formulations of the definitions given above can be found in (Arif, 2015).

Though we will not be able to go into details, we hope to provide the reader with a general understanding of what sentiment analysis is and the methods and tools with which it is carried out.

3.1 What is Sentiment Analysis?

Sentiment analysis is a relatively new field of research. It has blossomed rapidly since the 2000s. Even though there is some earlier work on this subject, research concerning sentiment analysis has surged up as a result of the social platforms, such as Twitter and Facebook getting prevalent (cf. Pang and Lee, 2008). Among the terms that refer to the same or similar fields of research are sentiment mining, review mining, opinion mining, opinion extraction, affect analysis, subjectivity analysis, emotion analysis, etc. The first scientific article where the term *sentiment analysis* was first used is probably a paper by Nasukawa and Yi (2003) in which the following statement appears: "The essential issues in sentiment analysis are to identify how sentiments are expressed in texts and whether the expressions indicate positive (favorable) or negative (unfavorable) opinions toward the subject" (Nasukawa and Yi, 2003, p. 70).

One of the most straightforward definitions is made in Liu (2012): "Sentiment analysis, also called opinion mining, is the field of study that analyzes people's opinions, sentiments, evaluations, appraisals, attitudes and emotions towards entities, such as products, services, organizations, individuals, issues, events, topics and their attributes" (Liu, 2012, p. 1).

Some concepts are closely related to sentiment analysis. Among them are opinion, view, belief, conviction, persuasion and sentiment. Pang and Lee (2008) point out that they all refer to a judgment that one holds as true. Below are the definitions of these concepts given by *Merriam-Webster's Online Dictionary* along with the examples of sentences provided by Pang and Lee (2008):

- *Opinion*: A conclusion thought out but open to dispute (e.g., 'Each expert seemed to have a different opinion').
- *View*: A subjective opinion (e.g., 'Tom is very assertive in stating his views').
- *Belief*: Often deliberate acceptance and intellectual assent (e.g., 'She has a firm belief in her party's platform').
- *Conviction*: A firmly and seriously held belief (e.g., 'The conviction that animal life is as sacred as human is what defines Shirley's character').
- *Persuasion*: A belief grounded on assurance (as by evidence) of its truth (e.g., 'He was of the persuasion that everything changes over time').
- *Sentiment*: A settled opinion reflective of one's feelings (e.g., 'Her feminist sentiments are well-known').

Schrauwen (2010) adds the following concepts to the list:

- *Emotion*: A strong feeling (e.g., 'I have difficulty in controlling my emotions when something like this happens').
- *Feeling*: An experience of affective and emotional states (e.g., 'I like her and apparently the feeling is mutual').

- *Thought*: A personal belief or judgment that is not founded on proof or certainty (e.g., 'That thought had never occurred to me').
- *Impression*: A vague idea in which some confidence is placed (e.g., 'Her first impression of him proved to be completely wrong').

3.2 How is Sentiment Analysis Carried Out?

3.2.1 An Overview of the Literature

Many experiment-based research articles have been published which give insight as to how to conduct sentiment analysis. Below is a list of such works, together with a brief explanatory information:

- Pang and Lee (2002): Sentiment analysis is carried out on the basis of product assessments using supervised machine learning.
- Liu et al. (2007): A sentiment model is developed for predicting marketing performance by analysing Web blogs.
- McGlohon et al. (2010): Assessments in web blogs are exploited in order to sort products and suppliers.
- Hong and Skiena (2010): Work is conducted on blogs and tweets in order to discover the relationship between public opinion and national football league bets.
- O'Connor et al. (2010): The connection is examined between sentiment analysis results concerning Twitter and public opinion polls.
- Tumasjan et al. (2010): Election results are predicted using sentiment analysis on Twitter data.
- Chen et al. (2010): An opinion scoring model is developed in order to explore political standpoints.
- Yano and Smith (2010): A method is put forward to generate a content-based prediction of the amount of comments that political blogs will receive.
- Asur and Huberman (2010); Joshi et al. (2010); Sadikov et al. (2009): Twitter data, comments on movies and blogs are examined in order to predict box-office returns of movies.
- Miller et al. (2011). Sentiment flow through hyperlink networks is analyzed.
- Mohammad and Yang (2011): An answer is searched for the question of how the genders differ from each other along with sentimental dimensions.
- Mohammad (2011): It is focused on sentiment analysis of novels and fairy-tales.
- Bollen et al. (2011): Stock markets are predicted through an analysis of Twitter data.
- Bar-Haim et al. (2011) and Feldman et al. (2011): Expert investors in stock microblogs are identified and followed in order to come up with a basis for developing models that predict stock rise.
- Zhang and Skiena (2010): Sentiment analysis is conducted on blog and news texts to determine trading strategies.

- Sakunkoo and Sakunkoo (2009): A model is presented to illustrate the relationship between existing new reviews of online books.
- Groh and Hauffa (2011): Natural language processing (NLP)-based sentiment analysis methods are investigated and evaluated to determine the characterization of social relations from textual communication.
- Tang et al. (2015): A neural network model is presented. It is intended to perform document-level sentiment classification. It is developed within a framework that incorporates user- and product-level information.
- Zhai and Zhang (2016): A semi-supervised denoising autoencoder model is proposed for document-level sentiment analysis. Sentiment information is taken into consideration during learning for obtaining good document vector representations.
- Dou (2017): A user-product deep memory network is proposed for capturing user and product information. A document is initially represented by using long short-term memory (LSTM) and then the deep memory network is applied for predicting the review rating.

A general overview of the literature as above reveals that there are basically three types of approaches to sentiment analysis:

1) Probability- or statistics-based approaches
2) Learning-based approaches
3) Rule-based approaches

Let us now have a look at each of these approaches.

3.2.2 Probability- or Statistics-based Approaches

One of the best-known instances of probability- or statistics-based approaches is the documents-modeling method relying on the notion of term *frequency* that traditional information extraction techniques have often resorted to. The main idea here is that if certain terms are employed more frequently in certain documents compared to the rest, then this means that these terms provide us with an idea about the topics of these documents. A not-surprising observation in the field of sentiment analysis is that it is more meaningful to focus on terms that are frequently found in some documents but not in others, rather than focusing merely on term frequency. For example, Pang and Lee (2002) improved their systems the following way.

Term position, like term occurrence, bears importance in sentiment analysis. N-grams are commonly used for determining the position of terms. Generally, an *n-gram model* is constructed to check the n-1 terms occurring prior to the term the position of which is in question (cf. Jurafsky and Martin, 2020; Russel and Norvig, 2003). What basically underlies this technique is the assumption that there is a close relationship between the occurrence probability of a term and the occurrence probabilities of the n-1 terms appearing prior to it. Many works on sentiment analysis where n-grams are employed can be found in the literature (Kim and Hovy, 2006; Pang and Lee, 2002; Wiebe et al., 2004).

Another probabilistic alternative for analyzing sentiments in texts is to use a hidden Markov model (Jiang et al., 2011; Mei et al., 2007; inter alia). A hidden Markov model is used for statistical modeling of chronologically organized data (Fink, 2014). In this technique, a temporal process is defined as a discrete random variable that takes probabilistic values that correspond to actual states.

3.2.3 Learning-based Approaches

Sentiment analysis is essentially a document classification task. Machine learning is one of the best-known techniques of classification (Apaydın, 2010; Mitchell, 1997; Quinlan, 1993; Russel and Norvig, 2003; inter alia). In general terms, machine learning is the technique whereby computers make generalizations resting on inductive inference strategies. More specifically, machine learning is learning a hypothesis that converges with a set of example input-output pairs to the function that maps the inputs to the outputs. Below is the list of steps that abstractly characterize the procedure for learning such a hypothesis:

(1) Collecting (positive and negative) examples.
(2) Determining the attributes that will impact the classification process.
(3) Annotating the collected attributes in accordance with these attributes.
(4) Splitting the annotated examples into a set of training data and a set of test data.
(5) Choosing or developing a learning algorithm.
(6) Applying the learning algorithm to the set of training data to generate a learning hypothesis.
(7) Calculating the performance of the learning hypothesis, using the set of test data.
(8) Repeating steps 4–7 with randomly chosen training data of varying sizes.

One of the most crucial questions that needs to be answered in order to concretize this abstract procedure is: Which learning algorithm to choose and use? Below are some of the classification algorithms used in machine learning (Kılıçaslan et al., 2009):

- *Naïve Bayes Classification Algorithm*: It relies on the assumption that attributes are conditionally independent of each other given the class of examples. Despite the fact that this hypothesis is often inappropriate for real world problems, where attributes strongly depend on each other, the Naïve Bayes approach can yield surprisingly successful classification results. Very briefly, to cite an example, X with a feature vector $(x1, \ldots, xn)$, the Naïve Bayes classifier looks for a class label C that maximizes the likelihood $P(X|C) = P(x_1,\ldots, x_n|c)$. This classification approach helps to reduce the effect of dimensionality by simplifying the problem.
- *K-Nearest Neighbourhood Algorithm*: Instance based or k-nearest neighbor (kNN) classification contrasts with other classification methods, namely the eager ones; in that it stores all the training examples as points in an n-dimensional space and does not build a classifier until an unlabelled instance is to be classified. When a new instance is to be tested, it is assigned the most common class among its k-nearest neighbors. When the kNN algorithm is given two data points, such

as $X = (x_1, ..., x_n)$ and $Y = (y_1, ..., y_n)$ in an n-dimensional space, the Euclidean distance between them is calculated by:

$$\sqrt{(x_1 - y_1)^2 + (x_2 - y_2)^2 + \cdots + (x_n - y_n)^2} = \sqrt{\sum_{i=1}^{n} (x_i - y_i)^2}$$

The algorithm performs well if the *k* value is appropriately chosen.

- *Decision Trees Algorithms*: In decision tree learning, trees are composed of decision nodes and terminal leaves. Given a new instance to be classified, test functions are applied to an instance recursively in decision nodes until hitting a leaf node which assigns a discrete output to it. A feature of the instance is tested in every node for branching. Information gain of selecting an attribute to form a tree must be calculated and a predefined number of the most informative attributes have to be selected in order to minimize the depth of the tree. Below is a decision tree that is used to determine whether or not to go out:

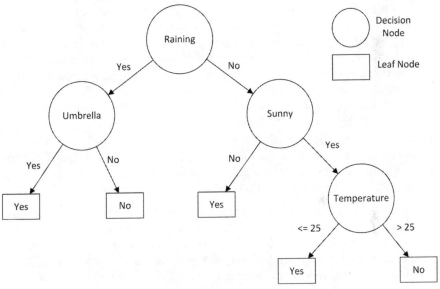

Fig. 6: Decision tree.

The attributes used are the following:

1. Raining: whether it is raining;
2. Umbrella: whether I have an umbrella;
3. Sunny: whether it is sunny;
4. Temperature: the value of the weather temperature (in Celsius).

- In cases where more than one hypothesis is extracted from the training set, ensemble learning methods are used to increase the efficiency of the classifier by selecting and combining a set of hypotheses from the hypotheses space. These hypotheses are combined into a single classifier that makes predictions by taking a vote of its constituents. One of the most used methods in ensemble learning is boosting. The boosting model is sequentially induced from the training examples where the example weights are adjusted at each iteration.

- *Support Vector Machines*: A support vector machine is a linear classifier. More explicitly, a support vector machine algorithm is intended to find a hyperplane in an n-dimensional space that distinctly separates the data points into different classes. There are, of course, many possible hyperplanes that could separate such data. However, the main idea of support vector classification is to find a plane that represents the largest separation between the classes. This is achieved by choosing the hyperplane, the distance from which to the nearest data point on each side is maximal. Such nearest data points are referred to as support vectors. If the data to be classified is not linearly separable, the original data space is mapped into a higher dimensional space, where a linear separation is possible by means of a kernel function.

- *Voted Perceptron*: A voted perceptron is a neural network algorithm, which modifies the original perceptron learning by changing the weighting process and enabling one to use a kernel trick (Freund and Schapire, 1999). The output of a classifier in perceptron learning is 1, if $w.x + b > 0$ where w is the weight vector, x is the input vector and b is the bias. In the original perceptron learning algorithm, in order to train the classifier, feature vectors are processed one after another and every time when an error occurs in the output of the network, the weights are updated. However, the original algorithm can only reach a good solution if the data is linearly separable.

- *Deep learning*: Deep learning is a subset of machine learning that focuses on neural networks and algorithms for training neural networks (Campesato, 2020). It involves a class of machine learning algorithms that use multiple layers to progressively extract higher-level features from the raw input.

Another crucial question that needs to be answered when doing sentiment analysis is: Which learning attributes to use? An answer to this question can be given by detecting which attributes are most informative for any given learning task. A common assumption in the field of sentiment analysis is that adjectives and adverbs are the most informative words and, hence, the words of other syntactic categories can be ignored. However, as demonstrated in work by Hu and Liu (2004), Pang et al. (2002), Pang and Lee (2004) and Riloff et al. (2003), certain nouns and verbs can also be informative for some sentiments.

One of the approaches to be adopted for word-based sentiment classification is to construct lexicons, where words are associated with numerical scores indicating (positive and negative) sentiment information. A common method to do this is to manually construct a sentiment lexicon, which can be either domain-specific (Das and Chen, 2007) or general-purpose (Hurst and Nigam, 2004; Yi et al., 2003). Another method is to start building up the lexicon with a small set that includes 'seed' words and enlarge it by detecting synonymous words in various online resources via bootstrapping (Ding et al., 2008; Hu and Liu, 2004; Kim and Hovy, 2004; Riloff et al., 2003; inter alia). One of the important online resources to be used for this purpose is WordNet. A sentiment lexicon, called SentiWordNet, has been built up employing WordNet and many works have been carried out using this lexicon (Hamouda and Rohaim, 2011; Ohana and Tierney, 2009; Saggion and Funk, 2010; Chalothorn and Ellman, 2013; inter alia).

As their construction is time-consuming (Whitelaw et al., 2005) and since answers provided by people as to whether a given word is positive or negative are not very consistent (Kim and Hovy, 2004; Pang et al., 2002; Wilson et al., 2005), hidden Markov models or statistical and/or learning-based methods, such as the maximum entropy model, have also been used instead of sentiment lexicons for similar purposes (Duric and Song, 2012).

The sentential positions of words, the syntactic structures of sentences, the semantic features of words and sentences and the discursive properties of texts can also be used as learning attributes when doing sentiment analysis with machine learning. However, the extraction of attributes of these kinds largely necessitates to do natural language processing. In what follows, we will have a brief look at natural language processing techniques.

3.2.4 Rule-based Approaches

Some researchers maintain that machine learning is sufficient as a technique to do NLP (Collobert et al., 2011). It is a fact that almost every contemporary approach to NLP involves a learning-based element, however, we still hold the view that linguistic knowledge bears non-negligible importance to this field, and hence, to sentiment analysis. The core work of rule-based NLP is to transform texts in natural language to general-purpose linguistic structures, such as phonemes, morphemes, syntactic categories, tree-structured representations of phrasal structures and logic-based representations of meaning. We share Eisenstein's (2019) view that such structures can and should be incorporated into learning-based architectures in natural language processing.

There are many ways in which rule- and learning-based techniques can be combined in sentiment analysis. Texts to be analyzed often need to be pre-processed for various reasons. Before feeding the text to the classifier, it might, for instance, be desirable to remove uninformative characters from it, to tokenize it into words, or to analyze its words into morphemes. Any of these tasks can be accomplished by using rule-based methods. Words are often used as learning features in sentiment analysis applications. Still, sometimes phrasal structures might be informative for a learning algorithm. It is true however that advanced machine learning techniques have cleaned up expert-engineered representations from the peripheral areas of NLP, namely those concerning phonetics and text/discourse pragmatics. But learning-based algorithms do not perform satisfactorily when the task is more abstract, such as detecting phrasal structures or conducting reasoning processes. Parsers based on syntactic knowledge or logic-based reasoners can handle such abstract tasks to some extent. Paradigms, like inductive logic programming, can serve to combine learning- and rule-based approaches when doing sentiment analysis.

4. Conclusion and Future Work

This chapter started with the statement that life is social and species can only survive within a well-defined structure. Humans also created different social structures. The study of these structures is not only an intellectual amusement but also vital for the species.

With the rise of information technologies, the creation and the analysis of social network analysis reached another quality, and not only is the quality affected, but also the quantity of social networks.

This chapter gave a brief overview on the most important mathematical and computational tools and methods used in social media analytics with an example of use, namely sentiment analysis.

The good news about the extensive usage of information technologies is that all data created is in a machine-readable form and we have now the strong computational powers to analyze them. The bad news is that it turns out to be a vicious circle; we have the ability to analyze big data much faster, but we also have the power to create much more data. With new technologies, like IoT, it will be not only the human creating the data but also machines will contribute on a large scale.

In a time where data is created very fast but also destroyed and forgotten, the need to understand human relations still exists and becomes more important. New approaches are needed and deep learning looks like a promising direction to handle the upcoming complexity and break the vicious cycle.

References

Alsina, C. 2017. *Graphentheorie von U-Bahn-Plänen zu neuronalen Netzen*, Librero.

Apaydın, E. 2010. *Introduction to Machine Learning*. The MIT Press.

Arif, T. 2015. The mathematics of social network analysis: metrics for academic social networks. *International Journal of Computer Applications Technology and Research*, 4(12): 889–893. https://doi.org/10.7753/ijcatr0412.1003.

Asur, S. and Huberman, B.A. 2010. Predicting the future with social media. pp. 492–499. *In: 2010 IEEE/WIC/ACM International Conference on Web Intelligence and Intelligent Agent Technology*. https://doi.org/10.1109/WI-IAT.2010.63.

Bar-Haim, R., Dinur, E., Feldman, R., Fresko, M. and Goldstein, G. 2011. Identifying and following expert investors in stock microblogs. *Proceedings of the 2011 Conference on Empirical Methods in Natural Language Processing*, pp. 1310–1319. Association For Computational Linguistics. Edinburgh, Scotland, UK.

Bollen, J., Mao, H. and Xiao-Jun, Z. 2011. Twitter mood predicts the stock market. *Journal of Computational Science*, 2(1): 1–8. https://doi.org/10.1016/j.jocs.2010.12.007.

Campesato, O. 2020. *Artificial Intelligence, Machine Learning, and Deep Learning*. Mercury Learning and Information LLC.

Cartwright, D. and Harary, F. 1956. Structural balance. A generalization of Heider's Theory. *Psychological Review*, 63(5): 277–293. https://doi.org/10.1037/h0046049.

Chalothorn, T. and Ellman, J. 2013. Affect analysis of radical contents on web forums using SentiWordNet. *International Journal of Innovation, Management and Technology*, 4(1): 122–124.

Chen, B., Zhu, L., Kifer, D. and Lee, D. 2010. What is an opinion about? Exploring political standpoints using opinion scoring model. *Proceedings of the AAAI Conference on Artificial Intelligence*, 24(1): retrieved from: https://ojs.aaai.org/index.php/AAAI/article/view/7717.

Collobert, R., Weston, J., Bottou, L., Karlen, M., Kavukcuoglu, K. and Kuksa, P. 2011. Natural language processing (almost) from scratch. *Journal of Machine Learning Research* 12: 2493–2537.

Comte, A. 1841. *Cours de Philosophie Positive, La Partie historique de la philosophie sociale*.

Das, S.R. and Chen, M.Y. 2007. Yahoo! for Amazon: Sentiment extraction from small talk on the web. *Management Science,* 53(9): 1375–1388. https://doi.org/10.1287/mnsc.1070.0704.

Ding, X., Liu, B. and Yu, P.S. 2008. A holistic lexicon-based approach to opinion mining. *Proceedings of the 2008 Conference on Web Search and Data Mining* (WSDM'08), pp. 231–240. Palo Alto, California, USA.

Dou, Z.-Y. 2017. Capturing user and product information for document level sentiment analysis with deep memory network. pp. 521–526. *Proceedings of the 2017 Conference on Empirical Methods in Natural Language Processing.*

Duric, A. and Song, F. 2012. Feature selection for sentiment analysis based on content and syntax models. *Decision Support Systems,* 53(4): 704–711. https://doi.org/10.1016/j.dss.2012.05.023.

Eisenstein, J. 2019. *Introduction t o Natural Language Processing,* The MIT Press.

Feldman, R., Rosenfeld, B., Bar-Haim, R. and Fresko, M. 2011. *The stock sonar – sentiment analysis of stocks based on a hybrid approach.* pp. 1642–1647. *Proceedings of 23rd IAAI Conference on Artificial Intelligence (IAAI-2011).*

Fink, G.A. 2014. *Markov Models for Pattern Recognition: From Theory to Applications,* Springer.

Freeman, L.C. 2004. *The Development of Social Network Analysis. A Study in the Sociology of Science.* Vancouver BC North Charleston S.C.

Freund, Y. and Schapire, R.E. 1999. Large margin classification using the perceptron algorithm. *Machine Learning,* 37(3): 277–296. https://doi.org/10.1023/A:1007662407062.

Grandjean, M. (n.d.). *Social Network Analysis and Visualization: Moreno's Sociograms Revisited,* Martin Grandjean. http://www.martingrandjean.ch/social-network-analysis-visualization-morenos-sociograms-revisited/.

Groh, G. and Hauffa, J. 2011. Characterizing social relations via NLP-based sentiment analysis. pp. 502–505. *Proceedings of the Fifth International AAAI Conference on Weblogs and Social Media (ICWSM-2011).*

Gross, J.L. and Yellen, J. 1999. *Graph Theory and Its Application,* CRC Press LLC.

Gross, J.L. and Yellen, J. 2004. *Handbook of Graph Theory,* CRC Press LLC.

Hamouda, A. and Rohaim, M. 2011. Reviews classification using sentiwordnet lexicon. *The Online Journal on Computer Science and Information Technology (OJCSIT),* 2(1): 120–123.

Hansen, D.L., Shneiderman, B., Smith, M.A. and Himelboim, I. 2020. *Analyzing Social Media Networks with NodeXL. Insights from a Connected World,* Morgan Kaufmann Publishers.

Harary, F., Norman, R.Z. and Cartwright, D. 1966. *Structural Models: An Introduction to the Theory of Directed Graphs,* John Wiley & Sons Inc.

Harary, F. 1969. *Graph Theory,* Westview Press.

Hong, Y. and Skiena, S. 2010. The wisdom of bookies? Sentiment Analysis versus the NFL Point Spread. pp. 251–254. *Proceedings of the Fourth International AAAI Conference on Weblogs and Social Media ICWSM.*

Hu, M. and Liu, B. 2004. Mining and summarizing customer services. *Proceedings of the Tenth ACM SIGKDD International Conference on Knowledge Discovery and Data Mining,* pp. 168–177. Seattle, Washington, USA.

Hurst, M. and Nigam, K. 2004. Retrieving topical sentiments from online document collections. *Proceedings of SPIE 5296, Document Recognition and Retrieval XI.* https://doi.org/10.1117/12.529422.

Jansen, D. 2003. *Einführung in die Netzwerkanalyse,* Grundlagen, Methoden, *Forschungsbeispiele,* Springer.

Jiang, Y., Meng, W. and Yu, C. 2011. Topic sentiment change analysis. Machine learning and data mining in pattern recognition, MLDM 2011. *Lecture Notes in Computer Science,* 443–457. https://doi.org/10.1007/978-3-642-23199-5_33.

Jurafsky, D. and Martin, J.H. 2020. *Speech and Language Processing: An Introduction to Natural Language Processing, Computational Linguistics, and Speech Recognition.* Pearson.

Kılıçaslan, Y., Güner, E.S. and Yıldırım, S. 2009. Learning-based pronoun resolution for turkish with a comparative evaluation. *Computer Speech and Language,* 23(3): 311–331. https://doi.org/10.1016/j.csl.2008.09.001.

Kim, S.-M. and Hovy, E. 2004. Determining the sentiment of opinions. pp. 1367–1373. *Proceedings of the International Conference on Computational Linguistics (COLING).* https://doi.org/10.3115/1220355.1220555.

Kim, S.-M. and Hovy, E. 2006. Automatic identification of pro and con reasons in online reviews. pp. 483–490. *Proceedings of the COLING/ACL 2006 Main Conference Poster Sessions.* Association for Computational Linguistics (ACL). https://dl.acm.org/doi/10.5555/1273073.1273136.

Liu, Y., Huang, X., An, A. and Yu, X. 2007. ARSA: A sentiment-aware model for predicting sales performance using blogs. pp. 607–614. *Proceedings of the 30th Annual International ACM SIGIR Conference on Research and Development in Information retrieval (SIGIR'07).* https://dl.acm.org/doi/abs/10.1145/1277741.1277845.

McGlohon, M., Glance, N.S. and Reiter, Z. 2010. Star quality: aggregating reviews to rank products and merchants. pp. 114–121. *Proceedings of the 4th International Conference on Weblogs and Social Media (ICWSM).*

Mei, Q., Ling, X., Wondra, M., Su, H. and Zha, C.X. 2007. Topic sentiment mixture: modeling facets and opinions in weblogs. pp. 171–180. *Proceedings of the 16th International Conference on World Wide Web (WWW '07).* https://dl.acm.org/doi/10.1145/1242572.1242596.

Milgram, S. 1967. The small world problem. *Psychology Today*, 1(1): 61–67.

Miller, M., Sathi, C., Wiesenthal, D., Leskovec, J. and Potts, C. 2011. Sentiment flow through hyperlink networks. *Proceedings of the Fifth International AAAI Conference on Weblogs and Social Media (ICWSM-2011).*

Mitchell, T.M. 1997. *Machine Learning,* McGraw-Hill.

Mohammad, S. 2011. From once upon a time to happily ever after: tracking emotions in novels and fairy tales. pp. 105–114. *Proceedings of the ACL 2011 Workshop on Language Technology for Cultural Heritage, Social Sciences and Humanities (LaTeCH'11).* https://dl.acm.org/doi/10.5555/2107636.2107650.

Mohammad, S.M. and Yang, T.(W.). 2011. Tracking sentiment in mail: how genders differ on emotional axes. pp. 70–79. *Proceedings of the ACL Workshop on ACL 2011 Workshop on Computational Approaches to Subjectivity and Sentiment Analysis (WASSA-2011).* https://dl.acm.org/doi/10.5555/2107653.2107662.

Moreno, J.L. 1934. *Who shall survive? A new approach to the problem of human interrelations.* Nervous and Mental Disease Publishing.

Nasukawa, T. and Yi, J. 2003. *Sentiment Analysis: Capturing Favorability Using Natural Language Processing.* https://doi.org/10.1145/945645.945658.

O'Connor, B., Balasubramanyan, R., Routledge, B.R. and Smith, N.A. 2010. From tweets to polls: linking text sentiment to public opinion time series. *Tepper School of Business*, Paper 559. https://doi.org/10.1184/r1/6705632.

Ohana, B. and Tierney, B. 2009. Sentiment classification of reviews using SentiWordNet. *Proceedings of the 9th IT&T Conference.*

Pang, B. and Lee, L. 2002. Thumbs up?: Sentiment classification using machine learning techniques. pp. 79–86. *Proceedings of the ACL-02 Conference on Empirical Methods in Natural Language Processing (EMNLP'02)*, 10. https://dl.acm.org/doi/10.3115/1118693.1118704.

Pang, B. and Lee, L. 2004. A sentimental education: Sentiment analysis using subjectivity summarization based on minimum cuts. pp. 271–278. *Proceedings of the Association for Computational Linguistics (ACL'04).* https://dl.acm.org/doi/10.3115/1218955.1218990.

Pang, B. and Lee, L. 2008. Opinion mining and sentiment analysis. *Foundations and Trends in Information Retrieval.* https://doi.org/10.1561/1500000011.

Pathak, R.A., Agarwal, B., Pandey, M. and Rautaray, S. 2020. Application of deep learning approaches for sentiment analysis. pp. 1–31. *In:* Agarwal, B., Mittal, N., Nayak, R. and Patnaik, S. (Eds.). *Deep Learning-Based Approaches for Sentiment Analysis.* Springer.

Quinlan, R. 1993. *Programs for Machine Learning.* Morgan Kaufmann Publishers.

Riloff, E., Janyce, W. and Wilson, T. 2003. Learning subjective nouns using extraction pattern bootstrapping. pp. 25–32. *Proceedings of the Seventh Conference on Natural Language Learning at HLT-NAACL 2003 (CONLL'03)*, 4. https://dl.acm.org/doi/10.3115/1119176.1119180.

Russel, S.J. and Norvig, P. 2003. *Artificial Intelligence: A Modern Approach*, Prentice Hall.

Sadikov, E., Parmeswaran, A.G. and Venetis, P. 2009. Blogs as predictors of movie success. *Proceedings of the 4th International Conference on Weblogs and Social Media (ICWSM).*

Saggion, H. and Funk, A. 2010. Interpreting SentiWordNet for opinion classification. *Proceedings of the Seventh International Conference on Language Resources and Evaluation (LREC'10).*

Sakunkoo, P. and Sakunkoo, N. 2009. Analysis of social influence in online book reviews. *Proceedings of Third International AAAI Conference on Weblogs and Social Media (ICWSM-2009)*.

Schrauwen, S. 2010. *Machine Learning Approaches to Sentiment Analysis Using the Dutch Netlog Corpus*. Computational Linguistics and Psycholinguistics Technical Report Series (CLiPS), CTRS-001.

Scott, J. 2000. *Social Network Analysis: A Handbook*, SAGE Publication.

Simmel, G. 1890. Über soziale Differenzierung Soziologische und psychologische Untersuchungen, 5. *Kapitel*: Über die Kreuzung sozialer Kreise, Duncker & Humblot.

Simmel, G. 1908. *Soziologie. Untersuchungen über die Formen der Vergesellschaftung*, Duncker and Humblot.

Tang, D., Qin, B. and Liu, T. 2015. Learning semantic representations of users and products for document level classification. pp. 1014–1023. *Proceedings of the 53rd Annual Meeting of the Association for Computational Linguistics and the 7th International Joint Conference on Natural Language Processing*, vol. 1, long papers.

Travers, J. and Milgram, S. 1969. An experimental study of the small world problem. *Sociometry*, 42(4): 425–443.

Tumasjan, A., Sprenger, T.O., Sandner, P.G. and Welpe, I.M. 2010. Predicting election with twitter: what 140 characters reveal about political sentiment. pp. 178–18. *Proceedings of the 4th International Conference on Weblogs and Social Media (ICWSM)*.

Whitelaw, C., Garg, N. and Argamon, S. 2005. Using appraisal groups for sentiment analysis. pp. 625–631. *Proceedings of the 14th ACM International Conference on Information and Knowledge Management (CIKM'05)*. https://dl.acm.org/doi/10.1145/1099554.1099714.

Wiebe, J.M., Wilson, T., Bruce, R., Bell, M. and Martin, M. 2004. Learning subjective language, *Computational Linguistics*, 30. https://dl.acm.org/doi/10.1162/0891201041850885.

Wikipedia Foundation (2021, February 27-a). Auguste Comte, *Wikipedia*. https://en.wikipedia.org/wiki/Auguste_Comte.

Wikipedia Foundation (2021, February 27-b). Graph Theory, *Wikipedia*. https://en.wikipedia.org/wiki/Graph_Theory.

Wikipedia Foundation (2021, February 27-c). Small-world experiment, *Wikipedia*. https://en.wikipedia.org/wiki/Small-world_experiment.

Wilson, T., Wiebe, J. and Hoffmann, P. 2005. Recognizing contextual polarity in phrase-level sentiment analysis. pp. 347–354. *Proceedings of the Human Language Technology Conference and the Conference on Empirical Methods in Natural Language Processing (HLT/EMNLP))*. https://dl.acm.org/doi/10.3115/1220575.1220619.

Yano, T. and Smith, N.A. 2010. What's worthy of comment? Content and comment volume in political blogs. *Proceedings of the 4th International Conference on Weblogs and Social Media (ICWSM)*.

Yi, J., Nasukawa, T., Bunescu, R. and Niblack, N. 2003. Sentiment analyzer: Extracting sentiments about a given topic using natural language processing techniques. *Proceedings of the Third IEEE International Conference on Data Mining (ICDM'03)*. https://dl.acm.org/doi/10.5555/951949.952133.

Zhai, S. and Z.M. Zhang. 2016. Semisupervised autoencoder for sentiment analysis. pp. 1394–1400. *Proceedings of the Thirtieth AAAI Conference on Artificial Intelligence (AAAI'16)*. https://dl.acm.org/doi/10.5555/3015812.3016017.

Zhang, W. and Skiena, S. 2010. Trading strategies to exploit blog and news sentiment. *Proceedings of the Fourth International Conference on Weblogs and Social Media, ICWSM 2010*.

7

Personal Brand Management using Conceptual Assessment Model

*Giedrius Romeika** and *Ingrida Griesiene*

INTRODUCTION

The brand is a combination of value-adding features and an image embedded in the minds of consumers, in 1997, Peters (1997, pp. 83–90) modernized this theory and adapted it to individuals by introducing terms as 'personal branding' or 'self-branding'. His research and aspects of modernization of the theory were based on the idea that everyone can have their own personal brand and they must promote themselves (Peters 1997, pp. 83–90). Both business and scientific literature often emphasize the importance of exclusivity in developing a personal brand, especially in the context of job search. However, personal branding may be of greatest significance perhaps in those areas where a person's financial situation and quality of life directly depend on the popularity of his or her image. This reason has led to a number of followers of the theory and further research, which revealed the diversity of the concept of personal branding and different angles of its justification. It remains until these days that personal branding is not a single theory simply because it is studied by researchers in different fields, involving even more diverse subjects of research (the representatives of art, culture, politics, sports, business, etc.). Having created a strong, consumer-friendly brand, its creators receive tangible benefits: world-famous personal brand creators attract thousands of followers on social media, politicians get more votes, athletes more advertising orders, abundant support of fans, employees are more valued by employers and vice versa.

The versatility and effectiveness of personal brand requires for a proper analysis of theoretical background, areas of application, management processes and tools which can maximize value creation.

Institute of Social Sciences and Applied Informatics, Kaunas Faculty, Vilnius University, Lithuania.
Emails: ingrida.griesiene@knf.vu.lt
* Corresponding author: giedrius.romeika@knf.vu.lt

In the interactive and virtual age of 21st-century individualism, the benefits and value of an authentic and distinctive personal brand in the competitive struggle have increased even more. According to Rangarajan et al. (2017), the most favorable environment for the development and emergence of a personal brand has evolved on the Internet in line with the rise of social media popularity. One of the main elements of social media is social networks; thus in this environment, the process of PB development and its proper management with selected elements will be examined according to the characteristics of different industries' representatives, key elements and distinctive procedural models.

Aim of the chapter is to develop a model for assessing the activity in social networks by refining the characteristics of developing different types of PB. *Objectives* of the chapter are:

1. To provide a general theoretical analysis of PB.
2. To classify the PB characteristics of the representatives in different fields of activity.
3. To identify the most effective PB development and management instruments for representatives of different fields of activity.
4. To provide a general model for the assessment of personal brand based on an analysis of quantitative and qualitative indicators.

Methods: Analysis and systematization of scientific literature, analysis for categorization, analysis of secondary data. The following main methods used in the study are analysis of scientific literature, the conception of the personal brand was investigated and formulated by the method of synthesis, by analyzing the insights and opinions of different authors by the study question, the concept of the personal brand was analyzed and formulated, categorical and secondary data analysis contributed to refining and revealing peculiarities in the classification of different types of personal brands. Also, other aspects of the study were examined by the method of systematization and generalization of information as well as a theoretical model was introduced.

1. Personal Brand (PB) Concept and Theoretical Overview

For a long time, brands were seen as belonging to products, companies and only later brands began to be associated with individual persons (Aaker, 1996). Personalities have been treated as commodities, as unique images. Table 1 provides a concise analysis of the different authors' concepts, based on the main aspects covering the definition of PB.

A comparison of the concepts of the authors shows a clear difference in the definition of a personal brand, i.e., it is not the essence itself, but the presentation and different characteristics. Some authors define the meaning of this term as a whole self-presentation while others describe more specific features—personal appearance, skills, reputation building and others according to the field and nature they represent and the brand of industrial representatives they research and analyze. However, there are also common features that reflect the views of most authors, such as the image,

Table 1: Main aspects of the concept under the approach of different authors.

Peculiarities/Features	Ryabykh and Zebra (2014)	Petrov (2016)	Patrachina and Vialkova (2015)	Gander (2014)	Holloway (2013)	Khedher (2015)	Petruca (2016)	Arruda and Dixson (2010)	Arai et al. (2014)
Promises and expectations	+							+	
Image in the audience's mind		+	+	+	+			+	
Created value			+		+			+	+
Communication of reputation					+				
Demonstration of skills, beliefs				+	+		+	+	
Receiving benefits						+			
Acquisition of distinctiveness						+	+		
Public person									+
Brand elements									+

associations, perceptions, a set of promises and expectations of a personal brand that are associated with a particular person, creating value through different elements.

Thus, having analyzed and structured the aspects of concepts provided by different authors, it can be argued that *personal branding is a combination of unique features and tools that help to create an image and reputation through communication and marketing and also disclose their whole as the product to the target audience which is related to the implementation of set objectives and direct benefits.*

Personal branding gives an opportunity to sell oneself and allows the person who wants to benefit from it to stand out from competitors (Tijūnaitienė et al., 2010, p. 128), to increase visibility and awareness (Bendisch, 2007, p. 15). This is particularly relevant in high-supply performance markets (such as sports, arts, cultural businesses, etc.) where representatives of individual industries that have developed their own brand, can make their name known, establish authority, increase sales and value of the products they create, communicate and represent.

The analysis of concepts suggests that it is a planned process in which characteristics of a personal brand are strategically designed and their positioning intends to influence the consumer and achieve the intended goals in different professions and industries. Therefore, it can be argued that highlighting one or other characteristics of a personal brand will make it easier to remember for the target audience and facilitate identification and recognition. As a result, representatives of different industries need to properly analyze their target audience and while developing their personal brand, strengthen it with authentic features, characteristics, detailed process models and instruments.

When analyzing the reasons for the emergence of personal brands, the opinions of different authors vary. Tijūnaitienė et al. (2010) state that personal brands are created by representatives of various fields of activity (business, religion, culture, art, sports, etc.); thus, the reasons for their development are different. According to scientific literature, two main groups of reasons for the formation of a personal brand can be distinguished (Fig. 1).

Figure 1 shows that Shepherd (2005) emphasizes that in the past, personal brands developed mainly due to a strong need for self-realization, the desire to make friends, professional success in the perspectives of one's activities, and more focused on material benefits. Material benefits as a reason are also emphasized by Montoya (2003, pp. 16–17), who stresses that a personal brand allows one to distinguish oneself from competitors, to gain recognition, which provides opportunity and enables to increase value as a person and associated activities or products. However,

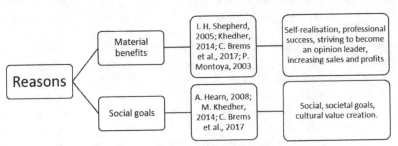

Fig. 1: Reasons for personal brand development.

other authors, for example Khedher (2014), Brems et al. (2017) in their works stress material or personal benefits due to social, societal goals and the desire to become opinion leaders. Although most authors agree that personal brands are developed for material gain, Hearn (2008) stresses that people find this process relevant in order to create a cultural value that unfolds in its own way in each area.

Assistance to the target audience in choosing a particular person can be identified as the main function of a personal brand. As a result, a personal brand has become an effective way of communication between the individual and society by distinguishing their uniqueness and values from competitors. The process of personal branding can be assessed from two main approaches defined in the scientific literature. The first one suggests that personal brand is developed strategically and consistently with a rigorous foresight and knowledge of reasons for PB development while the second states that personal brand is developed without a prior strategy, due to social attitudes and personal self-realization. However, in both cases, a set of expectations for a particular person is formed in the consumer's mind. If these expectations are fulfilled, the value created by a personal brand increases, reputation is established and recognition is earned.

2. Types of PB in Social Networks and Development Tools

Schawbel (2012) defines a personal brand as a process in which personalities and entrepreneurs individualize and stand out from the crowd by presenting competencies and resources in the personal or professional area to which the only one has access. This process is realized through various channels, presenting compact communication and image to achieve the set goal. In this way, a person can lay the foundations of value as a specialist, become reliable in one's field, gain confidence and career achievements.

Personal brand and support were first analyzed as one of the most significant activities of celebrities (Rein et al., 2007), politicians (Shepherd, 2005) but later it became an important object of research in analyzing the activities of entrepreneurs and business leaders Karaduman (2013), as well as athletes (Hodge and Walker, 2015), librarians (Ahmad et al., 2016), or students entering the market and seeking to establish themselves in the labor market (Lee and Cavanaugh, 2016). It is, therefore, necessary to define the possible personal brands found in literature and empirical research according to the represented industries, distinguishing the characteristic features specific to each of them (Table 2). As we can see in Table 2, the direction of personal brand activity can be also determined by different types and the areas they represent as well as the knowledge and distinctive features. It can be observed that almost all the analyzed authors related the classifications of types to a certain industrial category, the implementation of different goals and activity plans. Only Malinowska–Parzydlo (2015) presented a premium brand category that includes the fulfillment of all possible categories of areas at the highest level.

However, no matter what type of personal brand it is, the easiest and fastest way to present yourself to your target audience is through social networks. Nevertheless, it must be emphasized that the assessment of categories and instruments used in the prism of different types of personal brands may have separate instruments for their

Table 2: Classification of PB types.

Author, year	Types by Industry	Peculiarities and Features
Petrov (2016)	Show business.	A personal brand serves to create its own memorable image and arouses the interest of investors (producers).
	The face of the company.	The personal brand is designed to form the image standard, the correctness of the business for all representatives of the professional businesses.
	To distinguish a stand-alone brand.	In this case, a personal brand is a tool of open propaganda and self-promotion.
Ryabykh and Zebra (2014)	First category	Politicians, but mostly officials.
	Second category	Entrepreneurs.
	Third category	People in show business and sports.
	Fourth category	Employees who work in the service sector (lease).
Malinowska-Parzydlo (2015)	Premium personal brand	Reflects these qualities: shines with its unique light, not reflection; facilitates harmony in life; supports communicating the story through recognized values; shows one's 'own self' and capabilities as an expert and professional, a leader who is interested in a high-quality life.

management and support. In general terms, the main social networking instruments contribute to the implementation of the personal branding strategy (Table 3).

Since we live in times when there is a great focus on visual content, selfies are perhaps the most important instrument. Combining them with hashtags and photo caption may become an effective tool in shaping the desired image of a personal brand. Selfies are effective because they perfectly perform this function and create the image you want to convey, even if it is not true (Eagar and Dann, 2016, p. 17). Often selfies are combined with another instrument—content. In the world of social media, creating and sharing the content becomes an integral means of managing one's identity, leisure and social relationships (Livingstone, 2008, p. 394). Combining all the above instruments creates a certain story that dictates its image to the target audience.

Table 3: Table of the main instruments for developing a personal brand on social networks.

Name	Description
Selfies	A self-portrait photograph, taken with a smartphone and most often shared on social networks (Oxford, n.d.b).
Photos	Photographs posted on social networks.
Hashtags	A word or a phrase that is prefaced by the hash symbol and is used to indicate a specific theme or item (Oxford, n.d.a).
Photo caption	A brief description, conveying the desired thought or explaining what is happening in the photo (Merriam-Webster, n.d).
Content	This is quality and useful information that conveys the story in a way that evokes certain emotions or engagement (Cohen, 2013).
Tagging	A function where keywords (names, names of places, etc.) are used with the "@" sign.), allowing you to mark and specify to the audience what is depicted in the photo (Textbroker, n.d.).

PESO model: Paid, Earned, Shared and Owned:

- Paid (P)—content is paid by the user.
- Earned (E)—acquired content described and created on the same topic by other social network writers or bloggers.
- Shared (S)—shared content. This is content shared with other social media users on the same topic, including 'word-of-mouth' marketing.
- Owned (O)—owned or personal type of content. Content published through your own channel, site, Facebook profile. Sometimes with the help of persistent acquaintances, we can occur in other places too.

Table 4: Content types on the internet, PESO model (adapted from Miotk, 2015).

Acquired Media	Engaging Views of Leaders	Shared Media
Advertising Relations with media Relations with bloggers Investment relationships Relations with influencers	Responses to criticism Critics who became loyal Loyal who became lawyers	Social media Facebook, Twitter, Instagram.
Partnership Charity Volunteering Co-branding		
	Administration Shared content Engaging content Copyright assignment in search	
Promoted posts on Facebook Promoted tweets Fan search Lead generation	Incentives Associations Brand ambassadors Sponsored content National advertising	Content Expert texts Articles Personal brand journalism Webinars Podcasts
Paid media		Personal media

Thus, with the help of content management, a personal brand can appear in different places in different ways, allowing modeling of the effects of actions. The classification of these places corresponds to the division of social media into paid, earned, shared and owned. Paid media means various types of advertising, feedback received from its recipients, depending on one's efforts. Shared media means sharing personal messages, hints, or links, controlled by the recipients themselves, communication through personal media.

All the main listed instruments and many other instruments dictate to the audience the personal qualities of the person and form his image in the heads of the people belonging to the target audience, which accordingly affects their interest, admiration and faith in the person creating the personal brand.

According to Vallas and Christin (2018), social networks also educate personal brands for a perfect effect. This can be achieved through benchmarking, evaluation of competitors, as well as quantitative and qualitative analysis of the content most liked by the followers, thus reflecting two-way communication with the target audience. The personal brand that most engages the target audience includes not only a clear positioning message but also its fulfillment, audience monitoring and error correction. To do this, a call to action by a personal brand is very important: 1. activating the audience by encouraging them to discuss relevant issues; 2. the question of opinion; 3. response to comments and inquiries.

In order to maintain the interest of the audience, all three criteria must be met, since only in this way can the call for action receive a positive response, which is manifested in:

- writing comments;
- 'likes'
- 'shares'
- communication by 'word of mouth';
- writing reviews, recommendations;
- use of hashtags;
- sending messages.

Molyneux (2019) observed that men and women, working in the same sphere—journalism, form the image of a personal brand from different fields of vision. Men—professional field, women—personal, social. While the insights of Rangarajan et al. (2017) and Nolan (2015) have shown that managers of the organization develop a personal brand to enhance the image of the organization represented. The fact that the use of human, financial and social resources can be useful in pursuing a professional career has been highlighted by Hodge and Walker (2015). By systemizing the research conducted by the latter authors, it can be argued that different types of personal brands shape their strategy differently.

3. PB Development and Management Process

This part defines the importance of a personal brand and the influence of social networks, based on theoretical insights of various authors, such as Ryabykh and Zebra (2014); Malinowska-Parzydlo (2015); Tijūnaitienė et al. (2010); Rampersad (2009) that help to reveal the main stages of personal brand development and the peculiarities of its further management in social networks. In order to properly disclose the process of brand development, it is necessary to purify the cause and benefit elements, which is why the modeling of this process and the purification of stages and sequential processes are so important. Montoya and Vandehey (2002) distinguished that the essence of developing a personal brand is to influence other people's decisions, purchases and attitudes. Also, the author presented the advantages of developing a personal brand as it can help each person decide to develop their own personal brand.

Kang (2013) also wrote about the benefits of developing a personal brand and a comparative table shows the benefits and advantages identified by the authors in developing a personal brand (Table 5).

Summarizing the benefits of personal branding identified by the authors, it can be noted that a successful personal brand improves a person's image, increases its

Table 5: Reasons, advantages and benefits of developing a personal brand.

Advantages/Benefits	Montoya and Vandehey (2002)	Kang (2013)
gives priority status in mind	+	
gives authority and credibility to decisions made	+	+
gives leadership position	+	+
strengthens prestige	+	
Attraction	+	+
increases perceived value	+	
grants recognition	+	+
associates with successful trends	+	+
increases earnings potential	+	+
advocates ecosystem		+

influence in other people's minds and its relationship with other market participants or the goods or services they sell, adds value and increases consumer perceived value, and collectively, these benefits also provide financial benefits to a person with a strong personal brand. When comparing the advantages of a personal brand presented by the examined authors, a similar approach is observed in terms of reputation building, leadership towards others which leads to success in career and provides greater opportunities that usually bring financial benefits. Thus it can be said that people who build successful personal branding can earn more and achieve better results. Therefore, it can be argued that a successfully developed personal brand can bring significant benefits to a person in both his professional and personal life; therefore, in order to obtain the maximum benefits from personal branding, a systematic and consistent perception of the personal branding and management process is required.

The views of different authors on the development of a personal brand and strategy execution are similar, differing only in the names of the stages and their number (Table 6). Thus, it can be argued that each of them is not sufficiently detailed and authentic to develop a personal brand strategy in social networks with particular emphasis on their adaptability to different types of personal brands.

First of all, Tijūnaitienė et al. (2010) propose a competitor analysis before developing and implementing the PB strategy, although this step lays the foundations for the development of a person's identity as a brand. Analysis of competitors and identity creation are just a few examples of fundamental steps in the process of a personal branding strategy, but they are not mentioned (or not discussed enough) by all authors of the analyzed models. Therefore, no single process is sufficiently unique to allow the development and clear identification of a process that reflects the different types of authenticity.

When examining the ideas of Shepherd (2005) and Lair et al. (2005) the distinctiveness of a personal brand as a process was noticeable in emphasizing authenticity, which further stresses the different types of personal brand development stages discussed in this article (Fig. 2).

Table 6: Development of PB process.

Author	Stages
Ryabykh and Zebra (2014)	1. To determine the goal of developing a personal brand, distinguish tangible parameters (volume of publications, degree of availability), target audience, and formulate broadcast messages; 2. Presentation of a personal brand name or pseudonym, presentation of external appearance, non-verbal communication, and content; 3. Promotion of personal brand through different channels.
Frischmann (2014)	1. Definition of skills reflecting human functional value, professional abilities and competence skill set); 2. Creating the accessibility in search engines (getting found); 3. Identity formation; 4. Creating a positive first impression 5. Creation of aura, reflecting a person's emotional value and ability to communicate; 6. Brand experience.
Wincci and Mohamad (2015)	1. Personal brand development—exchange and distribution of social network content, communication between users; 2. Social media marketing—having and accessing accounts on different social networks, showing one's personality, belonging to certain social media networking communities; 3. Reputation management—relations and communication with other users, the establishment of clear values and positions on certain social issues.

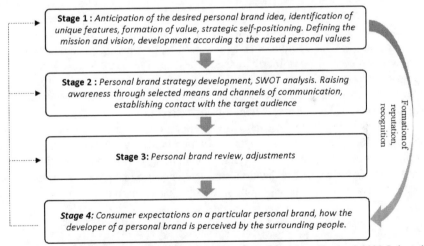

Stage 1 : *Anticipation of the desired personal brand idea, identification of unique features, formation of value, strategic self-positioning. Defining the mission and vision, development according to the raised personal values*

Stage 2 : *Personal brand strategy development, SWOT analysis. Raising awareness through selected means and channels of communication, establishing contact with the target audience*

Stage 3: *Personal brand review, adjustments*

Stage 4: *Consumer expectations on a particular personal brand, how the developer of a personal brand is perceived by the surrounding people.*

Formation of reputation, recognition

Fig. 2: The process of developing an authentic personal brand (adapted from Shepherd, 2005; Lair et al., 2005; Rangarajan et al., 2017).

The initial stage of a personal brand formation begins with self-knowledge, identification of the most prominent qualities and the identification of key roles. According to Lair et al. (2005), a personal brand developer must strategically anticipate in advance what personal brand he or she wants to develop. Rangarajan et al. (2017) argue that values, competencies and other strengths of a personal brand form a clear vision and mission.

In the second stage of developing a personal brand, a personal brand performs a personal SWOT analysis, which, through selected means and channels of communication, helps to increase a person's awareness and aims to reach the target audience. However, Peters (1997) emphasizes that the communication channels and the message sent to the target audience cannot be different from the actions of the personal brand holder, as this may affect the trust of the target audience. Thus, the nature of the public opinion (reputation) about a personal brand will depend on the nature of the selected communication.

In the third stage, personal brands have to constantly review their activities and adjust them to achieve the highest satisfaction of the target audience. Rangarajan et al. (2017) argue that a personal brand has to constantly monitor what image is desired and sought and how it is currently seen and perceived by users. This stage is considered to be a *reformulation of the personal brand* in order to achieve the objective and mission set out in the first stage.

The final stage of developing a personal brand *is to evaluate how it is seen and appreciated by the surrounding people.* This is an assessment of compliance with consumer expectations (Lair et al., 2005; Peters, 1997). Luca et al. (2015) emphasize that a personal brand establishes emotional connections with consumers, so the more their beliefs and values coincide, the greater links are established.

To summarize it can be stated that consistent implementation and execution of these activities in line with the stated objectives are required at all stages discussed, as well as a detailed review of the activities, which helps to correct existing errors on a feedback basis. According to Kapferer (2007), developing a personal brand is a long-term process based primarily on self-analysis. However, the uniqueness in this approach can be considered as specific reference groups (Fig. 3), the identification of which helps to achieve the success of a personal brand, it is important that the goals, aspirations and values of the reference group were similar.

Thus, it is important for each individual brand to have a clear identity, image and in the long run to form a reputation, which is achieved through the consistent implementation of the developed PB strategy, taking into account the discovery of similarities between self-realization and reference groups. According to Petruca (2016), successful implementation of these aspects in the PB strategy can be

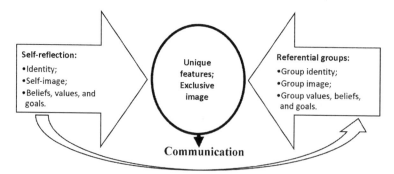

Fig. 3: Model of developing a personal brand (adapted from Kapferer, 2007).

achieved through the following actions in social networks: visibility; style; activity; promptness; engagement.

The fact that consistency and activity are key factors in the strategy of building a personal brand in social networks is also confirmed by Vilander (2017, p. 29). However, the author also distinguishes one more point—authenticity. To summarize the approaches of authors, it can be argued that a successful personal branding strategy on social networks should include both traditional personal brand development actions and actions related to social network specifics.

4. Methodology of PB Assessment

One of the most important aspects of developing a personal brand on social networks is determining the effectiveness. Many authors have identified and developed methodologies and described criteria that are useful and conveniently measured in order to assess the awareness of a personal brand. The most common reference in the academic literature is the identification of a personal brand by a quantitative assessment method—the number of posts, the number of followers and the size of the audience reached on social networks (Djafarova and Rushworth, 2017; Vilares et al., 2014). In this model, three impact factors are commonly used to analyze social network users: number of followers; shared posts; mentions of username. Analysis of specific qualitative data can also be used to identify social network influencers (Vilares et al., 2014).

McCann and Barlow (2015) identified the following several measurable indicators reflecting the awareness of a personal brand: number of followers, 'like' button clicks by users, number of visitors, in the case of a personal brand, mentions of a person in the communication of other users, number of positive and negative comments.

Meanwhile, to determine the efficiency on social networks, Murdough (2009) offers to monitor:

- social media *accessibility*
- *discussions*
- *results*

Booth and Matic (2011) presented an algorithm that helps to identify a personal brand on a virtual social network. The main idea of the authors is that the index (Table 5) helps to measure the relationships with direct users and the impact on them. Thus, to determine the numeric influence rating of the post, variables are measured both qualitatively and quantitatively. This index can be used by each PB to identify key 'assessment points'. The authors provided and described the following variables:

- *Viewers per month*. The number of visits per month is calculated.
- *Linkages*. The popularity of post links inbound and outbound are shown.
- *Post frequency*. The volume of posts per given time is calculated.
- *Media citation score*. The volume of media citations of the post is calculated.
- *Industry score*. The number of industry guru points based on industry events, such as keynotes, bylines, and panel participation is calculated.

- *Social aggregator rate.* Level of participation in social networks, for example, *Twitter*, *LinkedIn*, etc.
- *Engagement index.* Reader responses and comments.
- *Relevant topic-related posts.* Volume and questions on relevant topic-related posts.
- *Qualitative topic-related posts.* Qualitative review of topic-related posts.
- *Index score.* Identification and rank in the social network, based on the above variables.

Sociologists give a rating scale from 1 to 5, from poor to excellent. According to Booth and Matic (2011), specialists seeking to uncover a particular variable can delete or add variables in the developed algorithm according to their needs.

The measurements for the calculation of this index are presented in Tables 7, 8, and 9.

Co-founder of the social network *Instagram* Kevin Systrom states that *Instagram* is constantly changing the algorithm to increase the relevance of content (Isaac, 2016). This encourages brands and influencers to measure *Instagram* engagement rates on a weekly basis to make sure their posts remain relevant to their audience. Authors Ge and Grezel (2017) expressed engagement rate by the formula given below. The total number of 'likes' is added to the total number of comments and shares. The resulting figure is divided by the total followers of the profile. All figures in the engagement rate formula are measured over the last 20 days. The result is then multiplied by 100 in order to express the engagement as a percentage. The resulting percentage of engagement is usually between 0 and 10.

$$Engagement\ Rate(\%) = \left(\frac{LIKES + COMMENTS + SHARES}{TOTAL\ FOLLOWERS} \right) * 100$$

With a calculated percentage of engagement, it is necessary to analyze the obtained numbers. To compare the results, social networking specialists provide standard guidelines of social network *Instagram*:

- Less than 1 per cent—low engagement rate;
- Between 1 per cent and 3.5 per cent—average/good engagement rate;
- Between 3.5 per cent and 6 per cent—high engagement rate;
- Above 6 per cent—very high engagement rate.

Thus, by summarizing the quantitative assessment indicators of the personal brand in the social network (Table 10), it can be stated that many authors have distinguished similar indicators. The quantitative indicators most often mentioned by the authors are the number of followers, the size of the audience reached or the number of visitors, the number of posts and the number of mentions of the name or the post. Fewer authors emphasized the fact that the number of posts and comments was also important; however, the majority of them noticed it. The least popular indicator among the authors was the number of 'likes'.

Table 7: The measurements for the calculation of PB index (adapted from Booth and Matic, 2011, p. 187).

PB	Viewers per month	Linkages	Post frequency	Media citation score	Industry score	Social aggregator rate	Engagement index	Relative topic related posts	Qualitative topic related posts	Index score
Method	*AI technology leader*	*IT specialist*	*Manual identification*	*Google alerts*	*Manual identification*	*Manual identification*	*Online post distribution in blogs/no. of queries*	*Google trends/ online post distribution trends*	*Manual identification/ Google alerts*	*Average weighted score*
Rating system	< 500 = 1	< 100 = 1	Once a month = 1	< 2=1	1 = 1	1 point for use of tool	< 3 = 1	< 3 = 1	Extremely negative = 1	
	501–1,000 = 2	101–500 = 2	2–5 per month = 2	3–5 = 2	2–4 = 2	Microblogs and social networks	4–10 = 2	4–8 = 2	Negative = 2	
	1,001–5,000 = 3	501–1,000 = 3	6–10 per month = 3	6–10 = 3	4-6 = 3	Easy access on online list	11–15 = 3	9–12 = 3	Neutral = 3	
	5,001–15,000 = 4	1,0001–3,000 = 4	10–15 per month = 4	11–15 = 4	7–9 = 4	Access to videos/photos	16–20 = 4	13–16 = 4	Positive = 4	
	> 15,0001 = 5	> 3,000 = 5	> 15 per month = 5	> 15 = 5	> 10 = 5	Audio/video posts	> 20 = 5	> 16 = 5	Very positive = 5	

Table 8: PB index ratings (adapted from Booth and Matic, 2011, p. 187).

Ratings	
Excellent	5
Very good	4
Good	3
Fair	2
Poor	1

Table 9: PB index weights applied (adapted from Booth and Matic, 2011, p. 187).

Weights applied	
VPM	10%
Linkages	15%
Post frequency rate	5%
Media citation rate	15%
Industry score	10%
Social aggregator rate	10%
Relevant topic post rate	5%
Conversation index	20%
Quantitative	10%
Total	10%

Table 10: Comparison of quantitative assessment indicators.

Indicators	McCann and Barlow, 2015	Djafarova and Rushworth, 2017	Vilares et al., 2014	Booth and Matic, 2011	Ge and Grezel, 2017	Total
number of posts		+	+	+		3
number of followers	+	+	+		+	4
size of the audience reached on social networks	+	+	+	+		4
number of shared posts		+	+	+	+	4
number of username mentions	+	+	+	+		4
'like' button clicks by users	+				+	2
Comments	+			+	+	3

Thus, in general, when developing a personal brand model, it is necessary to take into account the most popular and most frequently discussed quantitative indicators by all authors. In terms of quantification, this analysis allows the model to refine the need for the most significant and most measurable indicators.

Meanwhile, as one of the strategic directions in developing a personal brand, Philbrick and Cleveland (2015) present an approach that reflects the treatment of one's identity as capital, in which constant investment is necessary because sooner or later each personal brand expects return expressed through human, social and economic capital components. *Human capital* reflects an approach linked to continuous learning. Continuous training and other personal training courses are necessary to strengthen professional competencies. *Social capital* is a wide network of relationships created not only with family members, friends and colleagues but also with everyone who can spread information, share opinions about a personal brand and its activities. A personal brand represents the investments of others in the brand. Awareness and recognition are some of the measures of a personal brand's success. *Economic capital* shows that people who create an authentic personal brand can also expect higher wages than people who do the same job but do not develop a personal brand (Arruda and Dixson, 2010).

To understand, develop, represent and manage a personal brand, Schawbel (2010) provides structured success factors that are presented in Fig. 4.

Although social networks do not directly generate revenue, according to Geurin-Eagleman and Burch (2016), they help to achieve this goal through the established follower flow movement allowing to reach other positive outcomes, such as increased interest and consumption, attraction of new sponsors and improvement in the personal brand awareness. These intermediate factors help to establish long-term relationships, find partners and sponsors, receive additional orders and gain a reputation of a professional in your field, which directly increase revenue and generate material benefits for the personal brand.

When developing a personal brand in social networks, a person's identity should first be created to be shown to the users of social networks. In identifying itself, a personal brand must examine in detail the industry in which it competes and identify the characteristics relevant to its activities because only then will it be able to anticipate its target audience. Personal brand support is formed by investing in the brand, including the elements of human, social and economic capital.

Continuous support of a personal brand would allow moving to the next stage of the personal brand development process through the follower flow regulation, which includes three main dimensions related to the expansion of the communication network, the result of which is directed to the image, the basis of which becomes the dimension of consumer engagement. In the model, consumer engagement is possible in two ways: positive engagement and rejection, which indicate some inefficiency in the process. Consumer engagement brings benefits to a personal brand: recognition, reputation development and material benefits. Due to certain signals of inefficiency

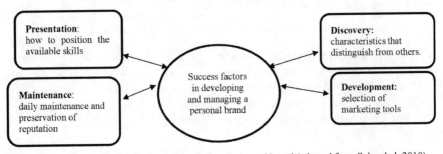

Fig. 4: Success factors in developing and managing a personal brand (adapted from Schawbel, 2010).

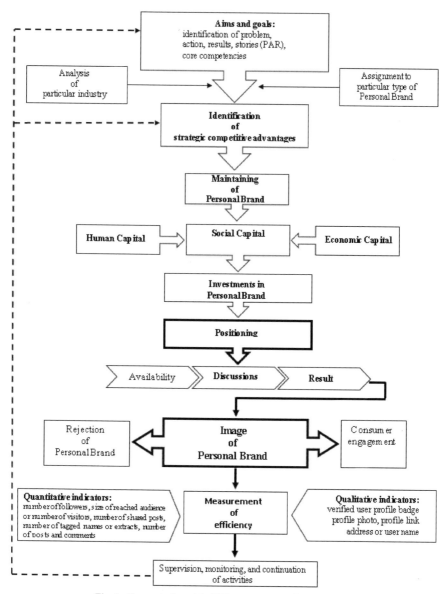

Fig. 5: Conceptual model of PB assessment and measurement.

or unsecured consumer involvement, the impact of the measures used on a personal brand, image and popularity should be monitored, followed by measuring the effectiveness of social network communication by using quantitative and qualitative performance indicators. Monitoring various statistics of social networks and assessing communication efficiency allow performing of review and monitoring, which are linked to feedback, ensuring business continuity.

After reassessing strengths, weaknesses, opportunities and threats, the communication with the target audience is continued in anticipation of its response. A personal brand presents its value to the target audience in such a way that consumers perceive it as unique and customized specifically to them. After the evaluation of the performance and correction of the mistakes, the personal brand returns to the communication on social networks through performance support tools, eliminating inefficiency indicators. Thus, a personal brand can be considered as a basis that allows creation of added value: formation of opinion, requests from advertisers and others.

5. Conclusion

1. The main reasons for the formation of personal brand phenomena are universal and material benefits. Therefore, it is important to emphasize that the main values of a person's brand are competencies, qualifications, and unique character traits. The biggest personal brands' mark is stored and pursued capital—consumer confidence, satisfaction and involvement. The scientific context of personal brand marking the development process is assessed from two main perspectives. The first personal brand mark is developed strategically and consistently and the second personal brand mark is created without preconditions strategy. However, in both cases, the consumer consciousness forms expectations and if these expectations are fulfilled, the value created by a person's brand grows, a reputation is formed and recognition is earned.

2. The analysis of the personal brand as a theoretical concept is multifaceted because it includes personal brands developed by different industries and fields of activity. Therefore, the deletion of individual categories and the analysis of commonly used instruments in personal brand management allow to categorize possible personal brands and the features applied to them, as well as different techniques. Personal branding and promotion foremost were analyzed as one of the most important aspects of promotion/advertising market access for celebrities, politicians, athletes, librarians, artists, entrepreneurs, students and professionals in their respective fields. Analysis of empirical researches conducted by different authors allowed to categorize separate personal brand categories based on the development and management processes, the usage of instruments, purification and specificity features, which generally allow to weigh, measure and adjust the components of own individual brand's unique features.

3. Main personal brands characters' creation, formation and expression tools and environment are social networks. Social networks are considered as one of most interactive virtual communication channels, where a big variety of communication forms could be created and long-term relationships maintained despite the geographical distance. Individual product brand creation is a long-term process generally covering four phases, primarily based upon self-assessment. Special additional attention should be paid to emphasis by individual authors/referencing groups whose identification helps to achieve the personal brand activities' aims and goals successfully. Therefore, in personal brand creation, it

is important to cover all stages of the development process and ensure that the goals, objectives and values of the reference group should be taken into account and reconciled. By following this way, personal brand awareness and image enhancement should be carried out more efficiently.

4. Social networks proved as very effective marketing tools whose effectiveness can be assessed by a variety of figures and data. Mostly used and analyzed in scientific literature is quantitative assessment of a person's brand, but there are opinions revealing the need for analysis of specific qualitative data too. Both these groups of evaluation methods have many criteria which, when used in combined form, measure the effectiveness of a personal brand as a key tool in the successful maintenance and development of a brand. Due to certain unwanted signals or insufficient user involvement, it is necessary to monitor the influence/efficiency of the particular used tools, the needs of reference groups' reconciliation with particular positioning and then start measuring the effectiveness of social network communication using quantitative and qualitative efficiency indicators. An overall (mixed quantitative and qualitative) performance appraisal is the basis for assessing the effectiveness of personal brands in different industries. It can be applied to all types and features of personal brands.

6. Future Research

In the future, as a perspective for potential research, we would like to propose application of the general model of personal brand evaluation which is presented in the research. Aspects of its application could vary and show significant results in the evaluation of personal brands in different areas, the evaluation and process of which may be exceptionally specific and significant in revealing the specificity of personal brands and efficiency factors in different industries. It is planned to investigate the major industries including fitness, culture, art, politics and business personal branding and develop particular areas, which are specifically adaptable models of efficiency in maintaining a personal brand on social networks.

References

Aaker, D.A. 1996. *Building Strong Brands*. New York, The Free Press.
Ahmad, R., Hashim, L. and Harun, N. 2016. Criteria for effective authentic personal branding for academic librarians in Universiti Sains Malaysia libraries. *Procedia-Social and Behavioral Sciences*, 224: 452–458.
Arai, A., Ko, Y.J. and Ross, S. 2014. Branding athletes: Exploration and conceptualization of athlete brand image. *Sport Management Review*, 17(2): 97–106.
Arruda, W. and Dixson, K. 2010. *Career Distinction: Stand Out by Building Your Brand*. New Jersey, John Willey and Sons.
Bendisch, F., Larsen, G. and Trueman, M. 2007. Branding people: towards a conceptual framework. *Working Paper Series*, 7(22): 15.
Booth, N. and Matic, A.J. 2011. Mapping and leveraging influencers in social media to shape corporate brand perceptions. *Corporate Communication: An International Journal*, 16(3): 184–191.
Brems, C., Temmerman, M., Graham, T. and Broersma, M. 2017. Personal branding on twitter: How employed and freelance journalists stage themselves on social media. *Digital Journalism*, 5(4): 443–459.

Cohen, H. 2013. *Definition of Content*; retrieved from: https://www.toprankblog.com/2013/03/what-is-content/.

Djafarova, E. and Rushworth, C. 2017. Exploring the credibility of online celebrities' instagram profiles in influencing the purchase decisions of young female users. *Computers in Human Behavior*, 68: 1–7.

Eagar, T. and Dann, S. 2016. Classifying the narrated #selfie: Genre typing human-branding activity. *European Journal of Marketing*, 9: 17.

Frischmann, R.M. 2014. *Online Personal Brand: Skill Set, Aura and Identity.* CreateSpace Independent Publishing Platform.

Gander, M. 2014. Managing your personal brand: Perspectives. *Policy and Practice in Higher Education*, 18(3): 100.

Ge, J. and Grezel, U. 2017. The role of humor in driving customer engagement. *Information and Communication Technologies in Tourism*, 2017: 461–474.

Geurin-Eagleman, A.N. and Burch, L.M. 2016. Communicating via photographs: A gendered analysis of Olympic athletes' visual self-presentation on Instagram. *Sport Management Review*, 19(2): 133–145.

Hearn, A. 2008. Meat, mask, burden: Probing the contours of the branded 'self'. *Journal of Consumer Culture*, 8(2): 197–217.

Hodge, C. and Walker, M. 2015. Personal branding: A perspective from the professional athlete-level-of-analysis. *International Journal of Sport Management and Marketing*, 16(1-2): 112–131.

Holloway, J. 2013. *Managing Your Personal Brand*. Webinar for Open University MBA alumni. Skipton, UK.

Isaac, M. 2016, March 15. Instagram may Change Your Feed, Personalizing it with an Algorithm. *The New York Times*; retrieved from: https://www.nytimes.com/2016/03/16/technology/instagram-feed.html.

Kang, K. 2013. *Branding Pays*, Branding Pays Media.

Kapferer, J.-N. 2007. *Бренд навсегда: создание, развитие, поддержка ценности бренда.* Вершина [Brand forever: creation, development, support of brand value, in Russian].

Karaduman, I. 2013. The effect of social media on personal branding efforts of top level executives. *Procedia – Social and Behavioral Sciences*, 99: 465–473.

Khedher, M. 2014. Personal branding phenomenon. *International Journal of Information, Business and Management*, 6(2): 29–40.

Khedher, M. 2015. Brand for everyone: Guidelines for personal brand managing. *Journal of Global Business Issues*, 1: 19–27.

Lair, D.J., Sullivan, K. and Cheney, G. 2005. Marketization and recasting of the professional self. *Management Communication Quarterly*, 18(3): 307–343.

Lee, J.W. and Cavanaugh, T. 2016. Building your brand: The integration of infographic resume as student self-analysis tools and self-branding resources. *Journal of Hospitality. Leisure, Sport and Tourism Education*, 18: 61–68.

Livingstone, S. 2008. Taking risky opportunities in youthful content creation: Teenagers' use of social networking sites for intimacy, privacy and self-expression. *New Media and Society*, 10(3): 394.

Luca, F.A., Ioan, C.A. and Sasu, C. 2015. The importance of the professional personal brand. *The Doctors' Personal Brand. Procedia Economics and Finance*, 20: 350–357.

Malinowska-Parzydlo, J. 2015. *Jestes markq. Jak odniesc sukces i pozostac sobq.*

McCann, M. and Barlow, A. 2015. Use and measurement of social media for SMEs. *Journal of Small Business and Enterprise Development*, 22(2): 273–287.

Merriam-Webster. (n.d.). Image. In Merriam-Webster.com dictionary. Retrieved August 28, 2018, from https://www.merriam-webster.com/dictionary/image.

Miotk, A. 2015, September 7. *PESO – Paid, Earned, Shared, Owned Media*. Annamiotk.pl.; retrieved from: http://annamiotk.pl/peso-paid-earned-shared-owned-media/.

Molyneux, L. 2019. A personalized self-image: gender and branding practices among journalists. *Social Media and Society*, 5(3): 2056305119872950.

Montoya, P. and Vandehey, T. 2002. *The Personal Branding Phenomenon: Realize Greater Influence, Explosive Income Growth and Rapid Career Advancement by Applying the Branding Techniques of Michael, Martha & Oprah*, Peter Montoya.

Montoya, P. 2003. *The Brand Called You: The Ultimate Brand Building and Business Development Handbook to Transform Anyone into an Indispensable Personal Brand*, New York: Personal Branding Press.

Murdough, C. 2009. Social media measurement: It's not impossible. *Journal of Interactive Advertising*, 10(1): 4–99.

Nolan, L. 2015. The impact of executive personal branding on non-profit perception and communications. *Public Relations Review*, 41(2): 288–292.

Oxford. (n.d.a). Hashtag. *In: English Oxford Living Dictionary*; retrieved on 4 January, 2021 from: https://en.oxforddictionaries.com/definition/hashtag.

Oxford. (n.d.b). Selfie. *In: English Oxford Living Dictionary*; retrieved on 4 January, 2021, from: https://en.oxforddictionaries.com/definition/selfie.

Patrachina, T.-N. and Vialkova, K.S. 2015. *Samprata, asmens prekės ženklas jo taikymo srityčių teoriniai aspektai. Jaunasis mokslininkas*, S., 294–297.

Peters, T. 1997. The brand called you. *Fast Company Magazine*; retrieved from: https://www.fastcompany.com/28905/brand-called-you.

Petrov, L. 2016. Что Нам Стоит Brand Построить; retrieved from http://www.leonidpetrov.ru/blog/articles?post=personalnyj-brending-intervju-dlja-biznes-zhurnala, [How we should Build Brand, in Russian].

Petruca, I. 2016. Personal branding through social media. *International Journal of Communication Research*, 6(4): 391.

Philbrick, J.L. and Cleveland, A.D. 2015. Personal branding: building your pathway to professional success. *Medical Reference Services Quarterly*, 34(2): 181–189.

Rampersad, H.K. 2009. *Authentic Personal Branding*. Information Age Publishing.

Rangarajan, D., Gelb, B.D. and Vandaveer, A. 2017. Strategic personal branding—and how it pays off, *Business Horizons*, 60(5): 657–666.

Rein, I.J., Kotler, P. and Shields, B. 2006. *The Elusive Fan: Reinventing Sports in a Crowded Marketplace*. New York, NY: McGraw-Hill.

Ryabykh, A. and Zebra, N. 2014. *Персональный бренд. Создание и продвижение*. Moscow: Mann, Ivanov and Ferber [Personal brand. Creation and promotion, *in Russian*].

Schawbel, D. 2012. Personal branding 2.0. Cztery kroki do sbudowania osobistej marki. Helion S.A., [Personal Branding 2.0. Four steps to building a personal brand, *in Polish*].

Shepherd, I.D.H. 2005. From cattle and coke to charlie: Meeting the challenge of self marketing and personal branding. *Journal of Marketing Management*, 21(5-6): 589–606.

Textbroker. (n.d.). *Tagging Glossary*; retrieved 9 January, 2021, from: https://www.textbroker.com/tagging.

Tijūnaitienė, R., Vaicekauskaitė, A., Bersėnaitė, J. and Petukienė, E. 2010. *Asmens prekės ženklo formavimo ypatumai muzikos rinkoje (Lietuvos muzikos atlikėjų pavyzdžiu), Ekonomika ir vadyba: aktualijos ir perspektyvos*. 2.

Vallas, S.P. and Christin, A. 2018. Work and identity in an era of precarious employment: How workers respond to 'personal branding' discourse. *Work and Occupations*, 45(1): 3–37.

Vilander, J. 2017. *Personal Branding in Social Media and Social Media-based Entrepreneurship*. Lahti University of Applied Sciences.

Vilares, D., Hermo, M., Alonso, M.A., Gómez-Rodríguez, C. and Vilares, J. 2014. Creating the state-of-the-art in author influence ranking and reputation classification on Twitter, pp. 1468–1478. *In: Cappellato, L., Ferro, N., Halvey, M. and Kraaij, W. (Eds.). Clef Rep Lab.*

Wincci, S. and Mohamad, W. 2015. Social media strategies for personal branding—A case study of malaysian celebrities on facebook. *American Journal of Economics*, 5(2): 240.

8

Social Media Analytics in Digital Marketing

Arti Yadav[1,]* and *Badar Alam Iqbal*[2]

INTRODUCTION

Over the past years, the world of business has been changing rapidly with the introduction of the digital platform and so is the concept of marketing in terms of digital marketing. The last three decades affected marketing with the mass adoption of Internet all over the world (Monnappa, 2020). The change has been witnessed in various steps, like the introduction of the telephone followed by the television and personal computers, which also led to the generation of various kinds of information for its users. Such type of information is also called born digital and 'big data', as it replaced the physical counterparts (films, optical, and paper) of the information and can be stored in large quantities (Digital Marketing Institute, 2016). Data plays a significant role in making understand what the target audience thinks by building the demographic profile of the customers through digital marketing analytics. Data analytics is the support system behind predictive analytics as it provides strength to the business in the form of making data-driven decisions, including the marketing decisions of what, when and where (Porteous, 2018). Moreover, the practice of analytics to utilize data by every type of organization (small, medium and large) has been facilitated by digital marketing through the exploitation of various opportunities in the form of websites, coupon codes and campaigns through email (Single Grain Team, 2017). There has been an expansion in the demand for vigorous digital marketing strategies with rapid growth of the digital platform and constant evolution has been observed in this dome, leading to abundant marketing strategies related to the digital ecosystem (Sidewalks Labs, 2019). So, to be in line with the continuous

[1] Indian Council of Social Science Research, Department of Commerce, Aligarh Muslim University, Aligarh, India.
[2] School of Transdisciplinary Research and Graduate Studies (STRGS), University of South Africa, Pretoria, South Africa.
Email: badar.iqbal@fulbrightmail.org
* Corresponding author: artiyadavdse@gmail.com

growth system of digital platforms, analytics of social media data is highly significant with its capacity to capture information based on various aspects (Nabler, 2020).

Social media is also one of the digital marketing tools that allow businesses to focus on their consumers based on their demographic profile. In addition to that, the concept of real-time analytics has also increased the desire to comprehend the customers for which the platform of social media is highly apt. To understand the perspective of the customers with regard to their desire, needs, wants and experience about a product, service, or even the organization, social media is the key (Alexander, 2019). Social media has emerged as a vital component of digital information, which has a big role to play in the digital marketing strategies of organizations. It provides opportunities for a better connection between the company and the customers. Social media analytics has become a significant tool for the marketing strategy of organizations, which can be monitored by checking the activities on every social media platform to maximize profit along with the welfare of the customers, competitors and society (Rondot, 2020). The need for social media analytics has promoted identification of the most effective strategies for analyzing the crowded and competitive environment of marketing (Batrinca and Treleaven, 2015). Social media analytics also helps in increasing business value through incorporating creativity and innovation, resulting from a deep investigation. Finance and retail-related organizations were the early adopters of analytics on social media data. The main motive in these organizations was to measure news data and market sentiments in finance, while for retail it is about structural analysis of the network, awareness of the brand, marketing strategies development, improvement of the product or service and proliferation of the news (Batrinca and Treleaven, 2015).

The core idea of the present study is therefore to contribute to the literature by synthesizing the role of social media analytics in digital marketing. This is particularly significant in the present world scenario where digital platforms are becoming more and more advanced and complementarities have been found between the growth of social media analytics and the sustainability of organizations development.

1. Literature Review

The world is witnessing a generation of masses of data every second through social media, which has become a fountain of consumer's knowledge in today's time. The collection of data and its analysis are part of the social media analytics process. Platforms like Instagram, TikTok, Twitter, and Facebook provide valuable insight into the data and the reach of these platforms has become easy due to extensive use of smartphones and the Internet (FlexMR, 2020). In the marketing environment, the potential of data through social media is increasing very fast as the generation and collection of data is in real-time settings. This has provided the organizations insight into what consumers are talking about, communicating or following, and buying. In addition to that, it also helps in analyzing the effectiveness of the marketing plans and policies (Barutcu, 2017; Iqbal and Yadav, 2021). Social media analytics provides data through various ways, for instance, Facebook provides information about the number of people to which a post reached along with their clicks and reactions; in the case of Twitter the number of tweets, mentions, profile visits, followers and tweet impressions are the source (Force, 2016). On the other hand, information about company pages, demographics of the followers is provided by LinkedIn. Some of the social media analytical tools are general that can be applied to various sites, while some are specific to a particular social media. Additionally, to get good results of the campaigns on social media tracking is indispensable (Appel et al., 2020). Social media analytics also played a significant role in the formation of business strategies by providing a better perspective of the marketing campaigns (Vasishta and Sreenivasa, 2016). There is a mass of accessible data on social media which helps in analyzing the associated issues and trends; however, the usefulness of the method employed for individual choices is the main task. Along with it, the organizations should make their social media strategy based on the engagement of various stakeholders so that the return on investment is highly acceptable (Sponder, 2012). At the beginning of the analytical process to ask the right questions plays a significant role as businesses are becoming more data-rich as the scale of data is increasing day by day, making it easy to lose focus; for example, without increasing the marketing budget how to increase the sales, for this, the amount to be invested and the selection of proper channel are the main questions. This will provide clarity in terms of developing a model to optimize spending across various channels (Gordon et al., 2012). Moreover, various studies have shown that investment in social media marketing has given fruitful gains to organizations, for instance, due to social media marketing, an increase of about two-thirds in search engine rankings and more exposure to around 88 per cent of the marketers has been witnessed. It signifies that compared to messages sponsored by companies, social media is more trusted by consumers. It also leads to the building of customer loyalty along with strong relationship in terms of shared product, values, vision and feedback (Green et al., 2018).

Fisher and Miller (2011) found that not only for business organizations, but social media analytics also has a significant role to play in the public or government sector as well. It will help them to identify the demographic information and the issues which are meaningful to them. It is further suggested that as the government institutions will enhance their use of social media data and analytics, it will help them in the incorporation of online dialogue with the public. It was also found that compared to the private sector, the government sector usually lags behind in the use of social media tools and analytics. Bekmamedova and Shanks (2014) suggested that organizations can find new methods for competitive gain and value creation with the help of social media analytics as it provides organizations with informed and insightful decision-making. Their study is case-based with a financial institution named Banko. The study showed that Banko has a competitive advantage in terms of its marketing campaign strategy. It uses various channels of social media to incorporate creativity and innovativeness in its marketing strategy. Moreover, social media analytics provides it with a significant approach to look into brand awareness, sentiments of the customers and their engagement with the organization. Dhawan and Zanini (2014) found that as the use of the Internet has gained popularity in terms of social media, emails, Web content, etc., the data generated from these sources also becomes useful. The data is mostly big from these sources and mostly in the form of non-text or text basis. Research based on 'big data' is used by various stakeholders, like the top management or the middle management as per their requirements. In this regard, the emergence of social media analytics helps organizations, based on their objectives (such as expansion of business, minimization of costs or risks, publicity, advertising or promotion of the product or service, long-term customer relationship and so on) on focusing on their market intelligence strategies from the data collected through customers' feedback, Web browsing, online shopping behavior, etc., though organizations must know that the data collected must be necessary or meaningful, as not all the data serve the main purpose behind their objectives.

Alzahrani (2016) highlighted three issues—dynamism, velocity and volume with respect to a huge amount of information associated with the social media platforms. Due to such types of complexities, the breakdown of the data for informal organizations is highly challenging. The author suggests the dissection of a large amount of information through the process of data mining, and that through data analytics, an insight into the success of the adopted method can be easily visible through the action plan and improvised marketing strategies of the organization. Wedel and Kannan (2016) have reviewed, in connection with the implementation of analytics of rich marketing data in organizations, the history, recent developments, opportunities and barriers, privacy, security and personalization of it. The study found that a broad skill-set is needed for the emerging big data environment and advanced analytical tools. Further, there is no analytical solution that fits all; therefore, marketing analytics should be need-based or customized as per the requirement for the development of the product, branding, advertisement, or promotion. Mindtree (2017) examined the ability of social media analytics in terms of its ability to act on a real-time basis. It found that over time, social media analytics provides a competitive advantage with its ability to make data speak. It further provides certain guidelines, like the development of a comprehensive set of capabilities to analyze and predict social media activity in terms of modeling, segmentation, profiling, management of the campaign and utilizing cyberspace for brand management for more efficient and effective results.

Singh et al. (2019) investigated social media analytics through detailed surveys and taking into consideration big data analytics. It also discussed data sets which are unstructured, different techniques like sentiment analysis, news analysis, scrapping, opinion mining and NLP. It further concludes that for product prediction, sentiment analysis works the best because it can be related to a specific purpose, like feelings, emotions and attitude. In addition to that, it throws light on tools like monitoring tools, scientific programming tools and business toolkits for social media analysis. Sivarajah et al. (2020) studied the transformation of the Web phenomenon which is the digital transformation and accumulation of various digital advancements. They found that the intelligence gathered through participatory Web leads to improved efficiency and productivity of every type of business, either big or small. Based on the qualitative results, their study reveals that for a business to become more profitable and remain sustainable through strategic operations and marketing-related activities, the ability of big data and social media analytics is highly significant for sustainability attainment. Perakakis et al. (2019) connote the significance of artificial intelligence as a tool for understanding customers and prospects on social media for marketing. The advantages are mainly in the form of reduction in human efforts, improvement in the level of accuracy and automation of the marketing-related tasks. Moreover, their study emphasized on issues, like monitoring of social media, analysis to find the right information, customized solutions and revealing of true scenarios in order to enhance the presence of a product or service on the digital platform, separation of positive and negative feedbacks and analysis of the competitors' strategy. The authors suggested that the adoption of artificial intelligence will help in marketing and sales improvement through the development of real-time data and its analysis along with improvement in creativity and innovation.

2. Digital Marketing and Social Media Analytics: A Conceptual Overview

The pattern of societal communication has changed since the introduction of the World Wide Web and social networking websites along with the relationship between organizations, consumers, government agencies and citizens (Grubmuller et al., 2013). The ability of social media to connect with each other in order to share information or to socialize, provides a broad sense of opportunities to organizations for a better achievement of their interests and goals (Bertot et al., 2010; Margo, 2012; Shirky, 2011). Various studies in the previous section have already shown the significance of social media for marketing and to be useful, the analytics of the social media data is crucial for the desired results. In addition to that, what attracted the organizations is the increased popularity and flexibility attached to social networking. Hence, the present section gives a conceptual overview of digital marketing and social media analytics has been discussed.

2.1 Digital Marketing

The crux of marketing lies in the better understanding of consumers' behavior through targeting and initiating significant offerings. It consists of efforts mostly in the form of the right person, right place and at the right time. Nowadays digital marketing has become a buzzword; however, a decade ago, traditional marketing tools mostly in offline modes, such as radio, print, television and billboards were used in the marketing campaigns of the majority of organizations (Lund, 2021; Mucka, 2020). On the other hand, email, blog posts and social media are the main sources of marketing in the present digital world. Since the 1990s there has been an emergence of the digital marketing era (Table 1); it is an upgrade over the traditional system which promises to deliver the right message at the right time to the right audience (Hemann and Burbary, 2013). It is further said in the present time, if a brand or business is not spending sufficient efforts and time on the digital platforms, it shows that they are missing out on several marketing opportunities associated with the growth of the business. It provides a space that encourages new visitors, is highly flexible in access and helps in retaining customers for an organization (Business Matters, 2020).

Digital marketing is basically an extension of the traditional marketing system wherein leading customers and prospects hold a significant place. It consists of leveraging online marketing tactics (like email marketing, social media marketing and search marketing) for the promotion and selling of products and services (Bala and Verma, 2018). In other words, it is a process of advertising and marketing

Table 1: Evolution of digital marketing over the years.

Year	Evolution of Digital Marketing
1990	• 'Digital Marketing' term came into existence • First search engine was launched 'Archie'
1993	• First clickable wed-ad banner
1994	• 'Yahoo!' was launched • Over Netmarket, first e-commerce transaction
1996	• LookSmart, Alexa and HotBot like small search engines were launched
1997	• First social media site SixDegrees.com was launched
1998	• Google came into existence • MSN was launched by Microsoft • Yahoo! Web search was launched by Yahoo!
2000	• Internet bubble bursts • Smaller search engines got extinct • Shutdown of SixDegrees.com
2001	• Universal music started first mobile marketing campaign
2002–2003	• LinkedIn, Myspace launched • Release of WordPress
2004–2005	• Gmail launched • Google goes public • Facebook goes live • Launch of YouTube
2006	• MS Live Search was launched by Microsoft • Launch of Twitter • E-commerce sale of Amazon cross $10 billion • Split testing in marketing introduced
2007	• Tumblr launched • Web-streaming service Hulu founded • iPhone launched
2008	• China overtakes US in number of Internet users • Spotify launched • Groupon goes live came into existence
2009	• Google launches instant for real-time search engine results
2010	• Google Affiliate Network Shutdown • Google Buzz launched • WhatsApp launched
2011	• Shutdown of Google Buzz • Launch of Google+ • Web-use overtakes figures for TV viewership among youth
2012–2013	• Social media budget up 64 per cent • Yahoo! Acquired Tumblr
2014	• Mobile exceeds PC internet usage • Facebook Messenger app, tailored ads on LinkedIn, iWatch, and Facebook's Look Back launched • Facebook acquired WhatsApp
2015	• Snapchat launches 'Discover' feature • The rise of predictive analytics, wearable tech and content marketing • Facebook launches 'Instant Articles'

Note: Adapted from *The History and Evolution of Digital Marketing* (Monnappa, 2020).

Fig. 1: Channels of digital marketing (adapted from *Digital Marketing vs Traditional Marketing: Which Produces Better ROI?* Sherman, 2019)

through online channels like email, search engine optimization, pay-per-click, social media and others (Fig. 1), of a product, service, business, or person (Andrus, 2020).

The Internet is the main reason behind the increasing importance of digital marketing by organizations. According to a report, in 2018, the global spending on digital transformation was around $ 1 trillion and by 2022 it is expected to grow to more than $ 2 trillion and due to the situation of the pandemic Covid-19, more than 79 per cent of the organizations accepting an amplification in digital transformation budget (Fitzpatrick et al., 2020; Reinsel et al., 2018). Such type of growth of digital technology has changed the behavior as well as expectations of the customers as they are the ones who are equipped with modern technology and also gives feedback first on the basis of their digital experience (Alida, 2017). Due to the easy accessibility of various services online, like purchasing and selling of goods and services, the system of online marketing is growing exponentially, making a definite edge for digital form (WebFx, 2021). One of the forms of digital marketing, i.e., inbound marketing (in which people find you; then you go out for the people) is the reason behind the continuous growth of digital marketing. With the growth and advancement of technology, it has now become easy to find the right audience and promote the product or service (Mishra, 2020). The main idea behind any form of digital marketing is to gain exposure by letting more and more people know about the product or service to build close customer relationships based on trust (Pettersson and Andersson, 2018).

2.1.1 Social Media Analytics

The concept of social media analytics has emerged from the evolution of social media and social media is based on the social network. A social network is based on actors (a social entity) and their associations, but in a defined set and a link over a social network between two or more actors is known as a 'connection' (Tabassum et al., 2018). The level of connectedness affects the concerned social network through structural and behavioral connectivity. In other words, the action of a single or more individual in a network surely affects the others and this enhances the significance of social media analytics from the business perspective (Pupazan, 2011).

Fig. 2: Framework of social media analytics (adapted from *Social Media Analytics for Business Analysis and Improved Decision Making* (Vasishta and Sreenivasa, 2016).

The concept of social media analytics has emerged from the increasing popularity of social media (It is a platform where people connect, interact with each other and share moments of their lives by sharing created content) (Fotis, 2015). According to Techopedia (2017), "Social media analytics refers to the approach of collecting data from social media sites and blogs and evaluating that data to make business decisions. This process goes beyond the usual monitoring or a basic analysis of retweets or 'likes' to develop an in-depth idea of the social consumer." The framework of social media analytics is shown in Fig. 2. In other words, it is the practice of making business decisions by gathering and analyzing data from the social media platform by applying social media analytics tools (Stieglitz et al., 2018). Not just Twitter and Facebook like sites, the social media sites also consist of news outlets, blogs as well as review sites, and forums where consumers are sharing their feelings, opinions and beliefs in an online mode (Leidig, 2021).

Social media analytics helps in finding out how activities on the social media platform are influencing the results of the business by measuring campaigns and tracking conversations. In addition to that, to get a complete picture of the consumers' experience, organizations mix notes of the call center agent, customer feedback, review sites and ratings, survey results with social analytics (Patel, 2020). The social media analytics work is based on various techniques, like:

2.1.2 Sentiment Analysis or Opinion Mining Technique

It is one of the significant tools to observe the social media platform to collect opinions of online clients; it controls system statistics and other analytical tools (Medhat et al., 2014). This technique mostly helps in evaluating the inadequacies of the product and its trends in marketing. Opinion mining techniques consist of Phrase Counts (based on the frequency of a product in the comments section), Semantic methods (includes the difference between good and bad comments) and Polarity Lexicon (consists of the good and bad comments on the products by users). Biasness is the key limitation of this technique (Ravi and Ravi, 2015).

2.1.3 Modeling of the Topic

This technique decodes from large quantities of a blog the common topics and these topics help (through data analytics) in processing the content that has more interests of the users. Advanced statistical and machine learning techniques are applied in the case of Topic Modeling (Ofcom, 2019).

2.1.4 Trend Analysis

Under trend analysis, behavior and future outcomes are predicted based on the data collected over time through methods, such as efficiency of PPC projection, stock market movement prediction and sales or client base development. Support vector machines, time-series analysis and neural networks are some of the methods used in trend analysis (Edwards, 2019).

2.1.5 Visual Analysis

In this technique, a visual interface involving logical analysis provides the information for marketing decisions. A combination of computer analysis and the human brain is used to extract information for the decision-making process (Keim et al., 2009).

2.1.6 Other Analytics Tools Based on Social Media Sites

Different social media platforms also have different analytical tools, like for Facebook it is Advert reports and Page insights; for Pinterest, it is having Pinterest Analysis; LinkedIn is having Analytics for individual users and business owners and Twitter have Twitter Analytics and third-party tools, such as SproutSocial, Quintly, Klout, Cyfe, TweetReach and so on (Lee, 2021). Social media analytics provides a glimpse of their actual feelings about products, services and organizations; it is much more than 'likes' and 'shares'. It also helps in understanding and improving the content which leads to an increase in the acceptance range for the users (McKinsey and Company, 2016). Even the performance of links, videos and images can be evaluated through image-focused platforms, such as Pinterest and Instagram that show which image appeals more to the customers (Fotis, 2015). It further provides a competitive edge in terms of tracking competitors' growth on social media and building counter strategies accordingly (Newberry, 2020). Moreover, a better understanding of the audience or the clients also develops along with the development of enhanced marketing strategies through analyzing the best and the worst works. Social media has provided invaluable opportunities due to its rapid growth in recent years, paving the way for organizations to market their products and services on the digital platform (Ramani, 2021; Tahmasebifard and Wright, 2018). However, various businesses are still not able to adopt the techniques and methodologies of social media analytics, which is hampering their growth. Social media analytics can be located as a business intelligence practice in terms of its capabilities, like prediction, monitoring and innovation to achieve the company's strategic objectives (Ruhi, 2014).

2.2 Role of Social Media Analytics in Digital Marketing

The significance to have an online presence can be analyzed from the data that around 57 per cent of the world's population is using the Internet in the present scenario. It is, therefore, imperative to have an online presence to get in touch with the target customer; and to accomplish this, digital marketing is the need of the hour and the analytics in it play a significant role in the desired consequences. With the emergence of social media platforms and an increasing number of users, it provides an opportunity to the marketers to extract the views of a large number of participants at selected platforms (McGaw, 2019).

In recent years, social media has provided a significant platform for digital marketing, which has made it occupy a substantial portion in the marketing budget of the majority of organizations. Furthermore, previously marketing was mostly

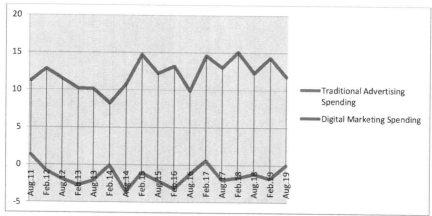

Fig. 3: Traditional advertising spending vs. digital marketing spending (adapted from *Highlights & Insights Report*, The CMO Survey, 2019).

based on speculation or guesswork as there were no techniques or tools available for analytics, like content engagement, sentiment analysis, etc. (Bhayana, 2020). Figure 3 shows the comparison between traditional and digital marketing spending by select US firms over a period of 12 months from 2011 to 2019, showing that over the years digital marketing spending has become highly dominant. Among all paid media alternatives, organizations emphasize print, search engine optimization and other paid digital media including trade shows and partnerships. This has further created the need for analytics as the organizations started tracking activities, leading to the emergence of concepts like Web analytics, email analytics and so on (Leone, 2020).

Digitally marketed products are easily available to consumers all the time and according to a survey by Marketing Techblog, Facebook is used to market by around 99 per cent of digital marketers, followed by Twitter (97 per cent use), Pinterest (69 per cent) and Instagram (59 per cent). In addition to that, Twitter, Facebook and LinkedIn are the three top sites used by marketers (Monnappa, 2020). According to Zeng et al. (2010), social media data is collected, monitored, analyzed and visualized using evaluating informatics tools of the social media analytics to get constructive patterns and intelligence. It provides a check on the campaigns along with the websites that are attracting the most traffic for the organization. The data analytics also differentiate between opinion and fact by giving the data-driven and creative foundation for marketing strategy, so as to attract and engage the new customers along with delighting the existing ones (McGaw, 2019).

Social media analytics can also address the concerns of customers along with fixing product issues and crafting messages for marketing. Moreover, the social media platform is exposed by social media analytics in finding out the best-suited marketing strategies for the organizations (Khan et al., 2014). Sentimental analysis is one of the advanced methods of social media analytics and is mostly applied to assess the clients' or customers' feelings towards the product or service. In this method, customers' comments about the brand are evaluated, using advanced methods of algorithms to detect their reaction (Batrinca and Treleaven, 2015; Drus and Khalid, 2019).

However, in today's time, the structure of social media and its analytics is becoming complex day by day with rapid and continuous changes, such as new tools and techniques, new sources of data, new media platforms and new and advanced devices for consumption, like tablets and mobiles (Dwivedi et al., 2020). This poses a challenge among marketers on how to create an environment in terms of marketing strategies that will lead to achieving the desired outcomes or objectives of the digital world. The following points show that even in the dynamic world, social media can help in achieving effective digital marketing strategies:

2.2.1 Best Strategy Evaluation Mechanism

Social media analytics helps in analyzing those strategies for marketing which influence positively towards maintaining the brand image at the digital platform, for example, to draw traffic, the consistency of quality content is the strategy which has been widely applied; however, the media analytics analysis helps in finding out the activity having highest influence, leading to shifting in the focus towards that as the parameters are clearer now (Fan and Gordon, 2014).

2.2.2 Development Assessment

Social media analytics helps in assessing the impact of the adopted marketing strategy in terms of its contribution towards the development of the brand (product or service) online. In addition to that, it helps in finding out the actual return on the investment based on the views, comments, likes and dislikes of the adopted marketing campaign (Li et al., 2021).

2.2.3 Escalating Effective Strategies

Social media analytics helps in finding out the effective strategies for marketing, thus providing a lead towards the best channel and intensification of the efforts for its application. As different platforms might need different strategies, the analysis of the data will surely help in choosing and making the online presence in a better way by customizing the content based on the profiles of the clients (Sears, 2018).

According to a Nielsen survey (2012), 92 per cent of the respondents said that compared to any other form of advertisement, they trust the recommendations about a product or service based on their family and friends; therefore, making social media marketing more valuable. In addition to that, the result further shows that around 70 per cent have faith in the consumer's online comments about a product or service. The marketing organizations are also encouraging the consumers to write reviews, comment and rate their products to get their feedback. So, the platform provides a much trustworthy evaluation of the marketing investment in terms of the returns based on the spread of the word-of-mouth.

In the digital world, data analytics helps in getting out the exquisiteness of social media and social networks by providing insights into the aspects of data for better and smarter future interactions (Ivanov, 2018). For instance, the Amazon e-commerce platform applied real-time behavioral data for sales recommendation. The behavioral data analytics on the Amazon website is based upon products' clickstream, time spent on the product or page, page switch between products, reviews, etc. The processing in the real-time analysis is not that simple with the continuously changing perspective or thoughts of the customers; so, the final outcome is based on several parts of the data that has to be integrated based on the algorithms (Krishnan and Rogers, 2015).

The role of social media analytics helps in deep understanding between various marketing channels adopted by an organization through their performance analysis and not only the individual performances, but it also has the power to analyze the combined performance of multiple channels, like email marketing, blog-related marketing, social media related, etc. (Crawford, 2021). The analytics of social media marketing, for instance, also provides a clear insight about how many individuals have clicked on the link of the website at the particular social media site along with those individuals' data that provide a lead for the business (Oyza and Edwin, 2015). Moreover, a comparison between the different marketing initiatives can be easily possible, like the content which the organization shared and which is more effective on Facebook or Instagram (Hudson, 2020). Loyalty of the target audience can also be easily testified with the support of social media analytics in terms of whenever a new content is posted by a marketer, do the customers come back to the website to have a look or not? This will help in long-term marketing strategies growth in order to gain the trust of the customers (LYFE Marketing, 2019). Tracking of the key metrics is also possible with the social media analytics that shapes the sales and goals of marketing. It will further strongly build profitable social media marketing decisions and help in minimizing the efforts on unproductive strategies of the marketing department (Makad, 2020). In other words, it is the social media analytics that helps an organization to find its present position, where it wants to go, i.e., the objectives and how it can get over there—the type of efforts to meet the goal (Owyang, 2009).

In the past, it was said that business is a kind of speculative venture up to a certain level as no tracking mechanism exists that can directly assess the impact of the advertisement. Moreover, 80 per cent of the data is unstructured (like call-logs, blogs, documents, etc.) as it is not as per the traditional database system and the flourishing nature of the social media data only increases the amount of the unstructured database (Tripathi, 2018). It was quite a hectic job to collect the data manually and even if the data was somehow collected, it was not easy to evaluate the data as per the needs without sufficient resources and tools (CLARABRIDGE, 2020; *Cognizant Reports*, 2013). However, in modern times when everything is based on the specific need of a consumer, not on the generalized principle, the platform of social media along with the presence of its analytical capability provides a broader perspective for the organizations to market their product or service with a sure possibility of success, if applied and reviewed cautiously (Deloitte Insights, 2020).

3. Conclusion

Smart and better business decisions are mostly driven by the data insights and no strategy is complete until backed by the data. Therefore, marketing departments are finding ways on social media platforms for analyzing customer engagement by collecting the data based on the visits to the website, popularity of the content and other developments based on the likes and comments. Across the digital platform, social media analytics has become an influential tool for examining the sentiments of the customers for the marketers. Social media analytics can make it factual that customer engagement is based on certain drivers of the content, such as the 'likes' will help in the development of strategies with stable content. The main motto of social media analytics towards digital marketing is to provide the right marketing campaign at the right time with the right idea. Social media analytics is an effective tool when it comes to defining what is right for the digital marketing environment. It also helps in building long-term customer relationships as data analytics can also measure the effectiveness of the content.

Moreover, with a wide range of social media platforms having scattered information in different formats, it is the need of the hour to find the correct strategy with the right combination as to what works on which platform and which is a crucial need for effective and efficient marketing of a product and service. Hence, key information for such types of strategies in a digital platform will only be possible if appropriate data is accompanied by the correct analytical tool and then comes into the picture as the most effective tool—social media analytics. Social media analytics will help in converting the data into insights through practical approach or actions and this approach is the base for a stout strategy of marketing. The combination of digital marketing and social media analytics also leads to the turning up of business objectives in outcomes that are in measurable terms, leading to support the line at the bottom by prioritizing the data reflecting individuals instead of views or likes.

The digital marketing approach has seen a significant change since the use of social media analytics in terms that the strategies nowadays are based on specific interests or demographics of the target customer base. Competitive advantage is also one of the contributions of social media analytics towards digital marketing, as it helps organizations to gain an edge over their competitors with superior information and knowledge about the product or service. Finally, the ultimate growth of the business that is profitability with long-term sustainability can be achieved through using the results of the social media analytics while framing a new policy or modifying the existing one. The present study is not free from limitations as it is based on secondary sources of data and is having a macro perspective, instead of micro, i.e., industry-specific. Therefore, the research can provide various future research avenues, like further research can be based on primary data or can be industry or firm-specific or it can be based on case studies using expert interview-based frameworks. Future studies can also be based on quantitative and qualitative analysis, using data or surveys and can use statistical techniques to prove their results.

References

Alexander, L. 2019. *The Who, What, Why and How of Digital Marketing*. HubSpot; retrieved from: https://blog.hubspot.com/marketing/what-is-digital-marketing.

Alida. 2017. *4 Ways Technology is Changing Consumer Behavior*; retrieved from: https://www.alida.com/the-alida-journal/4-examples-how-technology-changing-consumer-behavior.

Alzahrani, H. 2016. Social media analytics using data mining. *Global Journal of Computer Science and Technology*, 16(4): 1.0.

Andrus, A. 2020. *What is Digital Marketing and How do I get Started?* Disruptive Advertising Blog; retrieved from: https://www.disruptiveadvertising.com/marketing/digital-marketing/.

Appel, G., Grewal, L., Hadi, R. and Stephen, A.T. 2020. The future of social media in marketing. *Journal of the Academy of Marketing Science*, 48: 79–95.

Bala, M. and Verma, D. 2018. A critical review of digital marketing. *International Journal of Management, IT & Engineering*, 8(10).

Barutcu, M.T. 2017. Big data analytics for marketing revolution. *Journal of Media Critiques*, 3(11).

Batrinca, B. and Treleaven, P.C. 2015. Social media analytics: A survey of techniques, tools and platforms. *AI & Society*, 30: 89–116. https://doi.org/10.1007/s00146-014-0549-4.

Bekmamedova, N. and Shanks, G. 2014. *Social Media Analytics and Business Value: A Theoretical Framework and Case Study*. 7th Hawaii International Conference on System Science; retrieved from: https://ieeexplore.ieee.org/stamp/stamp.jsp?tp=&arnumber=6759066.

Bertot, J.C., Jaeger, P.T. and Grimes, J.M. 2010. Using ICTs to create a culture of transparency: E-government and social media as openness and anti-corruption tools for societies. *Government Information Quarterly*, 27: 264–271.

Bhayana, V.J. 2020. Evolving role of data analytics in digital marketing. *ET Brand Equity*; retrieved from: https://brandequity.economictimes.indiatimes.com/news/marketing/evolving-role-of-data-analytics-in-digital-marketing/79444234.

Business Matters. 2020. *Role of social media in digital marketing*; retrieved from: https://bmmagazine.co.uk/business/role-of-social-media-in-digital-marketing/.

CLARABRIDGE. 2020. *What is Social Media Analytics?* Retrieved from: https://www.clarabridge.com/customer-experience-dictionary/social-media-analytics/.

Cognizant Reports. 2013. Social media analytics: enabling intelligent. *Real-time Decision Making*; retrieved from: https://pt.slideshare.net/amitshah28/socialmediaanalyticsenablingintelligentrealtime decisionmaking.

Crawford, C. 2021. *Social Media Analytics: The Complete Guide*, socialbakers; retrieved from: https://www.socialbakers.com/blog/social-media-analytics-the-complete-guide.

Deloitte Insights. 2020. *Tech Trends*; retrieved from: https://www2.deloitte.com/content/dam/Deloitte/cz/Documents/technology/DI_TechTrends2020.pdf.

Dhawan, V. and Zanini, N. 2014. Big data and social media analytics. *Research Matters, UCLES*; retrieved from: https://www.cambridgeassessment.org.uk/Images/465808-big-data-and-social-media-analytics.pdf.

Digital Marketing Institute. 2016. *The Evolution of Digital Marketing: 30 Years in the Past & Future*; retrieved from: https://digitalmarketinginstitute.com/blog/the-evolution-of-digital-marketing-30-years-in-the-past-and-future.

Drus, Z. and Khalid, H. 2019. Sentiment analysis in social media and its application: systematic literature review. *Procedia Computer Science*, 161: 707–714.

Dwivedi, Y.K., Ismagilova, E., Hughes, D.L., Carlson, J., Filieri, R., Jacobson, J., Jain, V., Karjaluoto, H., Kefi, H., Krishen, A.S., Kumar, V., Rahman, M.M., Raman, R., Rauschnabel, P.A., Rowley, J., Salo, J., Tran, G.A. and Wang, Y. 2020. Setting the future of digital and social media marketing research: Perspectives and research propositions. *International Journal of Information Management*, 59: 102168.

Edwards, J. 2019. What is predictive analytics? Transforming data into future insights. *CIO India*; retrieved from: https://www.cio.com/article/3273114/what-is-predictive-analytics-transforming-data-into-future-insights.html.

Fan, W. and Gordon, M.D. 2014. The power of social media analytics. *Communications of the ACM*, 57(6): 74–81.

Fisher, B. and Miller, H. 2011. Social media analytics: how it can help shape government performance. *MicroTech White Papers*; retrieved from: https://www.microtech.net/sites/default/files/socialmediaanalytics.pdf.

Fitzpatrick, M., Gill, I., Libarikian, A., Smaje, K. and Zemmel, R. 2020. *The digital-led recovery from COVID-19: Five questions for CEOs McKinsey Digital*; retrieved from: https://www.mckinsey.com/business-functions/mckinsey-digital/our-insights/the-digital-led-recovery-from-covid-19-five-questions-for-ceos.

FlexMR. 2020. *Understanding the Role of Social Media Analytics in Market Research*; retrieved from: https://flexmr.medium.com/understanding-the-role-of-social-media-analytics-in-market-research-775fd24d87d6.

Force, J. 2020. The importance of social media analytics. *Sysomos*; retrieved from: https://sysomos. com/2016/06/14/the-importance-of-social-media-analytics/.

Fotis, J.N. 2015. *The Use of Social Media and Its Impacts on Consumer Behavior: The Context of Holiday Travel*. Doctor of Philosophy thesis, Bournemouth University.

Gordon, J., Goyal, M. and McGuire, T. 2012. Big Data and advanced analytics: Success stories from the front lines. *In: McKinsey and Company Report on Marketing & Sales: Big Data, Analytics, and the Future of Marketing & Sales* (2015); retrieved from: https://www.forbes.com/sites/mckinsey/2012/12/03/big-data-advanced-analytics-success-stories-from-the-front-lines/?sh=2d7abb4ab27a.

Green, D.D., Martinez, R., Kadja, A., Evenson, L., MacManus, L. and Dirlbeck, S. 2018. In a World of social media: A case study analysis of instagram. *American Research Journal of Business and Management*, 4(1): 1–8.

Grubmuller, V., Gotsch, K. and Krieger, B. 2013. Social media analytics for future-oriented policy making. *European Journal of Futures Research*, 1: 20.

Hemann, C. and Burbary, K. 2013. Understanding the digital media landscape. 1–12. *In:* Hemann, C. and Burbary, K. (Eds.). *Digital Marketing Analytics: Making Sense of Consumer Data in Digital World*, Que Publishing.

Hudson, E. 2020. How to Blend Web Analytics and Digital Marketing Analytics to Grow Better. *HubSpot*; retrieved from: https://blog.hubspot.com/marketing/digital-marketing-analytics.

Iqbal, B.A. and Yadav, A. 2021. Big data analytics: emergence, growth, issues and potential. *In:* Sousa, M.J. and Oliveira, M.Y. (Eds.). *Top 10 Challenges of Big Data Analytics*, 103–123, Nova Science Publishers, Inc.

Ivanov, I. 2018. What is big data analytics on social media? *Locowise*; retrieved from: https://locowise. com/blog/what-is-big-data-analytics-on-social-media.

Keim, D.A., Mansmann, F., Stoffel, A. and Ziegler, H. 2009. Visual analytics. pp. 3253–3440. *In:* Liu, L. and Özsu, M.T. (Eds.). *Encyclopedia of Database Systems*, Springer, Boston, MA.

Khan, N., Yaqoob, I., Hashem, I.A.T., Inayat, Z., Ali, W.K.M., Alam, M., Shiraz, M. and Gani, A. 2014. Big Data: Survey, Technologies, Opportunities and Challenges. *The Scientific World Journal*, 712826.

Krishnan, K. and Rogers, S.P. 2015. Social analytics in the enterprise. *Social Data Analytics Collaboration for the Enterprise*. MK Series on Business Intelligence, pp. 11–21.

Lee, K. 2021. Know What's Working on social media: 27 Paid and Free Social Media Analytics Tools. *Buffer Marketing Library*; retrieved from: https://buffer.com/library/social-media-analytics-tools/.

Leidig, P. 2021. What is Social Media Analytics and Why is It Important? *NETBASE QUID*; retrieved from: https://netbasequid.com/blog/what-is-social-media-analytics-why-is-it-important/.

Leone, C. 2019. How Much Should You Budget for Marketing In 2021? *WebStrategies Blog*; retrieved from: https://www.webstrategiesinc.com/blog/how-much-budget-for-online-marketing-in-2014.

Li, F., Larimo, J. and Leonidou, L.C. 2021. Social media marketing strategy: definition, conceptualization, taxonomy, validation, and future agenda. *Journal of the Academy of Marketing Science*, 49: 51–70.

Lund, J. 2021. How Customer Experience Drives Digital Transformation, Super Office; retrieved from: https://www.superoffice.com/blog/digital-transformation/.

LYFE Marketing. 2019. Understanding the Importance of Digital Marketing Analytics. *Blog*; retrieved from: https://www.lyfemarketing.com/blog/digital-marketing-analytics/.

Margo, M.J. 2012. A review of social media use in E-Government. *Administrative Sciences*, 2: 148–161.

Makad, S. 2020. The Importance of Social Media Analytics. *TNS*; retrieved from: https://thenextscoop. com/importance-of-social-media-analytics/.

McGaw, D. 2019. *The Importance of Analytics in Digital Marketing*. utm.io; retrieved from https://web. utm.io/blog/importance-of-analytics-in-digital-marketing/.

McKinsey and Company. 2016. *The Age of Analytics: Competing in a Data-driven World*. McKinsey Global Institute in Collaboration with McKinsey Analytics; retrieved from: https://www.mckinsey. com/business-functions/mckinsey-analytics/our-insights/the-age-of-analytics-competing-in-a-data-driven-world.

Medhat, W., Hassan, A. and Korashy, H. 2014. Sentiment analysis algorithms and applications: A survey. *Ain Shams Engineering Journal*, 5(4): 1093–1113.

Mindtree. 2017. *Social Media Analytics in the Insurance Industry*; retrieved from: https://www.mindtree. com/sites/default/files/2017-10/422%20mindtree-thought-posts-white-paper-social-media-analytics-in-the-insurance-industry_0.pdf.

Mishra, C.K. 2020. Digital marketing: scope opportunities and challenges. pp. 1–24. *In:* Ayman, U. and Kaya, A.K. (Eds.). *Promotion and Marketing Communications*. IntechOpen.

Monnappa, A. 2020. The History and Evolution of Digital Marketing. *Simplilearn*; retrieved from: https://www.simplilearn.com/history-and-evolution-of-digital-marketing-article.

Mucka, P. 2020. Consumer behavior: Practical application of marketing psychology in e-commerce (the ultimate guide), *Exponea Blog*; retrieved from: https://exponea.com/blog/consumer-behavior-marketing-psychology/.

Nabler. 2020. Why is Marketing Performance Analytics crucial for your Digital Marketing efforts? Retrieved from: https://www.nabler.com/articles/marketing-performance-analytics-crucial-digital-marketing-efforts/.

Newberry, C. 2020. *How to conduct a Social Media Competitive Analysis*. Hootsuite; retrieved from: https://blog.hootsuite.com/competitive-analysis-on-social-media/.

Nielsen. 2012. *State of the Media: The Social Media Report 2012*; retrieved from: https://www.nielsen.com/wp-content/uploads/sites/3/2019/04/nielsen-social-media-report-2012-final.pdf.

Ofcom. 2019. *Use of AI on Online Content Moderation. Cambridge Consultants*; retrieved from: https://www.ofcom.org.uk/data/assets/pdf_file/0028/157249/cambridge-consultants-ai-content-moderation.pdf.

Owyang, J. 2009. *Social media measurement: Dashboards vs. GPS*; retrieved from: http://www.web-strategist.com /blog/2008/10/16/social-media-measurement-dashboards-vs-gps/.

Oyza, I. and Edwin, A. 2015. Effectiveness of social media networks as a strategic tool for organizational marketing management. *Journal of Internet Banking and Commerce*, S2–006.

Patel, N. 2020. The 5 Easy Steps to Measure Your Social Media Campaigns. *The All-in-One SEO Tool*; retrieved from: https://neilpatel.com/blog/social-media-measurement/.

Perakakis, E., Mastorakis, G. and Kopanakis, I. 2019. Social media monitoring: an innovative intelligent approach. *Designs, MDPI*, 3: 24.

Pettersson, A.C.L. and Andersson, J.M.L. 2018. *Analyzing the usage of digital marketing and relationship marketing within Swedish SMEs in the B2B sector-Examining what is most effective*. Bachelor thesis, Linnaeus University.

Porteous, J. 2018. Target Audience Analysis: Everything Digital Marketers Need to Know, Socialbakers. *The Social Media Blog*; retrieved from: https://www.socialbakers.com/blog/target-audience-analysis-guide-everything-digital-marketers-need-to-know.

Pupazan, E. 2011. Social Networking Analytics. BMI Paper. *VU University Amsterdam*; retrieved from: https://www.math.vu.nl/~sbhulai/papers/paper-pupazan.pdf.

Ramani, K. 2021. Brand and Design: Top 10 Digital Wallets in India and UPI Payment App. *SocialBeat*; retrieved from: https://www.socialbeat.in/blog/category/brand-marketing-india/.

Ravi, K. and Ravi, V. 2015. A survey on opinion mining and sentiment analysis: Tasks, approaches and applications. *Knowledge-based Systems*, 89: 14–46.

Reinsel, D., Gantz, J. and Rydning, J. 2018. *The Digitization of the World from Edge to Core*. Data Age 2025, *IDC*; retrieved from: https://www.seagate.com/files/www-content/our-story/trends/files/idc-seagate-dataage-whitepaper.pdf.

Rondot, S. 2020. The Importance of the Social Media Analytics. *Hackernoon*; retrieved from: https://hackernoon.com/the-importance-of-social-media-analytics-qy1q30gc.

Ruhi, U. 2014. Social media analytics as a Business intelligence practice: Current landscape and future prospects. *Journal of Internet Social Networking and Virtual Communities*, 2014: 920553.

Sears, H. 2018. How to Use Social Data Analytics to Inform Your Marketing Strategy. *PIXLEE*; retrieved from: https://www.pixlee.com/blog/how-to-use-social-data-analytics-to-inform-your-marketing-strategy/.

Sherman. 2019. Digital Marketing vs. Traditional Marketing: Which Produces Better ROI? *LYFE Marketing Blog*; retrieved from: https://www.lyfemarketing.com/blog/digital-marketing-vs-traditional-marketing/.

Shirky, C. 2011. The political power of social media: Technology, the Public Sphere, and Political Change. Politics from a New Perspective. *Foreign Affairs*; retrieved from: https://www.cc.gatech.edu/~beki/cs4001/Shirky.pdf.

Sidewalk Labs. 2019. *Master Innovation & Development Plan Digital Innovation Appendix*; retrieved from: https://quaysideto.ca/wp-content/uploads/2019/11/Sidewalk-Labs-Digital-Innovation-Appendix.pdf.

Singh, S., Arya, P., Patel, A. and Tiwari, A.K. 2019. Social media analysis through big data analytics: A survey. *Proceedings of 2nd International Conference on Advanced Computing and Software Engineering*. http://dx.doi.org/10.2139/ssrn.3349561.

Single Grain Team. 2020. Why Digital Marketing Analytics Matter to Your Business. *Single Grain Blog*; retrieved from: https://www.singlegrain.com/blog-posts/analytics/why-digital-marketing-analytics-matter/.

Sivarajah, U., Irani, Z., Gupta, S. and Mahroof, K. 2020. Role of big data and social media analytics for business-to-business sustainability: A participatory web context. *Industrial Marketing Management*, 86: 163–179. https://doi.org/ 10.1016/ j.indmarman.2019.04.005.

Sponder, M. 2012. The uses and accuracy of social analytics data and platforms. *In:* Reiman, C. (Ed.). *Public Interest and Private Rights in Social Media*, Chandos Publishing Social Media Series, 2012, 175–196. https://doi.org/10.1016/B978-1-84334-693-7.50011-8.

Stieglitz, S., Mirbabaie, M., Ross, B. and Neuberger, C. 2018. Social media analytics—Challenges in topic discovery, data collection, and data preparation. *International Journal of Information Management*, 39: 156–168. https://doi.org/10.1016/ j.ijinf omgt.2017.12.002.

Tabassum, S., Pereira, F.S.F., Fernandes, S. and Gama, J. 2018. Social network analysis: An overview, *WIREs Data Mining and Knowledge Discovery*, Wiley Online Library.

Tahmasebifard, H. and Wright, L.T. 2018. The role of competitive intelligence and its sub-types on achieving market performance. *Cogent Business and Management*, 5: 1.

Techopedia. 2017. *Social Media Analytics (SMA)*. https://www.techopedia. com/definition/13853/social-media-analytics-sma.

The CMO Survey. 2019. *Highlights and Insights Report*. Deloitte, Duke Fuqua and American Marketing Association; retrieved from: https://cmosurvey.org/results/august-2019/.

Tripathi, S. 2018. Analytics on Unstructured data – Twitter, Facebook and social media. *Analytics Training*; retrieved from: https://analyticstraining.com/analytics-on-unstructured-data-%E2%80%93-twitter-facebook-and-social-media/.

Vasishta, H. and Sreenivasa, B.R. 2016. Social media analytics for business analysis and improved decision making. *International Journal of Advanced Networking & Applications*, 490–493; retrieved from: https://www.ijana.in/Special%20Issue/S108.pdf.

WebFx. 2021. *7 Reasons Behind the Importance of Internet Marketing*; retrieved from: https://www.webfx.com/internet-marketing/why-is-internet-marketing-so-important.html.

Wedel, M. and Kannan, P.K. 2016. Marketing analytics for data-rich environments. *Journal of Marketing, American Marketing Association*, 80: 97–121.

Zeng, D., Chen, H., Lusch, R. and Li, S.-H. 2010. Social media analytics and intelligence. *IEEE Intelligent Systems*, 25(6).

9

Measuring Digital Maturity
The Case of Economic Agents in the Tourism Sector in Portugal

Carlos Reis-Marques,[1] *Miguel de Castro Neto*[1] and
Ronnie Figueiredo[2,*]

INTRODUCTION

Economic agents and economic groups are often interested parties in the quest for digital maturity and innovation in industries. In addition, the diffusion of Information and Communication Technologies (ICTs) in the public sector has been significant over the last few decades (Merhi and Ahluwalia, 2018).

Maturity models (MMs) are valuable methodologies for helping manufacturing organizations track the progress of their I4.0 initiatives and guide their digitalization (Caiado et al., 2021). Nevertheless, it is a fact that Industry 4.0 is a relatively recent phenomenon for the academics and professionals who work in the area of manufacturing (Wagire et al., 2020).

In recent years, the concept of 'data' has come to mean a type of raw material and the foundation for a new infrastructure used to generate income, thus strengthening the evolution of society (Yablonsky, 2020). This technological revolution has spurred an evolution in society, catapulted by greater Internet access and the popularization of mobile devices. In the same manner, society's progress boosts technological evolution in a phenomenon called 'co-incorporated evolution' (Cukier and Kon, 2018).

In this way, significant advances in the areas of digitalization allow for the development, testing and implementation of continuously more advanced

[1] NOVA Information Management School (NOVA IMS), Universidade Nova de Lisboa, Lisboa, Portugal.
   Emails: crmarques@novaims.unl.pt; mneto@novaims.unl.pt
[2] Research Center in Business Sciences, NECE (UBI), Transdisciplinary Research Center of Innovation
   & Entrepreneurship Ecosystems, TRIE (ULHT), and Spinner Innovation Centre, Portugal.
* Corresponding author: contact@spinnercentre.com

autonomous solutions, creating the need to develop a maturity structure focused on businesses, their agents and their ecosystems (Thomson et al., 2021). This, in turn, makes it necessary to develop a maturity model to evaluate and guide research and development (R&D) organizations in the creation of sustainable, innovative products and services that stimulate growth (Hynds et al., 2014).

Since agents possess specific characteristics that differentiate them from large corporations, a model that can allow them to identify, leverage and develop their digital capabilities can help them advance in digital maturity (González-Varona et al., 2021). In this regard, Ghobakhloo (2020), advocates the identification and analysis of 'factors' that assist in the implementation of Information and Digital Technologies (IDT) for intelligent manufacturing. This has led to the perception that the change to digitalization, referred to as digital transformation (DX) in Anglo-Saxon terminology, is an important topic for companies in all sectors (Minonne et al., 2018).

For Lin et al. (2020), the development of a structure for evaluation of maturity based on a dynamic capacity that uses combined, integrated resources toward the transformation of traditional manufacturing into intelligent manufacturing is of extreme relevance. Thus, the adoption of new technologies is considered an important source for business opportunities (Mero et al., 2020).

According to Mettler and Pinto (2018), it has become increasingly important for decision makers to have a concise understanding of their current situation. For example, they should know which technologies they should consider to be 'white spots' (meaning, absent or poorly developed). This is understandable because the advance of business practices based on ICTs over the last few decades has transformed many, if not most, economies into e-economies and businesses into e-businesses (Molla and Cooper, 2010).

In respect to the digital maturity of tourism, Whyte (2019), describes how digital information, more widely disseminated every day, transforms models for project delivery. Nevertheless, for Lewis et al. (2013), the question is recognizing to what point a conceptual model derived from research into different implementations of Advanced Manufacturing Technology (AMT) can offer an explanatory vision for an economic agent who implements advanced service technologies.

For Vashishth et al. (2021), this depends on the impact of previous implementations of Integrated Management Systems (IMS) and their subsequent impact on the operational performance context for local economic agents. Nowadays, the growing demand from clients for customized products is a significant theme that is forcing digital transformation in industries (Sütőová et al., 2020).

From the viewpoint of Yablonsky (2020), innovation in Artificial Intelligence (IA) becomes useful when it enriches decision making that can be improved by the application of 'big data' (BD) and Advanced Analytics (AA), along with some element of human interaction, using digital platforms. While the Internet can make markets more competitive by improving decisions, it may at times be less than ideal because the maturity or level of development of tourism markets has not been studied sufficiently in terms of digital maturity (Bock et al., 2007).

In the absence of studies that consider initial perceptions and those measured as evaluated in accordance with the five domains of organization/management, digital technologies/solutions, digital innovation, digital innovation strategy and business models, a need arises for the study of the structuring of the domains of evaluation of maturity for the tourism sector in Portugal, in terms of practices and the adoption of digital, that is favorable to the digital transformation of economic agents in the sector. Therefore, our question for investigation is presented: How do economic agents in tourism in Portugal capitalize on digital transformation in the sector?

With this investigation, we hope to contribute to this field of study because, despite the existing investigations into digital maturity and digital transformation in different sectors of the industry, specially in 4.0, very few investigations have arisen with this focus, simultaneously with economic agents in Portugal.

In this manner, we are making a contribution to the literature, highlighting the importance of developing and understanding alternatives to include and measure digital maturity in the tourism sector, leading to international competitiveness.

We highlight that the quality of economic agents and economic groups display gaps in the conditions and necessities for implementation of practices of digital transformation in businesses. Given that the extent to which the perception on the part of agents and groups clarifies this vision, it contributes to the improvement of the results. We believe that the empirical results have important implications for researchers and for the creation of ecosystems of digital transformation in the tourism sector.

The structure of this article was established according to the following format: after an introduction, here in the first section, the second section presents a review of the literature related to the principal theme. The third section characterizes the methodology and the methods and data used. The fourth section makes an empirical analysis of the data. Finally, the fifth contains the results and the last adds final considerations, implications, limitations of the study and suggestions for future lines of investigation.

1. Theoretical Background

With the use of digital solutions, products, people and machines can be monitored and tracked. Digital technologies, such as intelligent sensors, make it possible for a company to collect a large volume of diverse data in real time together with external aspects, as an aide to decision making (Rocha et al., 2019).

These circumstances have demonstrated the vitality and capacity of industries to adapt to changes in a wide range of aspects (Tourism 4.0), developing new capabilities for analyses capable of including data based on social networks and reputational factors, promoting new partnerships and skills in human resources (Navío-Marco et al., 2018).

In fact, a study made on the determinants of innovation among Australian tourism companies proved that there was a positive correlation between collaborative actions (co-creation) and the 'quality' of human capital as a result of innovation (Divisekera and Nguyen, 2018).

Access to and the sharing of data is a fundamental factor in the generation of value in the digital era. The exchange of data between different platforms, facilitating interoperability between business partners, has led to the rise of intelligent ecosystems and an economy of costs. This situation, particularly when adjusted to the hospitality sector, makes it possible for owners of small and/or medium hotel units to have equal access to 'big data' and to perform strategic analyses, mitigating the advantages that international chains have with their greater access to data on a global scale, or to acquired data bases (Buhalis and Leung, 2018).

In tourism, the generation of data from a variety of sources opens up the potential for investigation and development and a field for collaboration to deepen the ties between economic agents and universities (Li et al., 2018).

This fact has a direct relationship today with other developments, such as the advent of 'smart cities', instigating the formation of options like 'smart destinations' and establishing what may be understood as 'smart tourism', allowing for immediate sharing of information and knowledge in regard to locations and the enjoyment of experiences associated with them (Jovicic, 2019; Liberato et al., 2018).

Digital transformation is a complex challenge for organizations, referring to the capacity to generate and share value through digital means. In this context, innovation emerges as a differentiating driving force that generates competitiveness and sustainability for businesses (Hausman and Johnston, 2014). This way, digital innovation is a lever for distributing value, making it the responsibility of the leaders of organizations to develop it and endow it with appropriate capabilities, not only in organizational and technical terms, but also in regard to the creation of cultures that propose debate and sharing of new ideas (Gill and VanBoskirk, 2016).

It is evident that the capacity to generate digital innovation implies the command of skills related to management processes and a strategy of innovation that goes beyond just digital technologies (Reis-Marques and Popovic, 2016). This allows for innovation not only in products and services (Holmstro and Nyle, 2015), but also with business models (Chesbrough, 2010; Cortimiglia et al., 2015) which are increasingly considered to be of great significance in the effectiveness of financial results (Cortimiglia et al., 2015).

The concept of digital maturity (DM) assumes particular relevance when the process through which organizations are learning about and gradually responding to emerging digital environments is understood and made clearer. This process is one which neither leaders, nor collaborators, or even digital natives are really qualified to predict (Kane, 2017).

On the other hand, enhanced by technological innovation, this new form of creating value (through digital model) comprises a set of actions that involve processes, the mobilization of people and the management of infrastructure and financial resources, which have redesigned industries in an increasingly digital world (Industry 4.0) (Günther Schuh et al., 2019; Kane, 2017; Piccinini et al., 2015).

Figure 1 presents, as a theoretical foundation, the conceptual model that we are proposing for our study on digital maturity. This model begins with the perception of digital maturity that companies have of themselves, consisting of the extent of digital innovation in the business environment, while complementarity assessing their degree of maturity in five domains.

Based on the results in each of the domains and the digital maturity demonstrated, a profile is created of the digital maturity of each company. This, when compared to

DIGITAL TRANSFORMATION

SECTOR/FIRM

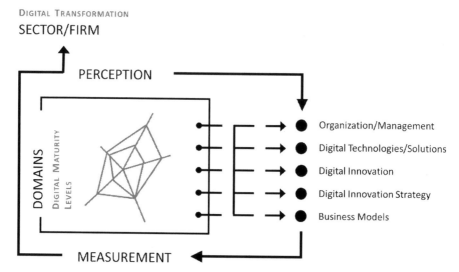

Fig. 1: MDML—Conceptual model of digital maturity levels Data Collection.

the digital maturity initially defined, allows us to understand the gap in the business's creation of value and define the actions that should be taken.

Finally, as in the studied case, when the model is applied to an economic sector, represented by a set of companies, it becomes possible to identify what the impact of digital transformation on the sector will be, measured in accordance with the digital maturity shown.

2. Collection Procedure

The used data was aggregated from the entire country, collected from a wide range of sources through the use of a survey, which provided a random sample stratified into two subgroups within the economic sector of tourism. Stratum 1 includes 35 economic agents (e.g., travel and tourism agencies and rent-a-car) and stratum 2 comprises two economic groups (Pestana Hotels and Sonel Hotels), representing 44 activities in the tourism sector (Table 1). The data was also classified in accordance with the size (Table 2) and internationalization of companies (Table 3).

Due to the nature of the collected data, the size of companies was characterized by the number of employees (Table 2).

With regards to internationalization, the majority of companies are internationalized (51 per cent). We highlight that hotel establishments (25 per cent), travel and tourism agencies (20 per cent) and rent-a-car agencies (5 per cent), are often integrated into international chains (Table 3).

Table 1: Activities in the tourism sector.

Nature of Economic Activity	No. of Companies
Hotel establishment	11
Tourist village	04
Tourist apartment	02
Local accommodation (AL)	02
Tourist complex	01
Rural tourism space	01
Camping park/caravan lodging	01
Tourism animation agent	03
Travel and tourism agency	09
Restaurant or similar	02
Golf course	01
Theme park	01
Cruise ships and nautical recreation	(Zero)
Casino	01
Rent-a-car agency	02
Air transport	(Zero)
Airport infrastructure	01
Promot. Spect. festival and expos (others)	01
Event organizer (others)	01
Total	44

Table 2: Size of enterprises in terms of number of employees.

No. of Employees (T)	Frequency
$T < 10$	42 per cent
$T < 50$	18 per cent
$T < 250$	24 per cent
$T >= 250$	15 per cent

Table 3: Internationalization of companies.

Internationalization	Frequency
Internationalized	51 per cent
Intention to Internationalize	11 per cent
Is not, doesn't intend to be	26 per cent
NS/NA	11 per cent

2.1 Measuring

The process of collecting the primary data was performed through an online questionnaire that sought to identify the maturity stage of the economic agents in terms of their DX processes, in the domains for analysis that are associated with them and can be considered to be their principal driving forces.

The questionnaire was structured to obtain the perceived DX profile measured by the responding companies themselves and divided into the following domains for analysis—Organization/Management, Digital Technologies/Solutions, Digital Innovation, Digital Strategy and Business Models—and to collect complementary information aimed at characterizing the responding companies.

In order to obtain the DX profile of each of the responding companies, statements were made corresponding to the effective stages of maturity for each of the domains analyzed, performing a classification of the 'level of agreement' pursuant to a hierarchical Likert scale on five levels (1–Totally Disagree; 2–Partially Disagree; 3–Neither Agree/Nor Disagree; 4–Partially Agree; 5–Totally Agree), resulting in a graduated interval of stages from beginners in maturity to full maturity: beginner, in transition, in development, significant maturity and full maturity.

The pre-test questionnaire was performed during the month of July 2019, using a sample of individuals who were sent a link for access to the form. Feedback was received from businessmen in the tourism sector and specialists in technologies and digital innovation, via email, which was complemented by a simulation of completing the form together with a technology specialist, a businessman in a tourism unit in a rural space and even elements from the Confederation of Portuguese Tourism (CTP).

Based on the contributions collected, a definitive version of the questionnaire was prepared, which was published online and distributed by the CTP to their associates with a request for them to promote/spread it among their respective associates, due to the legal nature of their relationship with the former. The period for collection ran from the month of August through November of 2019, with periodic reminders.

2.1.1 Domains of Digital Maturity

The following table presents the definitions of the domains used in the process of evaluation of the organizations (Table 4).

Table 4: Analysis dimensions.

Domains	Denomination	Definition
D1	Organization/ management	An evaluation of how the company is organized, structured and leads its teams with a focus on its digital skills.
D2	Digital technologies/ solutions	An evaluation of how the adoption of digital technologies is applied to the company's internal processes, its relationship with the market and support of decision making, as well as how it monitors the development of these technologies.
D3	Digital innovation	An evaluation of the adoption, diffusion, and implementation of practices of innovation, with a focus on the digital domain.
D4	Digital innovation strategy	An evaluation of decision-making processes for strategic positioning, especially in terms of the definition and development of actions of innovation, with a focus on the digital environment.
D5	Business models	An evaluation on the manner in which a company defines and implements its proposals for digital value and establishes its corresponding go-to-market strategies.

Table 5 presents a synthesis of the references that are used as a basis for the domains evaluated during the study.

Table 5: Analysis dimensions.

Domains	# Affirmations	References
D1	16	(Staggers and Rodney, 2012; Chapman and Plewes, 2014; Teece, 2014).
D2	12	(Tornatsky and Fleischer, 1990; Jokela and Saarela, 2001; Kieffer and Vanderdonckt, 2016).
D3	11	(Sward and Macarthur, 2007; Van Tyne, 2009; Rogers, 2003; Damanpour and Wischnevsky, 2006; Reis-Marques and Popovic, 2016).
D4	17	(Mostafa, 2013; Vasmatzidis et al., 2001; Holmstro and Nyle, 2015).
D5	10	(Earthy, 1998; Chesbrough, 2006; Teece, 2010; Zott, Amit and Massa, 2011; Baden-Fuller and Haefliger, 2013; Zott and Amit, 2013; DaSilva and Trkman, 2014).

2.2 Data Analysis

After the initial point, when the responding companies identified their perceived DM level, the following phases of the questionnaire aimed at identifying their real DM (measured) in each one of the domains presented.

Assuming that the affirmations correspond directly to the maturity stages and that the scale (Likert) is organized in an increasing level of concordance, or maturity, the stronger the level of concordance, the greater the maturity stage should be, in a spectrum that is represented in graphic form in Fig. 2.

An exploratory approach was used as a basis for the study and for analyzing the data, supported by a quantitative analysis. The data obtained was handled using Excel software (Version 365/2021).

Fig. 2: Digital maturity scale.

3. Results

3.1 Profile of Perceived Digital Maturity

In regard to the DM profile (Fig. 3) measured at the beginning of the study, the majority of companies consider themselves in an intermediate development stage (60 per cent), while the second group is made up of companies that consider themselves in a stage of maturity progressing toward full maturity (31 per cent) and the third consider themselves to still be in an early stage (9 per cent).

Most companies in the hotel sector, as well as travel agencies, are the ones that consider themselves in a stage of maturity progressing toward full maturity in regard to their DX processes. Nevertheless, the companies that consider themselves to still be in an early stage also fall into these categories.

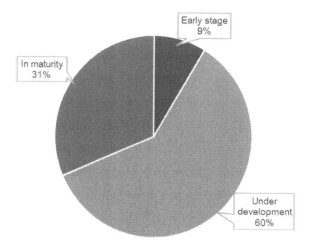

Fig. 3: Level of digital maturity (DM).

3.2 Profile of Digital Maturity–Measurement

3.2.1 Domain of Organization/Management

The domain 'Organization/Management' refers to aspects related to the way companies are organized, structured and manage/lead their teams, with a particular focus on the area of their digital skills. In this case, the responding companies were presented with a set of 16 statements that faithfully placed them in the maturity stages summarized as follows:

- 4.9 per cent in the early stage.
- 10.6 per cent in the transition stage.
- 18.1 per cent in the development stage.
- 40.4 per cent in the mature stage progressing toward full maturity.
- 26.0 per cent in the stage of full digital maturity.

Lack of regular practices of internal communication regarding innovation initiatives promoted by the company, or in which they have participated, is revealed as the less common practice and the recreation/acceptance of new ideas, even if they are very different, is referred to as the practices more frequently referred to as regular.

Given the results, the profile of the responding companies for the domain Organization/Management shows that they see themselves at a level of significant maturity and almost full maturity (Fig. 4).

3.2.2 Domain of Digital Technologies/Solutions

In the domain of 'Digital Technologies/Solutions', consisting of the adoption of these kinds of technologies for their internal processes, the relationship with the market and support of decision making, as well as the monitoring of the development of these technologies, the following results were registered, derived from 12 statements similar to those in the previous domain:

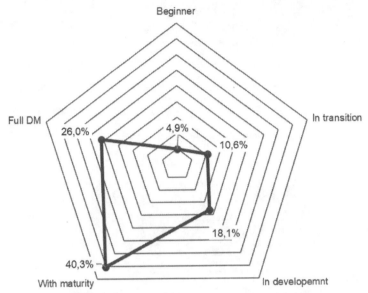

Fig. 4: Digital maturity profile: Domain of organization/management.

- 7.2 per cent in the early stage.
- 12.8 per cent in the transition stage.
- 20.5 per cent in the development stage.
- 33.5 per cent in the mature stage progressing toward full maturity.
- 26 per cent in the stage of full digital maturity.

Weak sharing of digital solutions with business partners is revealed as the less common practice, while concern over the use of duly licensed technologies is the practice more often referred to as the one most frequently adopted.

Given the results, the profile of the responding companies for the domain Digital Technologies/Solutions shows that they see themselves at a level of significant maturity and almost full maturity, as in the example of the previous domain (Fig. 5).

3.2.3 Domain of Digital Innovation

Considering that the domain of 'digital innovation' is related to the adoption, diffusion and implementation of practices of innovation at the company, with a particular focus on the digital domain, the companies were asked to consider 11 statements, with the responses divided according to the following aspects:

- 17.1 per cent in the early stage.
- 17.4 per cent in the transition stage.
- 30.0 per cent in the development stage.
- 22.0 per cent in the mature stage progressing toward full maturity.
- 13.5 per cent in the stage of full digital maturity.

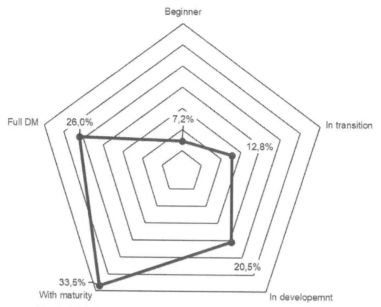

Fig. 5: Digital maturity profile: Domain of digital technologies/solutions.

Considering the profile of the companies in the domain for Digital Innovation, a more homogenous distribution was revealed. On the other hand, the creation of new tendencies and/or habits with consumers through the use of digital solutions developed is referred to as the element less commonly carried out, while specific actions performed to guarantee a differential and competitiveness through internal digital skills was referred to as being more commonly used.

Given the results, the profile of the responding companies for this domain is different from the others, revealing less maturity and showing more homogeneous distribution (Fig. 6).

3.2.4 Domain of Digital Strategy

Related to the company's decision-making processes and strategic positioning, in terms of its options, definition and development of actions/initiatives in innovation, especially within the digital environment, in the domain of 'Digital Strategy', 17 statements were placed to companies for consideration in order to identify their maturity in this domain:

- 22.9 per cent in the early stage.
- 16.0 per cent in the transition stage.
- 26.4 per cent in the development stage.
- 23.7 per cent in the mature stage progressing toward full maturity.
- 11.0 per cent in the stage of full digital maturity.

The element identified as most fragile is related to the absence of the company's own brands, as opposed to the collection of data through digital channels, notably on clients and which was referred to as the more common practice.

Given the results, a more homogeneous distribution is observed, demonstrating that the organizations are in a wide range of stages of development (Fig. 7).

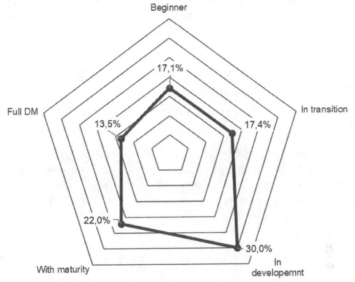

Fig. 6: Digital maturity profile: Domain of digital innovation.

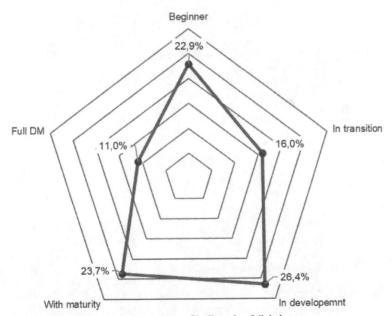

Fig. 7: Digital maturity profile: Domain of digital strategy.

3.2.5 Domain of Business Model

Refers to the manner in which the companies establish their definitions and implementation of their proposals for value and establish their approach to the market. Similarly, the domain of 'Business Models' is organized through response to 10 statements, complemented by other aspects, as can be seen.

- 6.3 per cent in the early stage.
- 10.9 per cent in the transition stage.
- 18.7 per cent in the development stage.
- 35.0 per cent in the mature stage progressing toward full maturity.
- 29.0 per cent in the stage of full digital maturity.

The aspect indicated as being the least developed pertains to the lack of Business Models in open platforms that integrate with other *players*, denoting insufficient strategic orientation toward innovation, particularly in terms of open innovation.

Given the results, most of the respondents indicate that they have reached significant levels of maturity (Fig. 8).

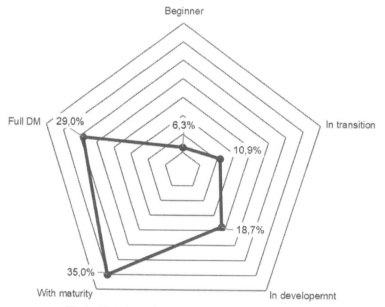

Fig. 8: Digital maturity profile: Domain of business model.

3.3 Profile of Digital Maturity Measured

For the aggregate analysis, as a result of the responses given for each of the domains and the respective maturity profile measurements, we can ascertain that the companies display high maturity levels in terms of the domains of 'Organization/ Management', 'Digital Technologies/Solutions' and 'Business Models', while the domains of 'Digital Innovation' and 'Digital Innovation Strategy' result in profiles with lower maturity, with some even in the beginning stage.

Considering the aggregate of the responses given, it can be said that the profile of digital maturity measured includes a great variety of options, as shown in Fig. 9, indicating stages of significant transition to maturity and consolidation of this reality.

In making a comparison between the 'profile of digital maturity' initially perceived and that actually measured, a correspondence can be seen between them, particularly in regard to the general stage of DM at the companies. Nevertheless, a detailed analysis of the various domains makes it clear which areas need improvement and which seem to have received less attention from the companies.

When the companies were asked to establish a hierarchy for the importance, they attributed to each of the dimensions for analysis in regard to their processes of digital transformation, they rated the domain of 'Organization/Management' as being the most important, followed by 'Business Models', 'Digital Technologies/Solutions', 'Digital Strategy', and finally 'Digital Innovation', a situation which is deserving of some reflection (Fig. 10).

With innovation being fundamental to the creation of value through digital model and being given less importance by companies in their DX processes, it is apparent that the relevance of this domain is not being perceived as well as the context in which these processes should occur. This affirmation is reinforced by the importance attributed to the domain 'Business Models', which, being rated as the second most important to companies according to the responses analyzed, indicates a failure to understand the transformative character of innovation in the digital context, reinforcing the idea of a failure to give value to that which is most critical.

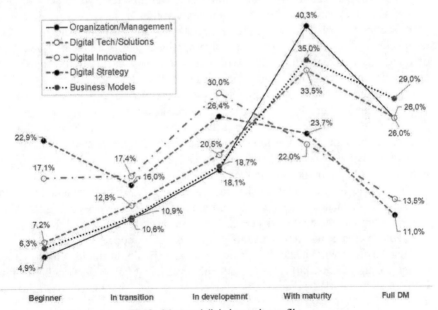

Fig. 9: Measured digital maturity profile.

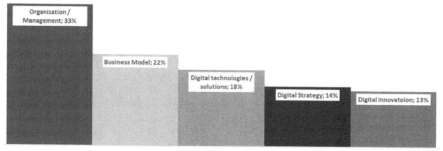

Fig. 10: Valuation of the dimensions of analysis.

4. Conclusion and Implications

An analysis of the answers demonstrates that there are a very diverse types of maturity stages in the sector in terms of digital transformation, while it is clear that some economic activities (ex: hotels) are more advanced.

On the other hand, being certain that digital innovation has a positive impact in terms of creation of value and the results obtained through the processes of digital transformation, it seems somewhat incoherent that companies (generally) consider themselves to be at a high level of maturity while they attribute a lesser relevance to digital innovation and a related strategy for innovation, elements that are fundamental and critical to these processes.

The fact that actions of innovation result less in the development of new products/services may come from a certain immutability in this area due to the nature of the sector. Nevertheless, the nature of the obtained data seems to indicate the need to develop a more distinctive, constructive approach that is a potential generator of value, specifically through the use of digital solutions leading to the enjoyment/anticipation of experiences, which, in the context of the pandemic provoked by Covid-19, find particular justification (ex: Augmented Reality).

Additionally, there are also elements that indicate that there is a lesser perception regarding the implications of digital transformation processes than there is of human resource management and the adoption of practices/principles related to the creation and dissemination of a culture of innovation. This, necessarily, implies improvements in processes of communication and teamwork (e.g., activities of co-creation).

Thus, one of the principal elements needed for the improvement of digital maturity of the economic agents is the training of human resources in digital skills, as well as innovation, teamwork and data analysis, as it is fundamental for the sector to be able to create and integrate value generated digital models.

On the other hand, it should be noted that the difficulty in attaining more skilled human resources (internal) is associated with insufficient involvement/collaboration with external entities in activities of creation and/or sharing of synergies for innovation.

Taking this into consideration and weighing in the fact that business models allow for little room to share elements of the value chain with partners, using the logic of networking may open up an opportunity to develop I&D+i ecosystems in tourism; particularly in the area related to actions of digital innovation, increasing the efficiency of DX processes, the competitiveness and sustainability of the sector, notably in terms of strategic positioning in relation to other markets.

We must also consider the opinions expressed by the companies themselves, which indicate the need to adopt measures in the following areas: (i) fiscal incentives, compensating investments in innovation; (ii) support for the training of collaborators in digital skills; (iii) support for activities of I&D+i, through specific programs; (iv) support for the acquisition of digital technologies; (v) greater flexibility in relationships with public administrative services offered via digital model; (vi) incentives to the establishment of associations as a way to create global value in the sector, particularly in I&D+i activities.

Taking into consideration some of the aforementioned measures and the existing programs that support I&D+I, the implementation of actions involving information, counselling and specific/effective support are justified in order to guarantee that economic agents in tourism have better awareness with regard to the available support, which, notably, allows for the hiring of people qualified in I&D+i, as well as the contracting of services and obtaining fiscal benefits.

In the case of processes as supporting elements for digital transformation, this is necessarily related to the aspects considered most critical to this reality. In this regard, we must point out the processes related to the management of innovation, the strategic options and the taking of these to the market, hopefully to offer new promotions with an advantageous value, or significantly altering the existing ones.

Thus, we see that the responding companies, generally speaking, are still lacking in the development and implementation of processes suited to the aforementioned, while still recognizing that digital transformation has been changing the manner in which a company's work is organized. This situation is evident in aspects like those related to processes that spur innovation, especially in terms of mechanisms for support and co-creation.

This fact results in a reduced availability of tools and methodologies for teamwork, accompanied by a reduced dematerialization of processes and utilization of digital platforms that are collaborative, demonstrating that there is still some ground to cover.

On the other hand, most of the companies admitted to not having indicators/ metrics associated with their actions of innovation, also recognizing that they do not publicize their initiatives in this regard, neither internally nor to the market. In addition, they have also recognized that policies for investments in digital models are weak.

This set of affirmations reveals the need for companies, in general, to think strategically about the way they can develop and share value via digital model, which is why they have not declined orientations in this regard as to the right way to organize and execute a set of tasks, this being an area where improvements can be implemented. That means that the design and implementation of processes for support and management of digital innovation, in support of options for strategies in this regard, should be viewed as essential.

In regard to the use of digital technologies, it is shown that the companies, generally speaking, either possess adequate technologies, or they are open to their acquisition—this having been the expressed opinion of the majority. Nevertheless, aspects such as the reduced sharing of technological solutions with partners, along with the low use of cloud solutions and technologies (and skills) for handling data (data mining) are evident. It can be pointed out that the companies that are not interested in investing in the adoption of these technologies relate that one of the main reasons is their high cost.

This is one of the areas that justifies careful intervention. Actually, there are many situations where we can perceive the need to improve existing practices and/or adopt new measures that allow companies, in general, to integrate more effectively into the irrefutable role that is required of people in the context of processes of digital transformation. This affirmation is based on the observation that there are responses that reveal some contradictions in this regard.

First, despite the fact that the majority of companies have stated that their leadership is guided and motivated by an interest in disseminating a culture of innovation, the adoption of innovation is also related to the sharing of the creation of ideas and processes of development/prototyping of solutions, both internally and in regard to outside their companies, and these have been registered as being of little significance.

On the other hand, as referred to before, the companies have registered an equal reduction in intervention in terms of teamwork in the area of innovation, in addition to difficulties in finding an equilibrium with digital skills in the creation of transversal teams. Included as one of the main reasons for this, and the fact that companies have not invested in digital technologies, is the lack of qualified HR personnel.

Thus, intervention with staff, particularly in terms of training for skills in the area of innovation and the creation of digital value, emerges as being fundamental for the improvement of companies—this having been referred to explicitly by the companies themselves.

Considering the contextual surroundings, there are two aspects that can be gleaned from the responses and that are equally characterized as being areas for intervention. The first relates to the lack of knowledge manifested by some companies in regard to the mechanisms that exist in terms of personnel training and fiscal advantages associated with the implementation of I&D+i initiatives, specifically with the establishment of relations of partnership/complementarity with other entities in this sphere.

In this regard, conditions should be created to allow companies to be able to access information and support mechanisms that can act as facilitators in these processes, with the dismantling of bureaucracy having also been referred to as a measure that contributes to this same effect.

On the other hand, there are many situations where it can be seen that there are no support ecosystems for innovation, which can function as agents for development and engagement of companies, in particular in terms of the sharing of resources and skills, as well as complementarities.

These ecosystems can (and should) assume a strategic dimension for the development of domestic tourism, specifically the ability to 'take advantage' of the movement of start-ups and establishing proximities with the academic world, articulating specific actions for value creation and sustained positioning of companies for the medium term.

5. Limitations and Future Research Trends

This research contains some limitations that must be considered as pointing to future directions for studies. The first category of limitations is related to the methodology. The data base used was aggregated data from Portugal, related to the tourism sector. Future studies may concentrate on data bases from other countries to reach conclusions on future decisions with regards to digital maturity based on the domains studied.

Secondly, the article employed a quantitative method to examine the results in five domains: Organization/Management, Digital Technologies/Solutions, Digital Innovation, Digital Innovation Strategy and Business Models.

Consequently, future studies can apply a qualitative approach to determine the quality of economic agents and economic groups as related to the transfer of knowledge, innovation and intellectual property. They may also use the same domains presented in the model in comparison to other international data bases and observe their behavior in relation to other economic agents and economic groups.

Finally, the domain to be inserted into future studies is the impact of digital transformation. As we know that there are inequalities between countries, it becomes important to disaggregate the studies by countries in order to perceive the differences between them and allow for different actions in each country through comparative analyses.

References

Baden-Fuller, C. and Haefliger, S. 2013. Business models and technological innovation. *Long Range Planning*, 46(6): 419–426. https://doi.org/10.1016/j.lrp.2013.08.023.

Bock, G.W., Lee, S.Y.T. and Li, H.Y. 2007. Price comparison and price dispersion: Products and retailers at different internet maturity stages. *International Journal of Electronic Commerce*, 11(4): 101–124. https://doi.org/10.2753/JEC1086-4415110404.

Buhalis, D. and Leung, R. 2018. Smart hospitality—Interconnectivity and interoperability towards an ecosystem. *International Journal of Hospitality Management*, 71(December 2017): 41–50. https://doi.org/10.1016/j.ijhm.2017.11.011.

Caiado, R.G.G., Scavarda, L.F., Gavião, L.O., Ivson, P., Nascimento, D.L. de M. and Garza-Reyes, J.A. 2021. A fuzzy rule-based industry 4.0 maturity model for operations and supply chain management. *International Journal of Production Economics*, 231(November 2019). https://doi.org/10.1016/j.ijpe.2020.107883.

Chapman, L. and Plewes, S. 2014. A UX maturity model: Effective introduction of UX into organizations. *Lecture Notes in Computer Science (Including Subseries Lecture Notes in Artificial Intelligence and Lecture Notes in Bioinformatics)*, 8520 LNCS (Part 4), 12–22. https://doi.org/10.1007/978-3-319-07638-6_2.

Chesbrough, H. 2006. *Open Business Models: How to Thrive in the New Innovation Landscape*. Boston, Massachusetts: Harvard Business School Press.

Chesbrough, H. 2010. Business model innovation: opportunities and barriers. *Long Range Planning*, 43(2-3): 354–363. https://doi.org/10.1016/j.lrp.2009.07.010.

Cortimiglia, M.N., Ghezzi, A. and Frank, A.G. 2015. Business model innovation and strategy making nexus: Evidence from a cross-industry mixed-methods study. *R&D Management*, n/a--n/a. https://doi.org/10.1111/radm.12113.

Cukier, D. and Kon, F. 2018. A maturity model for software startup ecosystems. *Journal of Innovation and Entrepreneurship*, 7(1): 1–32. https://doi.org/10.1186/s13731-018-0091-6.

Damanpour, F. and Wischnevsky, J.D. 2006. Research on innovation in organizations: Distinguishing innovation-generating from innovation-adopting organizations. *Journal of Engineering and Technology Management*, 23(4): 269–291. https://doi.org/10.1016/j.jengtecman.2006.08.002.

DaSilva, C.M. and Trkman, P. 2014. Business model: what it is and what it is not. *Long Range Planning*, 47(6): 379–389. https://doi.org/10.1016/j.lrp.2013.08.004.

Divisekera, S. and Nguyen, V.K. 2018. Determinants of innovation in tourism evidence from Australia. *Tourism Management*, 67: 157–167. https://doi.org/10.1016/j.tourman.2018.01.010.

Earthy, J. (1998). Usability maturity model: Human centredness scale. INUSE Project deliverable D, 5: 1–34; retrieved from: http://www.idemployee.id.tue.nl/g.w.m.rauterberg/lecturenotes/usability-maturity-model[1].pdf.

Ghobakhloo, M. 2020. Determinants of information and digital technology implementation for smart manufacturing. *International Journal of Production Research*, 58(8): 2384–2405. https://doi.org/10.1080/00207543.2019.1630775.

Gill, M. and VanBoskirk, S. 2016. The digital maturity model 4.0. benchmarks: Digital transformation playbook.

González-Varona, J.M., López-Paredes, A., Poza, D. and Acebes, F. 2021. Building and development of an organizational competence for digital transformation in SMEs. *Journal of Industrial Engineering and Management*, 14(1): 15–24. https://doi.org/10.3926/jiem.3279.

Günther Schuh, Reiner Anderl, Jürgen Gausemeier, Michael ten Hompel, W.W. 2019. Roadmapping towards industrial digitalization based on an Industry 4.0 maturity model for manufacturing enterprises. *Procedia CIRP*, 79: 409–414. https://doi.org/10.1016/j.procir.2019.02.110.

Hausman, A. and Johnston, W.J. 2014. The role of innovation in driving the economy: Lessons from the global financial crisis. *Journal of Business Research*, 67(1): 2720–2726. https://doi.org/10.1016/j.jbusres.2013.03.021.

Holmstro, J. and Nyle, D. 2015. Digital innovation strategy: A framework for diagnosing and improving digital product and service innovation. *Business Horizon*, 58(1): 57–67. https://doi.org/10.1016/j.bushor.2014.09.001.

Hynds, E.J., Brandt, V., Burek, S., Jager, W., Knox, P., Parker, J.P., ... Zietlow, M. 2014. A maturity model for sustainability in new product development. *Research Technology Management*, 57(1): 50–57. https://doi.org/10.5437/08956308X5701143.

Jokela, S. and Saarela, J. (1999, October). A reference model for flexible content development. *In Proceedings of the Second International Conference on Telecommunications and Electronic Commerce (ICTEC)*, pp. 312–325.

Jovicic, D.Z. 2019. From the traditional understanding of tourism destination to the smart tourism destination. *Current Issues in Tourism*, 22(3): 276–282. https://doi.org/10.1080/13683500.2017.1313203.

Kane, G.C. 2017. Digital Maturity, Not Digital Transformation; retrieved from *MIT Sloan Management Review* website: http://sloanreview.mit.edu/article/digital-maturity-not-digital-transformation/.

Kieffer, S. and Vanderdonckt, J. 2016. STRATUS: A questionnaire for strategic usability assessment. *Proceedings of the ACM Symposium on Applied Computing, 04–08 April*, 205–212. https://doi.org/10.1145/2851613.2851912.

Lewis, M., Åhlström, P., Yalabik, B. and Mårtensson, P. 2013. Implementing advanced service technology in the public sector: An exploratory study of the relevance and limitations of insights from private sector manufacturing technology implementation. *Production Planning and Control*, 24(10-11): 916–930. https://doi.org/10.1080/09537287.2012.666901.

Li, J., Xu, L., Tang, L., Wang, S. and Li, L. 2018. Big data in tourism research: A literature review. *Tourism Management*, 68: 301–323. https://doi.org/10.1016/j.tourman.2018.03.009.

Liberato, P.M.C., Alén-González, E. and Liberato, D.V.A. 2018. Digital technology in a smart tourist destination: The case of porto. *Journal of Urban Technology*, 0732. https://doi.org/10.1080/10630732.2017.1413228.

Lin, T.C., Sheng, M.L. and Jeng Wang, K. 2020. Dynamic capabilities for smart manufacturing transformation by manufacturing enterprises. *Asian Journal of Technology Innovation*, 28(3): 403–426. https://doi.org/10.1080/19761597.2020.1769486.

Merhi, M.I. and Ahluwalia, P. 2018. Digital economy and corruption perceptions: A cross-country analysis. *International Journal of Digital Accounting Research*, 18(December 2017): 29–47. https://doi.org/10.4192/1577-8517-v18_2.

Mero, J., Tarkiainen, A. and Tobon, J. 2020. Effectual and causal reasoning in the adoption of marketing automation. *Industrial Marketing Management*, 86(March 2019): 212–222. https://doi.org/10.1016/j.indmarman.2019.12.008.

Mettler, T. and Pinto, R. 2018. Evolutionary paths and influencing factors towards digital maturity: An analysis of the status quo in Swiss hospitals. *Technological Forecasting and Social Change*, 133(February): 104–117. https://doi.org/10.1016/j.techfore.2018.03.009.

Minonne, C., Wyss, R., Schwer, K., Wirz, D. and Hitz, C. 2018. Digital maturity variables and their impact on the enterprise architecture layers. *Problems and Perspectives in Management*, 16(4): 141–154. https://doi.org/10.21511/ppm.16(4).2018.13.

Molla, A. and Cooper, V. 2010. Green it readiness: A framework and preliminary proof of concept. *Australasian Journal of Information Systems*, 16(2): 5–23. https://doi.org/10.3127/ajis.v16i2.545.

Mostafa, M.M. 2013. More than words: Social networks' text mining for consumer brand sentiments. *Expert Systems with Applications*, 40(10): 4241–4251.

Navío-Marco, J., Ruiz-Gómez, L.M. and Sevilla-Sevilla, C. 2018. Progress in information technology and tourism management: 30 years on and 20 years after the internet-Revisiting Buhalis & Law's landmark study about eTourism. *Tourism Management*, 69(December 2017): 460–470. https://doi.org/10.1016/j.tourman.2018.06.002.

Piccinini, E., Hanelt, A., Gregory, R.W. and Kolbe, L.M. 2015. Transforming industrial business: The impact of digital transformation on automotive organizations. *36 th International Conference on Information Systems*, 1–20.

Reis-Marques, C. and Popovic, A. 2016. Managing digitally enabled innovation: A conceptual framework. *10th European Conference on Information Systems Management*, 313–316, Évora: Academic Conferences and Publishing International Limited.

Rocha, C.F., Mamédio, D.F. and Quandt, C.O. 2019. Startups and the innovation ecosystem in Industry 4.0. *Technology Analysis and Strategic Management*, 31(12): 1474–1487. https://doi.org/10.1080/09537325.2019.1628938.

Rogers, E.M. 2003. *Diffusion of Innovations* (5th ed.), New York: Free Press.

Staggers, N. and Rodney, M. 2012. Promoting usability in organizations with a new health usability model: Implications for nursing informatics. *In NI 2012: 11th International Congress on Nursing Informatics*, June 23–27, 2012, Montreal, Canada. (Vol. 2012). American Medical Informatics Association.

Sütőová, A., Šooš, Ľ. and Kóča, F. 2020. Learning needs determination for industry 4.0 maturity development in automotive organisations in Slovakia. *Quality Innovation Prosperity*, 24(3): 122–139. https://doi.org/10.12776/QIP.V24I3.1521.

Sward, D. and Macarthur, G. 2007, September. Making user experience a business strategy. pp. 35–40. *In: Law, E.* et al. (Eds.). *Proceedings of the Workshop on Towards a UX Manifesto* (vol. 3).

Teece, D.J. 2010. Business models, business strategy and innovation. *Long Range Planning*, 43(2–3): 172–194. https://doi.org/10.1016/j.lrp.2009.07.003.

Teece, D.J. 2014. A dynamic capabilities-based entrepreneurial theory of the multinational enterprise. *Journal of International Business Studies*, 45(1): 8–37. https://doi.org/10.1057/jibs.2013.54.

Thomson, L., Kamalaldin, A., Sjödin, D. and Parida, V. 2021. A maturity framework for autonomous solutions in manufacturing firms: The interplay of technology, ecosystem, and business model. *International Entrepreneurship and Management Journal*. https://doi.org/10.1007/s11365-020-00717-3.

Tornatzky, L.G., Fleischer, M. and Chakrabarti, A.K. 1990. Processes of technological innovation. Lexington books.

Van Tyne, S. (2009, July). Corporate user-experience maturity model. *In International Conference on Human Centered Design* (pp. 635–639). Springer, Berlin, Heidelberg.

Vashishth, A., Chakraborty, A., Gouda, S.K. and Gajanand, M.S. 2021. Integrated management systems maturity: Drivers and benefits in Indian SMEs. *Journal of Cleaner Production*, 293: 126243. https://doi.org/10.1016/j.jclepro.2021.126243.

Vasmatzidis, I., Arvind, R. and Christopher, H. 2001. Introducing usability engineering into the CMM model: An empirical approach. *Proceedings of the Human Factors and Ergonomics Society 45th Annual Meeting*, 45(24): 1748–1752, Sage CA: Los Angeles.

Wagire, A.A., Joshi, R., Rathore, A.P.S. and Jain, R. 2021. Development of maturity model for assessing the implementation of Industry 4.0: learning from theory and practice. *Production Planning & Control*, 32(8): 603–622. https://doi.org/10.1080/09537287.2020.1744763.

Whyte, J. 2019. How digital information transforms project delivery models. *Project Management Journal*, 50(2): 177–194. https://doi.org/10.1177/8756972818823304.

Yablonsky, S.A. 2020. AI-driven digital platform innovation. *Technology Innovation Management Review*, 10(10): 4–15. https://doi.org/10.22215/TIMREVIEW/1392.

Zott, C., Amit, R. and Massa, L. 2011. The business model: recent developments and future research. *Journal of Management*, 37(4): 1019–1042. https://doi.org/10.1177/0149206311406265.

Zott, C. and Amit, R. 2013. The business model: A theoretically anchored robust construct for strategic analysis. *Strategic Organization*, 11(4): 403–411. https://doi.org/10.1177/1476127013510466.

10

The Impact of the Pandemic on a Five-star Hotel's Digital Revival

Sofia Almeida[1] and *Sofia Magalhães*[2,*]

INTRODUCTION

Since last year the world has experienced dramatic changes. The arrival of the pandemic has profoundly altered the day-to-day life of h umanity. Social distancing has been imposed to prevent the spread of the virus and lockdown has become a reality to which we have all had to adapt. The tourism industry has come to a halt. Hotels and restaurants have closed, airplanes are parked in airports, car rental companies have suspended business and tourist entertainment companies are waiting for better times. This is a period of anguish, but also of hope. In different crises, opportunities have arisen and this crisis is no exception. The aim of the case study presented herein is to analyze the performance of a five-star hotel in the centre of Lisbon, Portugal. In 24 months (2019 and 2020), the hotel was only open to the public for eight months. This research shows how the succession of lockdowns were used to diagnose the hotel's digital strategy, to benchmark competitors' strategies and test some changes. The results are surprising and serve as a reminder that sometimes it is necessary to stop and to reflect.

This chapter covers a literature review on social media and Social Media Analytics, which are important to describe the digital strategy of this case study. These metrics are critical to measure and monitor consumer behavior in tourism, and also for important strategic decisions for the future. To explain this process, a case study will be examined, namely the Bairro Alto Hotel. This boutique hotel has improved its performance over the last year, despite the pandemic context with particularly harsh effects for the hotel sector. This case focuses on the digital strategy

---

[1] Centre of Geografic Studies, The Institute of Geography and Spatial Planning (IGOT), Universidade de Lisboa; Faculty of Tourism and Hospitality (FTH), Universidade Europeia.
 Email: aagua@campus.ul.pt
[2] Faculty of Tourism and Hospitality (FTH), Universidade Europeia.
* Corresponding author: sofia.cmagalhaes@hotmail.com

decision taken by the coordinator, one year ago. The objectives are as follows: (i) to demonstrate how social analytics are crucial to improve hotel performance; (ii) to identify social media best practices to improve engagement with guests. Following the definition of objectives, an analysis is conducted of the Bairro Alto Hotel at the beginning of the pandemic and over a period of 24 months. Finally, conclusions are presented, such as good practices to increase digital performance in Covid-19 times and future avenues for further research are advanced.

1. Social Media Concept

The Internet has always been a social medium. It is unique as it is the first many-to-many communication channel (Sterne and Scott, 2010, p. 16) and is at the root of social media. This is probably the main difference in comparison with other social communication media, such as radio and television, which also revolutionized communication in society (but in a one-to-many communication process). In fact, both cases have had an important role in history.

Social media is a current topic that has been developed over the last two decades (Choi et al., 2020; Leung et al., 2013; Misirlis and Vlachopoulou, 2018; Poecze et al., 2018). Over time, several authors have defined the concept of social media monitoring as: [...] "the process of scanning social media to identify and analyze information about a firm's external environment, in order to assimilate and utilize the acquired external intelligence for business purposes" (Mayeh et al., 2012, p. 2); still social media analytics tools allow to measure user-generated public content, through postings, comments, conversations in online forums, among others, based on user-generated public content (Grubmüller et al., 2013 p. 4).

Social media makes it possible for one to communicate with everyone. Based on the ideological and technological foundations of Web 2.0, social media corresponds to a group of Internet-based applications that allow people to create or exchange online content or user-generated content (UGS) distributed through online channels (Kaplan and Haenlein, 2010; Sterne and Scott, 2010).

Social media refers to the wide range of Internet-based and mobile services allowing users to participate in online exchanges, to contribute to user-created content, or join online communities (Dewing, 2010). Choi et al. (2020) define social media types as online reviews, social networking sites (SNS), online discussion groups, multi-data and social media platforms (e.g., Twitter, Amazon, Yelp, TripAdvisor). Furthermore, several authors have categorized these diverse Internet services (Bainbridge, 2007; Chen et al., 2014; Choi et al., 2020; Dewing, 2010; Kusumasondjaja, 2018; Lee et al., 2020; Leung et al., 2013; Lieberman, 2014; Mariani et al., 2016; Nadeem et al., 2015; Paek et al., 2013; Ribarsky et al., 2014; Romão et al., 2019; Shao, 2009; Tiago and Veríssimo, 2014; Xie et al., 2012; Yakushev and Mityagin, 2014; Yu et al., 2013) commonly associated with social media as:

(i)   Status-update services or blogs and microblogs (e.g., Blogger and Twitter), Paek et al. (2013); Ribarsky et al. (2014); Yakushev and Mityagin (2014); Yu et al. (2013).

(ii) Online communities (e.g., Facebook, RenRen and TripAdvisor).

(iii) Video sharing sites (e.g., Flickr and YouTube) Carim and Warwick (2013); Geurin and Burch (2017). YouTube focuses on sharing and viewing videos, and "can be regarded as a convergence of the traditional entertainment choices of television, music and film" (Shao, 2009, p. 12). In fact, social media videos are known to be more effective in engaging viewers than other postings, such as texts and photos (Kusumasondjaja, 2018; Romão et al., 2019).

(iv) Social bookmarking sites (e.g., Delicious).

(v) Virtual world sites (e.g., Second Life, World of Warcraft).

(vi) Forums (Leung et al., 2013).

(vii) Social network sites (SNS) (Chen et al., 2014; Lee et al., 2020; Lieberman, 2014; Mariani et al., 2016; Nadeem et al., 2015; Tiago and Veríssimo, 2014; Xie et al., 2012).

(viii) Social knowledge sharing sites (e.g., Wikitravel) and other tools in a collaborative manner (Dewing, 2010; Leung et al., 2013).

2. Social Media Analytics

The following section presents a literature review on social media analytics and its importance in the hotel digital sector.

Social media analytics (SMA) is defined by Sterne and Scott (2010, p. 27), "as the study of social media metrics that help drive business strategy". Kaplan and Haenlein (2010) define SMA as a process to collect, measure, evaluate and finally to interpret data. According to Zeng et al. (2010) "social media analytics is concerned with developing and evaluating informatics tools and frameworks to collect, monitor, analyze, summarize and visualize social media data, usually driven by specific requirements from a target application" (p. 14). The authors claim that social media analytics research serves several purposes, namely facilitating conversations and interactions between online communities and obtaining useful patterns and intelligence to contribute to ongoing and online dialogues. In their research, Poecze et al. (2018) describe social media as 'traditional' retrievable metrics (i.e., number of likes, comments, shares of posted contents) to achieve a deeper understanding of audience reactions to communication forms of self-marketing on social media, based on a Grounded Theory approach and the analysis of retrieved posts. By coding those posts, four core categories may be created: link, photo, status update and video.

3. Digital Transformation

Social media has an important value for business intelligence (BI), due to the data quality, voluminous data, real-time data and customer-generated data potentially valuable to commercial firms, stakeholders and researchers (Jimenez-Marquez et al., 2019). There are several factors that have contributed to the rise of social media, namely technological factors, such as increased broadband availability, the improvement of software tools and the development of more powerful computers and mobile devices; social factors, such as the rapid uptake of social media by younger age groups; and economic factors, such as the increasing affordability of computers and software and growing commercial interest in social media sites.

Social media data has an important value for businesses and has several benefits for strengthening relations with the target audience: (i) large volume of information on the sector, companies and the audience can be distributed online to digital channels and platforms (Chen and Lin, 2019); (ii) the pace of data generation is swifter than other communication channels (Mayeh et al., 2012); (iii) the growing number of social media users allows companies to access consumer thoughts and opinions, receive feedback on stimulus issues and monitor their behavior in a timely manner (Chen and Lin, 2019); (iv) social media has changed the way information is produced, transferred and consumed (Bindra et al., 2012). From a different point of view, social media produces a high volume of information that is easily measured and monitored, which is very useful for marketers to develop their marketing strategies and customer loyalty campaigns (Misirlis and Vlachopoulou, 2018). Nevertheless, there are some risks related to how information is manipulated on social media. Due to the huge volume of information, the swiftness with which it is simultaneously distributed by several social media (Dai et al., 2011) hinders the process of selecting interesting and reliable information.

4. Social Media Contributions to the Development of the Tourism and Hospitality Sector

Two 'mega-trends' are currently impacting the tourism system: social media and search engines (Xiang and Gretzel, 2010). Social media are being adopted by travellers to help them organize their trips: searching, organizing and sharing their travel experiences and travel stories (Sterne and Scott, 2010). Social media have an important role in decision making and in tourism management operations. Researchers have become aware of their importance and valuable research has been conducted on this phenomenon. Considering the important role of social media in both travellers' decision-making as well as in tourism operations and management, a plethora of research on the application of social media in tourism and hospitality has been catalogued in refereed journals (Almeida et al., 2021; Buhalis and Mamalakis, 2015; Leung et al., 2013; Sigala, 2016; Sigala et al., 2016; Xiang and Gretzel, 2010).

There is a very close relationship between the production of content generated by consumers and tourism. The experiences that the sector offers feed into the market as useful information for decision making on the one hand and on the other, as matter and content to promote, for example, a given destination or accommodation unit. Mehraliyev et al. (2020) present the relationship between social media platforms in the flow of online travel information. The model shows the communication process between service providers and consumers through social media platforms. Leung et al. (2013) added that UGC is composed of photos, videos and other readers' comments which can increase online presence and reviews. Almeida et al. (2021) pinpoint that other types of UGC, such as blogs, chatrooms and podcasts also encourage individuals to generate their own content and share personal experiences online. UGC is so important to the online sales process in tourism that Leung et al. (2013) identify the role of social media in different phases of this process: the pre-trip phase, during-trip phase and the post-trip phase of the Travellers' Travel Planning Process. UGC helps to create memories and record them forever and this constitutes important material for tourism companies. "Social media provides tourists with a platform for creating and storing a memory of their past experiences as well as for sharing, promoting and discussing their experiences" (Sigala, 2016, p. 87). Social media are a very important means in trip planning, above all as a source of information and a way of accessing the experiences of other travellers (Chung and Buhalis, 2008). At the same time, they allow stories to be shared on a 24/7 basis, usually in the post-trip phase (Almeida and Campos, 2020).

The proliferation of social networking activities around the world is clearly evident. As stated in the *Global Digital Overview Report* prepared by We Are Social and Hootsuite (2021), in 2020 a 9.2 per cent growth in active social media users was recorded, totalling 3.80 billion people worldwide, 3.75 billion (99 per cent) of whom accessed social media via a mobile phone.

Facebook

Founded in 2004 by Mark Zuckerberg, Facebook's mission is to give people the power to build and bring the world closer together by staying connected, discovering, sharing and expressing what matters to them (Facebook, 2019). It allows brands to create a public profile page to post business information or content related to their product or services by inviting their consumers to get in touch or by updating them on what is going on (Jayasingh, 2019).

According to the Statista w ebsite (2021), by the fourth quarter of 2020, Facebook had roughly 2.8 billion active users, making it the largest social network worldwide.

Instagram

Instagram was launched by Kevin Systrom and Mike Krieger in 2010. It is home to photo, video and visual storytelling (Instagram, 2021) and has excelled as an effective communication and marketing tool to display products with visual descriptions. Hence, it has become a useful social networking platform for individuals and companies (Ting et al., 2015). It performs like a social media channel "where individuals, companies, vendors and interest groups can easily join in […] speeding up the dissemination of information" (Chante et al., 2014, p. 18). Among other features, Instagram users apply dynamic, user-generated tagging, called 'hashtag' to make it possible for others to easily find photos and videos with a specific theme, thus allowing users to classify contents easily and informally (Malik, 2018). According to Instagram (2021), by 2018 this social network had over one billion active accounts every month and by 2019, 90 per cent of these were following business accounts.

LinkedIn

LinkedIn was created in 2003, by Reid Hoffman and it is the world's largest professional network with almost 740 million members worldwide (LinkedIn, 2021). Comer (2010) defines the strategic uses of LinkedIn as follows: building relationships, understanding prospects, handpicking specific prospects, attracting prospects to a particular brand and listening to clients, finding that users are successful and affluent. The social network's mission is to connect the world's professionals and make them more productive and successful by creating an economic opportunity for every member of the global workforce (LinkedIn, 2021).

5. Bairro Alto Hotel—The Case Study

The Bairro Alto Hotel is located in Lisbon, Portugal, between two emblematic neighborhoods: the cosmopolitan Chiado and the bohemian Bairro Alto. Its 18th-century contemporary building, full of history, was recently extended and renovated by Pritzker Prize-winner architect, Eduardo Souto de Moura. The hotel's timeless character and historical elements have been preserved but it now boasts of 87 harmonious rooms, 22 of which are suites. The BAHR restaurant and unique terrace overlooking the city's skyline pay homage to the bohemian artistic manifesto era. Communal areas, with identities of their own, have also been created, such as the mezzanine lounge bar and the in-house pastry shop. The meeting and events facilities have been enlarged and the hotel now has a total of three meeting rooms and an auditorium, an innovative Wellness and Fitness Centre and the original premises of the oldest volunteer fire station in the country has been reinvented in the tribute cocktail bar named '18.68'.

The rejuvenation of this pioneer 5-star boutique hotel, Leading Hotels of the World (LHW) (2021) member, has not only been structural but also digital.

5.1 Digital Revival

The extension and consequent modernization of this emblematic neighborhood in the city came with an improved and strengthened digital strategy. By joining forces with a design team, what was initially to be a logo restyling turned into a total rebranding of the Bairro Alto Hotel, as it is known today.

Key points in the digital marketing strategy included, but were not limited to, storytelling, new and enhanced websites with separate identities and concepts for the hotel itself, the restaurant and cocktail bar, email marketing campaigns sent monthly and at pre- and post-arrival, personalized guest-driven reputation management tools, a blog as a source for Search Engine Optimization (SEO) and finally social media. Although the hotel's DNA has remained intact, its new visual perception has made broader strategic decisions possible and this has resulted in the Bairro Alto Hotel's on-going digital revival.

5.2 Google Analytics: A Marketer's Best Ally

As a Web analytics tool for measuring website traffic, Google Analytics played an important role in the decision-making process regarding Bairro Alto Hotel's social media panorama. The hotel's main media platforms with active profiles were Facebook, Instagram, LinkedIn, Pinterest and Twitter, among others. Part of the strategy was to focus on the traffic drivers and to deactivate those with little to no presence or impact.

According to Google Analytics' Traffic Acquisition, from January to December 2020, Pinterest and Twitter were responsible for only 1.86 per cent and 0.74 per cent of the traffic driven by social media, respectively. Not only the follower count and reach were very low for accounts set prior to the renovation, but also the engagement rate and interactions were not significant. In addition, no conversions were recorded on any profile. Given the statistics, it appeared to be wiser to redirect the efforts towards Facebook, Instagram and LinkedIn, which make up approximately 90 per cent of the Bairro Alto Hotel's social media acquired traffic.

5.3 Bairro Alto Hotel's Social Media Strategy

In order to understand the Bairro Alto Hotel's social media behaviors, the status of the hotel since 2019 should be taken into consideration. As illustrated on the timeline below, for the first nine months the hotel was still undergoing a total refurbishment, only to reopen in October 2019.

Early in 2020, the World Health Organization (WHO) declared a pandemic caused by the ongoing dissemination of the coronavirus disease. In line with the rest of the world, government measures were put in place in Portugal and, consequently, the hotel closed in March of the same year, shortly after having reopened. The hotel opened again in September and closed once more in December, remaining closed at the time of this research, as shown in Fig. 1.

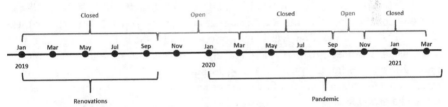

Fig. 1: Timeline of openness and closeness of Bairro Alto hotel during the lockdowns.

It does not come as a surprise that the pandemic impacted tourism and hospitality. The Bairro Alto Hotel was no exception. However, its social media platforms continued to develop and evolve throughout these circumstances and a long-term plan became a regularly revised monthly or weekly discussion on how to stand out in a crowded Web or how to remain relevant.

Digitally, the pandemic was seen as more of a challenge than an obstacle, but it impacted the digital revival set for the grand reopening of the Bairro Alto Hotel, as the strategy had to be rethought, replanned and adapted. If there is one thing that the pandemic brought, it was time. Hence, this reward was embraced as an opportunity to internally review approaches, procedures and plans and to reorganize the marketing methodologies. The ongoing storytelling approach was tailored to continue to keep the followers involved and connected by creating personalized one-to-one communication opportunities and a feeling of belonging through sharing the Bairro Alto Hotel's values, character and people. The main goal, aside from conversions, was to reach, interact, engage and boost its audience by telling the Bairro Alto Hotel's story.

Regarding this audience, its age demographics, ranging from 35 to 44 years in all the profiles analyzed, led to the decision to produce and plan all the social media content for Facebook. Being the main source of followers, reach and interactions, all the content is published on this platform. Instagram and LinkedIn publications are filtered and adapted to suit each social network purpose.

5.3.1 Facebook—@BairroAltoHotel

The action plan for the Bairro Alto Hotel's profile was initially to reduce response time, create a 360° picture to be used as its cover photo, generate exclusive online offers, reply to all the reviews and have the profile officially verified. In 2020, content was published on an average of 11 times a month, reaching over 24,000 people who interacted with the profile 1,900 times. An average engagement rate of 8 per cent was reported monthly and no conversions were recorded.

5.3.2 Instagram—@bairroaltohotel

In the Bairro Alto Hotel's profile less content is published when compared to other social networks. Preference is given to the most visually appealing content with an average of merely four feed publications per month recorded in 2020. During the same year, 5,533 people were reached in a total of approximately 576 interactions per month and an average engagement rate of 11 per cent was reported monthly. As on Facebook, no conversions were recorded.

The Bairro Alto Hotel's official hashtags are #bairroaltohotel, #wherelisbonis, and #lostinlisbon. At the time of this research, there were 8,020 entries for these hashtags as they are used in every publication made by the hotel and organically by some users. Hashtags of its partners and specific campaigns are also added to the publications. The hotel's plan regarding Instagram was to invest in stories, share guests' content, reach 10,000 followers in order to unlock other features and become a verified account.

5.3.3 LinkedIn—Bairro Alto Hotel

This social network is the hotel's second most active account. It recorded an average of seven publications in 2020, reaching 16,984 people and 1,086 interactions. There were no conversions and the engagement rate was the lowest of the profiles analyzed with only 6 per cent.

The plan set for LinkedIn, besides posting job offers, was to adapt Facebook's content to the professional tone the network is known for and to start building a community (group).

5.4 Content Creation

A wide range of marketeer-generated and user-generated content is shared on social media. By being a part of a digital society the Bairro Alto Hotel intends to be present and to constantly share its essence with those who love and relate to the brand.

Travellers often use the Internet for destination research prior to decision-making. Online Web applications and social media websites are critical elements in the travel planning process (Ruzic and Biloz, 2010) as they facilitate the creation and sharing of knowledge, information, media, ideas, opinions and insights and allow people to actively participate in the media itself (Buffardi and Campbell, 2008).

User generated content (UGC) is changing the structure and accessibility of travel information and travellers' knowledge and perception of many travel products (Litvin et al., 2008). Social media channels help promote awareness and create interest in a product or a destination (De Bruyn and Lilien, 2008), which is why the Bairro Alto Hotel complements its social media plan with recourse to some level of UGC. As for marketeer-generated content, it includes Board messages, awards, recipes, history, the hotel's blog, the teams, offers, clippings, unique selling points, job applications, food and beverage outlets, special occasions and videos.

As far as Board messages are concerned, Wang and Huang (2018) state that strategic leaders can use social media to contrive controversy and online debate with the intent of drawing attention to the firm. At the Bairro Alto Hotel, Board messages are written either by the CEO or the Hotel Manager and are published on special occasions, such as the hotel's anniversary or on the occasion of an important announcement. These types of messages are usually shared once or twice a year and result in a high engagement rate which reveals the importance of knowing the faces behind the brand.

As for awards, Nassar (2012) includes this type of content in the group of topics that are useful for hotels to spread and disseminate information widely and swiftly. The Bairro Alto Hotel shares awards and nominations given throughout the year as a means of showing appreciation to its guests and teams. Moreover, as content of interest for news creation, awards tend to be reliable generators of referral traffic to the hotel's website.

Tafesse (2016) categorized do-it-yourself content and history-related content as educational brand posts, stating that they empower consumers [...] to find creative ways of applying post suggestions in their daily lives by providing them with ample intellectual stimulation. At the Bairro Alto Hotel, the chefs' favourite recipes and the stories behind each dish are frequently shared in order to make them better known. Most cooking publications are made during the weekends when the reader is likely to have more spare time to put into practice the hotel's suggestions.

In the same proposed categorization of brand posts, Tafesse and Wien (2017) suggest that employee brand posts present employees' perspectives and offer customers direct access to their stories. These posts can motivate customers to connect with employees and the brand itself. At the hotel, the teams' achievements are publicly shared on social media since such posts have resulted in the most interactions.

The same authors also categorized promotional brand posts, recognizing them as an important approach to drive sales through social media. Offers or promotional posts are promoted on the hotel's social media channels once a week. During 2020 they did not convert but were a reliable source of traffic to the company's website. These campaigns usually include a visual identity and imagery of their own, depending on the message for which they are being advertised.

With regard to clipping, Shieh and Lai (2017) report that the marketing communications team maintains a media database. In the Bairro Alto Hotel's case, a news clipping database is kept in order to be shared. Articles from the most influential writers or websites mentioning the hotel are also posted. This type of publication is well received and shared by the audience.

As for blogs, Laboy and Torchio (2007) and Dellarocas (2003) state that they can be used for customer profiling, customer acquisition, customer engagement, brand awareness, brand reinforcement, reputation management and customer service. The history of Lisbon and the Bairro Alto Hotel is an undeniable part of the product. The city's architectural and historical heritage is shared once a month as part of the storytelling plan accomplished through the blog *Lost in Lisbon*. This is a strategic publication made exclusively to drive traffic to both the blog and website while improving its Search Engine Optimization ranking.

When referring to social media as part of a marketing strategy, Constantinides (2014) states that unique selling propositions should be responsible for delivering the expected product quality online. The Bairro Alto Hotel's unique selling points— USP—are the core of its social media presence and are published weekly. Aside from the hotel's location, these include the terrace, the rooftop, and the meeting rooms and auditorium.

Nikolaou (2014) considers social networking sites as an important medium for human resources professionals to advertise and acquire information on job seekers, effectively and efficiently. For the Bairro Alto Hotel, job application posts are a team effort carried out by the marketing and human resources departments. They are published when there is a job or internship opportunity and result in the most shared content.

Needles and Thompson (2013) mention that a restaurant can manage its online reputation by actively participating in social media. Thus, food and beverage outlets (places where food and beverages are served) are an important part of the Bairro Alto Hotel's social media platforms. Since there are five of them and they are all also a source of revenue, publications on this topic are shared as much as possible.

Tafesse and Wien (2017) categorize current event brand posts as popular holidays, anniversaries and/or special days. Fournier and Avery (2011) claim that they help keep the brand fresh and relevant in a highly dynamic environment and enable the brand to be invited into people's lives and their private conversations. Special occasions, such as the Bairro Alto Hotel's anniversary, Christmas, or New Year, for example, are always mentioned as the hotel likes to celebrate and acknowledge these special days.

Regarding videos, social media videos are known to be more effective in engaging viewers than other postings, such as texts and photos (Kusumasondjaja, 2018; Romão et al., 2019) and offer an increase by approximately 135 per cent in the organic reach of media users compared to photo posts. At the Bairro Alto Hotel, video content has always been shared at the time of a new campaign. Depending on the type and size of the video, teasers are published to entice interest in what is being advertised. For instance, when the BAHR restaurant opened, a full original video was released following a teaser strategy with different snippets.

The chef's stories can be labelled as emotional brand posts. According to Davis and Breazeale (2014), emotional brand posts arouse stronger feelings and emotions, enabling the brand to connect with consumers on an emotional level.

The Bairro Alto Hotel's most liked post types are related to the chef, Nuno Mendes. The Portuguese London-based Michelin Star chef is responsible for the hotel's and BAHR's gastronomic identity and his roots and stories stir the audience's

Table 1: Type of content vs. social media platform.

Content	Platform			References
	Facebook	LinkedIn	Instagram	
Board Messages	X	X		Wang and Huang, 2018
Awards	X	X		Nassar, 2012
Recipes	X			Tafesse, 2016
History	X	X	X	
Teams	X	X	X	Tafesse and Wien, 2017
Offers	X	X		Tafesse and Wien, 2017
Clipping	X	X		Shieh and Lai, 2017
Blog	X	X		Laboy and Torchio, 2007; Dellarocas, 2003
USPs	X	X	X	Constantinides, 2014
Job Applications	X	X		Nikolaou, 2014
Outlets	X	X	X	Needles and Thompson, 2013
Special Occasions	X	X	X	Fournier and Avery, 2011
Videos	X	X	X	Romão et al., 2019
Chef's stories	X	X	X	Davis and Breazeale, 2014

curiosity, making it worth sharing this type of content. Each social network has its own purpose and scope. Therefore, content is sorted differently through the different social media profiles.

According to Table 1, it is possible to confirm that Facebook is the hotel's focus, followed by LinkedIn and then Instagram. Additionally, Facebook is the primary source of information concerning the Bairro Alto Hotel. The only subject that is not published on LinkedIn includes recipes since it is a professional network where this information would not be relevant to followers.

Regarding Instagram, merely visually appealing content is published, therefore topics, such as the Bairro Alto Hotel's history, teams, USPs, outlets, special occasions, videos and the chef are preferable. Moreover, most of the visual content shared on Instagram is professionally generated.

At the end of each month, all the contents are evaluated in a performance report where metrics, such as followers, reach, number of publications, interactions and engagement rates are studied. Results are analyzed, discussed and measures to correct lower outcomes are taken in order to reach a broader audience and entice conversions.

To clarify some of the Bairro Alto Hotel's social media metrics, an overview of its outcomes comparing 2020 and 2019 is presented below. It should be noted that LinkedIn data was not available for 2019. The Bairro Alto Hotel's follower count increased very slowly over the course of studied time on Facebook and Instagram in 2019. Comparatively, as shown in Fig. 2, Instagram and LinkedIn had a similar behavior whereas Facebook was the only platform that recorded a loss of followers, resulting in a lower follower count at the end of the year.

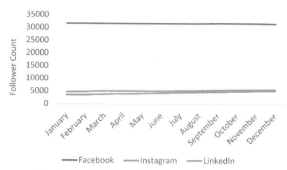

Fig. 2: Hotel's 2020 social network follower count.

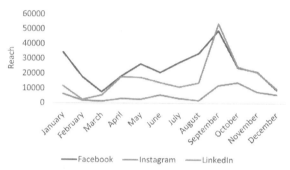

Fig. 3: Hotel's 2020 social networks audience reach.

In 2019, the largest audience was reached in April. Even though it was not the reopening month, which was in October, during the fourth month of the year, job offers performed better than other publications on social media. The first hotel sneak peeks were also shared, increasing the reach point values. In May, the hotel's anniversary was celebrated and in December, Christmas and New Year posts were responsible for the high numbers recorded. As seen in Fig. 3, in 2020, the highest reach points were anticipated and expected. January peaked due to New Year; in April, publications regarding the new cocktail bar were intensified; May was the month in which the Bairro Alto Hotel commemorated its anniversary and September was marked by the hotel's reopening. By the end of November, the hotel was closed again and a decrease may be noted.

When comparing both years, 2020 publications are observed to reach more people than 2019, even when LinkedIn is not taken into consideration.

The Bairro Alto Hotel's 2020 interactions may be seen in Fig. 4. In 2019, the highest interaction points occurred throughout April and June, and again in October, which are consistent with the year's recorded reach points. Figure 4 interaction curves are also similar to the reach observed in Fig. 3 during May and September. In April, a new video campaign was launched and that can also be seen in the interactions recorded on all the platforms. A peak in June on Instagram is the result of content published on one of the hotel's USPs—its rooftop.

Comparatively, 2020 was a stronger year for social networking interactions.

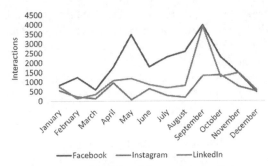

Fig. 4: Hotel's 2020 social network interactions.

The engagement rate behavior in 2019 is noteworthy since consistency on Instagram was not yet observed while on Facebook, from April to December, this rate was steady, albeit lower. If the low peaks of Instagram were not taken into consideration, the engagement rate would be highly similar to that of 2020 with figures around 5 per cent and 10 per cent. Figure 5 shows that the hotel's engagement rate in 2020 was steady throughout the year on LinkedIn. On Facebook, this rate peaked in May, the month of its anniversary and again in October, marking the award season for the hotel. As far as Instagram is concerned, the highest peak (30 per cent) occurred in April due to a video campaign launch. Disregarding the peaks, behavior was very similar.

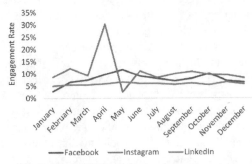

Fig. 5: Hotel's 2020 social network engagement rate.

In comparative terms, the average engagement rate in 2019 was 6 per cent while in 2020 it was 8 per cent.

Given the statistics presented on the Bairro Alto Hotel, the social media performance in 2020 is seen to have improved against 2019, as all the metrics analyzed showed enhanced results. This suggests that as the pandemic became more widespread and time spent on social media increased, resulting in the metric growth recorded.

6. Conclusion

The aim of this chapter is to highlight the importance of a social media digital strategy in the hotel sector. A case study was used to illustrate the importance of analytics in the decision-making process of a five-star hotel located in the centre of Lisbon, Portugal. During this research, the dynamics of the Bairro Alto Hotel on social networks and its performance were analyzed by means of the following metrics: social network followers; interactions; engagement rate and audience reach. Likewise, the content generated by the marketing team to feed the hotel's digital strategy on the website, its newsletter and social networks were also analyzed. This study points to the crucial role of social analytics to improve hotel performance. It clearly shows that despite the pandemic and lockdown, the hotel had better results than in the previous year. Moreover, through the hotel's social media actions, it is possible to identify social media best practices to improve engagement with guests. It is hoped that these best practices may be shared and followed by other hotels with a similar profile—namely, five-star boutique hotels in the city centre.

Covid-19 impacted the worldwide economy more significantly and harshly in some sectors, such as tourism and hospitality. With this reflection, the authors seek to demonstrate how this virus offered an opportunity for a hotel to reorganize and update its online strategy. The successive lockdowns enabled the marketing team to dedicate more time to thinking about its social media plan and improve it. Changes included the abandonment of some social media profiles, such as Twitter and Pinterest, focusing on those with higher return—Facebook, Instagram and LinkedIn. Decisions were made regarding content creation as during this period, more than ever, it was crucial to be present and to be seen online. Creating distinctive content was extremely important for the Bairro Alto Hotel in order to keep loyal guests engaged, reach a broader audience and generate new leads. The content varied from marketeer-generated to user-generated as the latter was more common on Instagram and only posted on special occasions, while experiences, unique photos and videos related to the hotel were shared. On the other hand, marketeer-generated content included hotel awards, recipes of the chef, the hotel's historical heritage, offers and job applications.

The decision to focus on specific social networks in such a difficult period as the pandemic had an important role in diffusing news and content, as confirmed by the social media analytics. The authors were able to verify a positive impact on all the profiles considered as the increased time spent online was responsible for the growth of the metrics analyzed. In addition, 2020 social media achievements were observed to outperform 2019 results. The analysis considered 24 months throughout 2019 and 2020 and the Bairro Alto Hotel was only open for approximately eight of these months, which points to the hotel's resilience and the challenges of creating and adapting social media strategies for two different moments with distinct purposes: Planning for an expected reopening following a long renovation period and planning for a pandemic.

Hopefully this case study will highlight the importance of social media analytics in a digital society and contribute to the innovation of a constantly evolving sector, as is tourism and hospitality, in a society where everyone is connected yet eager for reconnection.

References

Almeida, S. and Campos, A.C. 2020. *Termos nas áreas disciplinares de Marketing.* pp. 428. *In:* Correia, A. and Rodrigues, A. (Eds.). *Turismo e Hospitalidade de A a Z,* 428, Edições Actual, Almedina, Coimbra. ISBN: 9789896945053.

Almeida, S., Ivansecu, Y. and Campos, A.C. 2021. Creating an online brand identity: The case of the hotel. pp. 57–74. *In:* Dinis, G. (Ed.). *Impact of New Media in Tourism, IGI Global.* DOI: 10.4018/978-1-7998-7095-1. ISBN13: 9781799870951.

Bainbridge, W.S. 2007. The scientific research potential of virtual worlds. *Science,* 317(5837): 472–476.

Bairro Alto Hotel (n.d.). Timeline [Facebook page], *Facebook*; retreived from: https://www.facebook.com/BairroAltoHotel.

Bairro Alto Hotel (n.d.). Timeline [LinkedIn Page], *LinkedIn*; retreived from: https://pt.linkedin.com/company/bairro-alto-hotel.

Bairro Alto Hotel [@bairroaltohotel]. (n.d.). Posts [Instagram Profile], *Instagram*; r etrieved from: https://www.instagram.com/bairroaltohotel/?hl=pt.

Bairro Alto Hotel. 2021. Bairro Alto Hotel; retreived from: https://www.bairroaltohotel.com/en/.

Bindra, G.S., Kandwal, K.K., Singh, P.K. and Khanna, S. 2012. Tracing information flow and analyzing the effects of incomplete data in social media. *In: Proceedings of IEEE,* 235–240.

Buffardi, L.E. and Campbell, W.K. 2008. Narcissism and social networking web sites. *Personality and Social Psychology Bulletin,* 34: 1303–1314.

Buhalis, D. and Mamalakis, E. 2015. Social media return on investment and performance evaluation in the hotel industry context. *In:* Tussyadiah and Alessandro Inversini (Eds.). *Information and Communication Technologies in Tourism 2015,* 241–253, Springer, Cham.

Carim, L. and Warwick, C. 2013. Use of social media for corporate communications by research-funding organisations in the UK. *Public Relations Review,* 39(5): 521–525.

Chante, K., Jessica, C., Lindsay, B., Tyler, Q. and Robert, P.D. 2014. Dermatology on instagram. *Dermatology Online Journal,* 20(7): 1–6.

Chen, H., De, P., Hu, Y.J. and Hwang, B.H. 2014. Wisdom of crowds: The value of stock opinions transmitted through social media. *The Review of Financial Studies,* 27(5): 1367–1403.

Chen, S.C. and Lin, C.P. 2019. Understanding the effect of social media marketing activities: The mediation of social identification, perceived value and satisfaction. *Technological Forecasting and Social Change,* 140: 22–32.

Choi, J., Yoon, J., Chung, J., Coh, B.Y. and Lee, J.M. 2020. Social media analytics and business intelligence research: A systematic review. *Information Processing and Management,* 57(6): 102279.

Chung, J.Y. and Buhalis, D. 2008. Information needs in online social networks. *Information Technology and Tourism,* 10(4): 267–281.

Comer, J. 2010. *Marketing with LinkedIn,* Comer Consulting, p. 2011.

Constantinides, E. 2014. Foundations of social media marketing. *Procedia–Social and Behavioral Sciences,* 148: 40–57.

Dai, Y., Kakkonen, T. and Sutinen, E. 2011. SoMEST: A model for detecting competitive intelligence from social media. pp. 241–248. *Proceedings of the 15th International Academic MindTrek Conference: Envisioning Future Media Environments.*

Davis, R., Piven, I. and Breazeale, M. 2014. Conceptualizing the brand in social media community: The five sources model. *Journal of Retailing and Consumer Services,* 21: 468–481. 10.1016/j.jretconser.2014.03.006.

De Bruyn, A. and Lilien, G.L. 2008. A multi-stage model of word-of-mouth influence through viral marketing. *International Journal of Research in Marketing,* 25(3): 151–163.

Dellarocas, C.N. 2003. The Digitization of Word-of-Mouth: Promise and Challenges of Online Feedback Mechanisms; a vailable at: SSRN: https://ssrn.com/abstract=393042 or http://dx.doi.org/10.2139/ssrn.393042.

Dewing, M. 2010. *Social Media: An Introduction* (vol. 1), Ottawa: Library of Parliament.

Facebook. 2019. FAQs, *Facebook Investor Relations*; retrieved from: https://investor.fb.com/resources/default.aspx#:~:text=Founded%20in%202004%2C%20Facebook's%20mission,express%20what%20matters%20to%20them.

Facebook. 2021. Instagram. *Facebook for Business*; retrieved from: https://www.facebook.com/business/marketing/instagram.

Fournier, S. and Avery, J. 2011. The uninvited brand. *Business Horizons*, 54: 193–207. DOI: 10.1016/j.bushor.2011.01.001.

Geurin, A.N. and Burch, L.M. 2017. User-generated branding via social media: An examination of six running brands. *Sport Management Review*, 20(3): 273–284.

Grubmüller, V., Götsch, K. and Krieger, B. 2013. Social media analytics for future oriented policy making. *European Journal of Futures Research*, 1(1): 20.

Hootsuite and We Are Social. 2020. Digital 2020 Global digital overview essential insights into how people around the world use the internet, mobile devices, social media, and e-commerce, *Kepios*: retrieved from: https://datareportal.com/reports/digital-2020-global-digital-overview.

Hootsuite. 2021. *Digital Trends 2021*. Hootsuite; retrieved from: https://www.hootsuite.com/pages/digital-trends-2021.

Instagram. 2021. About Us, *Instagram*; retrieved from: https://www.instagram.com/about/us/.

Jayasingh, S. 2019. Consumer brand engagement in social networking sites and its effect on brand loyalty. *Cogent Business and Management*, 6(1): 1698793.

Jimenez-Marquez, J.L., Gonzalez-Carrasco, I., Lopez-Cuadrado, J.L. and Ruiz-Mezcua, B. 2019. Towards a big data framework for analyzing social media content. *International Journal of Information Management*, 44: 1–12.

Kaplan, A.M. and Haenlein, M. 2010. Users of the world, unite! The challenges and opportunities of Social Media. *Business Horizons*, 53(1): 59–68. Do I: 10.1016/ j.bushor.2009.09.003.

Kusumasondjaja, S. 2018. The roles of message appeals and orientation on social media brand communication effectiveness. *Asia Pacific Journal of Marketing and Logistics*, 30(4): 1135–1158.

Laboy, F. and Torchio, P. 2007. *Web 2.0 for the Travel Marketer and Consumer: A white Paper*. E-site Marketing and the International Association of Online Communicators; r etrieved from: http://www.esitemarketing. com/web2-travel-marketing.php.

Leading Hotels of the World. 2021. *Bairro Alto Hotel*; retrieved from: https://www.lhw.com/hotel/Bairro-Alto-Hotel-Lisbon-Portugal.

Lee, Jung Eun and Youn, Song-Yi. 2020. Luxury marketing in social media: The role of social distance in a craftsmanship video. *Asia-Pacific Journal of Marketing and Logistics*, 10.1108/APJML-09-2019-0551.

Leung, D., Law, R., Van Hoof, H. and Buhalis, D. 2013. Social media in tourism and hospitality: A literature review. *Journal of Travel and Tourism Marketing*, 30(1-2): 3–22.

Lieberman, M. 2014. Visualizing big data: Social network analysis. *In: Digital Research Conference*, 1–23.

LinkedIn. 2021. About LinkedIn. *LinkedIn*; retrieved from: https://about.linkedin.com/.

Litvin, S.W., Goldsmith, R.E. and Pan, B. 2008. Electronic word-of-mouth in hospitality and tourism management. *Tourism Management*, 29(3): 458–468.

Malik, M.N. 2018. A Theoretical Investigation into Instagram Hashtag Practices, Master's thesis. Carleton University, *CURVE*; retrieved from: https://curve.carleton.ca/2289951d-9632-4a84-a77b-bd9a315446ed.

Mayeh, M., Scheepers, R. and Valos, M. 2012. Understanding the role of social media monitoring in generating external intelligence. *In: ACIS 2012: Location, Location, Location: Proceedings of the 23rd Australasian Conference on Information Systems, 2012*, 1–10, ACIS.

Mariani, M. M., Di Felice, M. and Mura, M. 2016. Facebook as a destination marketing tool: Evidence from italian regional destination management organizations. *Tourism Management*, 54: 321–343.

Mehraliyev, F., Choi, Y. and King, B. 2020. Theoretical foundations of social media power in hospitality and tourism: A hierarchical model. *Cornell Hospitality Quarterly*. https://doi.org/10.1177/1938965520924650.

Misirlis, N. and Vlachopoulou, M. 2018. Social media metrics and analytics in marketing—S3M: A mapping literature review. *International Journal of Information Management*, 38(1): 270–276.

Nadeem, W., Andreini, D., Salo, J. and Laukkanen, T. 2015. Engaging consumers online through websites and social media: A gender study of Italian Generation Y clothing consumers. *International Journal of Information Management*, 35(4): 432–442.

Nassar, M.A. 2012. An investigation of hoteliers' attitudes toward the use of social media as a branding tool. *International Journal of Marketing Studies*, 4(4): 93–105. DOI :10.5539/ijms.v4n4p93.

Needles, A. and G.M. Thompson. 2013. Social media use in the restaurant industry: A work in progress. *Cornell Hospitality Report*, 13(7): 6–16.

Nikolaou, I. 2014. Social networking websites in job search and employee recruitment. *International Journal of Selection and Assessment*, 22(2): 179–189.

Paek, H.J., Hove, T., Jung, Y. and Cole, R.T. 2013. Engagement across three social media platforms: An exploratory study of a cause-related PR campaign. *Public Relations Review*, 39(5): 526–533.

Poecze, F., Ebster, C. and Strauss, C. 2018. Social media metrics and sentiment analysis to evaluate the effectiveness of social media posts. *Procedia Computer Science*, 130: 660–666.

Ribarsky, W., Wang, D.X. and Dou, W. 2014. Social media analytics for competitive advantage. *Computers and Graphics*, 38: 328–331.

Romão, M.T., Moro, S., Rita, P. and Ramos, P. 2019. Leveraging a luxury fashion brand through social media. *European Research on Management and Business Economics*, 25(1): 15–22.

Ruzic, D. and Bilos, A. 2010. Social media in destination marketing organization (DMOs). *Tourism and Hospitality Management Conference Proceedings*. Croatia, 178–190.

Shao, G. 2009. Understanding the appeal of user-generated media: A use and gratification perspective. *Internet Research*.

Shieh, H.S. and Lai, W.H. 2017. The relationships among brand experience, brand resonance and brand loyalty in experiential marketing: Evidence from smart phone in Taiwan. *Journal of Economics and Management*, 28: 57–73.

Sigala, M., Christou, E. and Gretzel, U. 2012. *Social Media in Travel, Tourism and Hospitality: Theory, Practice and Cases*, Ashgate Publishing Ltd.

Sigala, M. 2016. Social media and the co-creation of tourism experiences. pp. 85–111. *In*: Sotiriadis, M. and Gursoy, D. (Ed.). *The Handbook of Managing and Marketing Tourism Experiences*. Emerald Group Publishing Limited, Bingley. https://doi.org/10.1108/978-1-78635-290-320161033.

Statista. 2021. Number of monthly active Facebook users worldwide as of 4th quarter 2020, *Statista*; rerieved from https://www.statista.com/statistics/264810/number-of-monthly-active-facebook-users-worldwide/.

Sterne, J. and Scott, M.D. 2010. *Social Media Metrics: How to Measure and Optimize Your Marketing Investment*, Wiley.

Tafesse, W. 2016. An experiential model of consumer engagement in social media. *Journal of Product and Brand Management*, 25(5): 424–434. https://doi.org/10.1108/JPBM-05-2015-0879.

Tafesse, W. and Wien, A. 2017. A framework for categorizing social media posts. *Cogent Business and Management*, 4(1): 1284390.

Tiago, M.T.P.M.B. and Veríssimo, J.M.C. 2014. Digital marketing and social media: Why bother? *Business Horizons*, 57(6): 703–708.

Ting, H., Ming, W.W.P., de Run, E.C. and Choo, S.L.Y. 2015. Beliefs about the use of Instagram: An exploratory study. *International Journal of Business and Innovation*, 2(2): 15–31.

Wang, R. and Huang, Y. 2018. Communicating corporate social responsibility (CSR) on social media: How to message source and type of CSR messages influence stakeholders' perceptions? *Corporate Communications: An International Journal*, 23: 326–341.

Xiang, Z. and Gretzel, U. 2010. Role of social media in online travel information search. *Tourism Management*, 31: 179–188. 10.1016/j.tourman.2009.02.016.

Xie, B., Watkins, I., Golbeck, J. and Huang, M. 2012. Understanding and changing older adults' perceptions and learning of social media. *Educational Gerontology*, 38(4): 282–296.

Yakushev, A. and Mityagin, S. 2014. Social networks mining for analysis and modeling drugs usage. *Procedia Computer Science*, 29: 2462–2471.

Yu, Y., Duan, W. and Cao, Q. 2013. The impact of social and conventional media on firm equity value: A sentiment analysis approach. *Decision Support Systems*, 55(4): 919–926.

Zeng, D., Chen, H., Lusch, R. and Li, S.H. 2010. Social media analytics and intelligence. *IEEE Intelligent Systems*, 25(6): 13–16.

11

Social Networks Mediated by the Internet and Health Care

Carla Piscarreta Damásio[1,*] and *Breno Fontes*[2]

INTRODUCTION

The contribution of this chapter to this collection is part of a very innovative research agenda in the social sciences because it concerns a very recent phenomenon of this century that recently took on a very significant dimension: the increasingly widespread use of social media as a form of communication between people, sometimes replacing processes of interaction that previously, in most cases, were practiced based on the physical presence of the participants. Before the advent of the internet (especially Internet 2.0), communication between people at a distance was possible with some technological resources, such as the telephone or written correspondence. Indeed, they are important resources, but they do not correspond in any way to what was established with the digital revolution: the possibility of connecting people with audio and video resources; connections that are set at a very low cost (and more with access approaching universality, consequently, decreasing the *internet divide*).

This resource is spread over several forms of practices: conversation between friends, home office, interest groups, political platforms, e-commerce. Our argument, which will be the subject of this chapter, is the use of the Internet for the practice of care, whether it is professional (exercised by those enrolled in the field of medical practice), laypeople, or support groups of people who share the suffering caused due to illness (for example, among the many found on the Web, a support group for people with AIDS, transplanted people, people with mental disorders or with an oncological disease). Questions that we ask in a more specialized way, focusing on human health,

---

[1] School of Health Sciences, Polytechnic of Leiria, Portugal.
[2] Research Center on Social Networks and Power, Department of Sociology, Federal University of Pernambuco, Brazil.
Email: brenofontes@gmail.com
* Corresponding author: carla.damasio@ipleiria.pt

and that need more general answers: do the practices of social interaction mediated by the Internet have the same essence as those verified in face-to-face contacts? Does the phenomenon of social networks, a substrate for interactive practices, manifest themselves equally in their structural characteristics in the two reticular spaces? To work on these issues, in addition to the present introduction, we propose to organize the chapter as follows: (1) about social networks; (2) on social networks mediated by the Internet: the dimension of the phenomenon in contemporary times; (3) health, care and support practices based on information support: the example of people with oncological disease (4) conclusion.

1. About Social Networks

A first approximation of the social network phenomenon has been made for some time, based on the discoveries of the mathematician Euler and his Graph Theory. Unraveling a puzzle that has long been popular among mathematicians about the Könisberg bridges, Euler proposes, as a solution to this and other similar problems,[1] a new theory called graph theory, from which it is possible to mathematically formalize the relationship between nodes (in this case, bridges, from their connection to each other. Graph theory allows the understanding of the phenomenon of networks, which, in a simplified way, mean connections between points. These points, now called nodes, can be people, airport terminals, species (animals or plants in a food chain, among others). This way, the science of networks tries to establish general characteristics to this phenomenon, constructing structural indicators that allow us to observe the different types of reticular arrangements. Some authors even argue that the so-called network of science is an essential tool for understanding complex phenomena, of a reticular nature, with universal structuring patterns. Therefore, for example, sociability networks, observable among humans, would have some ingredients like the networks that characterize the metabolic network (Newman, 2010).

Recently, with the use of informatics, it was possible to build more powerful mathematical models, simulating reticular behavior with an important number of actors making it possible to test some hypotheses and reaffirm others. For instance, the idea of the random universe, where the ties were randomly distributed, proposed by the mathematicians Erdós and Rényi, later contested from the use of mathematical modeling using a significant volume of data and with the help of powerful computers. The networks' structure can occasionally behave randomly, giving equal chances to members of a reticular structure to connect with others. Still, there are also positions of actors in the structure that are more favorable to them, giving more chances of greater connections. It is a phenomenon called 'the rich get richer and richer' (the rich-get-richer).[2] Another interesting study, called six degrees of separation, conducted by Watts in the 1960s, in a nutshell, concluded that anyone could connect

---

[1] Euler concludes, for this case, that it is impossible to solve the problem, with the number of existing bridges (or nodes).

[2] Also known as 'power law'. On the subject, consult Barabási (2003). The study of Hungarian mathematicians was later known as random graph theory.

with anyone not known through the intermediation of a maximum of six other people (Milgram, 1967; Travers and Milgram, 1969). This study, initially done with a relatively small number of people, was later replicated aided by statistical modeling, using a considerable amount of information, with success.

The so-called 'Science of Networks' aims to establish a universal understanding of reality, based on a theory anchored on the assumption of complexity; a polysemic expression, but which fundamentally means that reality is only partially understood, based on successive approaches. The so-called Science of Networks[3] aims to establish a universal understanding of reality, based on a theory anchored on the assumption of complexity; a polysemic expression, but which fundamentally means that reality is only partially understood, based on successive approaches. Uncertainty is an ingredient that should not be forgotten among scientists.

The idea of social networks still metaphorically constructed, i.e., without the use of methodological tools developed by mathematicians, reached the social sciences at the beginning of the last century and developed relatively autonomously until the mid-1960s. It does not follow a specific tradition, but works with different fields of theoretical and methodological guidance. Indeed, there are records of important reticular phenomena described in Simmel (such as triads, social circles, homophily); contributions from social psychology, with the development of sociometry in Moreno (1951)[4] and Bott's (1957) famous study of family's contributions of structural anthropology, with the studies of Barnes (1954, 1969).

From the 1970s, research using graph theory and matrix algebra began to be used to investigate human behavior phenomena in society. With the introduction of informatics and software that allows network data processing, it was possible to work with larger databases.[5] Thus begins the time of social network analysis, an important specialty of the social sciences, with applications in sociology, anthropology, communication sciences, public health and epidemiology, among others. Network analysis has two fundamental assumptions: (a) that every phenomenon should be studied not from the attributes of the actors, but from the relationships they establish with others, thus moving away from the still dominant essentialist approach; (b) that the analysis is built from assumptions of a structural nature; i.e., there are reticular designs that impose patterns of behavior. The position of the variable in a network and its unique structure result in predictable patterns of behavior.[6]

For the case of an analysis of social networks, when applied to human behaviors— from the singular actor and his egocentric network to a broader reticular field, such as an organizational space—some important issues must be considered: on the one

---

[3] It's the expression used, for example by Barabási and Albert-Lászsló (2018).

[4] Some claim that Moreno was the one who introduced the graph technique for application in human behavior phenomena, but this thesis is controversial.

[5] Empirical research with reticular data has been carried out before, but with important methodological limitations. Bott's research (1957), for example, reports indices such as density, centrality or homophily, but without the sophistication that current investigations using network software currently achieve.

[6] Let us remember that even considering a structural approach, deterministic rigidity is absent in the analysis of social networks due to the extreme plasticity of its structure. Thousands of actors connected to each other organize a unique structural design, which can be modified at any time from the movement of these members of the network.

hand, the movement of these actors is guided from certain desires for interaction goals—of interest, affection, cooperation or conflict, among others—on the other hand, these objectives and practices of social interaction are inscribed in normative fields and standards of action orientation, depending on the cultural environment where the actors are located.

Thus, social network analysis uses methodological tools that are also used for other scientific disciplines.[7] Still, it necessarily incorporates patterns of human behavior that imply the consideration of normative fields that guide action and subjective considerations of desire and choice in the decision of interactive processes. Although the actor's place in a reticular structure often implies greater or lesser opportunities for action, an individual's role can be an important differential when it comes to interactive practice and achieving the objectives. In this sense, an important literature on social capital,[8] of different theoretical-methodological nuances, points out that people, even located in similar positions in the social structure and having similar reticular fields insertion,[9] search for similar goals in their interactive practices but different results can be achieved. They can mobilize diverse resources, or even build them, from strategically designed interactive practices, privileged positions in the reticular structure, i.e., the fact that they start from the same structural place does not mean that their destiny has already been defined. Individual performance is an important variable.

Some authors claim that relational thinking has spread to other disciplines in social sciences and social network analysis[10] is just a variant of a complex theme of the network phenomenon and the relational content of human behavior. In fact, the reference to the *relational turn* results in a research agenda that privileges methodological perspectives quite different from those traditionally constructed by the social sciences until then. Indeed, as Dépleteau (2018) shows us: "We are talking about questions, such as, should we think in terms of social substances or social processes? Should we rely on dualisms separating objectivism and subjectivism, social structures and agency, or societies and individuals? Should we give causal powers to social structures over individuals and groups? What about the importance of non-human interactions in sociological explanation?" (p.vi) Through this lens, the relational phenomenon is the subject of investigation by different authors in methodological orientations and temporal insertion, such as Tarde and Luhmann, in the example given by Dépleteau.

Thus, assuming that human behavior must be observed from a relational point of view and that it is also not possible to separate the agency from the structure,[11] the reticular analysis of social phenomena uses the social network analysis framework.

---

[7] Newman (2011), for instance, offers examples in the field of neuroscience, ecology, engineering, as well as mathematical experiences.

[8] The literature on social capital is extensive. On the subject, consult Coleman (1990), Bourdieu (2006), Lin (2001).

[9] What network theorists refer to as structural equivalence.

[10] Here understood as the one that makes use of the methodological instruments of graph theory and matrix algebra.

[11] One of the great dilemmas of sociology: Should one understand human behavior from the actions of individuals, or from the context of the social structure where it is located? Consult about: Fontes (2020).

Still, it also does not disregard the ingredients already widely studied by social scientists, indicating that the social phenomenon is, above all, a moral fact.[12]

2. On Social Networks Mediated by the Internet: The Dimension of the Phenomenon in Contemporary Times

Face-to-face interactions are the most complete way for a human being to meet another. Verbal, gestural communication, body posture and the environment where the interaction develops make it possible to have maximum efficiency in communicative practices.[13] But communicative processes are also possible when mediated by other communicative techniques: letters, print media, radio and television; and more recently, the Internet.

The world and people's behavior are constantly and rapidly changing because of connectivity. The expansion of online presence to new regions of the world allows for the development of new opportunities, especially in the qualification of young people from less developed countries, who now have access in a similar way to knowledge and virtual space like any other citizen in a more developed country, allowing the exchange of experiences and knowledge (Ribeiro, 2019). The Internet is the network of all networks (Gaspar, 2005), in which public and private, local and e-global, material and virtual cohabit (Silva, 1999). However, the Internet's communicative power is not yet a reality in some regions of the planet, where access is restricted by the accessibility limitations of important parts of the population. The phenomenon of digital exclusion concerns two orders: (a) the lack of access to Internet networks and to devices (computers, laptops, smartphones), and (b) the existence of poorly developed skills for the use of new technologies. The first point with a strong downward trend, mainly due to the popularization of smartphones and the reduction of costs for access to the network, is still a reality that significantly impacts an important portion of countries in the southern hemisphere. The second point has been observed even among populations that have resources to purchase equipment and pay the tariffs of network operators. Here the difficulties appear among older people, the illiterate and minority ethnic groups (Latinos and Afro-descendants in the United States, migrants of Arab, Pakistani and Turkish origin in Western Europe are examples well cited in the literature).[14]

Whenever we talk about Internet-mediated communications, the first question that arises is about the similarities with face-to-face interactions and the communicative power generated by this important technological innovation. On the one hand, with the emergence of Internet 2.0[15] and with the popularization of the means of access

---

[12] On the subject, consult: Bellah (1973).

[13] Even so, several noises can happen, which cause communication to fail. Merton's (1936) studies on the unintended effects of action are classic. Higgins (2011) makes an interesting review of the subject. On networks and communication theory, consult: Albrecht S. (2008).

[14] On the subject, consult: van Dijk (2017); Scheerder, van Deursen and van Dijk, J. (2017); Sorj and Guedes (2005).

[15] Basically, defined as a resource that allows the sharing of information and the possibility of online communication. Starting in the second half of the 1990s, platforms like Facebook emerged that had considerable effects on the way people interacted via the Net.

to the network, more and more people are making use of this new communication tool. Indeed, according to a survey conducted in 2015 by the Pew Research Center, 65 per cent of Americans made frequent use of Facebook.[16] Facebook proposes connecting friends and consequently expand the possibilities of interaction since physical distance is no longer an obstacle. In fact, it allows you to meet people, re-establish links and exchange information. At this point, there are quite evident convergences with networks anchored in face-to-face interactions. Still, it also has some characteristics that make this vehicle (and similar ones) a unique phenomenon. On the one hand, the expression *friend*, used to qualify Facebook contacts, has a different meaning than that used to describe the people with whom we interact in face-to-face interactions. A friend suggests intimate, long-lasting relationships with a strong affective bond. Research shows the contacts established between people in face-to-face interactions vary from 15 (for friends, people with whom we establish frequent communications) to around a thousand (people with whom we meet and establish some type of communication during our existence). Also, it informs that there is a cognitive limit of approximately 150 people with whom we establish stable social ties, which are kept at the same time (Dunbar, 1993). Therefore, we ascertain that the new media Internet-mediated plays an important role in the reaffirmation of social ties,[17] are also communicative instruments with different interest guidelines (political, cultural, entertainment, academic, among others).

Communication mediated by technology, in this way, allowed the maintenance of relationships that were already physically consolidated, the establishment of new relationships and the potentiation of strong or weak relationships (Antunes et al., 2005). The emergence of smartphones came to allow Internet access to be increasingly 'at hand'. Whether sick or healthy, people use them as an easy, fast and inexpensive source of information. Technological evolution has allowed new forms of interactions, such as the use of voice commands and gestural and touch interfaces, facilitating the inclusion of people with disabilities or with difficulties in using mobile phones.

The network conversation is an emerging dialogue whose fundamental point is the reconstruction of daily practices, expanded with the impact of mediation, bringing new challenges to understanding its influence on social actors (Recuero, 2012).

The changes we are experiencing with the emergence of the pandemic have also brought new communication methods. The world was forced to distance itself, but it looked for proximity strategies, resorting more and more to the video call. Talking is not enough; there is a need to illustrate the words with the image. The Internet, as we realize, profoundly changed communication practices; we can even say that today the use of the Internet becomes an essential activity; it is practically impossible, in the modern world, to fully meet the demands of society without access to communication tools in the digital sphere (and, therefore, the vast information that is made available). This fact runs through almost all activities, including, as we will see below—and the subject of analysis in this chapter—people's healthcare.

---

[16] Consult about it: Bidart et al., 2020.

[17] On this subject, Wellman (1971, 2001) has important contributions.

3. Healthcare and Support Practices based on Informational Support: The Example of People with an Oncological Disease

The practice of care implies a relationship between the people cared for and those who care, whatever the nature of this care is. For a therapeutic relationship, there must be proximity, which has been hampered in the context of a pandemic. On the one hand, tele and video consultations became a practice that was unthinkable in the recent past, but which are not a substitute for face-to-face care, touch, physical examination, and communication without digital interference. Health professionals have been called upon to recreate provision and care. On the other hand, this recreation has shown and made healthcare professionals and users aware of the benefits of these means in situations where physical distance made it impossible for some people to have access to healthcare available only in large urban centers, thus increasing social inclusion.

Information is the key to the person's involvement in health-related issues, whether for adopting healthy behaviors, prevention of disease, their treatment and rehabilitation. Knowledge empowers people to become independent and make decisions about life and, in this case, in relation to health.

The evolution of digital platforms, the ease of use and the availability of care providers for this new reality allows the training of the person for care, as well as for the choice of care appropriate to their condition, allowing care at home and avoiding institutionalization and consequently, also reducing costs. "The great trends that are emerging in the world point to a change in the experience of healthcare consumers, in three very specific directions: the use of methods of analysis in the treatment of health information data; the growth in demand for digital health tools and a very strong focus on analyzing the value of care" (Ribeiro, 2019, p. 60).

The Internet is a prestigious knowledge management tool for health, including civil society in general, health professionals, patients, family people, institutions providing care, the pharmaceutical industry and the scientific community (Pestana, 2010).

Health communities online are becoming increasingly popular among sick people, allowing them to connect with others with similar health problems and access much health-related information (Yan and Tan, 2017). Several forms of support use technology, including tele and video conferencing, and chat-rooms on the Internet, which promotes connections without geographical restrictions (Connel et al., 2006). In the case of blogs, these allow the creation of virtual communities (Amaral et al., 2009), whose subjects enable their authors to add a network around them (Rodrigues, 2004, 2006). Rheingold (1996) defines virtual communities as social aggregates arising on the network when the actors lead a debate with a sufficient number and feelings to form Webs of personal relationships in cyberspace.

Mutual help groups serve their members' interests in promoting a psychological sense of community, group ideology, an opportunity for catharsis and mutual criticism, role models, strategies for solving everyday problems and increased social networks (Levine and Perkins, 1987). In the case of oncology, support groups are recognized for their positive effect on mood disorders, such as anxiety and depression, as well as on the quality of life of patients, marital status and adaptation to the disease (Mikkelsen et al., 2008). In 2005, Im et al. estimated that in the United

States there were more than 400,000 online self-help groups for people with cancer, each with up to 2,065 members.

Olsen and Harder, in 2010, even suggested the concept of network-focused nursing, increasing awareness about non-traditional nursing practices in a hospital context, with potential for implementation in other areas of nursing. Nurses' emerging social role is based on the acceptance that the human being is a network within the entire social network. The reconstruction of nursing knowledge has an inherent responsibility to study patterns and structures that involve networks (Van Sell and Kalofissudis, 2010).

In this sense, Damásio (2019)[18] studied the process of building the mutual aid network throughout the transitions experienced by the person with oncological disease who has a blog.

It was a qualitative study, using Grounded Theory, based on the constructivist assumption (Strauss and Corbin, 2015). The researcher started by identifying people with oncological disease, carried out a structural analysis of the virtual social network (to identify the most active people on the network and identify the people who dominate it) and then went on to study the narrative of the person's blog posts. Identified in the previous phase as more active or dominant in the network and, finally, interviewed the dominant elements of the network to explore aspects that had not been developed in the previous phases, which have also been identified in the physical social network (Damásio, 2019; Damásio, 2020; Damásio and Nunes, 2018; Damásio et al., 2014). In this chapter we will focus on the motivation for creating the blog.

The identified network[19] is composed of 32 blogs, which make connections with people with an oncological disease and with people included in the network [30 individuals (93.7 per cent), two groups (6.25 per cent); 27 female blogs (90 per cent), three male blogs (10 per cent)]. Group blogs are related to individual blogs: blog 28, for integrating seven female participants, one of them also the author of one of the individual blogs; blog 32 represents a theater group and incorporates several authors from the network's individual blogs (Blogs 5, 13, 16, 21, 22, 30). Concerning the geographic location of the bloggers: 29 are in Portugal [distributed by the northern regions (3); Centro (7), Alentejo (2), Lisbon (14) and Algarve (1)], one in Rio de Janeiro, Brazil and one in Luanda (Angola) (Damásio 2019; Damásio, 2020; Damásio et al., 2014).

From the structural analysis of social networks, we resort to the concepts of density, reciprocity, Freeman's measure of centrality (outdegree and indegree), coefficient of variation and ego networks; we highlight that blogs with great potential for influence on the network are (in decreasing order) blogs 3, 13, 21, 7 and 15 (15.635 per cent). Blogs with less potential of network influence, or peripheral, are blogs 6, 11, 18, 24 and 32 (15.625 per cent). The remainder (1, 2, 4, 5, 8, 9, 10,

---

[18] The information explained here is based on the research data reported in the cited text.

[19] The network design represents an empirical section located in a defined virtual space, based on a blog studied in Damásio (2009), between February 26 and July 13, 2013, developed in Damásio et al. (2014). The non-probabilistic, intentional, snowball sampling method was used (Trochim, 2006), identifying the connections with which that person had connections.

12, 14, 16, 17, 19, 20, 22, 23, 25, 26, 27, 28, 29, 30, 31) (68.75 per cent), have an average potential to influence the network. These data reinforced the idea of the ease of circulation of information in this network, using the most influential blogs (3, 13 and 21), with 3 and 13 receiving the most information. Figure 1 shows the graph resulting from the relationship between the actors, carried out using the computer programs UCINET® 6 for Windows®, in Version 6.421 (Borgatti et al., 2002) and Netdraw 2.123® (Borgatti, 2002).

Fig. 1: Graph resulting from the relationship between the actors (*Source*: Damásio et al., 2014, p. 166).

As a result of the social network analysis that was carried out, the collection and analysis of blog posts started on blog 3, with the analysis of more than one blog planned. However, the size and richness of the data led the researcher to decide that the phenomenon would be explained by the analysis of blog 3, which also confirmed its dominance.

The motivations for creating the blog that were identified are the need for information about cancer and registration of experience, after having read other blogs of people in the same situation and computer problems. The need for information about cancer led blogger 3 to search and connect to the blogs of people in a similar situation.

"I created this blog out of necessity to absorb all the information about breast cancer. (...) In my numerous searches on the Net, I found several blogs where I read what I wanted to know because like me now, they were testimonies of life and that was what was looking for successes for me to fight against cancer with more certainty, strength and faith!"

March 2, 2009

This motivation involves the collection and dissemination of information (Baker and Moore, 2011; Baptista, 2004; Canavilhas, 2006; Dan Li, 2005; Kim and Chung, 2007; McKenzie, 2008; Nardi et al., 2004; Schmidt, 2009; Trammel et al., 2004). There was a search for health information (Fox, 2006b). The Internet was essential in this disease situation, attaching great importance to what is found on it (Fox 2006a, 2011). Behind blogging is the expression of emotions (Baker and Moore, 2011; Baptista, 2004; Dan Li, 2005; McKenzie, 2008; Nardi et al., 2004, Trammel et al., 2004) and feelings (Schmidt, 2009), comments and opinions on subjects of interest (Nardi et al., 2004). For this person (Blogger 3), blogging allows people to feel important in the thoughts of others by sharing what they think/feel, the clarification of thoughts and/or emotions, freedom from intense feelings/emotions (McKenzie, 2008), in which the player becomes an actor in the issue, in the production of content and sharing experiences (Lemos, 2009). There is the possibility of sharing information found or not on the Internet (Baptista, 2004), one's self-reflection for the purpose of personal expression (Dan Li, 2005; Pappacharissi, 2004, 2007; Trammel et al., 2004), social interaction (Trammel et al., 2004) with friends and acquaintances (Schmidt, 2009), which has the inherent cooperation for the dialogue to occur properly (Oliveira, 2006).

On the blog analysis and looking at the homepage, there is no evidence of its motivations; however, one can tell that it is either from someone with cancer disease or connected to someone in this situation by what is provided in its blogring (Dan Li, 2005): information on the line cancer, the breast cancer symbol, as well as the links that take us to related websites. There is also a link to blog 32, the theater group's blog.

We are facing the online expression of the disease narrative (Heilferty, 2009). It is a form of identification by diagnosis, also found in the study by Zancheta et al. (2016), as well as the mutual interests that make up the community (Dan Li, 2005; Canavilhas, 2006). Such information leads us to affirm that it is a *disease blog* (Heilferty, 2009), a thematic blog (Cruz and Carvalho, 2006), whose versed content encourages its aggregation in a network (Rodrigues, 2006).

Salvador Vaz da Silva (2008, p. 13), one of the network's bloggers, with the publication of his blog in a book, states his motivation at the beginning of the blog, using humor—"Making my life easier on the one hand, substantially reducing inevitability of writing the same over and over again (yes, the repetition of the word 'same' is purposeful) and making yours difficult, on the other hand (...)". In other words, his motivation is to inform those who care about you without having to repeat it over and over again.

Although not very expressive, it was a remarkable moment as the experience of the disease, associated with a person found by chance in the virtual world of blogs, who introduced her to the rest of the group. This online connection behavior is presented by Fox (2011), who argues that online conversation is driven by the motivation of people living in chronic conditions to connect with each other. Formal and informal connections and relationships are created (Eysenbach, 2008) and established with others who think/feel similarly (McKenzie, 2008; Technorati, 2011). Social ties are established and maintained (Gaspar, 2005; Recuero, 2004a) under singular cousins of common interests (Recuero, 2004a), in which there is an affinity at the level of established social relations (Rodrigues, 2006). The research culminated in readings in online groups, on website s or blogs, looking for others who were in a similar situation to follow his personal friends' health experiences (Fox, 2006a, 2006b, 2011). These cyber contacts were made with people with whom they had never had any social relationship in the physical space (Antunes et al., 2005) and evolved towards developing online friendships (Gaspar, 2005; Giddens, 2007; Schmidt, 2007). In addition to strangers, these relationships are also established with family and friends that are geographically distant (Heilferty, 2009), which in this case includes people from all over the country, Spain, Brazil, and Angola.

It is a virtual community, or a social network created and linked through electronic means (Eysenbach et al., 2004), a new opportunity for communication between ill people (Sullivan, 2003).

Computer problems are mentioned because after the construction of a first blog, there were readers who complained about the difficulty of accessing or commenting on it. Whoever writes wants to be read by someone, looking for visibility, credibility (Rodrigues, 2006), self-expression (Trammel et al., 2004; Dan Li, 2005) and self-promotion (McKenzie, 2008; Baker and Moore, 2011). The difficulty of accessing a blog may be a reason for losing credibility (Ferreira, 2001), nor does it allow connection with others who think similarly or receive feedback on what they publish (McKenzie, 2008), social interaction (Trammel et al., 2004), nor the sharing of his life (Nardi et al., 2004), initial motivations for entering the blog author's blogosphere. The second blog was created along the same lines and with the same purpose as the initial blog, while still having the inaugural blog online, which is extremely important for future memory regarding recording the experience.

"This blog has a great value for me—despite having a lot of pain and suffering it also has messages that I keep here and, in the heart 🖳 this one is not going to be closed. I am going to put something here to be open but I will pass to the other on the wings of an angel."

December 10, 2009

Such expression portrays self-documentation (Dan Li, 2005), chronicles recording of his life (McKenzie, 2008), self-expression (McKinnon, 2001), or documentation of the blog author's life (Nardi et al., 2004) in this period of illness. It can even be considered a logbook of life itself, in which some moments are made known (Silva, 2005). It is a mixed publication in which there is a mix of information with personal comments (Recuero, 2004a; 2004b).

4. Conclusion

The report of people who seek relief from suffering through communication with others who are also suffering, through blogs developed by people with oncologic disease, shows us the power of the Internet as a communication tool. It is a small facet of the phenomenon, but it shows us the centrality of the tools provided by the WWW in our daily lives. Health care actions are among those most recently developed. Among the innumerable initiatives, they are guided by communication networks established between people who are somehow involved with illness: people in distress, family members, specialists. In these different communication platforms (discussion groups, blogs, institutional pages), people get more information, more help and social support in the specific case studied here. Indeed, the suffering resulting from illness is mitigated to the extent that it is shared, with people who offer information, emotional support and even in some cases, support with mobilization of tangible resources like collecting for expenses, help in the care of daily routine, among others.

With the coronavirus pandemic, which affected an important part of the planet for almost the entire year of 2020, which promises to remain in 2021, the practices and care support anchored on the Internet reach a significant density. Perhaps it is now the beginning of a new era, where the Internet's communicative power reaches, definitively, several spheres of sociability, replacing (or representing an ever-increasing portion), including some traditionally anchored in face-to-face communication. Health care is perhaps the most emblematic example.

Acknowledgements

We thank the nurse Daniela Gonçalves, from Royal Infirmary Leicester, University Leicester Hospitals, who, with great promptness, offered to review the English.

References

Albrecht, S. 2008. *Netzwerke und Kommunikation. Zum Verhältnis zweier sozialwissenschaftlicher Paradigmen.* pp. 165–178. *In:* Stegbauer, C. (Eds.). *Netzwerkanalyse und Netzwerktheorie. vs Verlag für Sozialwissenschaften.* https://DOI .org/10.1007/978-3-531-91107-6_12.

Amaral, A., Recuero, R. and Montardo, S. 2009. Blogs: *Mapeando um objeto.* pp. 27–54. *In:* Amaral, A., Recuero, R. and Montardo, S. (Orgs.). *Blogs com Estudos sobre blogs.* São Paulo: Momento Editorial.

Antunes, M.J., Castro, E.A. and Mealha, O. 2005. *Implicações sócio-espaciais das interações online. Livro de Actas – 4º SOPCOM,* 1506-1518. *Biblioteca online de ciências da comunicação – bocc.* http://www.bocc.ubi.pt/pag/antunes-castro-mealha-implicacoes-socio-espaciais-interacoes-on-line. pdf.

Baker, J. and Moore, S. 2011. Creation and validation of the personal blogging style scale. *Cyberpsychology, Behavior and Social Networking,* 14(6): 379–385.

Baptista, J. 2004. *O Fenómeno dos Blogues em Portugal, Estudo realizado no âmbito da minha Tese de Licenciatura em Comunicação Social, no Instituto Superior de Ciências Sociais e Políticas,* http:// seminarioinvestigacao.blogspot.com/.

Barabási, A.-L. 2003. *Linked. How everything is connected to everything else and what it means for business. Science and Everyday Life,* New York: Plume.

Barabási, A.-L. 2018. *Network Science.* Cambridge: Cambridge University Press.

Barnes, J.A. 1954. Class and committees in a norwegian island parish. *Human Relations,* 7(1): 3927–5458. https://DOI .org/10.1177/001872675400700102.

Barnes, J.A. 1969. Graph theory and social networks: a technical comment on connectedness and connectivity. *Sociology,* 3(2): 21527–54232. https://DOI .org/10.1177/003803856900300205.

Bellah, R.N. (Ed.). 1973. *Emile Durkheim: On morality and Society Selected Writings,* edited and with an Introduction by Robert Bellah, Chicago: The University of Chicago Press.

Bidart, C., Degenne, A. and Grossetti, M. 2020. *Living in Networks: The Dynamics of Social Relations (Structural Analysis in the Social Sciences),* Cambridge: Cambridge University Press. https:// DOI:10.1017/9781108882392.

Borgatti et al. 2002.

Bott, E. 1957. *Family and Social Network,* London: Tavistock.

Bourdieu, P. 2006. *1. Le capital social. Notes provisoires.* pp. 29–34. *In:* Bevort, A. (Ed.). *Le capital social: Performance, équité et réciprocité.* Paris: La Découverte. https://DOI.org/10.3917/dec. bevor.2006.01.0029.

Canavilhas, J. 2006. *Blogues Políticos em Portugal: O dispositivo criou novos atores?* http://www. labcom.ubi.pt/files/agoranet/06/canavilhas_bloguespoliticosportugal.pdf.

Coleman, J. 1990. *Foundations of Social Theory.* Cambridge: MA, Harvard University Press.

Connel, S., Patterson, C. and Newman, B. 2006. Issues and concerns of young Australian women with breast cancer: Supportive Care in Cancer. *Official Journal of the Multinational Association of Supportive Care in Cancer*, 14(5): 419–426.

Cruz, S. and Carvalho, A. 2006. *Weblog como Complemento ao Ensino Presencial no 2º e 3º Ciclos do Ensino Básico. Revista Prisma.com – Revista de Ciências da Informação e da Comunicação do* CETAC, 64–87.

Damásio, C., Nunes, L. and Sobral, J.M. 2014. *A análise de redes sociais no estudo do processo da construção da ajuda mútua da pessoa com doença oncológica com blogue, Redes – revista hispana para el análisis de redes sociales*, 25(1): 153–189.

Damásio, C.P. and Nunes, L. 2018. *Blogues em caso de doença oncológica: efeitos da rede social na pessoa e na sociedade.* pp. 28–48. *In:* Fialho, J., Baltazar, M.S., Saragoça, J., Santos, M.O.S. (Orgs.). *Livro de Atas. CIReS. 2º Congresso Internacional de Redes Sociais. Redes Sociais: perspetivas e desafios emergentes nas sociedades contemporâneas.* Évora: CICS.NOVA – Centro Interdisciplinar de Ciências Sociais. http://www.cires.uevora.pt/livro_Atas_2cires2018.pdf.

Damásio, C.P. 2020. *Capítulo 17. A formação de uma rede de ajuda mútua de pessoas com doença oncológica. In:* Fialho, J. (Org.). *Redes Sociais. Como compreendê-las? Uma introdução à análise de redes sociais*, 337–355, Lisboa: Edições Sílabo.

Damásio, C.S.S.P. 2009. '*Blogue': Uma nova forma de ajuda mútua da pessoa com doença oncológica*; work carried out to apply for the public exam tender for the recruitment of two places for assistant professor, for the scientific area of Nursing Sciences at School of Health Sciences, Polytechnic Institute of Leiria, according to *Edita jl nº* 540/2009, published in the *Diário da República, 2nd Série, Nr 102*, of 27 of May, 21219–21220.

Damásio, C.S.S.P. 2019. *Do Blogue à Rede de Ajuda Mútua, Processo de Construção ao longo das transições da pessoa com doença oncológica*, doctoral thesis in Nursing. University of Lisbon, Lisbon. http://hdl.handle.net/10451/38933.

Dan Li, B.A. 2005. Why do you blog: A uses-and-gratification inquiry into bloggers' motivations, thesis submitted to the Faculty of the Graduate School, Marquette University, in *Partial Requirements for the Degree of Master of Arts*. https://commonsenseblog.typepad.com/common_sense/files/Li_Dan_Aug_2005.pdf.

Dépleteau, F. 2018. Relational thinking in sociology: relevance, concurrence and dissonance. pp. 03–35. *In:* Dépleteau, François (Éd.). *The Palgrave Handbook of Relational Sociology*, Cham (Ch) Palgrave, Macmillan. DOI: 10.1007/978-3-319-66005-9.

Dunbar, R. 1993. Coevolution of neocortical size, group size and language in humans. *Behavioral and Brain Sciences*, 16(4): 681–694. DOI:10.1017/S0140525X00032325.

Eysenbach, G., Powell, J., Englesakis, M., Rizo, C. and Stern, A. 2004. Health-related virtual communities and electronic support groups: systematic review of the effects of online peer to peer interactions. *BMJ*, 328: 1166–1172.

Eysenbach, G. 2008. Medicine 2.0: Social networking, collaboration, participation, apomediation, and openness. *Journal of Medical Internet Research*, 10(3): e22.

Ferreira, I. 2001. *Retórica na época da* Internet. http://www.bocc.ubi.pt/pag/ferreira-ivone-retorica-internet.pdf.

Fontes, B.A.S.M. 2020. *A singularidade da análise reticular: Entre a ação e a estrutura.* pp. 47–61. *In:* Fialho, J. (Org.). *Redes Sociais. Como compreendê-las?* 47-61, Lisboa: Editora Sílabo.

Fox, S. 2006a. *Finding Answers Online in Sickness and in Health.* https://www.pewresearch.org/internet/PPF/r/183/report_display.asp.

Fox, S. 2006b. *Online Health Search, 2006*: Most internet users start at a search engine when looking for health information online. Very few check the source and date of the information they find. https://www.pewresearch.org/internet/PPF/r/190/report_display.asp.

Fox, S. 2011. *The Social Life of Health Information, 2011.* Pew Internet & American Life Project. https://www.pewresearch.org/internet/files/old-media/Files/Reports/2011/PIP_Social_Life_of_Health_Info.pdf.

Gaspar, A.F. 2005. *O blogue e a sua dimensão organizacional, Análise de um objeto empírico.* http://www.bocc.ubi.pt/pag/gaspar-ana-blogue-dimensao-organizacional.pdf.

Giddens, A. 2007. *Sociologia* (5th ed.), *Lisboa: Fundação Calouste Gulbenkian*.

Heilferty, C.M. 2009. Toward a theory of online communication in illness: Concept analysis of illness blogs. *Journal of Advanced Nursing*, 65(7): 1539–1547.

Higgins, S.S. 2011. *O estudo dos efeitos não intencionais da ação intencional na teoria sociológica, Sociologias, Porto Alegre*, 28(set./dez. 2011): 258–282.

Im, E.O., Chee, W., Tsai, H.M., Lin, L.C. and Cheng, C.Y. 2005. Internet cancer support groups. A feminist analysis. *Cancer Nursing*, 28(1): 1–7.

Kim, S. and Chung, D.S. 2007. Characteristics of cancer blog users. *Journal of the Medical Library Association*, 95(5): 445–450.

Lemos, A. 2009. Prefácio. pp. 7–20. *In*: Amaral, A., Recuero, R. and Montardo (Orgs). *Blogs.com Estudos sobre blogs e comunicação*. São Paulo: Momento Editorial.

Levine, M. and Perkins, D. 1987. *Principles of Community Psychology – Perspectives and Applications*, New Jersey: Oxford University Press.

Lin, N. 2001. *Social Capital: A Theory of Social Structure and Action (Structural Analysis in the Social Sciences)*. Cambridge: Cambridge University Press. DOI:10.1017/CBO9780511815447.

McKenzie, H. 2008. *Why Blogging? Motivations for Adults in the United States to Maintain a Personal Journal*. Blog, thesis submitted to the Graduate Faculty of North Carolina State University in partial fulfilment of the requirements for the Degree of Master of Science. https://repository.lib.ncsu.edu/bitstream/handle/1840.16/2825/final.pdf?sequence=1&isAllowed=y.

McKinnon, M. 2001. King of the Blogs, *Shift Summer*, 64–69.

Merton, R. 1936. The unanticipated consequences of purposive social action. *American Sociological Review*, 1(6): 894–904; retrieved on March 17, 2021. http://www.jstor.org/stable/2084615.

Mikkelsen, T., Sondergaard, J., Jensen, A. and Olensen, F. 2008. Cancer rehabilitation: Psychosocial rehabilitation needs after discharge from hospital? *Scandinavian Journal of Primary Health Care*, 26(4): 216–221.

Milgram, S. 1967. The small world problem. *Psychology Today*, 1(1): 61–67.

Moreno, J.L. 1951. *Sociometry, Experimental Method and the Science of Society: An Approach to a New Political Orientation*, Beacon, N.Y: Beacon House.

Nardi, B.A., Schiano, D.J., Gumbrecht, M. and Schwartz, L. 2004. *Why we blog. Communication of the ACM*, 47(12): 41–46.

Newman, M. 2010-03-25. *Networks: An Introduction*, Oxford University Press. https://oxford.universitypressscholarship.com/view/10.1093/acprof:oso/9780199206650.001.0001/acprof-9780199206650.

Oliveira, J.A. 2006. *A Intenção na Internet*. http://www.bocc.ubi.pt/pag/oliveira-jair-intencao-internet.pdf.

Olsen, P.R. and Harder, I. 2010. Network-focused nursing: Development of a new concept. *Advances in Nursing Science*, 33(4): 272–284.

Pestana, S.E.F.S.C. 2010. *Saúde Web 2.0 – O papel das comunidades virtuais de doentes na área da saúde: Um Estudo de Caso para Portugal*. Master's dissertation in Statistics and Information Management, New University of, Higher Institute of Statistics and Information Management, Lisbon. https://run.unl.pt/bitstream/10362/5369/1/TEGI0272.pdf.

Recuero, R.C. 2004a. *Redes sociais na Internet: Considerações Iniciais*. http://bocc.ubi.pt/pag/recuero-raquel-redes-sociais-na-internet.pdf.

Recuero, R.C. 2004b. *Weblogs, webrings e comunidades virtuais*. http://www.bocc.ubi.pt/pag/recuero-raquel-weblogs-webrings-comunidades-virtuais.pdf.

Recuero, R. 2012. *A conversação em rede Comunicação mediada pelo computador e redes sociais na Internet*, Porto Alegre: Sulina.

Ribeiro, J.M. 2019. *Saúde digital. Um sistema de saúde para o século XXI*. Lisboa: Fundação Francisco Manuel dos Santos.

Rheingold, H. 1996. *Comunidade Virtual*. Lisboa: Gradiva.

Rodrigues, C. 2004. *Blogs: uma Ágora na Net*. http://www.labcom.ubi.pt/agoranet/04/rodrigues-catarina-blogs-agora-na-net.pdf.

Rodrigues, C. 2006. *Blogs e a fragmentação do espaço público*, Covilhã: Livros LabCom.

Scheerder, A., van Deursen, A. and Van Dijk, J. 2017. Determinants of Internet skills, uses and outcomes. A systematic review of the second- and third-level digital divide. *Telematics and Informatics*, 34(8): 1607–1624. DOI : 10.1016/j.tele.2017.07.007.

Schmidt, J. 2007. Blogging practices: An analytical framework. *Journal of Computer-mediated Communication*, 12(4): 1409–1427.

Silva, H.N. 2005. *Blogues, Experiência Portuguesa.* http://blog.lisbonlab.com/estudos/blogues-experiencia-portuguesa/.

Silva, M.J.L. 2002. *Perspetivas Weberianas da Sociedade Rede.* http://www.bocc.ubi.pt/pag/silva-lopes-perspectivas-weberianas.pdf.

Sorj, B. and Guedes, L.E. 2005. *Exclusão digital: Problemas conceituais, evidências empíricas e políticas públicas, Novos estudos CEBRAP,* 72: 101–117. https://DOI .org/10.1590/S0101-33002005000200006.

Strauss, A. and Corbin, J. 2015. *Basics of Qualitative Research: Techniques and Procedures for Developing Grounded Theory,* 4th ed., Thousand Oaks CA: Sage.

Sullivan, C. 2003. Gendered cybersupport: A thematic analysis of two online cancer support groups. *Journal of Health Psychology,* 8(1): 83–103.

Technorati. 2011. State of the Blogosphere 2011. http://technorati.com/state-of-the-blogosphere-2011/.

Trammel, K.D., Tarkowski, A. and Hofmokl, J. 2004. *Rzeczpopspolita blogów: Identigfying the Uses and Gratifications of Polish Bloggers.* Paper presented at the meeting of the Association of Internet Researchers Annual Conference, Brighton, United Kingdom, 19–22 September 2004. https://gsb.haifa.ac.il/~sheizaf/AOIR5/199.html.

Travers, J. and Milgram, S. 1969. An experimental study of the small world problem. *Sociometry,* 32(4, Dec. 1969): 425–443.

Trochim, W. 2006. Research Methods. Knowledge Base. *In:* http://www.socialresearchmethods.net/kb/index.php.

Van Dijk, J.A. 2017. Digital divide: Impact of access. *In:* Rösslerhe, P. (Ed.). *International Encyclopedia of Media Effects.* Wiley. Ihttps://DOI .org/10.1002/9781118783764.wbieme0043.

Van Sell, S.L. and Kalofissudis, I. 2010. *The Evolving of the Science of Nursing: A complexity Integration Nursing Theory,* 2nd ed., Chania, Crete Greece: The Authors.

Watts, D. 2003. *Six Degrees. The Science of a Connected Age.* New-Yourk: W.W. Norton & Company.

Wellman, B. 1979. The community question: The intimate networks of east yorkers. *American Journal of Sociology,* 84(5): 1201–1231.

Wellman, B. 2001. Computer networks as social networks. *Science,* 293(5537): 2031–2034.

Yan, L. and Tan, Y. 2017. The consensus effect in online healthcare communities. *Journal of Management Informations Systems,* 34(1): 11–39.

Zancheta, M.S., Cognet, M., Lam-Kin-Teng, M.R., Dumitriu, M.E., Renaud, L. and Rhéaume, J. 2016. From early detection to rehabilitation in the community: Reading beyond the blog testimonies of survivors' quality of life and prostate cancer representation. *Health and Quality of Life Outcomes,* 15(1): 171.

12

Social Analytics Influencing KOLs Profiling in the Dissemination of Innovations and Scientific Knowledge in the Life Sciences Industry

António Pesqueira[1],* and *Maria José Sousa*[2]

INTRODUCTION

In the life sciences industry, social media analytics are strategic to medical and commercial activities where key opinion leaders (KOL) assume a fundamental role in using new technologies for innovation dissemination and scientific knowledge. A focus group study was conducted to investigate how social media has been used to support decision-makers in life sciences organizations and in various areas (Fakharaei et al., 2015).

Using social analytics can benefit managers, doctors and other health professionals in the decision-making process, as is demonstrated by the literature that shows that organizations have successfully implemented analytics tools and are able to make more accurate decisions. Additionally, KOLs require better and faster access to key information, since the literature also indicates that they can influence the decisions of stakeholders in the pharmaceutical industry and the healthcare sector. Information that is required for decision making about the health industry is complex and tools such as social analytics may be able to help gather, organize and visualize it, as well as predict business results, customers' behaviors and to disseminate the most important innovations (Haataja, 2011).

The literature review was conducted to obtain a more in-depth understanding of the context in which KOLs develop their activities. In addition, a focus group of practitioners was conducted to cultivate a better understanding of how digital

---
[1] Bavarian Nordic A/S, Switzerland.
[2] Instituto Universitário de Lisboa, Portugal.
   Email: maria.jose.sousa@iscte-iul.pt
* Corresponding author: ampe@bavarian-nordic.com

environments and social analytics herald a new era in the life sciences industry and how new technologies are pushing new trends. Taking this into account, the present work consists of three parts: the methods, systematic literature review and results of the focus group, followed by the conclusion.

1. Methodology

This paper includes a methodology with two steps: the first step is a bibliometric analysis to identify the main trends in research published in journals, indexed in the Scopus database. The search was made using the key words 'Key opinion leaders' or 'KOLs'. And the results of the search were exported to the bibliographic management software EndNoteWeb, in order to analyze the temporal distribution; leading authors, institutions and countries; type of publication in the area, keywords and the most cited papers.

This type of analysis gives a visualization of the global image of scientific production, and, in this case, the goal was to respond to the following research question: Which are the main research topics studied regarding the role of KOLs in communicating innovations and scientific knowledge regarding the health sector?

The second step of the methodology used in this paper was to focus group interviews with 45 life sciences professionals during the first three months of 2021, with the goal to understand the role of KOLs in the dissemination of innovations and scientific knowledge.

2. Bibliometric Analysis

The bibliometric analysis performed was based on a search made on Scopus database using as main criteria the keywords 'Key opinion leaders' or 'KOLs'. The number of papers that resulted from the search was 503, in the period of 1991 to 2001.

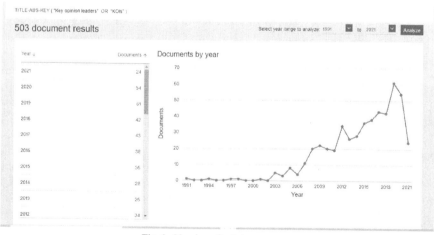

Fig. 1: Number of articles per year.

Regarding the authors, the results show that there several main authors with innumerous papers in this field, with Claassen, E. being the most prominent author, with more than 10 articles of reference published and indexed in Scopus.

Analyze search results

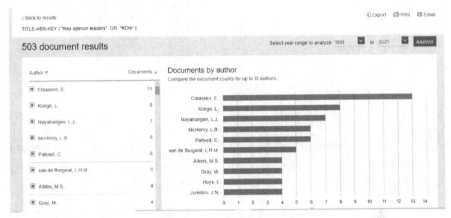

Fig. 2: Number of articles per author.

Among these authors, there are several of them who published together and this can be seen in the following figure representing the network of authors:

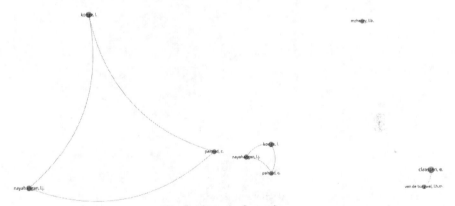

Fig. 3: Network of co-authors.

In respect to affiliations, authors from European universities are the most representative in researching the topic of key opinion leaders. However, the University of Toronto assumes the first position in this rank, with the University of California, San Francisco also acquiring a very high position in this research field.

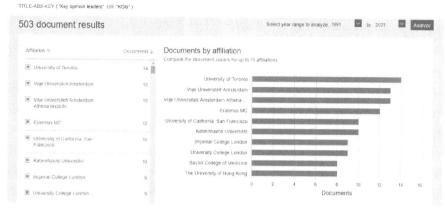

Fig. 4: Authors' affiliation.

The main type of publications of the articles searched are scientific articles (302), followed by reviews (70) and conference papers (61).

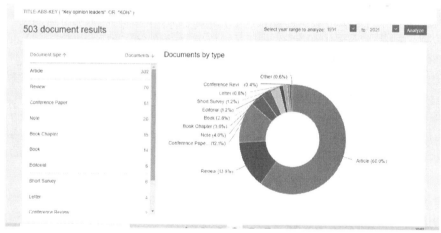

Fig. 5: Type of publications.

The most relevant field of the publication of articles that resulted from the search are medicine (362), biochemistry (60), pharmacology (51) and social sciences (46). This last one is surprising, as KOLs are normally associated with the health sector, as well as in fields of marketing and communication. However, more and more, the multidisciplinarity of the research in several fields, even in medicine and complementary disciplines, is emerging as a trend in contemporary research.

Regarding the keywords that indicate the main research topics claiming the researcher's attention and interest, it is possible to verify that, with regards to key opinion leaders, the pharmaceutical industry, clinical trials and social media are those with more relevance (Fig. 7).

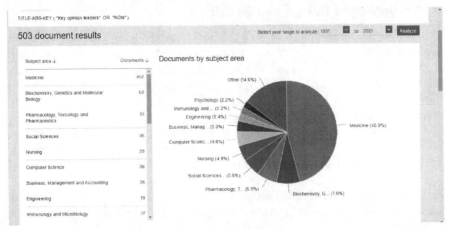

Fig. 6: Field of the publications.

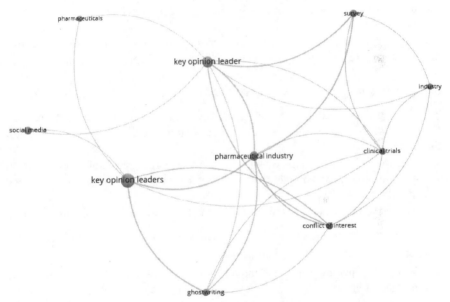

Fig. 7: Keywords.

The visualization of research over the last few decades shows that the theme of key opinion leaders has always assumed a higher importance, according to the number of publications in US and Europe, and also in other regions of the world. This is a consequence of the influence that KOLs exert in the way innovations and scientific knowledge of the health sector, and specifically in the pharma industry, are communicated and disseminated through digital and other channels directly, with social analytics being important tools that are used to convey accurate information to different stakeholders, as we can see in the following sections of this chapter.

3. Focus Group Design and Results

During the first three months of the year, we conducted focus groups with 45 life sciences professionals. In these interviews, we asked many different questions to learn all the participants' knowledge and experience of the authors. This worked in better understanding of the underlying research questions. Since the focus group participants represent industry leaders in leadership positions, their names cannot be disclosed to ensure anonymity (Morgan, 1997).

It was intended for the focus group study to explore how social media had been applied in the mentioned industries and how social media analytics are relevant to life sciences companies and decision makers from a variety of perspectives.

The study involved several focus group interviews with 45 participants, from 10 different countries, representing different industry leadership positions and roles, as well as contributors from the three major organizational areas: sales, marketing and medical affairs.

We conducted all focus groups in digital channels via Zoom or Microsoft Teams video conference technology, in January, February and March 2021.

Data sources, processes, use cases and metrics were the four major topics discussed in the focus group. By reviewing previous literature reviews and identifying areas that were relevant to the interview sessions, these topics were identified.

3.1 Participant Selection and Questions

The focus group participants were selected according to pre-defined criteria: role, topics knowledge, experience, processes understanding and availability to be part of the study.

One of the key objectives was to have a good representation of pharmaceutical and biotechnology professionals and experts, with practical experience in the selected topics and domains.

The participants (n=45) were selected from the following job positions and roles:

- Sales, marketing and medical affairs managers, directors and vice presidents.
- Commercial operations and digital project managers and directors.
- Marketing operations analysts and business leaders and local affiliated sales and marketing directors.

We conducted a total of 18 online and remote sessions using the Zoom and Microsoft teams, starting from January 6 to 11 March, 2021. The participants were selected and sorted into small groups with similar expertise and responsibilities, to create a more comfortable and harmonized environment in the sessions and allowing for deeper peer-to-peer discussions. The sessions were 60 minutes in length and PowerPoint presentations were used to facilitate and manage the interviews, to better steer the participants into the desired outcomes in terms of quality and quantity of valid comments and observations to the study (Rabiee, 2004).

3.2 Research Objectives

Using a focus group and literature review methodology, this paper discusses the different social media analytics approaches used during the past few years. This research paper aims to identify and describe how social media analytics is used to generate insights that support scientific knowledge and disseminate innovation across multiple strategic processes within life sciences, such as key opinion leader identification, profiling and tiering.

As this study aims to learn how social media analytics and decision-making processes interrelate, the research question aims to determine how these two processes interact and determine whether these two processes are compatible and if media analytics has an influence and connection to the described process area.

In this research paper, we will also be exploring the examples and practicalities of social media analytics in relation to life sciences, and better understanding which topics and subtopics are most relevant for our chosen area, as well as how to create and distribute knowledge through social media analytics.

The graphic below illustrates the study structure in an illustrative way.

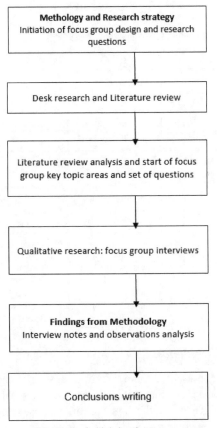

Fig. 8: Study high-level structure.

The focus group study consisted of a total of 12 related focus group questions that were grouped into four key topic areas.

The focus group study design was developed through a collective set of observations and conclusions from the previously presented literature review. The process was validated with a sub-set of the selected participants and experts in the selected area, where the overall design was discussed, including samples of the questions and topics collected from the literature review.

To simplify the data collection process and maintain consistency in the design and implementation phase of the focus group study, the authors produced a simple roadmap and processual interview 'script' to facilitate and support the management of all interviews with the 45 participants.

Also, other detailed documents were produced and applied, which included invitation letters to all participants, letters of information of data privacy and participants' identity protection, consent form, introductory PowerPoint slides for the interview and a moderator guide (including ranking exercise templates and topic questions).

In the following table, we can also observe in more detail what were the steps and activities performed during the different study phases (Table 1).

Table 1: Methodology phases and phases.

	Phase I	**Phase II**	**Phase III**	**Phase IV**
Planning for analysis	• Defined research and analysis group. • Choose a recording method.	• Targeted the desired outcomes and analysis methodology.	• Developed the focus group questions.	• Research timeline, objectives, and resources.
Information collection and interpretation	• Review recorded sessions and collected notes.	• Debrief with focus group and follow up questions	• Start of analysis from collected notes and audio sessions.	• Qualification of initial collected observations for consistency and quality assessments.
Conclusions	• Group-interview observations and analysis.	• Groups discussions and additional points analysis and interpretation.	• Assessment of research questions answered during interview sessions.	• Conclusion's completion and recommendations.

3.3 Risk and Inconveniences

This focus group study presented some risks of discovering sensitive and confidential information, for instance, concerning commercial or medical practices, or specific metrics and key performance indicators that might pose specific competition and confidential information concerns.

In the focus group introduction and debriefing, the focus group facilitators emphasized that participants would have all the necessary time to review all of the collected notes and observations from the focus group interviews, and, in case of any correction or inconveniences, the facilitator and moderator would avoid and remove all potential risks.

Some such situations and risks occurred during the study and, to protect the identity of the participants and respective working organizations, it was previously decided in the focus group sessions that all organizations, diseases, products and participants' names would not be referred to and would, therefore, be retracted. The participants were also informed about these matters in the informed consent form, whereby the participants agreed to maintain the confidentiality of the information discussed by all participants and researchers during the focus group session.

3.4 Composition of Focus Groups

In addition to composing the focus groups based on their main area of research, the composition strategy also entailed an orientation towards the practical usage and application approaches in terms of how social media analytics are used in the pharmaceutical and biotechnology business spaces and for what purposes. The following outline shows the division of groups according to these sampling and topics criteria:

a) One focus group was based on data and technical organizational capabilities and connected processes: areas like data tracking, social media metrics monitoring, data analysis, systems, and tools.

b) Other groups included all relevant professionals from a more holistic and strategic perspective in terms of business development, commercial excellence and digital strategy.

c) The third group was based on people and human resources perspectives in terms of employees and organizational functions skills and competencies to develop social media analytics.

d) The fourth group consisted of professionals from medical science and medical affairs (including clinical operations) to allow a more scientific and medical application usage of social media analytics and its purposes and use cases.

In the following points, we can understand and observe the different overviews of participants in the social sciences focus group interviews.

3.5 Interview Design

During the focus group interview sessions, the aim was to secure data that could answer the research questions most precisely and effectively, confirm empirical and contextual assumptions and be useful for academics. We intended that the interviews would enrich previous understandings with new insights, observations and knowledge as well as provide context and substantial importance.

With a focus on social media analytics in the pharmaceutical industry, the interview questions were organized as exploratory and open-ended questions.

The list of topics selected for the sessions was qualified and characterized by each focus group while some also ordered the topics according to the information and

Table 2: Overview of participants in the social sciences focus group interviews.

Focus Group Number	Disciplines Represented	Topics for In-depth Discussion	Stakeholders Titles Represented	Country	Online Interview	Number of Participants
1	Information Technology Systems management Digital Commercial and Marketing operations	Data and technical organizational capabilities	Head/Global Head of IT (2 stakeholders) Vice President and Head Commercial Excellence (3 stakeholders) Digital Manager (4 stakeholders) Global Head of IT (2 stakeholders)	Sweden Switzerland US Canada Spain	4 Interviews using Zoom and Microsoft Teams	11
2	Commercial Excellence Sales Management Marketing Market Access Training and learning development Business Development	Business development, commercial excellence, and digital strategy	Member of executive management team Marketing Head Sales Director Commercial Operations Key Account Manager	Italy Switzerland Germany UK US	5 Interviews using Zoom	12
3	Human Resources Business Development Training and learning development Digital Commercial and Marketing operations Analytics and Digital	Organizational skills and competencies	Marketing Head Sales Director Commercial Operations HR Head HR Manager HR/People management Vice President	US Switzerland UK France Belgium Singapore	4 interviews with Microsoft Teams	10
4	Medical Affairs Clinical Operations and management Global processes management Analytics Digital	Scientific and medical application usage of social media analytics	Medical Affairs Vice President Medical Affairs Systems and Processes Head Medical Affairs Manager Clinical Operations Head Regulatory and Compliance manager	Switzerland US UK France	5 interviews with Microsoft Teams	12

Table 3: Overview of key topic areas and questions.

Key Topic Area	Question
1. Data and technical organizational capabilities	a. Can you please describe the data sets, data points, and sources for your social media analytics processes? b. Please provide us an overview of the used systems and tools and use cases examples. c. Which processes and decisions are your social media analytics being able to support?
2. Business development, commercial excellence, and digital strategy	a. Currently, what are the processes that are being supported with social media analytics techniques and data? b. Is your organization currently using social media analytics for specific digital and business development metrics? c. What are the systems and tools being used for social media analytics?
3. Organizational skills and competencies	a. What are the most relevant organizational competencies and skills in performing social media analytics? b. What was the investment made in people skills and competencies to improve the quality of social media analytics? c. What are the most relevant individual skills and competencies when performing social media analytics?
4. Scientific and medical application usage of social media analytics	a. How are medical affairs and clinical operations using social media data? b. What the use cases for social media analytics in medical and clinical contexts? c. Currently, social media is being used to perform key opinion leader's identification, tiering, and profiling?

experience within the topic and provided the facilitator with all the needed details. The following table provides an overview of key topics and questions addressed during the focus groups.

The following sub-section explores how the answers to the above questions were presented, the key insights from the focus group interviews and the key discussion topics.

3.6 Focus Group Key Topic Areas, Key Takeaways and Raised Points

Through the focus group interviews, we explored the questions' knowledge areas to increase our understanding of how social media analytics may foster and advance business practices, disseminate innovation and support strategic processes like key opinion leaders' (KOLs) profiling and many others.

The following analysis draws on the transcripts of the four focus groups. The participants in these groups discussed and prioritized several different topics and a select number of topics were discussed in-depth, as shown in the tables below. The results of these discussions were addressed in the following sub-sections topic-wise and summarized in separate displays.

Data and technical organizational capabilities focus group interviews

Table 4: Focus group interview sessions topics/subtopics, key takeaways and additional raised points.

Topic/Subtopics	Key Takeaways	Additional Raised Points
Question 1: Data sets, data points, and sources	• Social media can provide a wide range of information critical to the organizations with some examples in customer listening and competitor's information gathering. • Social media listening is being incorporated into brand strategy plans and market landscapes – oncology. • Hootsuite and salesforce.com social studio is used in rare diseases, vaccines, and big pharma contexts to better understand relevant stakeholders profiles and support some events management activities— invitations and speaker selection for preceptorship, speaker programs, and congresses. • In the diabetes, cardiology, and dermatology units, social media is being used by marketing and some local affiliates or local operating countries to find KOLs influencers, medical speakers and discover insights that could lead to new market opportunities and to understanding some of the competitors positioning. • Social media insights are produced in ad-hoc reports and not using structured data feeds or systematic internal tracking methods. • Most of the access is done via external or third party providers tools and data not being incorporated into corporate data warehouses or data lakes structures.	• Its departments are considering more systematic approaches like social listening APIs connections with public data sources like Twitter, PubMed, ResearchGate, and LinkedIn. • Sentiment analysis and opinions related to products or brands are extremely important to be tracked and currently, only marketing is adding those insights and inputs into the brand plans and some competitive intelligence analysis. • Most relevant analysis methods: statistical from social media content, social networks, sentiment, trend, and digital content. • Tracking sources: Twitter, Facebook, Instagram, specific medical websites and Weblogs. • Tracking methods: most frequent are external providers and system access via browser but also APIs and HTML parsing. • Tracking approaches: keywords, topic-based and explorative URLs.
Question 2: Examples	• Some examples of data analysis are automated content analysis, trend analysis, and sentiments tracking. • Multichannel and commercial excellence typically provide available reports and analysis to business decision-makers and provide regular updates in some of the cases—mainly from Big Pharma. • Some relevant metrics examples: reach, velocity of reach, share of voice, sentiment index, net promoter scoring, loyalty, and innovation track.	• Analysis purposes: reputation, brands and products, and influencers management. • General monitoring or social media applied to clinical and medical contexts are also applied. • Social media segmentation—currently already several companies are performing segmentation via social media data and information for influencers, recommenders, detractors, prospective speakers based on geographic, content, involvement in communities or societies with also demographics information.

Question 3: Processes and decisions	• Social media currently supports already several processes areas like the ones we describe below:
	  o Sales processes: segmentation, profiling, competitive intelligence, surveys management, multichannel strategy definition, incentive compensation schemes.
	  o Key Account Management: key accounts plan management, accounts prioritization and ranking, and sales progress monitoring.
	  o Marketing: brand plan development, digital campaigns, and events management.
	  o Medical: medical inquiries and medical communities raised concerns about management and medical events and meetings management.
		• Most of the access is done via external or third party providers' tools and data not being incorporated into corporate data warehouses or data lakes structures.
		• The major concept of social media and web monitoring lies on top of having sporadic or sometimes regular needs or questions that need to be addressed to collect in real-time specific words and behaviors and attitudes to some search terms.
		• Sales teams sometimes need social media analysis to be able to better plan their visits and engagement activities, and knowing how to adapt product key messages and tackle product objections with more information available and allows sales teams to build closer and more personalized relationships with very well informed medical and critical audiences.

Open discussions	• Tracking competition activities and getting access to the brand, diseases, therapeutic areas, and medical products mentioned across social, news, blogs, videos, forums, podcasts, and social media platforms are essential for a more contextual understanding of key areas, opportunities, and insights generation. • Analysis of the number of mentions and social media reach are extremely important for KOLs identification and profiling as it is necessary to better understand the sentiment of some key influencers and to understand where the products and company are being mentioned.	• The available time from the sessions did not allow to have additional notes collected for this point.

Business development, commercial excellence and digital strategy focus group interviews

Table 5: Focus group interview sessions topics/subtopics, key takeaways and additional raised points.

Topic/Subtopics	Key Takeaways	Additional Raised Points

Question 1: Processes with social media techniques and data	• Applied to commercial excellence, business development, and digital strategy, the following processes were mentioned as being relevant:
	  • Segmentation.
	  • Brand listening.
	  • Crisis and reputation risks management.
	  • Promotional campaigns monitoring.
	  • Influencer networks and KOLs monitoring.
	  • Content analytics.
	  • Multi channels or distribution and supply chain monitoring.
	  • Opportunities mapping for merge and acquisitions.
	  • Patient support.
	  • Competitive intelligence (most mentioned process during this interview phase).
		• It is important to implement a rigorous and creative process to consistently understand what relevant healthcare professionals, institutions, patients, and KOLs are discussing about the company, competitors, and products.
		• Companies that do not perform these analyses lose the capacity to gain a competitive advantage and therefore having a better and more informed engagement level and relationships with the community.

Question 2: Digital and business development metrics	• The highlighted and presented metrics were:
	  o Number of mentions.
	  o Social media reach.
	  o Interaction tracking and success.
	  o Positive and negative sentiment.
	  o Top public profiles.
	  o Most active public profiles.
	• Currently, biopharma needs to improve the capacity to estimate and understand the social media reach and digital content. Still, not a lot of companies are examining social and non-social media consistently and better understand the content performance.
	• The audience also provided clear examples of key performance indicators that are being used, such as:
	  o Brand awareness and reputation: total number of conversions mentioned, real-time analysis for new products launches of sentiment and opinions.
	  o Marketing effectiveness: Total number of followers across all relevant social platforms, influencer engagement, and cost/benefit analysis with ROI of social campaigns and total number of industry influencers.
		• Analysis purposes: reputation, brands and products, and influencers management.
		• General monitoring or social media applied to clinical and medical contexts are also applied.
		• Social media segmentation—currently already several companies are performing segmentation via social media data and information for influencers, recommenders, detractors, prospective speakers based on geographic, content, involvement in communities or societies with also demographics information.

Question 3: Systems and tools applied to commercial excellence, business development, and digital strategy	• Several tools were mentioned as being used like:
	  o Informa.
	  o Content studio.
	  o Falcon.
	  o Salesforce.com studio.
	  o Brand24.
	  o G2.
	  o Digimind.
	  o Google Alert.
	  o Mention.
		• N/A

Open discussions	• Social media was mentioned as a major need for business development and commercial excellence in terms of synthesizing large pieces of information, allowing the creation and building of robust data sets to support the delivery of the correct and appropriate product and disease messages to the medical and scientific community. • Email reports and notifications were also mentioned as being useful and relevant to inform quickly Backoffice and strategy definition teams like competitive intelligence and commercial data science. • Other processes mentioned randomly during the discussions: engaging the medical and patient's audience to foster trustful relationships. • Managing the brand reputation and creating disease awareness when relevant. • Conducting market research and primary and secondary data research support. Identify relevant healthcare professionals, rising stars in the medical community and understand key patient groups and advocacy influencers.	• The available time from the sessions did not allow for additional notes collected for this point.

Organizational skills and competencies focus group interviews

Table 6: Focus group interview sessions topics/subtopics, key takeaways and additional raised points.

Topic/Subtopics	Key Takeaways	Additional Raised Points

Question 1: Most relevant organizational skills and competencies	• Knowledge sharing processes to empower social media analytics from different functions to incentivize exchange, distribution, and content reception are typically not well developed and disseminated from an organizational perspective.
	• Several organizations still struggle with core capabilities for social media understanding or readiness like digital, key account management, content development, and technical capabilities.
	• The technical capabilities were mentioned several times as most of the organizations still do not fully grasp or can reach the full technical potential to be able to effectively operate with social media analytics.
	• Most highlighted organizational skills:
	   ○ Coordination.
	   ○ Creative Thinking.
	   ○ Effectiveness.
	   ○ Handling Details.
	   ○ Identifying Problems.
	   ○ Identifying Resources.
	   ○ Prioritization.
	   ○ Productivity.
	   ○ Situational Assessment.
	   ○ Task Analysis.
	   ○ Workflow Analysis.
	   ○ Workflow Management.
	   ○ Analysis.
	   ○ Analyzing Issues.
	   ○ Budgeting.
	   ○ Business Intelligence.
	   ○ Data.
	   ○ Deadlines.
		• Facebook, Instagram, specific medical websites, and Weblogs.
		• Tracking methods: most frequent are external providers and system access via browser but also APIs and HTML parsing.
		• Tracking approaches: keywords, topic-based and explorative URLs.

- o Decision Making.
- o Forecasting.
- o Information Gathering.
- o Problem Solving.
- o Program Management.
- o Project Management.
- o Strategic Planning.
- o Strategy Development.
- o Attentive Listening.
- o Collaboration.
- o Communication.
- o Confidence.
- o Evaluating.
- o Facilitating.
- o Goals.
- o Goal Setting.
- o Group Leadership.
- o Implementation.
- o Implementing Decisions.
- o Multitasking.
- o Negotiation.
- o Teamwork.
- o Time Management.
- o Training.
- o Decision Making.
- o Proactivity.
- o Resourcefulness.
- o Self-motivation.
- o Strategic Planning.

Table 6 contd. ...

...Table 6 contd.

Topic/Subtopics	Key Takeaways	Additional Raised Points
Question 2: Investment made	• Some relevant metrics examples: reach, velocity of reach, share of voice, sentiment index, net promoter scoring, loyalty and innovation track. • Investment summary in relevant stakeholders classification and profiling analysis, as well in terms of social media awareness internal campaigns and change management measures to increase the methods for data and information sharing. • From a long-term perspective, social media listening should be considered by the organizations as an important capability in terms of skills and time investment, where the right combination of people, processes, and tools is ensured. • Some of the key challenges highlighted in terms of future investments that might be needed were around a solid qualitative and quantitative balance between the produced insights and outputs from social media analysis, where having a clear and initial set of guidelines and procedures to what are the goals and objectives for any social media analytics project are critical.	• The current increase in adoption of AI in social media analytics is creating more needs for investments in terms of increasing presence in social media platforms. • Sales and marketing and commercial operations teams and managing already different customer journeys and digital personas tracking and making more contributions in terms of adoption of social media analytics solutions and needs to internal teams to have a new set of skills and technical competencies. • Some social media ROI considerations were also made: efficiency, reputation, innovation, building trust, influencers' disease awareness, and perception shifting.

Question 3: Individual skills	• Some of the most highlighted skills were: o Strategic thinking. o Data understanding. o Analytical thinking. o Data analytics and business. Intelligence. o Understand the business needs. o Leadership. o Audience centric. o Derive insights. o Influence decisions. o Establish metrics. o Create reports. o Apply insights and critical thinking. o Understanding of compliance, legal and data privacy. • Connected feedback also made mention to existing creative competencies and to being able to build and understand the social media platforms and to monitor dynamics of social sharing, responses and user behavior. • Additional skills were highlighted with a broader perspective: • Personal effectiveness: goal-orientation, interpersonal skills, and cross-functional collaboration. • Business acumen: analytical thinking, understanding of disease areas and products. • Usage of relevant systems and tools.	• Some of the participants highlighted that typically the skills management for social media analytics is not at the top of the priorities for the organizations and especially for human resources departments when it is being planned and executed for corporate learning and training development programs. • The involvement from legal and compliance teams in SOP understanding and clarification to support social media analytics was presented as an area that most of the professionals need to be aware of. • Privacy policies for HCPs data treatment are extremely important to be considered by all employees that manage and produce social media analytics.
Open discussions	• The available time from the sessions did not allow us to have open discussions for this group.	• The available time from the sessions did not allow for additional notes collected for this point.

Scientific and medical application usage of social media analytics focus group interviews

Table 7: Focus group interview sessions topics/subtopics, key takeaways and additional raised points.

Topic/Subtopics	Key Takeaways	Additional Raised Points
Question 1: Clinical operations and usage	• Different healthcare professionals value the engagements and interactions with medical affairs. In most of the cases, we can understand from social media what the major clinical, scientific challenges are that need to be addressed collectively within medical communication. Moreover, we can understand some public opinions or areas that can be addressed and further discussed during medical events organization. • Social media analytics are also used to understand diagnosis, research therapies and coverage, patient adherence or challenges, and to understand any possible medical follow-ups.	• Tracking sources: Twitter, Facebook, Instagram, specific medical websites, and Weblogs. • Tracking methods: most frequent are external providers and system access via browser but also APIs and HTML parsing. • Tracking approaches: keywords, topic-based and explorative URLs.
Question 2: Use cases	• By using independent websites, publications, and social networks, new opportunities can be assessed in terms of medical education and clinical events organization. • Assessing and understanding how community KOLs are expressing opinions and comments, as well to better understand new dimensions for KOLs tiering and clinical profiling. • Assess information relevance, medical or scientific exchange visits or activities cadence and needs. • Generating the ability to bring innovation and new thinking in terms of medical and scientific community engagement. • In some of the cases social media analytics are used to understand how deep scientific discussions can happen from a medical management perspective. • Publications and scientific reports. • Enterprise and propriety data. • Real-world data understanding from very specific public information sources.	• Some observations were made in terms of sporadic use cases, such as social media listening, to provide more generic details in terms of patient advocacy, policies, and patient support. • Medical affairs are still not advanced in using social media analytics as a source of insights, as compliance and privacy concerns typically arise in those discussions.

| Question 3: KOLs identification, tiering, and profiling | • Medical Affairs provides data and proceed with analysis from public data sources like PubMed and Clinical Trials.gov and to support the key experts and relevant institutions and laboratories globally.
• Data extractions are performed from public data sources with information about names, locations, working institutions, number of connections, and other relevant information.
• Activities are done to deliver actionable intelligence that facilitates optimal data management and social media analytics maintenance.
• In some situations, medical data science teams have been applying social media analytics to generate intelligent insights, prescriptive guidance, and automated actions to improve internal decision-making processes, ensure business intelligence system availability, and automate the proactive, predictive maintenance of data and insights around the globe. | • In some cases, social media analytics have been used for fair market value calculations and develop and customize policies and standard procedures.
• Also in some sporadic situations, social media has been able to provide relevant data to real-world data outcomes in multiple forms like clinical setting data from medical available data, patient surveys from forum sites, claims data derived from reimbursement information, conference abstracts, and specific clinical insights driving proactive decisions. |
| Open discussions | • In some of the cases medical affairs information has been used to evidence generation strategies, sales training presentations to add more public social media available data, and as content review in terms of online data sources like websites, weblogs, etc.
• Social media listening in the context of medical affairs is performed to seek and understand the emotions and sentiments from pre-identified KOLs and understand relevant future scientific discussion topics.
• Social media analytics is performed with qualitative and scientific and medical relevant numbers and data such as involvement in medical publications, connections and involvement in clinical research activities. | • The available time from the sessions did not allow us to have additional notes collected for this point. |

4. Key Observations from the Focus Group Interviews

In general, the participants assigned high relevance and a good commitment and dedication to all interviews, where they also highlighted that having the pre-reading of the questions was extremely useful and important for the interview's preparation.

On a more abstract level, several participants referred to the idea of having a more well-developed organizational culture of social media analytics and overall data management and science capacity from all involved functions, where the different challenges of this industry in making the most out of social media analytics have to be deeply reflected upon.

The ultimate objective should be to have a structured and a well-defined social media analytics framework that is applied and adapted to the life sciences industry and with clear case studies for benefits and opportunities management.

The participants in the focus group interviews mentioned the difficulty in applying very general guidelines and practices to social media analytics in their own processes. Some participants indicated that existing social media reports and data analytics activities still need a lot of improvement, where a practical understanding of what social media analytics data is expressing will be important for a successful implementation.

In addition to the general opinion among all participants that a framework and best practices guidelines and training should be further discussed, two specific suggestions were given on how to deal with this issue. The first was to use consulting companies to create and provide niche training, while the second was to create a framework between academics and professionals that detailed how social media analytics could be taken to another level and be applied to the entire life sciences sector.

The focus group interviews, the related answers and the observations provided by the participants also highlighted a range of other important issues that pertain to be explained during this section. The major conclusions and takeaways from the collected information and knowledge from the interview sessions are highlighted:

1. Social media analytics are being used to listen to customers and gather competitor information.
2. Most relevant data sources used in the life sciences industry (including pharmaceuticals) are Twitter, PubMed, ResearchGate and LinkedIn.
3. Applied use cases in the industry and according to all focus group discussions:
   - Social media content and network analysis.
   - Sentiment analysis towards brands, products, therapeutics areas.
   - Managing the brand reputation and creating disease awareness when relevant.
   - Conducting market research and primary and secondary data research support.
   - Identify relevant healthcare professionals, rising stars in the medical community and understand key patient groups and advocacy influencers.
   - Brand listening and Promotional campaigns monitoring.
   - Crisis and reputation risks management.

- Influencer networks and KOLs monitoring.
- Multi channels or distribution and supply chain monitoring.
- Opportunities mapping for merge and acquisitions.

4. Relevant metrics examples:
   - *Operational metrics*: Reach, Velocity of reach, Share of voice, Sentiment index, Net promoter scoring, Loyalty, Innovation track.
   - *Qualitative metrics*: Number of mentions, Interactions tracking and success, Positive and negative sentiment, Top public profiles and most active public profiles.

5. Examples of used systems and tools to perform social media analytics: Informa, Content Studio, Falcon, Salesforce.com studio, Brand24, Digimind and Mention.

6. Social media currently supports already several processes areas like the ones described below:
   - *Sales processes*: Segmentation, profiling, competitive intelligence, surveys management, multichannel strategy definition, incentive compensation schemes.
   - *Key Account Management*: Key accounts plan management, accounts prioritization and ranking, and sales progress monitoring.
   - *Marketing*: Brand plan development, digital campaigns, and events management.
   - *Medical*: Medical inquiries and medical communities raised concerns about management and medical events and meetings management.

7. The most highlighted individual skills for social media analytics were:
   - Strategic thinking.
   - Data understanding.
   - Analytical thinking.
   - Data analytics and business intelligence.
   - Understand the business needs.
   - Leadership.
   - Audience centric.
   - Derive insights.
   - Influence decisions.
   - Establish metrics.
   - Create reports.
   - Apply insights and critical thinking.
   - Understanding of compliance, legal and data privacy.

8. One of the most relevant and rich focus group interview sessions was the scientific and medical application of social media analytics, where the key observation was the understanding of major social media clinical and scientific challenges that need to be collectively addressed by medical communication, as well as the understanding of some public opinions or areas that can be addressed and further discussed during medical event organization.

9. Most discussed use cases of social media analytics applied to medical affairs and clinical operations context:

- Social media analytics are also used to understand diagnosis, research therapies and coverage, patient adherence or challenges, and understand any possible medical follow-ups that are possible.
- Assessing and understanding how community KOLs are expressing opinions and comments but as well to better understand new dimensions for KOLs tiering and clinical profiling.
- Assessing information relevance, medical or scientific exchange visits or activities cadence and needs.
- Generating ability to bring innovation and new thinking in terms of medical and scientific community engagement.
- Some of the cases we use social media analytics are to understand how deep scientific discussions can happen from a medical management perspective.
- Understanding real-world data from very specific public information sources.
- Using, in some of the cases, medical affairs information to evidence generation strategies, sales training presentations to add more available public social media data and content review in terms of online data sources like websites, weblogs, etc.
- Social media listening in the context of medical affairs is performed to seek and understand the emotions and sentiments from pre-identified KOLs and understand relevant future scientific discussion topics.
- Performing social media analytics is with qualitative, scientific and medically relevant numbers and data, such as the involvement in medical publications, connections and involvement in clinical research activities.

5. Conclusion

The authors conducted focus group interviews with 45 life sciences professionals in the first three months of 2021 and asked several different questions to understand all the participants' knowledge and experiences and provide all the necessary background knowledge and foundation to better understand the research questions.

Participants generally attributed high relevance and good commitment to all interviews and pointed out that pre-reading of the questions had a tremendous effect on getting ready for the interview.

Studying four focus groups to discover how different use cases apply to social media analytics, as well as how each relates to a variety of business decision demands, was the objective of this focus group study.

The analysis discussed previously draws attention to specific business situations and cases in the life sciences industry where social media analytics are being implemented and to what are the most important organizational and individual skills as well as key performance indicators and metrics that deserve to be mentioned as examples and best practices.

Several discussions emphasized the importance of social media analytics to industry and seemed to be a recurring theme. According to the focus group interviewees, a systematized social media analytics process would be effective in addressing and disseminating a variety of business problems and decision-relevant topics.

Several comments underscored the strategic direction and business importance of identifying and managing key opinion leaders in the focus groups. One of the participants of the focus group where the issue was specifically raised for in-depth discussion emphasized that, in most cases, KOLs and HCPs identification and behavioral and attitude management are considered as dedicated processes that require internal efforts from departments like commercial operations, medical affairs and analytics.

Further, the focus group offered some concrete suggestions for possible future elements, including the need to supervise IT activities and investments, as well as to provide training and mentoring for all relevant skills concerning social media analytics. To avoid any reputational or legal risks and to ensure a good, correct and ethical use of all collected data, it is necessary to draw clearer boundaries around potential risky behaviors or any legal, privacy and compliance key considerations.

Risk management and compliance, which are crucial for effective management of social media analytics processes, are key areas that were considered extremely relevant when it came to incorporating social media into internal policies and procedures.

Understanding and being clear in this focus group interviews' study of social media analytics was crucial for gaining insight and value. Even more, social media analytics policies must make it clear what employees can and cannot do in terms of any social media analytics procedure or step. A consistent, ongoing oversight process can detect potential issues and lead to prompt corrections. Furthermore, approval processes can minimize inadvertent errors in data analysis and other areas.

For anyone using social media for business communications, employee training is critical to ensuring they are aware of the policy, as well as the potential risks.

Most of the requirements and risks referred to fall into three categories, such as privacy and data security, confidentiality and access to data and archiving of data.

The final idea that was raised by many participants is that it is imperative to develop better processes for ad-hoc and systematic social media analytics and senior management to have a better understanding of all benefits and opportunities. An organization and individual can benefit from formal and informal skills' development initiatives, internal and external training and learning development opportunities that increase their skills and competence. There are some existing processes of this kind in some organizations, but executive management or related functions are not always aware of them.

References

Fakhraei, S., Onukwugha, E. and Getoor, L. 2015. *Data Analytics for Pharmaceutical Discoveries*, 599–623.

Haataja, J.E. 2011. Social Media as a Source of Competitive Intelligence in a Pharmaceutical Corporation, 30–92.

Morgan, D.L. 1997. *Focus Groups as Qualitative Research* (2nd ed.). Thousand Oaks, CA, US: Sage Publications, Inc.

Rabiee, F. 2004. Focus-group interview and data analysis. *Proceedings of the Nutrition Society*, 63(4): 655–660.

13

The Social Media Usage and Impact on Performance of SMEs
A New Entrepreneur Behavior on Policy Implementation

Francesca Di Virgilio

INTRODUCTION

In the age of modern technologies, social media have become a strategic tool in the environment for all business sectors (Di Virgilio, 2018a,b; Gaál et al., 2015; Yassin et al., 2013). Studies highlight and explain how technological development has involved companies of diverse categories and the relative impact on their economic equilibrium (Gensler et al., 2013; Nisar and Whitehead, 2016).

In particular, this ongoing process has started with an innovative perspective on the prospective of the customer in the managerial process with a central role. Nowadays, organizations are finding ways to satisfy their customers' needs and expectations (Chang et al., 2015; Culnan et al., 2010; Di Virgilio and Antonelli, 2018; Kim and Ko, 2012; Sashi, 2012). Social media have the power to strengthen this relationship and generate consistent effects on performance that are continuously changing to combine strategies with technological means in their business processes (Gaál et al., 2015). Thus, the ability to manage information becomes a firm core competence in creating competitive long-term strategies. The development of online communities by using social media has expanded the interconnectivity between businesses and consumers that have access to different sources of shared information from other customers and this influences their purchasing decisions (Chen et al., 2011; Di Virgilio and Antonelli, 2018). Moreover, the development of online communities has expanded the interconnectivity between businesses and consumers, enabling the latter to faster exchange information, even at international level (Aichner and Jacob, 2015). This ongoing process has started with an innovative

Department of Economics, University of Molise, Italy.
Email: fradivi@unimol.it

prospective of the customer in the company structure where the social media usage plays the central role to manage information. It becomes a firm core competence in creating competitive long-term advantages and improving performance.

In this regard, social media is considered a 'must have' in every single firm. Nowadays, the principal goal is the satisfaction of client's needs and expectations. Social media have the power to strengthen this crucial relationship and generate consistent effects on company performance that is continuously changing to combine firm aims with technological means (Tajvidi and Karami, 2017). The measurement to evaluate a firm's performance is through efficiency and profitability. The most acknowledged measurement to evaluate efficiency and profitability of an investment is the return on investment (ROI) index. In particular, by analyzing the state-of-the-art, several studies have been conducted to define a unique and definitive calculation of ROI concerning social media (Lenskold, 2003; Hoffman and Fodor, 2010).

Furthermore, there are no studies focused on social media use, the relationship with performance and the role of entrepreneurs from small and medium enterprises (SMEs) in South Italy, to promote policy implementation, to increase dynamic range and power of their communication and marketing. Considering the goal of this paper, it is also important to analyze the influence of social media policy implementation on the performance and profitability of small and medium enterprises (SMEs) in South Italy, in particular during this pandemic period. Because of the global pandemic, due to the coronavirus (Covid-19) outbreak since the beginning of 2020, in Italy and worldwide, there has been a dramatic interruption of activities during lockdown, with effects on the global economy and in businesses that were forced to shut down. The dramatic interruption of activities during lockdown, in all sectors worldwide (Ratten, 2020), has had significant effects on firms' performance, especially that of SMEs.

The findings of the study show the multiple relationships between the principal variables. The Pearson's Chi-square index was fundamental for the overall analysis through the decryption of the relative correlation between social media effects on firm performance, highlighting the considerable and notable association with ROI measurement.

In this scenario, the chapter is organized as follows: in the first part, the chapter presents a background about social media policy implementation, its definition, its advantages and disadvantages and its relationship with the firm's performance. The second part focuses on methodology, the research questions derived from theory and empirical results with the main findings. Lastly, the chapter concludes with a discussion, implications for practice and theory, limitations, and future research directions.

1. Conceptual Background

1.1 Social Media Policy Implementation: An Innovative Entrepreneurs' Opportunity

The Resource Based View theory (RBV) deepens the role of firms' capabilities and resources to create sustained competitive advantages and superior performance (Barney, 2001; Davcik and Sharma, 2016; Wernerfelt, 1984).

Social media as a communication tool helps enterprises to connect with a large number of potential customers in order to spread information about their services and products (Schaupp and Belanger, 2013) and to accomplish different organizational objectives in different areas, including marketing, advertising, branding, customer service and human resources recruitment (Di Virgilio, 2018; 2021; Greenwald, 2010; Kim and Park, 2013; Nisar and Whitehead, 2016). In this scenario, and according to RVB theory, the firm provides a foundation for the link between social media usage and value creation with competitive advantages for firms (Palacios-Marques et al., 2015).

In general, social media are Web-based services that allow individuals or organizations to construct a public or semi-public profile within a bounded system, articulate a list of other users with whom they share information and view and traverse their list of connections and those made by others within the system (Ellison and Boyd, 2007). In particular, it is possible to individualize two competitive advantages of social media: the technological and the social one. On one hand, the technological facet refers to numerous innovations in the Information technology (IT) sector that has changed people's life through the introduction of computers and smartphones (Yadav et al., 2015), with multiple functions that support a constant communication via the Internet, in particular via the most popular social media as Facebook, Instagram, Twitter, TikTok and so on. On the other hand, the social dimension is based on the opportunities offered by social media to communicate with people and firms all around the world (Di Virgilio, 2021).

Such is the potentiality of social media that the majority of companies decided to involve these strategic tools in their structure for diverse areas, as marketing and communication. Colicev et al. (2018) classify companies into two sectors: owned social media (OSM) and earned social media (ESM).

OSM indicates social media activities managed and shared by the firm on its personal profiles, like a Facebook page, a YouTube channel, etc., whereas the second one defines all other SM expressions not directly controlled by the organization. In particular, ESM encompasses multiple content related to the brand that different people can spread on online assets. In this case, the role of consumers is fundamental due to the impact on two ESM's dimensions: valence and volume. ESM valence is the sentiment that a company's online theme generates in the users, while ESM volume points out the number of the impressions received by followers under the firm's posts and the ones that fans create or share, mentioning the company itself, like retweeting (Barreda et al., 2015; Nisar and Whitehead, 2016). It is the brand fan following (BFF) that comprehends the sphere of people who constantly manifest their support through millions of likes, comments, shares, etc. (Dineva et al., 2020). It is another metric that allows the evaluation of a brand's meaningful impact on the audience and it could be used to create eventual customized content or to embrace passive fans with specific posts (Chen et al., 2011; Gensler et al., 2013; Hudson et al., 2016; Nisar and Whitehead, 2016; Dineva et al., 2020).

1.2 *Advantages and Disadvantages in Adopting Social Media Policy Implementation*

Social media brings with it many opportunities but also challenges that become evident with their unsuitable use. Because of this, companies have been forced to study more deeply this extraordinary and demanding application tool (Di Virgilio, 2018; 2018a).

In the existing literature, it is possible to find numerous definitions and measurements of the main advantages for companies to use social media in all sectors, such as sales growth (Kumar et al., 2013); brand value (Gensler et al., 2013; Hudson et al., 2016; Nisar and Whitehead, 2016); e-commerce and social commerce opportunities (Hajli, 2014); knowledge sharing (Di Virgilio, 2018; Munar and Jacobsen, 2014); customer relationship management (Rosman and Stuhura, 2013), recruiting tools to attract new employees and pre screen potential future employees (Greenwald, 2010). Indeed, firms have a great opportunity to determine consumers' requirements and needs by involving consumers in panel questionnaires and interviews (Chang et al., 2015; Culnan et al., 2010; Di Virgilio and Antonelli, 2018; Kim et al., 2012). Online ratings are another potential tool to catch the customers' eyes. Positive rankings could attract future consumers who will feel confident in buying your items because other people have done it and rated it as an important/ effective purchase (Labrecque et al., 2013). Thus, the ability to manage information becomes a firm's core competence in creating competitive long-term advantages and improving performance.

Although numerous advantages have been examined in the usage of social media by a company, principal and daunting risks can be highlighted. Firstly, damage to an organization's reputation may occur when a customer or an employee posts negative comments about its products or policies (Brivot et al., 2017; O'Leary, 2011). Moreover, hackers may infiltrate an organization's social media accounts and post false or misleading information (Castillo et al., 2011). Reputation is defined as a set of characteristics which are socially constructed for an organization, based on the organization's previous actions (Aula, 2008). In addition, social media risks can stem from the organization's use of it, from employees' use, from external sources to the organization, or from a combination of these factors (Ollier-Malaterre et al., 2013). An overuse of social media for personal purposes during working hours may result in productivity losses and misuse of resources (Field and Chelliah, 2012; Khansa et al., 2017). Brivot et al. (2017). Hence, care has to be taken on controlling reputational risks and multiple conflicting viewpoints on social media risks.

Thus the risk regarding security issues is important for various aspects of social media policy implementation in order to establish a credible, safe and lasting social platform (Demek et al., 2018; Di Virgilio, 2021; Zhang, 2017), because "each risk comes with a potential cost" (Di Virgilio, 2018, pp. 12–16).

2. The Relationship between Social Media Usage and Firm Performance

Existing literature highlights the combination between knowledge technological resources and organizational skills representing a competitive advantage because it reveals itself as a driver of impressive performance, which will lead to high future incomes and to better responses to market demand (Garcia-Morales et al., 2018).

Performance management is a continuous process of identifying, measuring and developing the performance of individuals and teams and aligning performance with the strategic goals of the organization (Schleicher et al., 2018).

It is considered as a fundamental tool to be integrated in multiple segments, like the evaluation of market research that will undoubtedly be involved in numerous departments or companies: the RoI index (Lenskold, 2003).

The RoI (Return on Investment) index measures profitability and economic efficiency of an investment. It reveals the amount of the return on a specific investment, relative to the investment's cost. The Return-on-Investment formula is as following:

$$\text{RoI (\%)} = \frac{\text{Total Revenue } - \text{Total Cost}}{\text{Total Cost}} \times 100$$

RoI is calculated by subtracting the cost of an investment from the proceeds received from the investment, divided by that same investment cost. Because RoI is measured as a percentage, it can be easily compared with returns from diverse types of investments against each other (David et al., 2012). Nowadays, each organization has to clarify why its sector is so relevant and RoI is considered as one of the principal indexes to provide scientific reasons that support the market research being conducted in the firm.

A reliable RoI measurement enables an understanding of the perfect area and the size of market research activities, improves and allows the achievement of budget goals and enables the firm to quantify and develop performance (Hoffman and Fodor, 2010).

Thus, the extent of social media use will directly influence social media policy implementation and will positively influence a firm's performance.

To empirically measure social media, the principal issue is the use of traditional metrics that do not offer the possibility of answering questions, like 'How measure the RoI generated by SM?' (Trier and Jensen, 2018).

To efficiently describe social media, their assessment indicators are clicks, likes, shares, comments, brand mentions, profile visits and active followers. The quality of the title and the specific image catch the user's attention. At the same time, the number of clicks with insufficient amount of likes and shares shows the interest of the client. On the other side, if a post receives numerous likes, the specific content is one of the first research results. Shares represent the attractiveness of the link and its quality, while comments could be positive or negative and, consequently, increase or diminish marketing. Brand mentions are one of the fundamental key performance indicators (KPIs) for social media because they indicate the number of conversations on a certain brand and maintain top-of-mind awareness (Podobnik, 2013). In general, the aforementioned KPI's for social media can be divided into two main groups: the involvement and the range (Gräve, 2019). The first one is represented by numbers regarding users registered in the database, redirections to external websites, sending invitations to friends, recommending actions, posts, comments on websites, clicks of cool, like it, threads, posts on forums, completing questionnaires, submitted competition entries, users taking part in competitions, votes for contest entries, installing applications, games or playing games. On the other hand, the range relates to numbers of unique user/visitor (UU), page view/impression (PV), click through ratio (CTR) in diverse target groups (age, gender, education, place of residence), clicks of creations, website visits, page views, conversion rate (CR) or the number of UU on websites. As a result, so fundamental is the implementation of KPIs of social media in the organization that it represents the basis for an overall assessment of the strategy adopted and continuously improved upon (Gräve, 2019; Kóscielniak, 2018).

3. Research Design and Data Collection

The aim of this study is to explore the impact of the social media usage and policy implementation by SMEs on performance, focusing on the relationship with RoI. The following main research question was asked:

RQ_1:   *What is the impact of social media usage on performance and profitability in SMEs?*

To answer the main research question, the research design was guided by two derived research questions:

RQ_{1a}: How high is the correlation between the sector of each firm and profitability generated by the use of social media?

RQ_{1b}: How high is the correlation between the age of entrepreneurs and profitability generated by the use of social media in their firms?

For doing so, an online survey was conducted to gather data. The participants were 210 entrepreneurs of SMEs in a region of South Italy called Molise.

The data were collected within a period of three months, between March 2020 and May 2020, during the first lockdown in Italy due to the outbreak of Covid-19. Participants were randomly selected from the list of the Chamber of Commerce of the region and they were representative of the larger population of SMEs of the region.

The online survey was divided into two sections. The first section was used to gather data relating demographic profile of entrepreneurs, such as age, education and operational field. The second section includes an overview regarding the implementation of social media. It is divided into four sections: Social Media Use (six items) (Demek et al., 2018; Eschenbrenner et al., 2015; Schaupp and Bélanger, 2014; Trinkle et al., 2015;), Social Media Risk of Use (6 items) (Ollier-Malaterre et al., 2013), Social Media Policy Implementation (6 items) (Carlson et al., 2016; Scott and Jacka, 2011) and Firm Performance (five items) (Kim et al., 2015; Tajvidi and Karami, 2017; Watson, 2007; Yen and Tag, 2015).

With regard to data analysis process, Pearson's Chi-square index was used to analyze the descriptive data.

The calculation of the Pearson's Chi-square index was done in order to understand the interdependence of the two attributes. When a connection of independence or logic dependence between two variables is not possible to be established, the interdependence will be analyzed and it equals the individualization of the bidirectional link between the two attributes. Moreover, this index measures the association for disconnected (or nominal) qualitative attributes. This means that variables express a quality of the unit and it is only possible to verify if the variables are the same or different. It is defined, in mathematical terms, as:

$$\chi^2 = \sum_{i=1}^{H} \cdot \sum_{j=1}^{K} \frac{(n_{ij} - n'_{ij})^2}{n'_{ij}}$$

Where χ^2 is Pearson's Chi-square index, n_{ij} are the observed frequencies and n'_{ij} are the theoretical frequencies of independence. If the two attributes are perfectly independent, $n_{ij} = n'_{ij}$ and the $\chi^2 = 0$. On the contrary, if the two attributes are associated or interdependent, χ^2 will be positive and it will be as high as the observed frequencies will differentiate more than the theoretical ones (Bryant and Satorra, 2012).

4. Findings

4.1 SME Characterization and Demographic Profile of Respondents

To increase the single frequency and achieve consistent results, the first crucial modification was the assortment of business sector's items into 19 macro areas. The resultant values were associated with the total frequencies of elements comprehended in each macro area. Frequency of an event is the number that expresses how many times one event occurs in an experiment or study (Irpino and Verde, 2015). In the following Table 1, every sector is displayed with its frequency in the sample.

The correlation between the variable sectors with the education one is the object of the first part of this statistical study to point out a specific background regarding the entrepreneurs' level of education that has a consistent influence on company management.

There was a strong statistical significance at $\alpha = .0.05$ level, when these two variables were cross tabulated using Chi-Square (Table 2).

It demonstrates a high dependence between the sector variable and the educational one. It means that the majority of entrepreneurs of SMEs have achieved an educational certificate to improve their own abilities and knowledge. In particular, green data are the most significant and not only do they prove that 24.52 per cent of professional offices have a high school diploma, but 71.99 per cent of them are positively correlated with participation in a professional degree. Another interesting

Table 1: Sectors with respective frequencies.

Sectors	Frequencies	Percentage (%)
Handicraft	17	8.09
Trade	46	21.90
Marketing and Communication	10	4.76
Restaurants	21	10
Services	39	18.57
Professional services	65	30.95
Tourism	12	5.71
Total	**210**	**100**

data point is in the handicraft category, where 84.44 per cent have a strong dependence on the acquisition of a middle-school diploma.

Finally, other fundamental factors should be analyzed: like age, in order to individualize the interval designed by the following classes, where the majority of interviewed entrepreneurs are included (Table 3). Table 3 presents the age of entrepreneurs. All respondents were men—around half of them were between 41–50 years old and 6.19 per cent aged up to 30 years.

Table 2: The Chi-square matrix of sector and education.

Sectors	High School	Bachelor Degree	Middle School	Professional Course	Total
Handicraft	3.0	1.5	41.9	3.2	8.09
Trade	4.0	0.1	0.1	8.8	21.90
Marketing and Communication	0.0	3.8	0.5	1.9	4.76
Restaurants	6.5	4.5	0.0	4.0	10
Services	1.1	0.0	2.0	0.8	18.57
Professional services	14.1	0.3	1.7	41.3	30.95
Tourism	3.1	1.0	0.6	2.3	5.71
Total	**31.8**	**11.2**	**46.9**	**62.3**	**100**

Table 3: Entrepreneurs' age.

Age	Frequencies	Percentage (%)
Up to 30	13	6.19
31–40	40	19.05
41–50	86	40.95
51–60	48	22.86
Over 60	23	10.95
Total	**210**	**100**

4.2 The Relationship of Social Media Effects on Profitability: The Role of Sector and Entrepreneurs' Age

The research question RQ_{1a} inquires how high is the correlation between the sector of each entrepreneur's company and profitability generated by the use of social media. Firstly, it should be explained what is intended by profit and profitability. The first one is an absolute number that indicates the revenues that a company generates above and beyond the incurred expenses. Contrarily, profitability is a relative amount that expresses the aim of a company's profit in relation with the size of the business. It is a measurement of efficiency. Furthermore, it is a business's capacity to generate a return on investment across its resources in comparison with an alternative investment. In other words, a company can realize a profit but it does not necessarily mean that the company is profitable (Tulsian, 2014).

Table 4: The Chi-square matrix of sector and social media effects on profitability.

Sectors	0 Null	1 Minimum	2 Sufficient	3 Good	4 Excellent	Total
Handicraft	2.2	1.8	4.1	1.0	13.0	22.1
Trade	8.0	0.0	5.5	0.1	0.1	13.7
Marketing and Communication	0.5	0.6	0.1	0.1	0.3	1.5
Restaurants	1.5	1.0	0.2	0.0	0.6	3.3
Services	3.2	0.7	0.6	2.8	0.0	7.3
Professional services	0.4	0.4	0.3	0.8	1.9	3.7
Tourism	3.9	0.6	0.5	2.4	1.3	8.6
Total	**19.7**	**5.0**	**11.3**	**7.2**	**17.1**	**60.3**

The profitability is an ordered qualitative attribute because it expresses a quality of the unit and, at the same time, a natural order between the diverse variables can be defined. Consequently, every value is equal to a specific estimation as is shown in the following matrix (Table 4).

What can be deducted is the slight dependence between the sector variable and the effects on profitability and it is shown, in statistical terms, through the total result of 28.70 per cent. This means that the sector does not have an influence on profitability promoted by the integration of social media in the organization. The only value that manifests a higher association between the two factors reveals that the implementation of this innovative tool is strongly correlated with the handicraft sector, where 58.92 per cent of entrepreneurs have obtained excellent benefits in their organizations.

The second aspect of RQ_{1b} offers an interesting analysis that could be the interpretation of the relationship between the age variable and social media effects on performance. In particular, the latter is an ordered qualitative attribute and each value is equal to a determined estimate shown in the next Table 5. The method to follow is the formulation of the chi-square matrix, in order to decipher the significance of their connection.

The final result demonstrates that the two factors present a slight dependence of 29.22 per cent (Table 5). This means that the effects generated by social media on company performance are not strongly influenced by the entrepreneur's age.

Despite 32.38 per cent of entrepreneurs obtaining a null effect on their organizations, 30.48 per cent and the 30 per cent respectively achieved minimum results and good ones. Consequently, it can be deduced that in SMEs, more time is needed to individualize the most effective strategy to efficiently integrate social media in order to guarantee future significant results on company performance.

The research question RQ_1 asks for examination of the relationship between two ordered qualitative attributes and the most appropriate method to implement presents multiple levels: the formulation of the contingency table will be the base for next calculations regarding the definition of the Goodman-Kruskal's gamma index, that includes two further steps in the identification of the N_c, the number of couples

Table 5: The Chi-square matrix of age and social media effects on performance.

Age	0 Null	3 Minimum	7 Good	9 Excellent	Total
22	0.5	0.8	0.0	0.4	1.7
25	0.1	0.0	0.5	0.3	0.9
28	1.1	0.9	0.0	0.2	2.2
32	0.7	0.4	0.4	0.5	1.9
34	0.1	0.1	1.5	1.2	2.9
35	0.5	1.8	2.7	0.8	5.7
36	0.1	1.8	0.3	1.0	3.2
38	1.3	0.2	0.6	2.9	4.9
41	0.2	0.1	0.2	0.4	1.0
43	1.2	1.5	0.2	0.4	3.2
44	0.9	0.4	2.7	0.0	4.1
45	0.1	0.1	0.8	3.6	4.5
48	0.0	0.0	0.0	0.1	0.1
49	0.5	0.3	0.0	0.1	0.9
51	0.2	0.4	0.3	2.3	3.2
52	1.5	0.3	0.3	0.1	2.3
56	0.1	0.0	0.0	0.9	1.1
57	0.2	0.0	0.0	0.7	0.9
58	1.6	0.2	1.5	1.2	4.5
60	3.5	0.2	1.5	0.4	5.5
62	1.2	0.2	0.2	0.4	1.9
63	0.5	0.0	0.8	0.4	1.7
65	1.5	1.1	0.2	0.2	3.0
Total	**17.4**	**10.8**	**14.8**	**18.3**	**61.4**

Table 6: The matrix of social media effects on performance and social media effects on profitability.

SM Effects on Performance	0 Null	3 Minimum	6 Sufficient	8 Good	9 Excellent	Total
0-Null	68					68
3-Minimum		6	25	33		64
8-Good			63			63
9-Excellent		4	5		6	15
Total	**68**	**10**	**93**	**33**	**6**	**210**

equally ordered on both attributes and N_d, the number of couples differently ordered on both attributes (Tables 6 and 7).

The value expresses the N_c calculated through the sum of the marginal total of the SM effects on performance variable or the sum of the marginal total of the SM effects

Table 7: The matrix of social media effects on performance and social media effects on profitability for the concordance definition.

SM Effects on Performance	0 Null	3 Minimum	6 Sufficient	8 Good	9 Excellent	Total
0-Null	9556					9556
3-Minimum		444	150	198		792
8-Good			378			378
9-Excellent						0
Total	9656	444	528	198	0	10826

on profitability. Each n'_{ij} is obtained through the product between every n_{ij} of the contingency table and the sum of variables of the contingency matrix comprehended in the imaginary rectangle situated in the right area of the n_{ij} considered, from the subsequent row of the n_{ij} value to the last one (without the row that presents marginal total) (Table 7). In this case, the final total expresses a positive concordance.

Numerical example:

$$n'_{11} = 68 * (6 + 25 + 33 + 63 + 4 + 5 + 6) = 9656$$

The value expresses the N_d calculated through the sum of the marginal total of the SM effects on performance variable or the sum of the marginal total of the SM effects on profitability one (Table 7). Each n'_{ij} is obtained through the product between every n_{ij} of the contingency table and the sum of variables of the contingency matrix comprehended in the imaginary rectangle situated in the left area of the n_{ij} considered, from the subsequent row of the n_{ij} value to the last one (without the row that presents marginal total). In the current case, the final total expresses a positive discordance (Table 8).

The gamma index of this analysis is calculated as it is shown in the next formula:

$$Y = \frac{10826 - 2728}{10826 + 2728} = 0{,}5975 = 59{,}75\%$$

The result demonstrates that social media effects definitely improve company profitability and performance. Moreover, an aspect has to be highlighted regarding the RoI index because it is an acknowledged measure of profitability and a notable

Table 8: The matrix of social media effects on performance and social media effects on profitability for the discordance definition.

Total	0 Null	3 Minimum	6 Sufficient	8 Good	9 Excellent	Total
0-Null						0
3-Minimum			100	2376		2476
8-Good			252			252
9-Excellent						0
Total	0	0	352	2376	0	2728

indicator of performance that supports entrepreneurs' decisions in the investment area (Broccardo and Zicari, 2020). The analysis proves that in 60 per cent of cases, an increase of profitability equals a respective growth of performance and this correlation has a direct impact on an undoubted enhancement of the RoI index related to social media.

5. Solutions and Recommendations

The statistical results of the chapter are a further demonstration that social media are definitely confirmed as a fundamental element to be involved in the company equipment for multiple reasons.

To sum up, the integration of social media has enhanced social media RoI in SMEs enterprises through a significant development in their efficiency, efficacy and alignment with it's own strategic goals (Blanchard, 2011). Nonetheless, higher results could be achieved to overcome the sufficient or good level towards the excellent one. Consequently, positive outcomes will be guaranteed, firstly, on internal sectors, to intensify the communication between employees and departments or to sustain the recruitment of personnel, and, secondly, on external ones, to reinforce the relationship with the crucial element of the company structure to the customer.

At the same time, significant barriers are encountered by entrepreneurs in South Italy for social media measurement (SMM). Entrepreneurs should identify a specific social media channel and associate it with a specific aim, measurable with qualitative information. Social media metrics are incommensurable across related channels due to the lack of common drivers and aggregated outcomes. In addition, in a generic company, each role assumes a personal perspective related to the aims to achieve that are based on different selections of the same SMM. Consequently, this organization prevents internal collaboration—a lack of effective organizational processes to associate local SMM through comparisons or aggregations. In fact, the fractionalization across departments with different levels of maturity and proficiency is one of the principal effective problems for the RoI calculation. It is evident that the divergence of adopting basic metrics such as likes or reach in contrast to measuring real-time data with high-quality dashboards (Hoffman and Fodor, 2010).

The difficulty is in creating a social media management aligned with strategic organizational layers. It corresponds to the absence of connection with decision making and marketing KPIs (Gräve, 2019). Furthermore, a coherent analysis of the customer is difficult to design due to the complexity of combining SMM with existing marketing channels.

The tool-driven measures guarantee continuity only in a short time period. Moreover, social media metrics are generated by diverse platform providers, causing a lack of continuity and an excessive number of produced data.

Tool-driven measures do not have the comprehensiveness to translate user behavior and motivations. Therefore, better qualitative metrics are required, like the creation of a dashboard with the assessment not only of quantitative metrics, but qualitative ones, like consumer feedback.

In conclusion, although the number of promoted models to individualize the optimal measurement of social media RoI has increased in the last years and a general strategy that can be followed in all enterprises has been designed, a final solution and a formula of the Return-on-Investment index for SMMs has still not been defined for SMEs.

6. Conclusion

Due to the outbreak of Covid-19, a number of precautionary measures (e.g., travel restrictions, lockdown) were taken to restrain this pandemic. These measures have negative consequences on the performance of firms, with results in the global economy and businesses shutting down in all sectors worldwide (Ratten, 2020). To this end, the current study sought to evaluate the relationships between SMU, entrepreneur's orientation to use social media and impact the performance of SMEs. The empirical findings depict that social media use positively and significantly affects the firm performance. Additionally, it significantly and positively impacts RoI. In addition, it is considered one of the limited attempts that examines the associations between social media use and the relationship with age of the entrepreneurs and educational level among entrepreneurs' SMEs, particularly in South Italy. Concerning the managerial implications, this research represents clear insights related to the benefits of using social media for SMEs in all sectors. Furthermore, based on the empirical results, it is evident that top management orientation to use social media has a positive impact on the performance as well as mediates the association between SMU and the performance. That is, manager's and/or owners' orientation towards using or adopting social media has critical consequences on the enterprise's performance.

Furthermore, the study's results revealed that social media has a positive link with the RoI of SMEs in all sectors. In this vein, it can be concluded that social media gives the possibility for entrepreneurs to freely decideabout the use of tool in the company management for several reasons.

Firstly, they have the principal functionality of customer care, in particular Twitter, Instagram and Facebook, to create a tangible relationship with the consumer. A satisfied client will certainly research its preferred brand on social media to receive news or to suggest it to his or her friends through word of mouth. Otherwise, in case of complaining, they will have the opportunity of contacting the firm directly and obtaining specific explanations. As a result, the enterprise will show itself as transparent, reliable, reputed and will invest in this strategic tool to understand and respond to customer's expectations.

Secondly, once a brand has caught the client's attention, approval and loyalty, it gains an unmeasurable advantage on its competitors for having created a specific image in the customer's mind. Such is the potentiality of social media that they can utterly contribute to the intensification of brand awareness and subsequent brand engagement process to receive positive feedback from the consumer. He will immediately recognise the brand through some distinctive signs, like colours and confirm his convinced preference for its well-known offer.

Thirdly, social media exponentially has improved company performance and profitability. In fact, they support innovation ability, productivity of invested resources and knowledge interaction between employees and managers. It was defined as a specific economic index to measure the economic value of social media, called

Social Media Return on Investment. Several frameworks and models were designed to achieve a unique formulation of this index in diverse categories of organizations. The discussion is still open and numerous economists have tried to solve this issue.

In accordance with this, Blanchard (2011) sustains an economic concept known as opportunity cost. It relates to the courses of one action, investment in business activity, chosen instead of another. For example, a social media program could have the objective of increasing customer loyalty and whose measurement of feelings and emotions remains challenging. Consequently, the measurement ought to be done on metrics that directly impact the plan. What matters the most in adopting the program is the performance measurement in achieving goals with the integration of social media. Therefore, he suggests that relevant measurements be identified and social capital be leveraged in order to comprehend the community in the brand-awareness process. The social media manager should embrace the methodology to persuade people to spend more money per transaction because, if only a follower were converted into a client, the company could consider them as a business client. To conclude, Blanchard (2011) affirms that the enterprise should point out clear goals to reach with the implementation of social media. At the same time, unique or standard strategies have not been defined for SM measurement. For this reason, each firm including SME has the possibility of adapting and customizing them according to the aims it wants to achieve.

However, reviewing and synthesizing the literature indicate that there is a gap in the area of social media use behaviour of firms in dealing with online networks to increase their performance. Using the theory of Resource-based Review and guided by the theoretical approaches from related research in firm performance, this chapter provides an analytical framework to explore social media use, investigating the influence of group variables. This study is one of the first to examine the age of entrepreneurs and educational level for each sector as a boundary condition of the firm performance in the context of social media for SMEs of South Italy.

This study shows that there are some important potential applications of social media management models in the study of social media strategy, with an outline of the major theoretical approaches to these applications. Practitioners can use this theoretical model to evaluate behavior of firms and employees and better target future social media interventions towards those groups which are most likely to benefit. This study opens a new avenue of research on how social media policy implementation can take place through the interactive effect of a firm's performance involvement in social media strategy.

7. Future Research Directions and Limitations

From a research perspective, this chapter sets a broad agenda for future research. Given the increasing prominence of social media phenomenon, there are many interesting opportunities for new research. Future research could analyze and develop a training system for employees and companies to gather data from the security with respect to variables governing the dynamics within the individual or a group. The issue of how to effectively design and deploy social media management model in this approach is an additional future research direction to follow.

Because only limited research on firm performance and the role of social media exists in the field of organizational business, this study can act as a catalyst for future scientific enquiries in this important area. A future research direction is to test the research questions regarding the role of security and to understand how social media can be successfully applied to interpret the function of determinants on a firm's performance. This study could be tested by a group of firms on this topic (e.g., Delphi methodology). This study also aims to contribute to the management and organizational disciplines in two principal and differentiated, but related ways.

First, future studies should compare firms that use this approach of social media tools with those that do not and determine the impact on a firm's performance. On a larger scale, a comparison could be made between a firm that uses this approach and one that does not in terms of the impact on job satisfaction, employee loyalty and development of new ideas.

Second, future research could analyze and develop a training system for employees and companies to gather data from the security with respect to variables governing the dynamics within the individual or group. From a better understanding of the determinants, a company will have a greater understanding of the true needs and expectations of human resources.

Despite efforts, response rate is relatively low, potentially undermining findings' external validity. The model assumes unidirectional relationships among constructs yet bidirectional linkages exist and need further investigation.

The present research has some limitations to be outlined and addressed for further research directions. Firstly, this chapter examined the impact of using social media on the profitability of SMEs in a region of South Italy. Thus, future research is recommended to test this link among other sectors within the tourism and hospitality field (e.g., hotels, motels, resorts, travel agents, etc.). Secondly, this research employed an online survey, as a data collection tool, to gather the primary data from concerned surveyors. Therefore, other data collection instruments (e.g., a self-administrative questionnaire, a semi-structured interview, a face-to-face interview, etc.) can be used to achieve this purpose. Thus, future studies can examine the research model within another region of the same country (e.g., northern Italy, western Italy, etc.). A comparative study is also suggested in this regard to provide clear and solid findings and implications. Moreover, the research model can be investigated in another country with a similar culture and conditions (e.g., a West European country) and/or a nation with different culture and conditions (e.g., a country from the Middle East and North Africa, Asia, South America, etc.). This can help in providing rigorous results and outlines concerning the links between the studied constructs. Lastly, the current study focuses on the perspective of owners of the SMEs in South Italy. As a result, future research can focus on the perspectives of other stakeholders, such as employees, locals, and/or customers using different variables and items.

References

Aichner, T. and Jacob, F. 2015. Measuring the degree of corporate social media use. *International Journal of Market Research*, 57(2): 257–275.

Aula, P. 2008. Social media, reputation risk and ambient publicity management. *Strategy and Leadership*, 38(6): 43–49.

Barney, J.B. 2001. Is the resource-based 'view' a useful perspective for strategic management research? Yes. *Academy of Management Review*, 26(1): 41–56.

Barreda, A.A., Bilgihan, A., Nusair, K. and Okumus, F. 2015. Generating brand awareness in online social networks. *Computers in Human Behavior*, 50: 600–609.

Blanchard, O. 2011. *Social Media ROI: Managing and Measuring Social Media Efforts in Your Organization*. Boston: Pearson Education, Inc.

Brivot, M., Gendron, Y. and Guenin, H. 2017. Reinventing organizational control: meaning contest surrounding reputational risk controllability in the social media area. *Accounting Auditing & Accounting Journal*, 30(4): 795–820.

Broccardo, L. and Zicari, A. 2020. Sustainability as a driver for value creation: A business model analysis of small and medium enterprises in the Italian wine sector. *Journal of Cleaner Production*, 259(1): 1–41.

Bryant, F. and Satorra, A. 2012. Principles and practise of scaled difference chi-square testing. *Structural Equation Modeling: A Multidisciplinary Journal*, 19(3): 372–398.

Carlson, J.B., Zivnuska, S., Harris, R.B., Harris, K.J. and Carlson, D.S. 2016. Social media use in the workplace: A study of dual effects. *Journal of Organizational and End User Computing*, 28(1): 15–31.

Castillo, C., Mendoza, M. and Poblete, B. 2011. Information credibility on twitter. pp. 675–684. *In: Proceedings of the 20th International Conference on the World Wide Web*. Association for Computing Machinery.

Chang, Y., Yu, H. and Lu, H. 2015. Persuasive messages, popularity cohesion, and message diffusion in social media marketing. *Journal of Business Research*, 68(4): 777–782.

Chen, Y., Fay, S. and Wang, Q. 2011. The role of marketing in social media: How online consumer reviews evolve. *Journal of Interactive Marketing*, 25(2): 85–94.

Colicev, A., Malshe, A., Pauwels, K. and O'Connor, P. 2018. Improving consumer mindset metrics and shareholder value through social media: The different roles of owned and earned media. *Journal of Marketing*, 82(1): 37–56.

Culnan, M., McHugh, P. and Zubillaga, J. 2010. How large U.S. companies can use twitter and other social media to gain business value. *MIS Quarterly Executive*, 9(4): 243–259.

Davcik, N.S. and Sharma, P. 2016. Marketing resources, performance, and competitive advantage: A review and future research directions. *Journal of Business Research*, 69(12): 5547–5552.

David, M., Gilfoil, D.M. and Jobs, C. 2012. Return on investment for social media: A proposed framework for understanding, implementing and measuring the return. *Journal of Business and Economics Research*, 10(4): 637–650.

Demek, K.C., Raschke, R.L., Janvrin, D.J. and Dilla, W.N. 2018. Do organizations use a formalized risk management process to address social media risk? *International Journal of Accounting Information Systems*, 28(3): 1–34.

Di Virgilio, F. 2018a. Exploring determinants of knowledge sharing: the role of social media in business organizations: Overview and new direction. pp. 1–30. *In:* Di Virgilio, F. (Ed.). *Social Media for Knowledge Management Applications in Modern Organizations*. Pennsylvania, USA: IGI Global.

Di Virgilio, F. (Ed.). 2018b. *Social Media for Knowledge Management Applications in Modern Organizations*. Pennsylvania, USA: IGI Global.

Di Virgilio, F. and Antonelli, G. 2018. Consumer behavior, trust and electronic word-of-mouth communication: toward a model of understanding of consumer's purchase intentions online. pp. 58–80. *In:* Di Virgilio, F. (Ed.). *Social Media for Knowledge Management Applications in Modern Organizations*. Pennsylvania, USA: IGI Global.

Di Virgilio, F., Valderrama Santomé, M. and López Bolás, A. 2018. Social media strategy within organizational communication: major open issues and challenges. pp. 205–225. *In:* Cantoni, F. and Mangia, G. (Eds.). *Human Resource Management and Digitalization.* Torino: Giappichelli Routledge.

Di Virgilio, F. 2021. Bringing social media into work: the positive and negative effects on policy implementation—an introduction to theory and research. pp. 121–142. *In:* Yadav, R., Panday, P. and Sharma, N. (Eds.). Pennsylvania, USA: IGI Global.

Dineva, D., Breitsohl, J., Garrod, B. and Megicks, P. 2020. Consumer responses to conflict-management strategies on non-profit social media fan pages. *Journal of Interactive Marketing*, 52: 118–136.

Ellison, N.B. and Boyd, D.M. 2007. Social network sites: definition, history, and scholarship. *Journal of Computer-Mediated Communication*, 13(1): 210–230.

Eschenbrenner, B., Nah, F.F.H. and Telaprolu, V.R. 2015. Efficacy of social media utilization by public accounting firms: Findings and directions for future research. *Journal Information System*, 29(2): 5–21.

Field, J. and Chelliah, J. 2012. Social-media misuse a ticking time-bomb for employers: Robust policies and procedures needed to reduce the risks. *Human Resource Management International Digest*, 20(7): 36–38.

Gaál, Z., Szabó, L., Obermayer-Kovács, N. and Csepregi, A. 2015. Exploring the role of social media in knowledge sharing. *The Electronic Journal of Knowledge Management*, 13(3): 185–197.

Garcia-Morales, V., Martin-Rojas, R. and Lardòn-Lòpez, M. 2018. Influence of social media technologies on organizational performance through knowledge and innovation. *Baltic Journal of Management*, 13(3): 345–367.

Gensler, S., Volckner, F., Liu-Thompkins, Y. and Wiertz, C. 2013. Managing brands in the social media environment. *Journal of Interactive Marketing*, 27(4): 242–256.

Gräve, J.-F. 2019. What KPIs are key? Evaluating performance metrics for social media influencers. *Social Media and Society*. July–September, 1–9.

Greenwald, D. 2010. Social media: Changing the world of business communication. In: *Proceedings of the 75th Annual Convention of the Association for Business Communication*, October 27–30, IL, Chicago.

Hajli, M.N. and Lin, X. 2014. Developing tourism education through social media. *Tourism Planning & Development*, 11(4): 405–414.

Hoffman, D.L. and Fodor, M. 2010. Can you measure the RoI of your social media marketing? *Sloan Manage Review*, 52(1): 41.

Hudson, S., Huang, L., Roth, M.S. and Madden, T.J. 2016. The influence of social media interactions on consumer brand relationships: A three-country study of brand perceptions and marketing behaviors. *International Journal of Research in Marketing*, 33(1): 27–41.

Khansa, L., Kuem, J., Siponen, M. and Kim, S.S. 2017. To cyberloaf or not to cyberloaf: the impact of the announcement of formal organizational controls. *Journal Management Information System*, 34(1): 141–176.

Kim, A.J. and Ko, E. 2012. Do social media marketing activities enhance customer equity? An empirical study of luxury fashion brand. *Journal of Business Research*, 65(10): 1480–1486.

Kim, S. and Park, H. 2013. Effects of various characteristics of social commerce (s-commerce) on consumers' trust and trust performance. *International Journal of Information Management*, 33(2): 318–332.

Kim, W.G., Lim, H. and Brymer, R.A. 2015. The effectiveness of managing social media on hotel performance. *International Journal of Hospitality Management*, 44: 165–171.

Kóscielniak, H. 2018. Key performance indicators of social media in enterprise management. *Polish Journal of Management Studies*, 18(2): 176–184.

Kumar, V., Bhaskaran, V., Mirchandani, R. and Shah, M. 2013. Practice prize winner creating a measurable social media marketing strategy: Increasing the value and ROI of intangibles and tangibles for hokey pokey. *Marketing Science*, 32(2): 194–212.

Labrecque, L.I., Vor Dem Esche, J., Mathwick, C., Novak, T.P. and Hofacker, C.F. 2013. Consumer Power: Evolution in the Digital Age. *Journal of Interactive Marketing*, 27(4): 257–269.

Lenskold, J. 2003. *Marketing ROI: The Path to Campaign, Customer, and Corporate Profitability* (1st ed.), New York: McGraw-Hill.

Munar, A.M. and Jacobsen, J.K.S. 2014. Motivations for sharing tourism experiences through social media. *Tourism Management*, 43: 46–54.

Nisar, T.M. and Whitehead, C. 2016. Brand interactions and social media: Enhancing user loyalty through social networking sites. *Computers in Human Behavior*, 62: 743–753.

O'Leary, D.E. 2011. Blog mining-review and extensions: from each according to his opinion. *Decision Supporting System*, 51(4): 821–830.

Ollier-Malaterre, A., Rothbard, N.P. and Berg, J. 2013. When worlds collide in cyberspace: How boundary work in online social networks impacts professional relationships. *Academy Management Review*, 38(4): 645–669.

Palacios-Marques, D., Merigo, J.M. and Soto-Acosta, P. 2015. Online social networks as an enabler of innovation in organizations. *Management Decision*, 53(9): 1906–1920.

Podobnik, V. 2013. An analysis of Facebook social media marketing key performance indicators: The case of premier league brands. *Proceedings of the 12th International Conference on Telecommunications*, 131–138, Zagreb, Croatia.

Ratten, V. 2020. Coronavirus and international business: An entrepreneurial ecosystem perspective, *International Business Review*, 1–6.

Rosman, R. and Stuhura, K. 2013. The implications of social media on customer relationship management and the hospitality industry. *Journal of Management Policy and Practice*, 14(3): 18.

Sashi, C.M. 2012. Customer engagement, buyer-seller relationships and social media. *Management Decision*, 50(2): 253–272.

Schaupp, L.C. and Bélanger, F. 2014. The value of social media for small businesses. *Information System*, 28(1): 187–2.

Schleicher, D.J., Baumann, H.M., Sullivan, D.W., Levy, P.E., Hargrove, D.C. and Barros-Rivera, B.A. 2018. Putting the system into performance management systems: a review and agenda for performance management research. *Journal of Management*, 44(6): 2209–2245.

Scott, P.R. and Jacka, J.M. 2011. *Auditing Social Media: A Governance and Risk Guide*. John Wiley & Sons, Hoboken, NJ.

Tajvidi, R. and Karami, A. 2017. The effect of social media on firm performance. *Computers in Human Behavior*, 1–10.

Trier, M. and Jensen, C.V. 2018. Social media management metrics for business analytics—Investing managerial challenges. *Twenty-sixth European Conference on Information Systems*. Portsmouth, UK.

Trinkle, B., Crossler, R. and Bélanger, F. 2015. Voluntary disclosures via social media and the role of comments. *Journal Information System*, 29(2): 101–122.

Tulsian, M. 2014. Profitability Analysis. A comparative study of SAIL and TATA Steel. *Journal of Economics and Finance*, 3(2): 19–22.

Watson, J. 2007. Modeling the relationship between networking and firm performance. *Journal of Business Venturing*, 22(6): 852–874.

Wernerfelt, B. 1984. A resource-based view of the firm. *Strategic Management Journal*, 5(2): 171–180.

Yadav, M., Joshib, Y. and Rahmanc, Z. 2015. Mobile social media: The new hybrid element of digital marketing communications. *Social and Behavioral Sciences*, 189: 335–343.

Yassin, F., Salim, J. and Sahari, N. 2013. The Influence of organizational factors on knowledge sharing using ICT among teachers. *Procedia Technology*, 11: 272–280.

Yen, C.L.A. and Tag, C.H.H. 2015. Hotel attribute performance, e Wom motivations, and media choice. *International Journal of Hospitality Management*, 46: 79–88.

Zhang, M., Guo, L., Hu, M. and Liu, W. 2017. Influence of customer engagement with company social networks on stickiness: Mediating effect of customer value creation. *International Journal of Information Management*, 37(3): 229–240.

14

Understanding the Impact of TikTok
A Study of TikTok's Strategy and Its Impact on Users' Lives

Julianna Kovács,[1] *Lilian Barbosa,*[1] *Lucas Barros,*[1]
Yuli Della Volpi,[1] *Cláudia Miranda Veloso,*[2]
Cicero Eduardo Walter[3] *and Manuel Au-Yong-Oliveira*[4,*]

INTRODUCTION

Today, people use mobile devices in order to immerse themselves into a media content world and to acquire some entertainment or knowledge. This can be achieved through social media and the consumption of mobile videos. According to some authors (Wang, 2020), the trend of consuming increasingly shorter videos may, to some extent, result from the fast pace of modern life.

In the social media world, apps need to evolve according to the way of life of users and their needs. Although Facebook is still the most popular social media platform in the world, with more than two billion active users, in July 2020 (Statista, 2020a), studies have demonstrated that in the past few years social media users tend to prefer sharing short-form videos due to convenience and content duration (Wright, 2017).

Short videos became a way of interaction that can transfer content in a really short period of time. Social media platforms present multiple features and videos can range from a few seconds to a few minutes (Su, 2018). TikTok emerged by generating

[1] DEGEIT, University of Aveiro, 3810-193 Aveiro, Portugal.
  Emails: kovacsjulianna09@gmail.com; lilianbarbosa@ua.pt; lucasfrb45@ua.pt; yuli.dvolpi@ua.pt
[2] GOVCOPP, ESTGA, University of Aveiro, 3810-193 Aveiro, Portugal.
  Email: cmv@ua.pt
[3] Federal Institute of Education Science and Technology of Piauí, Brazil; GOVCOPP, DEGEIT, University of Aveiro, 3810-193 Aveiro, Portugal.
  Email: eduardowalter@ifpi.edu.br
[4] GOVCOPP, DEGEIT, University of Aveiro, 3810-193 Aveiro, Portugal; INESC TEC, Porto, Portugal.
* Corresponding author: mao@ua.pt

entertainment content through users' experiences and with stimulation mechanisms, allowing them to share it with the app community, opening opportunities for a collaborative, engaging and effective learning experience for users (Zhou, 2019). This is probably the reason why TikTok is becoming one of the most popular social media platforms nowadays, especially among the younger generation.

Based on that, this article aims to understand the impact of this social media on its users' lives. The literature review on TikTok's history and strategy is presented in the next section, followed by the methodology and the results of the survey applied to TikTok's users. Finally, the last section is dedicated to the conclusion.

1. Literature Review

1.1 Short Videos Trend in Social Media: TikTok's History

TikTok is a short-video sharing app that started from two other applications: Musical.ly and Douyin. Musical.ly was launched in Shanghai in 2014 and its main purpose was to allow users to create short lip-sync videos that combine popular songs with the user's video creation. According to the marketing agency Brandastic (Brandastic, 2020), by the end of the first semester of 2017, the Musical.ly app already had over 200 million users.

In 2016, ByteDance, a technology company from China, created an application named Douyin with a similar service where users could create and share lip-sync and other kinds of videos based on different challenges. In 2017, ByteDance bought Musical.ly and one year later the Chinese company merged the two apps into one, under the name of TikTok.

Launched initially in China, TikTok is now available in over 150 markets around the world, in 39 languages. The site Business of Apps (Business of Apps, 2020) published, in October 2020, the latest available official statistics which show that there are 500 million TikTok users around the world (monthly active users).

The strategy to merge Musical.ly and Douyin can be considered also as a way for ByteDance to enter the United States market, where Musical.ly already had a position. It was the beginning of TikTok's global expansion.

Unlike Facebook, for example, TikTok was not created after some new fresh idea or need. It was a merge of two very popular social media apps with a clear strategy—build a world short-video platform based on the trend of consumption of millennials and Generation Z and a highly qualified merging of artificial intelligence and image capture (Jaffar et al., 2019).

Today, TikTok can be considered a global phenomenon since it became one of the fastest-growing apps worldwide. TikTok jumped from 269th to 4th in the global app download rank in February 2019 and has remained in the top-20 in February 2020 (Apptrace, 2020).

Research shows that short video platforms have become the most popular type of social media among millennials in China (*The Japan Times*, 2018) and in the world. Almost entirely short video platforms are mobile applications where users can create, edit, share and view videos ranging from a few seconds to a few minutes (Zhao and Wang, 2015). The interesting content generation and its fast transmission in a community makes the short-videos platform convenient and attractive. This seems to be the initial and core strategy of TikTok.

1.2 Why TikTok became so Popular

Some of the possible reasons to explain TikTok's popularity are (Influencer Marketing Hub, 2020):

a) Celebrity endorsements (the app is used by several celebrities and, over time, created partnerships with some of them to promote the app).

b) The localized content, expressed by a 'divide to conquer' methodology to gain popularity region by region. This is done in multiple ways, like capturing local trends and promoting local challenges through the use of localized hashtags. This also helps users in the creation of videos that could go viral. In addition, TikTok also runs the 'one million audition' contest in several countries. It is a contest where users from the same country have a set of themes to create videos and the top ones are rewarded.

c) The fact that it is easy to use. Because videos are so short, there is a big advantage towards other platforms, due to the small amount of time it takes to upload. Additionally, these videos are played as soon as the user opens the app, which helps to capture the user's attention and keep it there. It is kind of addictive.

1.3 TikTok's Growth Strategy

TikTok's strategy is based on adapting to the personality, lifestyle and taste of young people in a short video social platform. This application function pushes content according to the user's preferences, highlighting the desire of expressing opinions and stories about themselves, enhancing their creativity (Yanget al., 2019). This creativity makes TikTok grow at a rapid pace because of its sophisticated stylish content and interesting advertising ideas and makes this the meaning of the short video existence.

TikTok's growth also relies on a theory: the mass communication theory. According to the literature (Chaffee and Metzger, 2001), mass communication means different things to different people. The word mass in a mass communication allows a communicator to reach a much larger and more geographically dispersed audience.

Sharing your life and/or getting a marketing message out to younger customers is a challenging task, especially after the millennials. The media consumption patterns differentiate from generation Z (those born in the late 1990s) to the new generations shifting specifically to social media platforms, such as Instagram or TikTok. While users on Facebook tend to be in their 40s, Instagram seems to attract consumers in their 30s, and TikTok in their 20s. This shows a different media consumption pattern, and, for the younger people, influencer marketing is particularly important (Haenlein et al., 2020).

Social media with user generated content represents one of the most consumed on-line products. Figure 1 shows the time spent (in hours) per week watching selected types of online video content according to online viewers worldwide, in

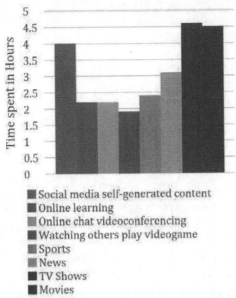

Fig. 1: Time spent watching online video content [based on Statista (2020b)].

August 2020. The survey was applied in an age group of 18 years and older with 5,000 respondents (Statista, 2020b).

But why does TikTok get so much attention from younger people? What makes TikTok different is the availability of several kinds of background music, challenges, dance videos, magic tricks and funny videos that fascinate younger consumers to connect with the app. Another reason is that it requires less time to create a video, which is an advantage for the users and makes TikTok totally different from other apps. This unique design is a plus for the product and supports its development and growth. Additionally, the first short video app to use 'big data' analysis is TikTok. They have used 'big data' analysis to understand the liking of the users so that they can suggest new contents to them, making it easier for the users to select what they prefer (Hou, 2018).

Thus, it is possible to understand that TikTok provides all sorts of tools, filters and augmented reality effects so their users can create their own videos or engage in a variety of challenges that aim to duplicate other video creators' content (Zhang, 2020) and that one of the major advantages in the development of TikTok was its strong algorithmic technical support (Xu et al., 2019).

Zhang Yiming, CEO of Bytedance, valued an algorithm-driven approach and considered that machines could perform better than humans when regarding the distribution of information (Zhang, 2020). Furthermore, their investment in innovative technological features becomes more and more evident to the public with the development of new functions, such as the 'dance function', created to recognize people's dance moves and match them with the postures featured on the app (Xu et al., 2019).

Based on this, it is possible to say that TikTok developers got the timing right. Hence, TikTok's success could not have been the same without the development of artificial intelligence technologies (AIT) that happened in the past few years. After all, it was the development of AIT that enabled the platform to analyze user preferences in a precise way and promote their favorite content in order to improve user satisfaction (Xu et al., 2019).

Although very important, artificial intelligence technologies are not the only factor responsible for the company's accomplishments. TikTok also invested in a variety of marketing strategies that proved to be effective. Some examples of these strategies worth mentioning, are (Xu et al., 2019):

a) TikTok invited a couple of Chinese celebrities to record and post their videos online during the Spring Festival of 2017.

b) The company invests in advertising that reaches their target group, appearing in the advertisement of the variety show 'China has hip hop', for example.

c) TikTok marketing is not restricted to online promotion. The company also cooperates with others in the development and promotion of offline activities, such as the 2017 National Youth Talent Competition, thus increasing its visibility.

d) The adoption of an international strategy, recruiting partners and expanding globally.

e) The company also cooperates with major music platforms in order to have many music copyrights.

In fact, TikTok's marketing team seems to be very good when it comes to fulfilling their customers' needs. The recent crisis caused by the rise of Covid-19 forced a lot of entertainment organizations, including museums and movie theatres around the world, to stop their business for a while due to quarantine periods. TikTok saw this as a business opportunity and launched a series of new services to meet the consumers' needs. Among these services, online exhibitions, online movie playback and online education in the live-streaming sector stand out (Wang et al., 2020).

Each of those strategies played a part in the company's current success. It is important to note that TikTok has been increasing its focus on monetizing opportunities. Working with e-commerce platforms, the company has recently introduced new shopping features (Zhang, 2020). Additionally, TikTok recently launched a fund to pay video creators directly for their content (The Verge, 2020).

The pace at which the competition in many world industries is changing is relentless and continuously increasing (Hitt et al., 2009). Due to globalization and the fast changes in the technology market, it is important for companies to keep innovating and creating value for their product.

Thus, organizations need to offer more value than their competitors to present a competitive advantage (Hitt et al., 2009). Thus to maintain its popularity and not to be replaced or lose its market share to another application with similar features in a short period of time, TikTok must keep improving and innovating its strategies.

However, besides the challenges imposed to all companies that stand out in a globalized and competitive economy, it is noteworthy that TikTok also needs to face a bigger challenge and overcome the distrust of some potential users. A fast search on the Internet shows a series of newspaper articles questioning its transparency and possible political implications (El País, 2020) or reporting attacks against the company (Forbes, 2020). TikTok was also the target of an executive order issued by the President of USA, Donald Trump, to ban its use (Koleson, 2020). The President later back tracked on his decision. Hence, TikTok's marketing and strategy team must focus on improving their international image related to transparency to build trust in its business.

1.4 How TikTok Affects the Users' Lives

TikTok is constantly growing and becoming one of the most popular smartphone applications. It was designed to connect content producers and users who have the same interests.

The algorithm collects data on how much time a person is watching a video, what it is about and whether he or she clicks on the comment section, shares or likes the video. Therefore, as previously discussed, the users receive a completely personalized home page about the topics they are most interested in.

As the authors of this paper had the opportunity to see when installing the app, the so-called TikTokers—video makers—on the platform are surprisingly open and share many details about their personal lives. Videos giving advice on social anxiety, cyberbullying, relationships, etc., are very common. Therefore, it is possible that those who have these issues do not feel like they are the only ones dealing with that problem and feel confident to share their experience.

However, using the application may have some negative effects as well. To begin with, some users complain about wasting too much of their time on the app. They open it, thinking they will probably watch just a few videos, but then catch themselves scrolling through hundreds of videos for hours. On one hand, this means that they enjoy their time on the application; however, on the other hand, it is not beneficial for their time-management. Besides that, users are also complaining about how much TikTok has affected their concentration time span. Since the videos are very short—maximum one-minute long—users have become used to receiving new information very quickly (Zhou, 2019).

Regarding their time spent on the app, it is interesting to note that TikTok provides some tools for the user to control it. For instance, TikTok alerts users when they spend more than two hours on the app.

It is also important to note that TikTok, as with most social media nowadays, can be seen as an opportunity for people to become famous quickly, which might dictate the way and frequency in which users share their content.

1.5 Scopus Literature Search—TikTok

A search on Scopus on 23-01-2021, with the term TikTok, returned 81 documents. When narrowing the search to 'TikTok and strategy', a total of seven documents were found. Table 1 shows the results of the latter search on Scopus.

Note how Table 1 focuses on: (1) all-in-one app ecosystems and their (in) security; (2) how TikTok has become an outlet used by athletes through which they may effectively communicate—via short videos—with their fans—current and new;

Table 1: A search on scopus on 23-01-2021—with the term 'TikTok and Strategy'.

Authors	Source	Title of the Article	Contribution – from the Abstract
Lu et al., 2020	Proceedings of the ACM Conference on Computer and Communications Security, pp. 569–585	Demystifying Resource Management Risks in Emerging Mobile App-in-App Ecosystems.	'App-in-app is a new and trending mobile computing paradigm... to enrich the host app's [e.g., Wechat, Baidu, TikTok and Chrome] functionalities. All-in-one app ecosystems are seen to be insecure as the host (such as Wechat, Baidu, TikTok and Chrome) reveals high-impact security flaws, which allow the adversary to stealthily escalate privilege (e.g., accessing the camera, photo gallery, microphone, etc.) or acquire sensitive data (e.g., location, passwords of Amazon, Google, etc.).'
Su et al., 2020	International Journal of Sport Communication Volume 13, Issue 3, September 2020, pp. 436–446	Fan engagement in 15 seconds: Athletes' relationship marketing during a pandemic via TikTok.	'As Covid-19 lockdowns force most sport leagues into hiatus, engaging fans has emerged as a key challenge confronting the sport industry. While navigating social distancing protocols, athletes are experimenting with new ways to connect with their fans.' TikTok has emerged as an outlet through which athletes may effectively communicate—via short videos—with their fan base (existing and new), especially during Covid-19 lockdowns. These videos are seen to be playful and authentic and may be integrated into athletes' online branding strategies.'
Jia and Ruan, 2020	Internet Policy Review Volume 9, Issue 3, 2020, pp. 1–22	Going global: Comparing chinese mobile applications' data and user privacy governance at home and abroad.	'Examine and compare data and privacy governance by four China-based mobile applications and their international versions: Baidu, Toutiao and its international version TopBuzz, Douyin and its international version TikTok, and WeChat ... Baidu has the most unsatisfactory data and privacy protection measures, while ByteDance's TikTok/Douyin and TopBuzz/Toutiao offer more comprehensive user protection from different jurisdictions.'
Chen et al., 2020	Mobile Media and Communication	The co-evolution of two Chinese mobile short video apps: Parallel platformization of Douyin and TikTok.	'TikTok is the international twin of China's mobile short video app, Douyin, and one of the fastest growing short video platforms in the world. Owned by Chinese tech giant, ByteDance, TikTok and Douyin share many similarities in terms of appearance, functionality, and platform affordances; however, they exist in radically different markets and are governed by radically different forces. Using the app walkthrough method informed by platformization of culture production theory, this study highlights the similarities and distinctions between these two platforms.' 'This provides an interesting case study to investigate how an emerging internet company adapts its products to better fit divergent expectations, cultures, and policy frameworks in China and abroad.'

Author	Source	Title	Summary
De Veirman et al., 2019	Frontiers in Psychology Volume 10, 3 December 2019, Article number 2685	What Is Influencer Marketing and How does It Target Children? A Review and Direction for Future Research.	Both children and adults post attractive content online, nowadays. 'The famous child vlogger Ryan of Ryan's World, for instance, has more than 19 million viewers and he is (at age seven) a social media influencer.' Influencer marketing includes such vloggers as a communication tool/as advertisers. 'Sponsored content appears to be highly influential and may affect young children's brand preferences.' Children under age 12 are vulnerable to such advertising and communication processes. 'Many influential vloggers now receive free products from brands in return for a mention in one of their videos and their other social media (e.g., TikTok or Instagram) and some are even paid to create a sponsored post or video and distribute it to their followers.' 'We then discuss the few studies that have been conducted on influencer marketing among young children (under 12), based on a systematic literature review, and take these findings to formulate societal and policy implications and develop a future research agenda.'
Peng et al., 2019	2019 International Conference on Wavelet Active Media Technology and Information Processing (ICWAMTIP) 9067687, pp. 100–104	Public Opinion Analysis Strategy of Short Video Content Review in Big Data Environment.	'With the rapid development of mobile Internet and 4G, short video apps came into being. Internet companies have launched such explosive short video platforms as "weishi", "TikTok" and "kuaishou" in response to the fragmented reading habits of the public.' 'Internet users can more easily browse public opinion news, express opinions and emotions.' 'This paper proposes a big data public opinion analysis strategy which integrates short video content comments.' Then, according to the characteristics of online public opinion, a model is proposed to quantitatively express the emotional value of public opinion comments.
Cheng et al., 2019	2019 International Conference on Virtual Reality and Intelligent Systems (ICVRIS)	Practice of a New Model Fusion Structure in Short Video Recommendation.	'In recent years, the popular short video content understanding, and recommendation technology, has become a research hotspot. This paper presents a new mixed short video recommendation algorithm' based on the content, and on other aspects.

(3) data and privacy protection measures—examining and comparing governance in the case of four China-based mobile applications—including their international versions; (4) a 'case study to investigate how an emerging Internet company adapts its products to better fit divergent expectations, cultures and policy frameworks in China and abroad' (Kaye et al., 2020, from the abstract); (5) 'many influential vloggers now receive free products from brands in return for a mention in one of their videos and their other social media (e.g., TikTok or Instagram) and some are even paid to create a sponsored post or video and distribute it to their followers. ... We then discuss the few studies that have been conducted on influencer marketing among young children (under 12)' (De Veirman et al., 2019, from the abstract); (6) 'Internet companies have launched such explosive short video platforms as "weishi", "TikTok" and "kuaishou" in response to the fragmented reading habits of the public. ... Internet users can more easily browse public opinion news, express opinions and emotions' (Peng et al., 2019, from the abstract); (7) short video recommendation technology, in the case of short video apps, such as TikTok.

1.6 May Two Chinese Mobile Short Video Apps Co-evolve? The Cases of Douyin and TikTok

ByteDance app TikTok was fined, in February 2019, a record 5.7 million USD for violations to the United States' Children's Online Privacy Protection Act. The entity responsible for this was the US Federal Trade Commission. The act was 'failing to obtain parental consent and deliver parental notification' [illegally collecting data belonging to children under 13 years of age] (Jia and Ruan, 2020, p. 2). Clearly, operating in China or abroad has its differences, with TikTok and Douyin possessing designated policies for domestic versus international users. TikTok's privacy policies and service terms tend to be most regional-specific. TikTok has three different approaches, for the USA, European Union, as well as for global users (not counting the USA or the European Union) (Jia and Ruan, 2020).

'TikTok, first created in 2016, was rebranded with ByteDance's US$ 1 billion acquisition of Musical.ly in 2018. The Chinese version of TikTok, Douyin, was released in 2016 by ByteDance as the leading short-video platform in the country. The Douyin app has several different features that are particular to the Chinese market and regulation. For example, the #PositiveEnergy was integrated into the app as an effort to align with the state's political agenda to promote Chinese patriotism and nationalism (Chen et al., 2020; Jia and Ruan, 2020, p. 7)'. What is 'positive energy' (*zheng nengliang*), really, according to Chinese political discourse? It is 'a popular expression that has embodied mainstream political ideology in China since 2012. This term has also become prominent on Douyin, a prominent Chinese short-video platform. By June 2018, over 500 Chinese governmental accounts on Douyin had promoted positive energy in videos, and the content was viewed over 1.6 billion times. Douyin even created a separate trending section, Positive Energy, for videos that promoted the dominant state ideology' (Chen et al., 2020, p. 97). What is the opposite of positive energy, argues the Chinese government? Vulgarity (Chen et al., 2020), which has also been occurring on such networks and platforms.

Chen et al. (2020) performed a content analysis, involving in excess of 800 videos, from the Positive Energy area of Douyin and it may be concluded that, in a playful way, patriotism, and China's state political agenda, may be promoted online, quite ingeniously.

According to Zhao (2021, p. 1), 'Douyin has accumulated more than half of the Chinese netizens as its daily active users'. Indeed, Douyin addiction (and the viewing of its short videos) is a known and widespread phenomenon (Zhao, 2021). A big part of the above is the recommendation algorithm used, to keep users satisfied and happy and to meet their needs (Zhao, 2021). The recommendation algorithm is accurate and personalized, and often makes use of traps.

As mentioned above, 'the algorithm principles positively affects users' continuance intention. Meanwhile, the more frequent the user uses Douyin, the more accurate the algorithm will be. If not intervened, the addiction may be severely exacerbated' (Zhao, 2021, p. 1). This is thus a current problem, which requires attention by authorities and stakeholders alike.

The need for users to express themselves and to project a full and good life is very strong. This may in fact be achieved via very short videos ranging from 15 seconds long to 60 seconds long, often very funny videos and on a wide number of topics. What we now call 'short form' videos is a popular and growing trend on the Internet.

How is Douyin different from other apps? 'The most conspicuous feature that distinguishes Douyin from other similar products is that it is an algorithm-driven, content-oriented product, which means that its popularity is largely dependent on the powerful AI [Artificial Intelligence] algorithms and content distribution strategies.' (Zhao, 2021, p. 1).

Namely, 'with the recommendation of the algorithm, each user will receive a completely personalized video feed based on the matching between their own personalities, content labels and the characteristics of their environment' (Zhao, 2021, p. 1)'. This is the success formula. The personalized content recommended is passively accepted by the user in question, without the necessity for a search (in itself, this is a significant revolution as regards the Internet, involving less effort and apparently more freedom). This activity has been labelled as an 'innovative channel of information dissemination' (Zhao, 2021, p. 1), the usage of algorithms in communication. Hours of (addicted and also harmful) viewing may be the result, of which the long-term consequences are still largely unknown. In effect, Douyin's (at times abusive) algorithms are 'sticky' and help not only attract, but also maintain, users.

While on Douyin, and though the videos are very short, time will 'fly by', without the user being conscious of it. Douyin usage is thus simple and effortless, and screen-swipes are often the only more obvious cost involved. Smartphone usage is hence at an all-time high, especially amongst the younger generations, who appear to be addicted to mobile short-form videos. Such usage has grown over six times, from 2017 to 2019, for such Chinese apps alone (Meeker, 2019). 'Short videos have been considered high-frequency applications, with 41.3 per cent of users using multiple times a day and 56.9 per cent of users using more than 60 minutes per day (Big Data-Research, 2019). Douyin, as one of the most popular short video platforms in China today, is even higher than this overall average' (Zhao, 2020, pp. 2–3).

2. Methodology

First, a literature review was conducted in order to understand TikTok's history, features and strategies that explain its fast growth and popularity.

Secondly, a survey was conducted in order to obtain more information about the impact of TikTok as it is perceived by users. This survey was aimed at people who had already had contact with this particular social media platform and included open and closed questions. The survey was conducted online from November 2 to November 20 and was shared throughout different social media networks. Thus, the sample was a convenience sample. The survey returned 51 valid answers. Most of the participants were residents in Portugal or other European countries.

The questions can be classified in two types: User a ttribute related and TikTok's usage related.

The questions related to users' attributes are meant to collect information about the users. This type of information aims to find patterns among users to build knowledge about not only the impact and usage of TikTok by users in general but also by those with the same attributes. To help doing so, we developed a Python program that takes the data from the questionnaire and plots bar figures divided both by gender and age related to each question. To plot the figures, the library matplotlib was used.

The questions related to TikTok's usage gave useful information to produce findings regarding the impact of TikTok on users' lives. Here is a list of these questions:

- How did you discover TikTok?
- What are/were your interests for using TikTok?
- Have you ever stopped using TikTok?
- If so, why? (related to the previous question)
- How often do you use TikTok nowadays?
- How much time per day do you spend on the app?
- Did you increase the time spent on your phone since downloading TikTok?
- Have you ever bought anything you saw advertised in TikTok?
- Do you think TikTok has affected your personality, like your shyness, for instance?

As perceived by the questions, this questionnaire was meant not only for TikTok's current users but also for former users/people who once downloaded it. We wanted to understand not only what drives people to use this app but also what drives them away from it after checking what it is about.

3. Results and Discussion

First, we are going to present the survey's participants (TikTok's users) who we will denominate 'users' from this point forward in this paper. We had a total number of 51 answers to the survey. Among these 51 users, more than 64 per cent are teens (< 18 years) and young adults (18–21 years old), 19.6 per cent are between 22 and 25 years old and 15.7 per cent are more than 26 years old.

Figures 2 and 3 present the results for the question: 'How often do you use TikTok nowadays?' both by gender and age.

By analyzing these figures and our data, there are two conclusions that can be inferred from the sample. First, women use TikTok more than men and are less likely to stop using the app after trying it. This last information is confirmed with the answers to the question: 'Have you ever stopped using TikTok?' in which almost 70 per cent of men confirmed they have and only 16.6 per cent of women said the same. Moreover, we also analyzed the results to the question: 'How much time per

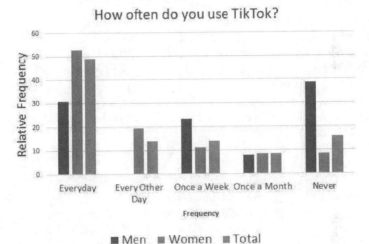

Fig. 2: Answer to the question: 'How often do you use TikTok?' by gender.

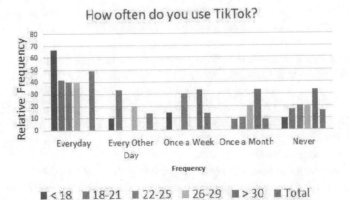

Fig. 3: Answer to the question: 'How often do you use TikTok?' by age.

day do you spend on the app?' by gender and more than 60 per cent of men spend less than 30 minutes while only 27.7 per cent of women spend less than 30 minutes on it, which is in line with what we have stated. This can be explained in two ways: either TikTok's content is more appealing to women or women get more attention and are more likely to have followers and success. To try to understand this, we then analyzed the answers to the question: 'What are/were your interests for using TikTok?'. The great majority of answers to this question were related to watching funny videos, spending time and having fun. There were also some females who answered 'peer pressure' which might indicate that women are more easily influenced by their social group than men.

Second, younger people use TikTok more and are less likely to stop using it than older people. Regarding the reasons why people quit using TikTok, we analyzed the answers to the question: 'If so (stopped using TikTok), why?' The majority of answers were related to losing interest and finding the content boring. Some answers also showed users' concern of becoming 'addicted' to TikTok and also data security issues.

By analyzing the answers to the question: 'Did you increase the time spent on your phone since downloading TikTok?', it is possible to note that 51 per cent of users did not, while 49 per cent stated that now they spend more time on their phone. It is important to highlight that 0 per cent claimed spending less time on their phone. This suggests that TikTok has replaced some of the time spent on other social media networks for most of the users while increasing the screen time of the others. Furthermore, most of the users who reported using TikTok every day spend more time on their phones than before downloading it.

When analyzing the answers to the question: 'Have you ever bought anything you saw advertised in TikTok?', it was possible to note that approximately 80 per cent of the participants answered 'no'. When analyzing the gender and age graphic, practically all users that had already bought something after seeing it advertised on TikTok were more than 21-years old. This finding suggests that older users are more likely to buy products advertised in TikTok than teenagers. Further study or research must be carried out to understand this behavior.

Finally, regarding the question: 'Do you think TikTok has affected your personality like your shyness for instance?', 45.09 per cent of the participants gave a positive answer and 54.9 per cent gave a negative one. Concerning the positive answers, some users said that they in fact became less shy due to posting videos and seeing the reactions from other people. There were also some users who said that watching videos of other people who dealt with the same issues as them and speak openly about these problems had helped them to overcome these issues. Some users also said that posting videos had made them feel more comfortable being themselves. Finally, there was also a small percentage of users who were foreigners living in Portugal and who said that TikTok had helped them to better understand the Portuguese sense of humor.

To finalize, we applied the chi-square test to check if the variables 'Do you think TikTok has affected your personality like your shyness for instance?' and 'Did you increase the time spent on your phone since downloading TikTok?' were related. For that, we first created a contingency table (Table 2) with the appropriate values.

Table 2: Time spent on the phone increased x consequences of TikTok in shaping one's personality.

Did you increase the time spent on your phone since downloading TikTok?	Do you think TikTok has affected your personality like your shyness for instance?		
	Yes	No	Total
Yes	15	10	25
No	8	18	26
Total	23	28	51

Then, the expected values were calculated for each observation and so on until we got the test statistic. These are presented in Table 3. The degrees of freedom (number of columns - 1) x (number of rows - 1) = 1 x 1 = 1. Hence, Yates' correction was applied as there was only one degree of freedom.

Table 3: Analysis—time spent on the phone increased x consequences of TikTok in shaping one's personality.

O	E	O-E	IO-EI-0,5	(IO-EI-0,5)2	((IO-EI-0,5)2)/E
15	11,275	3,725	3,225	10,4	0,922
10	13,725	–3,725	3,225	10,4	0,758
8	11,725	–3,725	3,225	10,4	0,887
18	14,275	3,725	3,225	10,4	0,729
					3,296

After checking the table of the chi-square distribution, at the 5 per cent significance level we note that our test statistic (3.296) is less than the critical value obtained from the table (3.841). We thus confirm the null hypothesis (H_0) that there seems to be no association between the variables, 'Do you think TikTok has affected your personality like your shyness for instance?' and 'Did you increase the time spent on your phone since downloading TikTok?'. We hence reject the alternative hypothesis (H_1) that there is such an association, at the 5 per cent significance level. The variables are independent.

4. Conclusion

The chapter's methodology included a literature review as well as primary data research, in this case a survey, which had 51 answers from TikTok users.

Based on our research, it is possible to conclude that TikTok's popularity has been increasing around the world in the past few years (Apptrace, 2020). Its strategy is ambitious and it aims at big markets, such as the North American market. In this sense, the merge with Musical.ly was a big move towards this goal.

On the other hand, Douyin, in China, shows that, quite clearly, operating in China or abroad has its differences. For example, Douyin, for the Chinese market and by the same firm as TikTok, follows a different perspective, including a 'positive energy' (*zheng nengliang*), Chinese political discourse. TikTok, perhaps not used to the USA market, recorded a record fine there. TikTok and Douyin possess designated policies for domestic versus international users. TikTok's privacy policies and service terms tend to be most regional-specific.

Furthermore, addiction is a new malady and occurs due to the sticky algorithm which TikTok and Douyin use, based on AI, to attract and maintain users. No searches are needed to receive personalized content for each user, based on personality, past actions (which are registered) and on the specific environment. Users are spending ever more time online on these short-form video platforms.

The survey results also demonstrated that TikTokers' profiles are mostly from people under 26 years old and the majority of people who use the app every day also increased their screen time in their mobile phones, reinforcing the idea that TikTok is capable of keeping users' attention for a long time (Influencer Marketing Hub, 2020); sometimes longer than they would like, which is competitive in the current social media market.

Furthermore, this article aimed to show the impact of TikTok on the users' lives and, even with a small sample, it can be confirmed through the results that people have been spending more time on their mobile phones searching for entertainment and information, which impacts on their behavior and opens a door to a faster and more agile consumption of information and possibly products.

We did some inferential statistics, namely, the chi-square test, but no statistically significant association was found. There seems to be no association between the variables, 'Do you think TikTok has affected your personality like your shyness for instance?' and 'Did you increase the time spent on your phone since downloading TikTok?'.

It is important to observe that this research is not exhaustive, but rather that it is exploratory, thus presenting some limitations, such as the size of the sample. Although it is useful to bring some insights on the TikTok users' perspective regarding the impact of this social media on their lives, further research is still needed in order to better understand some questions raised by the article. For example, future research could focus on understanding why older users seem to be more willing to buy products they see advertised on TikTok or why this social media is more appealing to women. We also recommend that further research focuses on the psychological effect of TikTok on the users' lives.

References

Apptrace. 2020. *TikTok Statistics*; retrieved from: https://www.apptrace.com/app/com.zhiliaoapp. musically.

Big Data-Research. 2019. *China Short Video Market Research Report for the 3rd Quarter of 2019*; retrieved from: http://www.bigdata- research.cn/content/201911/1010.html.

Brandastic. 2020. *What is TikTok? Why is it so Popular?* Retrieved from: https://brandastic.com/blog/what-is-tiktok-and-why-is-it-so-popular/.

Business of Apps. 2020. *TikTok Revenue and Usage Statistics*; retrieved from: https://www.businessofapps.com/data/tik-tok-statistics/.

Chaffee, S.H. and Metzger, M.J. 2001. The end of mass communication? *Mass Communication and Society*, 4(4): 365–379.

Chen, X., Kaye, D., Bondy Valdovinos and Zeng, J. 2021. #PositiveEnergy Douyin: Constructing 'playful patriotism' in a Chinese short-video application. *Chinese Journal of Communication*, 14(1): 97–117.

Cheng, J., Li, Z., Wang, L. and Bian, Q. 2019. Practice of a new model recommendation. pp. 27–30. *In*: *IEEE Computer Society, 2019 International Conference Systems (ICVRIS)*. Jishou, China, 14-15 September.

De Veirman, M., Hudders, L. and Nelson, M.R. 2019. What is influencer marketing and how does it target children? A review and direction for future research. *Frontiers in Psychology*, 10(3): December 2019.

El País. 2020. *The Dark Side of TikTok, a Chinese Social Network of Short Videos*; retrieved from: https://brasil.elpais.com/tecnologia/2020-01-19/o-lado-escuro-do-tiktok-a-rede-social-chinesa-dos-videos-curtos.html.

Forbes. 2020. *Anonymous Hackers Target TikTok: Delete This Chinese Spyware Now*; retrieved from: https://www.forbes.com/sites/zakdoffman/2020/07/01/anonymous-targets-tiktok-delete-this-chinese-spyware-now/#48eafc2c35cc.

Haenlein, M., Anadol, E., Farnsworth, T., Hugo, H., Hunichen, J. and Welte, D. 2020. Navigating the new era of influencer marketing: how to be successful on Instagram, TikTok, & Co. *California Management Review*, 63(1): 5–25.

Hitt, M.A., Ireland, R.S. and Hoskisson, R.E. 2009. *Strategic Management: Concepts and Cases: Competitiveness and Globalization*, 8th ed., South-Western Cengage Learning.

Hou, L. 2018. Study on the perceived popularity of TikTok. *Partial Fulfilment of the Requirements for the Master's in Communication Arts*. Graduate School, Bangkok University.

Influencer Marketing Hub. 2020. *What is TikTok?—The Fastest Growing Social Media App;* retrieved from: https://influencermarketinghub.com/what-is-tiktok/.

Jaffar, A.B., Riaz, S. and Mushtaq, A. 2019. Living in a Moment: Impact of TikTok on Influencing Younger Generation into Micro-fame. *Journal of Content, Community and Communication*, 10: 5.

Jia, L. and Ruan, L. 2020. Going global: Comparing Chinese mobile applications' data and user privacy governance at home and abroad. *Internet Policy Review*, 9(3): 1–22.

Kaye, D.B.V., Chen, X. and Zeng, J. 2020. The co-evolution of two Chinese mobile short video apps: Parallel platformization of Douyin and TikTok. *Mobile Media and Communication*.

Koleson, J. 2020. TikTok is on the clock, will democracy stop? *SLU Law Journal Online*.

Lu, H., Xing, L., Xiao, Y., Zhang, Y., Liao, X., Wang, X. and Wang, X. 2020. Demystifying resource management risks in emerging mobile app-in-app ecosystems. pp. 569–585. *Proceedings of the ACM Conference on Computer and Communications Security*.

Meeker, M. 2019. *Internet Trends Report*. Retrieved from: https://www.bondcap.com/report/itr19.

Peng, A., Liu, J. and Gao, Q. 2019. Public opinion analysis strategy of short video content review in big data environment. *2019 International Conference on Wavelet Active Media Technology and Information Processing (ICWAMTIP)*, (100–104): 9067687.

Statista. 2020a. *Social Media and User-generated Content*; retrieved from: <https://www.statista.com/statistics/784403/time-spend-watching-online-video-by-content-worldwide/.

Statista. 2020b. *How Many Hours of Online Video do you Watch Per Week*? Retrieved from: <https://www.statista.com/statistics/784403/time-spend-watching-online-video-by-content-worldwide/>.

Su, T. 2018. *Research on Influencing Factors of the New Generation User's Behavior Intention Toward Mobile Short Video App*. Master's thesis, Jinan University, Lebanon.

Su, Y., Baker, B.J., Doyle, J.P. and Yan, M. 2020. Fan engagement in 15 seconds: Athletes' relationship marketing during a pandemic via TikTok. *International Journal of Sport Communication*. September, 13(3): 436–446.

The Japan Times. 2018. *Tiktok Video App has Become a Petri Dish for Youth Culture*; retrieved from: https://www.japantimes.co.jp/news/2018/08/25/national/media-national/tiktok-video-appbecome-petri-dish-youth-culture/#.XIda5ohKjid.

The Verge. 2020. TikTok is launching a $200 million fund to pay creators for their videos; retrieved from: https://www.theverge.com/2020/7/23/21335404/tiktok-creators-monetization-fund-followers-youtube-content-videos.

Wang, Y. 2020. Humor and camera view on mobile short-form video apps influence user experience and technology-adoption intent, an example of TikTok (DouYin). *Computers in Human Behavior*, 110.

Wang, Y., Hong, A., Li, X. and Gao, J. 2020. Marketing innovations during a global crisis: A study of China firms' response to Covid-19. *Journal of Business Research*, 116: 214–220.

Wright, C. 2017. Are beauty bloggers more influential than traditional industry experts? *Journal of Promotional Communications*, 5(3).

Xu, L., Yan, X. and Zhang, Z. 2019. Research on the causes of the 'TikTok' app becoming popular and the existing problems. *Journal of Advanced Management Science*, 7(2).

Yang, S., Zhao, Y. and Ma, Y. 2019. Analysis of the reasons and development TikTok as an example. pp. 340–343. *In*: Xu, J. (Ed.). *9th International* Conference on 2019), Manila, Philippines, 12–14 July.

Zhang, Z. 2020. Infrastructuralization of TikTok: Transformation, power relationships, and platformization of video entertainment in China. *Media, Culture and Society*.

Zhao, Y. and Wang, Y. 2015. The research on the dissemination of short videos. *Research on Digital Media*, 32(3): 54–58.

Zhou, Q. 2019. *Understanding User Behaviors of Creative Practice on Short Video Sharing Platforms—A Case Study of TikTok and Bilibili*, PhD thesis, University of Cincinnati, USA.

Index